THE HISTORY OF HENRY FIELDING

PUBLISHED ON THE FOUNDATION
ESTABLISHED IN MEMORY OF
WILLIAM McKEAN BROWN

Henry Fielding
From an engraving by James Basire after a sketch by Hogarth

THE HISTORY
OF
HENRY FIELDING

BY

WILBUR L. CROSS

AUTHOR OF
THE DEVELOPMENT OF THE ENGLISH NOVEL
THE LIFE AND TIMES OF LAURENCE STERNE

VOLUME ONE

NEW HAVEN
YALE UNIVERSITY PRESS
LONDON · HUMPHREY MILFORD · OXFORD UNIVERSITY PRESS
MDCCCCXVIII

PREFACE

The title of this book will recall Fielding's favourite use of the word history; by which the great novelist meant a biography, either fictitious or real, that places in the proper social background all the incidents in the life of a man essential to knowing him, in conjunction with a sufficient account of the persons who bore upon that life for good or for evil. This was the aim of "The History of Tom Jones"; and this has been the aim of "The History of Henry Fielding." By accident, perhaps, the two histories contain about the same number of words.

Obviously, real history differs from fictitious in its art. "Tom Jones" has a plot which Coleridge described as a masterpiece; wherein incident is manipulated so as to determine character, and character is manipulated so as to determine incident, to a degree which does not prevail in actual life; wherein, too, lurk preconceived views or principles of conduct—a thesis almost—to be quietly and unobtrusively illustrated and maintained. None of these artistic devices are at the disposal of the honest historian of a man who has really lived and done his work in this world. Chance plays her part in the affairs of men; events happen which ought never to have happened; they are there and they cannot be removed in the interest of a faultless order. Facts are stubborn things; they cannot be ignored nor altered; they must be given, if they can be discovered, just as they are. In brief, the art of real history or biography consists in a coherent narrative of what actually occurred, with the addition of necessary comment and interpretation. Inference and conjecture are legitimate, but they should be held in restraint.

THE HISTORY OF HENRY FIELDING

This is not to say that real and fictitious history do not approach each other at some points. The Earl of Orrery lamented that Mr. Fielding, who had described many imaginary men and women, had no leisure to depict with a kindred art the career of the late Jonathan Swift. A biographer who keeps his mind upon human nature as it is and upon facts as he finds them, will surely discover that the outcome, far from being a mere collection of events, more or less discordant, will be groups of events which on reflection fall into a connected series having a beginning and an end and never quite breaking asunder. In other words, the incidents of real life as well as of fiction have their import and their logic. At length a sort of natural plot, lacking the precision of perfect art, emerges, and at last the man's character and achievements become reasonably clear.

This history of Henry Fielding I began several years ago with only one prepossession—a surmise which soon grew into the conviction that the author of "Tom Jones" could not have been the kind of man described in innumerable books and essays. In these volumes I have presented, so far as I could ascertain them, the details of Fielding's career; I have observed what was recorded for and against him by his contemporaries; and I have tried, extending the history, to thread the maze of controversy since his death over his personal character and the proper estimate to be placed upon his books. Doubtless positive errors have been made in the statement of facts; doubtless also, I have sometimes failed to interpret rightly such facts as have been at my disposal. All I can hope is that the story I have told, after being amended and amplified by others, will in general stand the test which time brings to history and biography and to all things. Inasmuch as Fielding published in part anonymously, the compass of his writings will be enlarged here and there by the addition of new items; and a few minor pieces whose authenticity is now regarded as doubtful will be definitely cast aside or definitely assigned to him.

To the shame of all who write and speak our mother tongue, no one has yet brought together the works of a great master who, like Shakespeare, was careless of his fame. Nor have the biographers given more than casual attention to anything beyond what a very mediocre journalist once selected for them; all the rest, except such stray pieces as they happened to read in the most cursory manner, they have in turn consigned to the land of matters forgot because they knew nothing of them. I have attempted to discover what these secondary works are, to fix their dates, and to give some account of them in connection with the half-known plays and the famous novels. These rejected publications have been a primary source of this biography; they have let light in upon the long-prevailing darkness. Their number, their scope, their character, make absurd the dissipated Fielding of tradition; they are a monument to Fielding's energy and earnestness, which once established time cannot remove.

Probably most that was printed about Fielding within the period of his lifetime has not escaped observation. If I have not referred to some things in praise or censure mentioned by other biographers, if I have left undisturbed in the old newspapers half the scurrility that was heaped upon his head, I have omitted nothing which if present would give the reader a different impression of the reaction of Fielding's work and personality upon his contemporaries. No one would care to see reprinted certain indecent passages from the pens of Grub Street on Fielding's physical infirmities and personal appearance when he was worn down by disease. Just as in the case of Pope, all this unrestrained invective was thrown against Fielding by men who were stung by his irony, or enraged by his enforcement of the law when he presided over the Bow Street court as the principal justice of the peace for London and Westminster. With slight or no change of phrase, these venomous paragraphs might be hurled at one man as well as another. They hardly concern biography; they concern more the capacity of the English language for vituperation. Still, where I have not quoted in full, I have given the substance of the worst that was ever said of Fielding in order that he may be viewed on all sides. No greater mistake could be made than to apply a reticent art to the author of "Tom Jones."

Of the countless opinions that have been passed upon the man and his novels since his death, and of his immense influence on British and Continental fiction, I have given fewer details; I profess to have done little more than touch the high places. The depth and breadth of that influence have not been recorded here; nor all the vagaries of those opinions. Of both influence and opinion, the reader, I daresay, will have enough. It will be seen that, despite all statements to the contrary, "the most English of English authors"—"the untranslatable"—has been very well known in France, Holland, and Germany (not unknown, too, in Italy, Spain, and Russia), and that the majority of his countrymen who have written of him have at once lost their poise and judgment, while some of them became, before they finished their work, fit subjects for the madhouse. James Russell Lowell saw Fielding most nearly as he was.

It is indeed difficult for a biographer of Fielding to keep a just and even course. He has no large body of personal correspondence to guide him and set him right in doubtful places. Why this is so has long been a matter for conjecture or for positive assertion. It has been said that Fielding's correspondence, supposed to have been in the keeping of his brother, was destroyed during the Gordon riots of 1780, when the Bow Street house of Sir John Fielding was wrecked and burned by the mob. It has also been said, no authority or reason being given, that Fielding's correspondence was destroyed by members of his family— by his widow, his brother, his sister or his children, or later descendants, acting singly or in concert. The first conjecture would indeed account for the loss of official letters to Fielding while he was a justice of the peace; but it would not account for the loss of any letters written by himself at that time except some addressed to his brother John. The second conjecture, which probably had its origin in the insufficiency of the first, would account chiefly for the loss of letters to various members of his household. Neither conjecture gives due weight to Fielding's career and character or to the ordinary ways in which letters disappear.

Fielding led too busy a life to be a voluminous letter-writer. He lived so much among his friends that he had less need than some of writing to them. And yet in the aggregate he must have been the author of hundreds of letters. When at Eton, he must have written to his father and grandmother. When in London, he must have written to his friends at Bath and Salisbury. There were surely numerous letters to Allen, to Lyttelton, to his sister Sarah, and to Charlotte Cradock. What has become of these? They have simply gone the journey that all letters go unless some special effort be made to preserve them. Many of them were read and cast aside and so perished immediately. Others like those to Charlotte were doubtless kept for a time and then lost in some hidden place. One of his letters, said to have been very playful over a huge cake, long reposed, we know, in the drawer of an old bureau and afterwards fell into the hands of someone who, desiring only the bureau, probably threw away the letter. This is the way of the world.

Very likely scores of Fielding's personal letters were in existence at the time of his death. Had he possessed the vanity of Sterne, he would have left directions to Mrs. Fielding where she could have found them; he would have told her to ask his friends for them, to sell them to his publisher, and to drive as hard a bargain as she could with him. Or had Arthur Murphy been endowed with the instinct of a biographer, he would have collected them and published them with the Works of Henry Fielding, Esq. But the man who never sat for his portrait had no vanity, and the man who first wrote his Life was without the instinct of the biographer. So, having never been assembled when they might have been, Fielding's letters were exposed to all the accidents of time in town and country.

Preposterous is the assumption that members of his family gathered them in and then burned them, just as the old spinsters in "Cranford" read and cast into the fire the letters of the deceased rector and his wife. Without doubt some of Fielding's letters were incinerated in the flames kindled by Gordon's mob on an evening in June; but they could not have composed the larger part of them. At that time John Fielding, broken in health, had retired to Brompton, where he died early in the next September. Of Henry's letters that have survived, three long ones were addressed to Brother Jack, and two of these were kept in the family for more than a hundred and fifty years. How is this fact to be explained on the theory of the Gordon riots or wilful destruction? But speculation or lament over the disappearance of Fielding's letters cannot restore them. A biographer is confronted with the cold fact that most of them are gone, and he must see what he can do without them—what he can do by making the best use of those that remain with the aid of information to be obtained elsewhere.

Here a remark of Sir Walter Scott is most pertinent. When Dr. Dryasdust told him that his projected "Ivanhoe" would be a failure because there was no extended contem-

porary account of the private life of their remote Norman
and Saxon ancestors on which to base a modern narrative,
the novelist replied that the materials for his story, though
scattered, were nevertheless abundant, that it would be his
business to collect these materials, to study them, to compare and adjust them; in short, to let his mind play upon
them until they should all be fused into a consistent whole.
These words of Sir Walter are also true in a large measure
when applied to the problem of constructing a biography
of Fielding. The materials, though not abundant, are
nearly adequate, but they are dispersed in a thousand
places. Fielding was a public character from the time he
took over the management of the Little Theatre in the Haymarket down through his political pamphlets and newspapers to his death as a Bow Street justice. In his almost
continuous political and literary warfare we see him as nowhere else in his full prime, thoroughly alive, striking his
opponents right and left. If we must discount much that
his enemies said of him, the fact remains that they have
given to posterity the man in action. The necessary corrections to the caricatures which they drew are to be found
in the casual remarks of his friends, in what he said of himself in his periodicals, pamphlets, and prefaces, and in the
prevailing characteristics of the man apparent in his works
when they are considered not singly but as a whole.

Moreover, the loss of his correspondence is not without
some compensations. Though we have none of his letters
from Eton, we have the later allusions to his life there, and
we know from an old Chancery suit what was then occurring
in the family at Salisbury and East Stour. The verses addressed to Charlotte Cradock are a good substitute for the
love epistles he indited to the charming girl. The preface
to the "Miscellanies" sufficiently describes his distress of
mind and body when his fortunes were at their lowest ebb,
and "A Voyage to Lisbon" is a true relation of the last

months of his life. Nor are letters in Fielding's own hand wholly wanting. A majority of them deal with matters of business connected with the Bow Street court, and for this reason they found their way into safe archives. Disappointment has often been expressed that these official letters do not tell us much about Fielding himself. True, their purpose necessarily precludes that unrestrained wit and gaiety for which their author is famous; but to a biographer they are of very great value in that they furnish clues to Fielding's activities and enlarge the number of his associates and friends. They also exhibit two of Fielding's prime qualities: they are all perfectly courteous in tone, and self is always forgotten in favour of some friend or the public weal.

And if more of Fielding's intimate letters had withstood the wreck of fortune, it is not likely that they would show him other than he appears in the one to Lyttelton and in the three to his brother John. They would of course give us a more complete portrait, and they would enable us to disprove more easily the slanders of Richardson and other enemies. This would be much, but it would be all. Not only the letters but such pieces of documentary evidence as we have, apart from satire and obvious abuse, merely confirm what may be read of Fielding in "A Voyage to Lisbon." This book, showing no trace of a desire to conceal either the author's weaknesses or his virtues—whichever they may be called—is as frank and as candid a piece of autobiography as ever came from any pen. Our knowledge of Fielding is of course derived only in a very small part from "A Voyage to Lisbon"; but where questions arise about his habits and character, that book must always be in a biographer's mind to rectify what he finds said of him by others. When Fielding wrote the account of his last journey, it should be remembered, he was not an old man; he was but on the threshold of his forty-eighth year.

PREFACE

Though his heart and arteries were breaking under the strain of labour, he still attempted to order his daily life on the lines of his former habits. He must eat, he must drink, in the ways he had eaten and drunken. His intellect was still vigorous and his temper was not soured. Nor was he disillusioned. He must have a companion to talk to, he must observe men and things, he must read and write, or else die. He was gentle towards women, he honoured and admired them, and resented the least indication of insult towards them. He insisted upon all the minor proprieties as well as upon a due consideration of his rank and learning; and yet his mind was on others more than on himself.

As Fielding was then he had always been; only he was then less buoyant and less the animal than in his youth. Remembering an earlier time, Lyttelton once remarked to the poet Beattie: "Henry Fielding, I assure you, had more wit and humour than all the persons we have been speaking of put together." They had been speaking of Pope and Swift, whom Lyttelton had known well. Withal, Fielding lived, contrary to the usual opinion, as single and consistent a life as most men. We miss in him the vagaries supposed to be necessary to genius. God, nature, and circumstance made Henry Fielding what he was. His was a full-blooded youth and a full-blooded manhood. Of this man I have written.

There are but few words more to say here. It is always a question whether quotations should be reproduced exactly in the old spelling, capitals, and punctuation, or whether they should be made to conform to present-day standards. In a biography of Fielding, where many writers of various styles and periods are concerned, the easier way would be to modernize them all; but this course would be quite unsatisfactory to readers who wish to see the author of "Tom

xv

Jones'' and his contemporaries in the dress which they habitually wore. Accordingly, I have struck a sort of compromise. Fielding's own spelling and punctuation have been everywhere retained; but for the sake of appearance, I have usually degraded initial capitals, if present usage would not permit them, in verse and dramatic dialogue, and in other quotations incorporated in my own paragraphs. When passages of prose, except from the plays, stand by themselves they have been given with all their capitals as Fielding printed them, and in the case of available manuscripts with all the abbreviations as Fielding wrote them. Perhaps I have not been equally consistent in quoting from other authors; but always where their typographical peculiarities are of real interest they have been re-exhibited here. In general all nouns in Fielding's books published under his own supervision began with capitals, and proper names were printed in italics. Most exceptions to the rule seem to be due to the carelessness of compositors. Fielding's friends thus appear, when he had his own way, as Mr. *Hogarth,* Mr. *Garrick,* and Mr. *Pitt.* In all his autographs which I have seen he signed himself Ffielding, the first two letters being united by a ligature.

The bibliography has been prepared in collaboration with Mr. Frederick S. Dickson, who supplied the larger part of the material for the bibliographical descriptions. Besides many other details, I have, however, added from the newspapers, wherever I was able, the exact day of publication, and for the plays the exact day of the first performance also. The aim has been to describe the first editions of Fielding's undoubted works and to give a record of subsequent editions which were published during his lifetime, with the addition of many of the others which have appeared since his death. There are subjoined lists which cover works doubtfully or not certainly Fielding's; works which, though at various times curiously attributed to him,

PREFACE

are known to have been written by others; plays founded upon his books or upon traditional incidents in his life; and the manuscripts, those lost as well as those existing, so far as there is any record of them,—alas! too few in number. Altogether, the bibliography shows the extraordinary place which Fielding occupies in modern literature.

To Mr. Andrew Keogh of the Yale University Library I am indebted for the index; and I should not forget to thank several other friends for their comment and criticism while the book was in press.

WILBUR L. CROSS.

Yale University, June, 1918.

CONTENTS

VOLUME ONE

ILLUSTRATIONS

VOLUME ONE

THE HISTORY OF HENRY FIELDING

CHAPTER I

ANCESTRY AND CHILDHOOD

"It is the custom of all biographers, at their entrance into their work," said Fielding humorously, "to step a little backwards (as far, indeed, generally as they are able) and to trace up their hero, as the ancients did the river Nile, till an incapacity of proceeding higher puts an end to their search." So it once was with Fielding's own biographers, who, relying upon the genealogists, traced his ancestral stream back through six centuries, and then in the darkness of the Middle Ages feigned a source for it in one of the most ancient and illustrious houses in Europe. The family was allied, it used to be said, with the gods, meaning thereby emperors and kings. Who does not recall that splendid passage from Gibbon quoted by Thackeray?—"Our immortal Fielding was of a younger branch of the Earls of Denbigh, who draw their origin from the Counts of Hapsburg, the lineal descendants of Ethico in the seventh century, Duke of Alsace. Far different have been the fortunes of the English and German divisions of the family of Hapsburg. The former, the Knights and Sheriffs of Leicestershire, have slowly risen to the dignity of a peerage; the latter, the Emperors of Germany and Kings of Spain, have threatened the liberty of the old, and invaded the treasures of the new world. The successors of Charles the Fifth may disdain their humble brethren of England, but the romance of 'Tom Jones,' that exquisite picture of human manners, will outlive the palace of the Escurial, and the Imperial Eagle of the House of Austria."

1

THE HISTORY OF HENRY FIELDING

These Hapsburgs whence the Fieldings have been derived, take their name from the old castle of Hapsburg on the river Aar in the Swiss canton of Aargau, which once formed a part of their extensive possessions in Switzerland and the Rhine valley. The Fieldings, it was usually claimed, descended from the younger branch of the family, whose seat at the beginning of the thirteenth century was Laufenburg or "the Castle of the Rapids," on the Rhine to the east of Basel. To the domains of this younger branch the Fielding genealogists have added Rheinfelden, lying midway between Basel and Laufenburg. According to the story, "Geoffrey, Count of Hapsburg, Laufenburg and Rheinfelden," was impoverished by his cousin Rudolph, who afterwards ascended the German throne. His territory, it is said, was overrun by the bands of this cousin and his lands were mostly wrested from him. In these hard circumstances, Geoffrey sent his son and heir, likewise named Geoffrey, over to England to retrieve the fortunes of his family in the service of Henry the Third. While in England, this Geoffrey married Maud de Colville without the consent of his family and was forthwith disinherited for it by the old Count on the Rhine. Thus forced to settle in England, Geoffrey assumed the name of Felden (*anglicé* Felding, Feilding, or Fielding) in memory of Rheinfelden. His eldest son, another Geoffrey, tried in vain to recover the estates of his grandfather, which had then fallen into the hands of Rudolph of Germany. He married Agnes de Napton; and with him was established the long line of Fieldings as an offshoot of those Hapsburgs who later became German kings and Austrian emperors.

Such in brief is the romantic story, so complete in all essential details that it was long held as true history, doubtless by Henry Fielding himself as well as by others, including the great Gibbon. The legend is now thoroughly discredited. Twenty-odd years ago all the deeds, charters,

2

and pedigrees on which the Fieldings based their claims to Hapsburg blood were found to be unmistakable forgeries concocted for the family in the seventeenth century after it had been raised to the peerage.* The Count Geoffrey, it has been shown, to whom the Fieldings linked their line, had no connection whatever with Rheinfelden. He was merely Count or Lord of Laufenburg, which he held from the neighbouring abbey of Säckingen; and he was so styled in his own time. Rheinfelden was clearly included in the titles of the Count of Laufenburg by the forgers, who were unaware that the castle and the lands did not then belong to the Hapsburgs, in order that they might derive the name *Fielding* from the German *felden*. This was a neat and necessary detail. Unfortunately, however, for the derivation, *felden,* as well as its dialectic variations in *ing,* is also a good old English word, meaning, when applied to a man, one living or labouring in the field. All this points to the Fieldings as being in origin not Hapsburgs but plain English yeomen or small landowners. From early times their arms bore as crest a nuthatch pecking at a fructed hazel bough, with the motto beneath: *Virtutis praemium honor.*

As in the case of Shakespeare, the family in early times spelled their name variously. But after obtaining the earldom of Denbigh in the seventeenth century, the main line agreed mostly though not completely on *Feilding,* while the younger line, to which the novelist belonged, retained the more common *Fielding,* though there were very many exceptions to this practice. Concerning the correct form of the name, tradition records an amusing conversation between Henry Fielding and the Earl of Denbigh of his

---

* For the spurious genealogy, see Collins's ''Peerage of England,'' as revised by Sir Egerton Bridges, 1812, III, 265; for the story of the forgeries, ''Our English Hapsburgs'' by J. H. Round in ''The Genealogist,'' 1894, New Series, X, 193.

time. "Why is it, Harry," inquired the Earl, "that you put the *i* before the *e,* writing it *Fielding,* while we put the *e* before the *i,* writing it *Feilding?*" "I cannot tell, my Lord," replied the humorist, "except it be that my branch of the family were the first that knew how to spell."* It was, if true, a bold jest, implying that the Earl possessed the titles and the wealth but not the brains of the family.

Though the Hapsburg descent once claimed for the Fieldings (we shall spell the name this way) must be abandoned, the family is nevertheless among the most ancient and honourable in the English peerage; and the story of its rise to large estates and many dignities until it became the source of a novelist of the first rank is still interesting without the glamour of legend. The family apparently emerged from the yeomanry in the time of Edward the Third with that Geoffrey Fielding who married Agnes, daughter and heir of John de Napton, and acquired thereby Misterton, a manor near Lutterworth in southern Leicestershire. Their son William married a granddaughter and heir of Robert de Newnham and thus came into possession of the large manor of Newnham Paddox, just over the border in Warwickshire. Ever since those days Newnham, as old as the Doomsday Book, has remained the chief seat of the family, which in subsequent centuries included many knights and sheriffs of Leicestershire and Warwickshire.

In the next generation, for example, John Fielding, it is said, served in the French wars and was knighted for his bravery. His son William took part in the War of the Roses, fighting on the side of the Lancastrians, and was slain at Tewkesbury. By his marriage, it is alleged, into the younger branch of the family of St. Liz, he allied himself with the Earls of Northampton and Huntingdon, and

* John Nichols, "Literary Anecdotes of the Eighteenth Century," 1812, III, 384.

incidentally added to his estates the lordship of two or more manors, including Martinsthorpe in Rutland. In turn his son Everard, twice sheriff of the counties of Warwick and Leicester, held a command in the army of Edward the Fourth at the battle of Stoke, and was subsequently created, under Henry the Seventh, a Knight of the Bath. During the reigns of the Tudors, one Fielding after another increased the family estates by fortunate marriages among the landed gentry and wealthy merchants. Besides being almost invariably sheriffs, they occasionally appear in the immediate service of their sovereigns.

This succession of Fieldings is rather shadowy. In all likelihood their importance has been exaggerated by the genealogists, and certainly knighthood has been too often conferred upon them as an adornment to their names in the family pedigree. The story, barring details, must be, however, essentially true, for it is but typical of the rise of all great English families from the yeomanry and perhaps earlier servitude to the dignity of squires and country gentlemen. The next step in the rise is to an earldom. Here we reach authentic history and men and women whose personal characteristics we may know.*

The earldom came to the family by a happy marriage. At the beginning of the reign of James the First, the head of the house was William Fielding, a young man recently graduated at Oxford and soon to be knighted by the King. He married Susan, daughter of Sir George Villiers of

* For the Fieldings of the seventeenth century, see the Earls of Denbigh in Burke's "Peerage"; S. R. Gardiner, "History of the Great Civil War," London, 1886-1891, and "History of the Commonwealth and Protectorate," London, 1894-1903; Clarendon, "History of the Rebellion," Oxford, 1888; Ludlow, "Memoirs," edited by C. H. Firth, Oxford, 1894; C. Dalton, "English Army Lists and Commission Registers," from 1661 to 1707, London, 1892-1902; and various Reports of the Historical Manuscripts Commission, especially the Fourth (1874), the Sixth (1877-1878), the Seventh (1879), and the Eighth Report (1881), together with "Report on the Manuscripts of the Earl of Denbigh" (1911).

5

Brooksby Hall, Leicestershire, and settled as a "plain
country gentleman" at Newnham Paddox. His wife's
brother, then nothing but a boy, afterwards became the
King's favourite, none other than the powerful Duke of
Buckingham whom the world knows. No sooner did the
Duke obtain his own titles than he began, as dispenser of
the King's grace, to bestow similar ones upon his family
and friends. Sir William Fielding was created in succession Baron of Newnham Paddox, Viscount Fielding (1620),
and Earl of Denbigh (1622). He likewise became in succession deputy-master and master of his Majesty's great
wardrobe. As a follower of Buckingham, the Earl was also
appointed to various commands in the army and the navy,
but he was found rather inefficient. On the other hand, the
Countess possessed in a measure the talent and brilliancy of
her brother. Their eldest son, Basil Fielding, educated at
Emmanuel College, Cambridge, was taken into the household of Buckingham, to whom he became most closely attached in love and devotion, offering on one occasion to
shield the Duke from threatened assassination by disguising
himself at the risk of his own life in Buckingham's great
cloak and hat. But the Duke would not permit this sacrifice; for he valued, he said, his nephew's life far more than
his own.*

After the death of Buckingham, who in due time had a
knife put through his heart, the Fieldings still retained the
favour of the King. The Earl made a semi-official journey
to the East and then retired to the family seat. Basil, who
in the meantime had been summoned to the House of Lords
as Baron Fielding, fought in the Low Countries, travelled
and studied in Germany, and was subsequently sent as
Ambassador Extraordinary to the Republic of Venice
(1634-1639). But on the outbreak of the great Civil War,
the house of Denbigh became divided against itself. The

* Sir Henry Wotton, "Reliquiae Wottonianae," London, 1651, p. 110.

Earl went with the King; and though well advanced in
years, served bravely as a volunteer in the horse of Prince
Rupert. Basil, against whom hostility had arisen at the
English Court during his last years at Venice, being practically, though indirectly, dismissed from his post for
reasons not now very clear, turned against the King, raised
a troop of horse, and accepted a command under the Earl
of Essex. It thus happened that father and son fought on
opposite sides at Edgehill, the father under Prince Rupert
and the son in command of the right wing of the Parliamentary forces. Thereafter events moved rapidly. The
aged Earl died of many wounds received in the capture of
Birmingham (April, 1643). A few weeks later his son
Richard, senior colonel of the King's garrison at Reading,
surrendered the town to Essex on conditions so favourable
to Parliament that he was brought before a court-martial
at Oxford and sentenced to death as a traitor. "Twice he
mounted the scaffold, and twice he was withdrawn; the
second time at the pleading of the young Prince of Wales"
with the King. Heart-broken over the disaffection of Basil
and the suspicions against Richard, the Countess of Denbigh, at that time with the Queen as first lady of her
Majesty's bedchamber, poured forth her deep grief in
touching letters to her eldest son, imploring him to return
to the King. On the death of her husband, she wrote most
pathetically: "I beg of you, my first born, to give me the
comfort of that son I do so dearly love, that satisfaction
which you owe me now, which is to leave those that murdered your dear father. . . . O my dear Jesus, put it into
my dear son's heart to leave that merciless company that
was the death of his father, for now I think of it with
horror, before with sorrow. Now is the time that God
and nature claims it from you. . . . The last words your
dear father spoke of you were to desire God to forgive you
and to touch your heart. Let your dying father and

unfortunate mother make your heart relent; let my great sorrow receive some comfort. If I receive joy, you shall receive blessing and honour.''*

But Basil, now second Earl of Denbigh by the death of his father, had committed himself too far to the Parliamentary cause for retreat, though he felt indeed some prick of conscience for his disloyalty to the King. At the very time his mother was pleading with him to break with his Majesty's enemies, he was appointed commander-in-chief of the Parliamentary forces in the midland and western counties, and during the next year (1644) captured several Royalist strongholds, receiving therefor the formal thanks of Parliament. A few weeks later the sorrowful Countess went into exile with the Queen. While in Paris, she befriended the poet Crashaw, living there in great distress, who addressed two poems to her, urging that she ''render herself without further delay into the communion of the Catholic Church''; and afterwards, as he lay dying, requested that his volume of ''Sacred Poems'' be dedicated to her ''in hearty acknowledgement of his immortal obligation to her goodness and charity.''

Meanwhile, on the passage of the Self-Denying Ordinance (1645), Denbigh followed Essex in laying down his command, and was subsequently employed by Parliament in the final overtures to King Charles. When these negotiations failed and the first ordinance for the King's trial reached the House of Lords with Denbigh's name inserted by the Commons in the list of the Commissioners forming the court before which the King was to be brought, the Earl spoke with intense emotion against the measure, vowing that ''he would choose to be torn to pieces rather than have any share in so infamous a business.'' After the execution of Charles, the Earl nevertheless became a member of the first two Councils of State under the Commonwealth; but

* ''Historical MSS. Commission. Fourth Report,'' p. 260.

later rendered only cool support to the Protectorate, and was among the first to greet Charles the Second on his return to England. Going into retirement, the Earl put forth, during his last years, formal claims to descent from the Hapsburgs, and introduced into his arms, in place of the old nuthatch, the imperial eagle of the House of Austria.

This second Earl of Denbigh had also a brother George, born in 1616, from whom Henry Fielding the novelist directly descended. When the Duke of Buckingham was ennobling the family, he did not forget George, the second surviving son of his sister, who, though a mere boy, was elevated in 1622 to the Irish peerage as Baron Fielding of Lecaghe, Viscount Callan, with the provision that he should become Earl of Desmond on the death of Sir Richard Preston, who then held the title. In 1628 Sir Richard was drowned at sea, and the youngster duly succeeded him in the Irish earldom. On the coronation of Charles the First, George was made a Knight of the Bath, and at a tournament four years later was one of the tilters before the King. While yet in his teens, the family married him to Bridget, daughter and coheir of Sir Michael Stanhope of Sudbury in Suffolk. Leaving his wife under the care of his mother and the old Countess of Buckingham, he set out on his travels in France and Italy. He was for a time with his brother Basil at Paris and Turin, and for six months attended an academy at Paris for perfecting himself in knightly exercises. His wife was clearly annoyed, to say the least, at the long absences of her husband, for in 1635 she brought suit against him for divorce on the ground of his "insufficiency to please a reasonable woman." The boy met the charge with a jest, saying, in a letter to Basil, that he had heard of few Fieldings against whom such a charge could be established.*

* "Historical MSS. Commission. Report on the Manuscripts of the Earl of Denbigh," p. 14.

THE HISTORY OF HENRY FIELDING

In the case of George the charge was certainly not established; for subsequent to this misunderstanding, there were born of the marriage five sons and three daughters. During the Civil War the Earl of Desmond sided with the King, and after the Restoration took his seat in the Irish Parliament. At his death in 1665, his titles descended to his eldest son, William, "a very good and hopeful young man" and then "captain of a troop of horse in Ireland." His uncle Basil dying without issue in 1675, William also succeeded to his titles, thus becoming the third Earl of Denbigh as well as the second Earl of Desmond in the new line. George, the second son of the first Earl of Desmond, married an heiress in Suffolk, the daughter of Sir John Lee of Lawshall; and the third son, Sir Charles Fielding, had a distinguished career as an officer in the army, military governor, and member of the Privy Council in Ireland. About the fourth son, named Basil from his uncle, Pepys, writing in his "Diary" under date of May 9, 1667, tells a pretty story were it not so tragic. Basil, a mere stripling in the household of "my Lady Sandwich," fell into a quarrel with one of his brothers (both being drunk) at a London tavern called the Three Tuns, and was killed before the fracas was over. Pepys, who used to dine at the Three Tuns, went there to see the corpse and was present at the trial of the nameless brother when convicted of murder and sent to Newgate. There was probably no punishment for the crime beyond a brief imprisonment.

The youngest brother of these boys was John Fielding, the grandfather of the novelist. As he was not born until 1650, he was rather young to be the brother who killed Basil in the tavern brawl. Nor is it probable that William was guilty of this rash act, for we find him a few months later in the North with the army. The Cain of the family appears to have been Charles, then twenty-two years old. John Fielding, evidently of quieter temperament than his

10

military brothers, studied at Cambridge, where, in 1671, he proceeded directly to the degree of Master of Arts without taking a Bachelor's degree—a privilege once accorded to the sons of noblemen. Then or somewhat later, he was also elected a Fellow of Queens' College, Cambridge. Entering the Church, his rise was rapid, though he never reached the highest dignities. His first appointment was to Piddletown, an extensive parish five miles northeast of Dorchester. When Benjamin Woodroffe, afterwards Principal of Gloucester Hall, Oxford, obtained this vicarage in 1673, through the favour of the Earl of Huntingdon, he chose John Fielding as his curate; and two years later resigned the living, valued at £120 a year, to the young man. John Fielding, it is said, subsequently held the vicarage of Codgrave in Nottinghamshire, but there is no evidence of his ever residing there. In 1677, he was appointed. Prebendary of Yatesbury and Canon Residentiary in Salisbury Cathedral. The next year he was permitted to exchange Yatesbury for Beaminster; and in 1682 for Gillingham major, then one of the richest stalls in the Cathedral. The prebend of Gillingham included lands at Motcombe, and East and West Stour, places since intimately associated with Henry Fielding's life in the country. A few months afterwards (March 25, 1683), John Fielding was raised to the Archdeaconry of Dorset, then in the diocese of Bristol. He apparently tried for further honours; for at this time the Bishop of Salisbury was recommending him to the Archbishop of Canterbury "as a very good man and an honour to the Church, deserving your Grace's favour and his Majesty's promotion." If he was striving for a bishopric, he missed it.

As Archdeacon of Dorset, John Fielding proved himself most efficient in his office. Near the time of his first visitation, he published in 1683 a little book called "Articles to be Ministered, Enquired of, and Answered, concerning

Matters Ecclesiastical"—for the guidance of church-wardens in the well-ordering of their parishes. He came into especial prominence in 1687, when James the Second issued his first Declaration of Indulgence suspending the laws against Roman Catholics and Dissenters. His bishop, Sir Jonathan Trelawny, ordered him to summon his clergy to sign an address to the King in favour of the Declaration; but the Archdeacon at first stoutly refused, and afterwards obeyed the order only on the most peremptory command, perhaps only after learning that Trelawny wished the clergy assembled that they might be persuaded not to sign the address. Very few of them signed it. Trelawny was one of the Seven Bishops brought to trial the next year on a charge of seditious libel for presenting to King James a petition against the second Declaration of Indulgence. On the accession of William and Mary, Trelawny was translated to the See of Exeter; and John Fielding was enrolled among his Majesty's chaplains, with a Sunday in February assigned to him for preaching in the royal chapel. In October, 1689, he accompanied King William on a visit to Cambridge, where he received, while a conduit was made to run wine instead of water in honour of his Majesty's presence, the degree of Doctor of Divinity. The ecclesiastic's career, however, was cut short by death, which came to him early in 1698, before he had reached the age of fifty. So it was to happen in the case of his famous grandson.

Two places are especially connected with the life of John Fielding. They are Salisbury and Piddletown, of which the latter has been strangely overlooked by the biographers. As Canon Residentiary of Salisbury, he lived at the Canonry in the southwest Cathedral Close. The house has since been rebuilt upon the old foundations and is now occupied by the Archdeacon of the diocese. His predecessor, it is worth while to observe, was William Lloyd,

one of the Seven Bishops; and his successor was Isaac
Walton, a son of the angler. When a young man, John
Fielding married Bridget, daughter of Scipio Cockayne
(or Cokayne), a Somerset squire, related to an old family
which had its chief seat at Ashbourne in Derbyshire.
Scipio Cockayne was thus a distant cousin of Sir Aston
Cokayne, the poet and dramatist, whose works are described
on their title-pages as more "excellent" than they really
are. His direct descent, however, was from a branch of
the family then established at Cockayne Hatley in Bed-
fordshire. Sometime after his marriage, John Fielding
settled at Piddletown, where were born and baptized, as
the parish register shows, several of his many children—
Bridget, Dorothy, Edmund, and William. The family
histories mention another daughter, Elizabeth, and two
other sons, John and George, all of whom were born earlier.
John, the eldest son, became secretary to the first Duke
of Portland, and Captain-General and Governor of Jamaica,
where he died in 1725. George, the second son, became
Lieutenant-Colonel of the Royal Regiment of Blues, and
groom of the bedchamber to Queen Anne and George the
First. Dying in 1738, he lies buried in St. George's
Chapel, Windsor. Edmund, the third son, born on January
20, 1680, was the father of Henry Fielding.*

* The main sources for this account of John Fielding are J. Nichols,
"History and Antiquities of Leicester," 1807; J. Hutchins, "History and
Antiquities of Dorset," 1861-1873; E. Chamberlayne, "Angliae Notitia,"
1694; "Life and Times of Anthony Wood," edited by A. Clark, 1891-1900;
Collins's "Peerage," 1812; J. Le Neve, "Fasti Ecclesiae Anglicanae," 1854;
H. R. Luard, "Graduati Cantabrigienses," 1873; Anthony Wood, "Athenae
Oxonienses," edited by Bliss, 1813-1820; W. H. Jones, "Fasti Ecclesiae
Sarisberiensis," 1879; "First Report" of the Historical MSS. Commission,
1870; "Cockayne Memoranda," giving the pedigree of Scipio Cockayne, in
the British Museum; transcripts of the diocesan records at Salisbury and of
the parish register of Piddletown, made in 1911. According to the old style,
Edmund Fielding was born on Jan. 20, 1679. Of John Fielding's other children
the parish register of Piddletown gives the following baptisms: Bridgett, June
26, 1675; Dorothy, Dec. 20, 1677; and William, Sept. 1 (or 5), 1685.

THE HISTORY OF HENRY FIELDING

Edmund Fielding followed the military traditions of his family. Towards the close of the seventeenth century there was scarcely an English regiment without a Fielding—a brother, a cousin, or an uncle—among the officers. Before Edmund was seventeen years old, the family obtained for him an ensigncy in the First Regiment of Foot Guards, which under Lord George Hamilton greatly distinguished itself in the capture of Liége. At the close of this campaign in the autumn of 1702, the ensign, having doubtless served as a lieutenant, became a captain in the Queen's Regiment of Foot, then commanded by Colonel Webb, and forming a part of the army with which the Duke of Marlborough subdued the Netherlands and invaded Germany. Webb, who was soon promoted for his gallantry, is the brave and handsome Brigadier-General to whom Thackeray detailed Henry Esmond as aide-de-camp, though he failed to give us a scene between Esmond and the father of the man who wrote "Tom Jones." Captain Fielding's name appears, in the summer of 1704, among the officers who led their men in Webb's terrific attack upon the French at Blenheim, chasing them from the field and capturing their commander. For his part in the exploit, he received along with other captains of his regiment a bounty of thirty pounds. In 1705, perhaps after Webb's victory at Helixem in July, Edmund Fielding returned to England; for he was appointed on April 12, 1706, major of Lord Tunbridge's Regiment of Foot, which was sent to Ireland. Three years later, he succeeded Colonel Brazier in command of a regiment raised for service in the Spanish peninsula. He may have fought at Malplaquet; but if his regiment ever went to Spain, he did not go with it. Nor was he always during this period in active service. In 1711, his regiment was reduced and the next year its officers were placed on half pay.*

* For Edmund Fielding's early military career, see especially C. Dalton, "English Army Lists and Commission Registers," index to vol. V; R. Cannon,

14

ANCESTRY AND CHILDHOOD

Subsequent to the battle of Blenheim, without doubt in 1706, Edmund Fielding married Sarah, daughter of Sir Henry Gould, a judge of the Queen's Bench, who had been knighted in 1694. Her mother was formerly Sarah Davidge of Dorchester. There were at least three children born into the Gould family—Davidge, who succeeded to the estates, Katherine, who, dying in childhood, was buried on November 24, 1681, and Sarah, who was baptized on December 28, 1682.* Sarah was thus nearly three years younger than her husband. Her marriage to Edmund Fielding, it was afterwards alleged by the mother, was without the consent of the bride's parents; that is, it was probably a runaway match. But, as usually happens in romances of this kind, the son-in-law duly made peace with his wife's family. By a will executed March 8, 1706 (or 1707 according to the new style), Sir Henry gave and devised to his son Davidge Gould and William Day of London three thousand pounds in trust for the sole use of his daughter during her lifetime and for the maintenance and education of her children in case of her death. The fund was to be placed at interest until it could be employed in "a fitting purchase either of a church or college lease or of lands of inheritance."† Distrustful of his son-in-law, the old judge directed that "the interest and profits of the estate" should be paid to his daughter herself and that "her husband should have nothing to do nor intermeddle

"Historical Record of the First or Royal Regiment of Foot," 1847; "Historical Record of the Eighth, or the King's Regiment of Foot," 1844; and "Historical Record of the King's Liverpool Regiment," second edition, 1883. Edmund Fielding is described as a colonel, for the first time, in the parish register of St. John's Church, Glastonbury, on the baptism of his daughter Ursula, Nov. 2, 1709. His later appointments are given in "Notes and Queries," 12 S. III, 267 (April 14, 1917).

* Register of St. John's Church, Glastonbury.

† The will, now at Somerset House, was discovered by Thomas Keightley. See "Notes and Queries," 3 S. II, 199 (Sept. 6, 1862).

15

therewith.'' The will, with these provisions, was made only a few weeks before the birth of her first child, Henry Fielding, on April 22, 1707.

Concerning this date there can be no doubt, for it was so given by Edmund Fielding in the Chancery proceedings to be hereafter described. It is not certainly known, however, where the novelist was born. According to Arthur Murphy, his first biographer, the place was Sir Henry Gould's seat at Sharpham Park, a manor near Glastonbury, where the family had been settled for a half century. But in the registers of Glastonbury and neighbouring parishes no entry of Henry Fielding's birth has yet been found. It has been surmised that the boy was born in Ireland, on the assumption, I take it, that Mrs. Fielding accompanied her husband when he went over there as major in Lord Tunbridge's regiment. ''Some say,'' it was remarked long after Fielding's death, that ''the celebrated writer'' was born ''in Capel Street, Dublin.''* But the parish registers of Dublin likewise fail to give the desired entry. From such facts as we have, the natural inference is that Mrs. Fielding fled to Ireland with her husband, but that she returned to England before her father, partially reconciled to her marriage, made provision for her and her prospective child in his will. Perhaps Henry was born while his mother was staying with some member of her family. The boy was named after his grandfather, who, if custom was followed, was present at the christening, wherever it may have been. All things considered, it is my opinion that Henry Fielding was born, like his two sisters who followed him, at Sharpham Park, and that he was likewise baptized at St. John's Church, Glastonbury. The reason why the desired record has not been discovered is because the registers of St. John's

* D. E. Baker, ''Biographia Dramatica,'' as revised by Stephen Jones, 1812.

16

SHARPHAM HOUSE.

for the years preceding 1708 are in great disorder and apparently incomplete.*

If not born at home, the infant was at any rate brought by his mother to Sharpham Park, where he was nursed through his first years and where he later visited his grandparents and uncle, absorbing in his memory the surrounding scenes, the most extensive of which was to be described in "Tom Jones." His grandfather's seat had, too, an interesting history, for anciently Sharpham Park belonged to the vast domain of the Benedictine Abbey at Glastonbury. The manor, lying two or three miles southwest of the town on a rise of ground known as Polden Hill, overlooking the Somerset moors, contained, say the old chroniclers, in circuit two long miles of good meadow and pasture, sufficient to keep four hundred deer and forty large cattle. The whole district from Glastonbury to Sharpham, once surrounded by water or deep marshes, was formerly called the Isle of Avalon, and became associated in Celtic romance with the land of immortality, where King Arthur went to be healed of his wounds. Near the beginning of the sixteenth century, Abbot Bere, one of the great abbey builders, erected at Sharpham a noble house, containing a large hall, parlours, kitchen, and chambers. In the rear was a beautiful chapel, which had an east window with

* The Vicar of the parish kindly searched the records for me in 1916, when he found the baptism of Sarah Gould and the burial of her sister Katherine; and again in July, 1917, when he found among the "Christnings" of 1708 and 1709 respectively: "Catherine daughter of Edmund Fielding Esqʳ and Sarah his wife was Born July 16 & was Baptiz'd August 11"; and "Ursula daughter of Coll. Edmund Fielding and Sarah his wife, Born October the 3 and Baptized November the 2."

The Vicar writes that the registers are "very involved, some in Latin and much mixed up with marriages, funerals, baptisms, etc."; and more specifically that "a wide hiatus occurs before 1708, so that the baptism of Henry Fielding does not occur." See also Mr. J. Paul de Castro in "Notes and Queries," Nov., 1917, p. 468. A more careful search than has yet been made may have better results.

mullions, representing, in the painted glass, Christ between John the Baptist and St. John the Evangelist. The approach from Glastonbury was through a long avenue of trees known as the abbot's ride, extending westward far beyond the park. During those years of trouble and confusion when Henry the Eighth was dissolving the monasteries, Sharpham was a favourite retreat of Richard Whiting, the last of the abbots; it was here while sitting in the kitchen, that he was arrested for treason by the King's commissioners, and led away to trial and eventually to execution on Tor Hill above the great abbey and the valley of Avalon.

As a part of the abbey lands, Sharpham Park thus passed to the Crown, and was granted to Edward Dyer, Esq., from whose descendants it came to the Goulds after the Civil War. In Fielding's time the manor was little changed from what it had been in the days when Abbot Whiting sought refuge there against the King's messengers. Since then the mansion, much dilapidated, has been converted into a farmhouse, the trees have mostly disappeared, and the chapel has been nearly wrecked. Time, however, has not dealt so severely with the stone walls and stone floors of the main building or with the heavy oak door at the east entrance, covered with huge ornamental hinges. Passing through the hall, one may still climb the stairway to a room called the Harlequin Chamber, where according to tradition Fielding was born. This chamber, directly over the monks' kitchen and facing the west, is finished in oak panels, with many cupboards, one of which opens into a dark hole known as the ghost's room. Looking out upon the ruined chapel is a small window, beneath which was once carved in the stone, hardly traceable now, a Harlequin, with crossed legs, playing upon a viol or a similar instrument.*

* For Sharpham Park, see W. Phelps, ''History and Antiquities of Somersetshire,'' 1836, I, 560. An engraving of the house is given by R. Warner in ''A

ANCESTRY AND CHILDHOOD

A novelist, seeking a chamber for Harry Fielding to sleep in when a boy, could imagine none more appropriate than one dedicated to Harlequin, where the disciples of St. Benedict had many times stretched their legs for the night after an evening of mirth in the old stone kitchen below. Fielding's descent, too, is much as one would have it. If we must give up the old Hapsburg story, we can put in its place an ancient family ennobled by a marriage with Buckingham's sister. Besides his supreme sense of humour, a hint for which is indicated in the first Earl of Desmond, Fielding was a man in whom were mixed many elements, here and there discernible among his ancestors. As proud of his race as was the second Earl of Denbigh, he insisted, though he hardly had the means for it, upon living the life of a gentleman. In combat he was as fearless as his military kinsmen, though he fought with the pen instead of the sword. Like one of his grandfathers, he became a scholar and moralist; and like the other, whose name he bore, he had a natural bent towards the law.

The scene of Fielding's childhood early shifted from the Somerset hills to the beautiful undulating country of Dorset. The boy remained at Sharpham for no more than two years and a half; and before that time he was crowded out of the Harlequin chamber by two sisters—Catherine, born on July 16, 1708; and Ursula, born on October 3, 1709. While the family of Edmund Fielding was thus rapidly increasing, Sir Henry Gould anticipated in part the provisions of his will with reference to his daughter and grandchildren by purchasing a farm for them at East Stour, a thatched village in north Dorset. The property had formerly belonged to Sir Robert Napier and was sold to the judge by the baronet's surviving daughters, Anne and Theodosia, of Puncknowle, in the same county near the sea.

History of the Abbey of Glaston,'' Bath, 1826, plate xv. It is reproduced here, facing page 16.

The house which formed a part of the estate was the ancient rectory, a large stone mansion having stone pavements, massive oak doors, oak panels, and a carved fireplace. It adjoined the parish church, with gardens and orchards beyond, and pastures and meadows extending down the hills into the valley of the river Stour. Altogether there were several hundred acres of enclosures and commons, for which Sir Henry paid £4,750. He also sent thither oxen to plough the land and cows for a dairy; while he himself, leaving Sharpham to his son Davidge, planned to spend part of the year at East Stour, doubtless to look after the estate during the absence of Edmund Fielding with his regiment.

But on March 26, 1710, a few months after the family was settled at East Stour, Sir Henry died, before he had placed the estate, as was his intention, in trust for his daughter and her children. Accordingly, the trustees named in his will, after considerable delay, employed the £3,000 therein provided for them in the purchase of the homestead and the major part of the lands at East Stour, valued variously at £120 and £150 a year. And that the property might be kept entire, Edmund Fielding reluctantly bought with his own money the remaining lands of Davidge Gould, paying for them £1,750. These family transactions were all carried through in September, 1713; and Edmund Fielding, now a colonel on half pay, was transformed into a gentleman farmer and justice of the peace. His household continued to grow apace. The parish register records the birth of Sarah on November 8, 1710, Anne on June 1, 1713, Beatrice on June 20, 1714, and the baptism of Edmund on April 22, 1716. Anne died in August, 1716; Sarah lived to be a friend of Samuel Richardson and an author of moral essays and tales; while Edmund was destined to follow the profession of his father, though he never rose above the rank of lieutenant. It is probable that Lady Gould, who long survived her husband, settled for a time with her daughter at East Stour to watch over the many children; and later came, too, Mrs. Catherine Cottington, apparently Lady Gould's sister, to take her place. There was a nurse named Mary Bentham, and a governess named Anne de la Borde. There was a succession of nursery-maids and house-maids besides a cook and a butler. A steward did the buying and selling and kept the men on the farm at their work. It was a typical establishment of a country squire who would live in good style.

East Stour was a quiet and healthful place for children to grow up. Through the farm ran several brooks down to the Stour, good for fishing. There were ponds for ducks and geese, and warrens for hares and partridges; and near the house rose a large locust tree, above fifty feet high, out of whose trunk curiously grew an elder tree to the height of twenty-four feet. A mile or two across the fields to the south lay Stour Provost; and westward across the river, West Stour—small villages both; while farther away, to the northeast, was Motcombe, having a gentleman's seat. Years afterward Fielding wrote of "the pleasant banks of sweetly winding Stour," along which he and his sisters used to play, and of "wakes and fairs," and of "Jemmy Tweedle," the wandering fiddler, who cheered "rural nymphs and swains" up and down the valley. Now and then appear in his novels, it is thought, scenes and prospects not unlike those from the uplands of the Fielding farm. Indeed, he loved so well the district, which he knew for many miles around, that he went back there to live for a time after his marriage. The main drawback to life in so remote a place was the education of children. Girls, it is true, did not then count for much, for they were expected at most to learn to read and write—hardly that—in addition to becoming expert with the needle; but a squire's son must be put seriously to his books before going to one of the great public schools and the university.

THE HISTORY OF HENRY FIELDING

Everybody, of course, would like to know under whose guidance Fielding set out on the road to learning. The boy, according to Arthur Murphy, "received the first rudiments of his education at home under the care of the Rev. Mr. Oliver, to whom, we may judge, he was not under any considerable obligations from the very humorous and striking portrait, given of him afterwards, under the name of Parson Trulliber in 'Joseph Andrews.'" This Trulliber, says Fielding in his novel, "was a parson on Sundays, but all the other six days might more properly be called a farmer. He occupied a small piece of land of his own, besides which he rented a considerable deal more. His wife milked his cows, managed his dairy, and followed the markets with butter and eggs. The hogs fell chiefly to his care, which he carefully waited on at home, and attended to fairs; on which occasion he was liable to many jokes, his own size being with much ale rendered little inferior to that of the beasts he sold. He was indeed one of the largest men you should see, and could have acted the part of Sir John Falstaff without stuffing. . . . His voice was loud and hoarse, and his accent extremely broad. To complete the whole, he had a stateliness in his gait, when he walked, not unlike that of a goose, only he stalked slower." As further described, Parson Trulliber was a hypocrite through and through, he never showed a sign of intelligence except when his purse was concerned, and he resembled the swine he fed no more in appearance than in character.

It is very difficult to imagine this coarse, rather than humorous, country parson coming from the pigsty to give Harry Fielding his lessons; and I suspect that Murphy, writing from hearsay, fell into some confusion. The biographer probably named the tutor correctly when he called him Oliver, but was almost certainly mistaken when he identified him with the original—if there was an original—of Parson Trulliber. Oliver, be it said, was a very com-

mon name in the neighbouring parishes. There was, for
example, a gentleman of the name at Stour Provost, whose
son John graduated at Magdalen College, Oxford, in 1704,
and afterwards became a Canon of Chester. Better still,
there was a "Rev. Mr. Oliver" who was holding the curacy
at Motcombe in 1738. According to one antiquary, it was
the Oliver of Stour Provost who taught Harry Fielding;
according to another antiquary, it was the Oliver of Motcombe. As the clergyman of Stour Provost left the valley
in Fielding's childhood, tradition naturally settled upon
the Oliver of Motcombe, whose widow, it is said, was questioned with reference to his relations with the humorist.
She evidently did not know whether her husband, when a
young man, had been Fielding's tutor, but she rightly
denied that he could have sat for the portrait of Parson
Trulliber; for "the Rev. Mr. Oliver" of Motcombe appears
in the parish register, not as an avaricious Parson Trulliber, but as a kind-hearted curate devoted to charity among
his people.

Fortunately there is another slight clue, hitherto overlooked, to the real character of Fielding's tutor in an anonymous burlesque of Richardson's "Pamela," called "Shamela" (1741), which was very generally, and I think correctly, attributed to Fielding at the time of its appearance.
In this humorous skit, the author makes a country parson
named Oliver his mouthpiece for an attack on the immorality of Richardson's novel, a copy of which had been sent
him from London by the Rev. Mr. Tickletext. Parson
Oliver as portrayed in "Shamela" in no respect resembles
Parson Trulliber. He is a man of some humour, some reading, very plain in speech, standing up for the old ways of
the country against the casuistry of Richardson and his
clerical friends in town. Here, I daresay, are some characteristics of Harry Fielding's tutor as well as his name.
In short, the honour of teaching the future novelist his

accidence probably fell to the Rev. Mr. Oliver of Motcombe; but the schoolmaster was in appearance and character a gentleman quite different from the sordid brute depicted as Parson Trulliber.*

The family seems to have thrived well enough at the Stour farm for a time. Children were born, and Harry was kept at his books. But after a few years of it, Colonel Fielding either found life in the country too tame for a soldier, or the presence of his mother-in-law in the household was rather more than he could bear. At any rate, a strange Bill of Complaint, discovered by Miss Godden among the records of the Court of Chancery, shows that the Colonel was staying in London in 1716 at a time when it would have been better for him had he been with his wife and children at East Stour. As related by himself in a very naïve and amusing narrative, Edmund Fielding fell a victim that year to a group of gamesters. It was his custom when he felt the need of recreation, according to his Bill of Complaint to the Lord High Chancellor of Great Britain, to frequent Prince's Coffee-House in the parish of St. James, where he encountered a man calling himself Robert Midford and claiming to be a captain in the army. The Captain pretended "very great kindness" for the Colonel and "an extraordinary value" for his company, introducing him to other so-called officers in his Majesty's service, who displayed equal fondness for him. Often the conversation would turn to the "pleasure or delight" of the ancient game of faro; and one day the Colonel, who knew nothing of gaming (God bless his innocence!), was prevailed upon to try his luck "for a small matter, purely

* For East Stour, the Fielding farm, and the neighbouring parishes, see J. Hutchins, "History and Antiquities of the County of Dorset," second edition, III, 1813, containing on page 211 the two engraved views of the house which are reproduced opposite this page. Additional information has been derived from local records, from Chancery proceedings, and original indentures relative to the East Stour estate, now in private hands.

House inhabited by Henry Fielding at East Stour.

Another View; with the Locust Tree.

for diversion.'' Once in the game, he was so fascinated by it that he played on until he lost to the sharpers £500 and eventually became involved for no less than £780.

Not having so much money as this by him, he gave notes and bonds, covering his debt of honour, to various confederates of Robert Midford in trust for that gentleman. There were bonds of fifty guineas, of thirty guineas, and one of two hundred pounds to a woman who posed as an unmarried sister of the Captain. Her name was Barbara. Some of these notes and bonds, including the one to Barbara, Colonel Fielding was persuaded to pay; but several of them remained unpaid so long that Midford and his associates began to press hard for a final settlement. On one of the obligations a judgment was obtained in a lower court and an execution was threatened against the debtor's goods. Thereupon Colonel Fielding appealed to the Lord Chancellor for protection in a Bill of Complaint dated October 22, 1722. He prayed that the proceedings at law against him be stayed, and that Midford and his sister be summoned before his lordship to show cause why they should not surrender all the notes and bonds which they then held against the plaintiff and repay all sums that they had hitherto received from him. Though an action of several heads, it was really a suit for the recovery of money lost at faro, on the ground that the game was dishonest and illegal. In accordance with Edmund Fielding's humble petition, writs of subpoena were addressed to Robert and Barbara Midford, commanding them to appear and make answer to the Colonel's Bill of Complaint; but needless to say, neither Robert nor Barbara could be found, for they knew that an Act of Parliament declared all gambling debts uncollectable and that they could not conceal from the Lord Chancellor their obvious attempt to evade the law by distributing an unfortunate gentleman's notes among their friends. We may be certain that these gamesters never more troubled Colonel Fielding and that they never returned the guineas which they took from him.*

Already misfortunes were falling thick and fast upon the family at East Stour. Not only did Edmund Fielding give his notes to gamblers and their accomplices, but he was also borrowing money of relatives and friends— £700, for example, from Mrs. Cottington, the godmother of Catherine. Presumably all the money went to the gaming-table and the dissipations of the town. In the summer of 1716, his little daughter Anne, as has been related, sickened and died; and two years later—April 13 or 14, 1718—the household was broken up by the death of Mrs. Fielding. Mother and child were both buried at East Stour. The death of Mrs. Fielding appears to have been unexpected, for she died intestate, leaving unfortunately no directions for the conveyance of her farm and lands at East Stour to her children. Colonel Fielding, as their natural guardian, took possession of the estate, receiving, contrary to the agreement of 1713, the rents as his wife had done before him, and using them, he said, for the maintenance and education of the children—but according to Lady Gould for his own benefit mostly. He did not, however, remain long in the country after his wife's death to watch over the family and the estate. He settled Mrs. Cottington in charge of the children and installed Thomas Grafton as his agent at East Stour, and then went up to London, where he obtained on March 11, 1719, his commission as Colonel of the Invalids, and a few weeks later married a widow named Anne, or Eleanor, Rapha. Not much is known of this woman; but rumours reached Stour and Sharpham that she was an Italian and a Roman Catholic; that she

* Fielding *v.* Midford. London Record Office. Chancery Proceedings, 1714-1758. Division Reynardson. Bundle 2726. Also Edmund Fielding Esq. *v.* Robert Midford Deft. Chancery Decrees and Orders, 1722. No. 339. fo. 5. As Robert Midford could not be found, the Court ordered, on November 7, 1722, that a subpoena be served on his attorney at law.

"kept an eating house in London," and had "two daughters
in a monastery beyond the sea." Grandmother and aunt
were angry at the Colonel's conduct and alarmed for the
welfare of the children. A year which had slipped by in
quiet at East Stour thus ended in confusion.

Mrs. Cottington (as we learn from affidavits in Chancery proceedings soon to be described) was the first to get
authentic news. A letter from the Colonel early in May
informed her that he was married and that a servant,
named Mary Howard, was already on the road to East
Stour to prepare the house for the reception of himself
and wife. A day or two later, Mary Howard arrived and
made a peremptory demand upon Mrs. Cottington for all
the keys, telling her that she was now the housekeeper; and
when Sunday came, she called for a horse to ride to a
Presbyterian meeting, though her real design was to ride
to a Mass in a neighbouring parish. Keys and horse were
flatly refused. But when in the course of ten days the
Colonel appeared on the scene with his new wife, he delivered the keys to Mary Howard, and committed to her,
under the direction of Mrs. Fielding, the entire management of the family. Thereupon Mrs. Cottington retired
to her apartments in the house, where she could observe
or learn from the children how they fared at the hands of
their stepmother and her housekeeper. According to her
story, Mrs. Fielding avowed herself a Roman Catholic and
forbad the children from further instruction in the Catechism of the Church of England; she locked up the Bible
and the History thereof, and left the Romish Prayer Book
in the windows where they might see and read it. Moreover, if their former governess is to be believed, the children
were used by Mrs. Fielding and her maid "in a most barbarous, cruel, and inhumane manner." The bread provided for them she declared to be so poor that they could
not eat it, the butter so rank that they could not come near

27

it, and the beer and ale so insipid or sour that they "were forced to drink water for several days together." When they rebelled against their intolerable food and drink, their father, urged on by his wife, beat and otherwise abused them. Altogether it was a miserable summer for the children.

Naturally the story was told quite differently by the servants directly dependent upon Edmund Fielding and his wife. They swore on their corporal oaths that the children were treated with unusual kindness and affection, that they were permitted to read and recite the Catechism in Mrs. Cottington's rooms, that they constantly dined with the Colonel and his lady, that there were never less than two very good dishes of meat at table, and that there were usually three or four dishes, besides fruits and plenty of strong beer and ale, "of which they always partook." To be sure, the baking or the brewing sometimes miscarried, and then the family suffered equally. Though a Roman Catholic, Mrs. Fielding had no desire to bring up the children in her faith; and if any restraint was placed upon their intercourse with their aunt, it was only a necessary precaution against her endeavours to alienate their affections from their father and stepmother. The truth doubtless lies between the two stories, but the accusations are to be believed rather than the apologies. To say the least, the family was grossly mismanaged by Mrs. Fielding and Mary Howard. The children, who liked better the old way of living with their aunt and governess, resented the intrusion of others upon their peace and quiet. From the standpoint of their father, they became "very headstrong and undutiful," owing to the evil influence of Mrs. Cottington. "The eldest son in particular," it was alleged by the housekeeper, cook, and butler, carried himself "very unhandsomely towards the whole family in general"; that is, towards his father, stepmother, and their servants.

Henry was then twelve years old; and it may be assumed that as the ringleader he felt the worst effects of the rod.

The Colonel, however, was unable to beat his household into order. So he resolved to disperse it. In August, 1719, he placed his four daughters in a boarding-school at Salisbury kept first by Mrs. Deer, and afterwards by Mrs. Mary Rookes, in order that they might "learn needlework" and "know how to carry or behave themselves." His son Edmund, who was of tender age, was consigned, at her urgent request, to the care of Lady Gould, who left Sharpham and Stour and took a house at Salisbury,* where she could oversee the education of her grand-daughters. At this point Colonel Fielding and his wife returned to London, after arrangements had been made that Henry should go to Eton. Apparently against his will, the boy was sent to this famous school in October, 1719, where he soon displayed, says his father, "good proficiency," or aptness for learning.

This disposition of the children bears all the marks of being a compromise between Colonel Fielding and Lady Gould, according to which the nominal control of the children was to remain with their father while the personal supervision of all except Henry was to be entrusted to their grandmother. For a year or more each party seems to have lived up to the tacit agreement, though there was some friction; but a little later the relations between the Colonel and his mother-in-law became greatly strained. Lady Gould grew displeased with the Colonel's management of the farm at East Stour. Children were also being rapidly born of the new marriage. There were already one, two, and three of them. Naturally Lady Gould became alarmed for the welfare of her own grandchildren, and so felt justi-

---

* The parish records at Salisbury show that Lady Gould was assessed on her house in St. Martin's Church Street, from 1720 to 1733, the year of her death. Her house was the fourteenth assessment from St. Martin's Church.

fied in manoeuvring to get them absolutely in her own power, away from a father certain to neglect them in the interest of his new family and away from a stepmother who might contaminate them with the doctrines of the Church of Rome. As soon as the Colonel saw what was happening, he demanded the custody of the children. His design was to take his son Edmund from Lady Gould and to remove his daughters from the school at Salisbury. Thereupon arose a bitter quarrel over the children and their estate. Of the various questions involved in the dispute, the main one became whether the father or the grandmother was in legal phrase "the next friend"—or the natural guardian—of the children, now that the Colonel had married again. Each party sought the advice of lawyers, and each was advised differently, as is usual in such cases. Lady Gould, though nearly seventy years old, was still a woman of determination—a stubborn snag, indeed, for her son-in-law to encounter. While he was merely indulging in loud threats, she took positive action by bringing a Chancery suit against him in the name of the children to oust him from the management of their estate.

Lady Gould's Bill of Complaint,* filed in the Court of Chancery on February 10, 1721, recited with many feminine touches, which her lawyer's phrasing could not conceal, the essential details in the history of the property at East Stour; it told how Sarah Gould intermarried with Edmund Fielding "without the consent of her . . . father or mother and contrary to their good liking"; how her father later bequeathed £3,000 in trust for his undutiful daughter and her children; how his executors satisfied the trust by purchasing, as Sir Henry desired, the farm at East Stour;

* Fielding v. Fielding. Chancery Proceedings, 1714-1758. Division Sewell. Bundle 259. No. 37. London Record Office. The same Bundle contains Edmund Fielding's Answer, and the Answers of Davidge Gould and William Day in a subsequent suit. The Bills and Answers in this case were discovered by Miss G. M. Godden. See her "Henry Fielding," London, 1910.

how, in accordance with the intent of the will, Edmund
Fielding agreed "that he would not intermeddle with the
rents and profits of the said estate, but would permit and
suffer . . . his wife and the said trustees quietly and peace-
ably to receive the same" for the benefit of Sarah and her
children; how on the death of his wife he nevertheless took
possession of the estate, collecting and appropriating to
his own purposes the rents without any interference on the
part of the trustees, Davidge Gould and William Day, as
if they were in confederacy with him to defraud the children
of their income; and how in consequence the children would
have been left without adequate care and support had not
their grandmother removed to Salisbury, where three of
the children were at school and the two youngest were living
in her own house. And then it was set forth that the father,
who had almost deserted his children, was now threatening
to take them all from her supervision in order to rear them
in the Roman Catholic faith. Of this intention Edmund
Fielding's recent conduct, Lady Gould declared, was sufficient evidence; for not only had he married a Roman
Catholic out of an Italian eating-house, whose children by
her former husband were in a convent abroad, but he
himself had "openly commended the manner of education
of young persons in monasteries."

On these representations Lady Gould humbly petitioned
that his Majesty's most gracious writs of subpoena be
directed to Edmund Fielding, Davidge Gould, and William
Day, summoning them to appear and make full and proper
answer to her charges. In case the trustees, who had let
Edmund Fielding do as he pleased with his children's
estate since the death of his first wife, should hereafter
refuse to perform their duty, it was asked that they assign
their trust to some other person or persons to be appointed
by the Court. It was further asked that Edmund Fielding
be enjoined from receiving the rents at East Stour and

from removing his children from the places where they then were, to the end that they might be properly maintained and saved from spiritual ruin at the hands of a stepmother who professed to be a Papist.

Edmund Fielding promptly filed his Answer to Lady Gould's Complaint on the twenty-third of the same month, in a courteously phrased document, half-admitting, half-denying the allegations of his aged mother-in-law, with whom he did not care to "controvert anything . . . further than of necessity." Whatever may have been, he declared, the circumstances of his marriage to Sarah Gould, he was "afterwards well approved of and received by" the family, especially by Sir Henry Gould, who not only put him into possession of the farm at East Stour, but supplied him with the necessary "stock and utensils of husbandry" and expressed a desire to live with him during a part of each year. With his mother-in-law, too, there had been no trouble until his present marriage, which had "occasioned some jealousy and displeasure, . . . though without just grounds." In the main he did not question Lady Gould's statement of the intent of her husband's will or of his own share in the subsequent settlement of the estate at East Stour in trust for Mrs. Fielding and her children. But far from there being any collusion between himself and the trustees, he would call attention to the fact that his brother-in-law, Davidge Gould, as executor of Sir Henry's will, forced him, in order to complete the purchase, to pay a large additional sum not contemplated by the old judge when he made provision for the trust. Notwithstanding his rights in equity to a part of the estate, the Colonel claimed that he had nevertheless expended the entire income of £150 and much besides upon his children, and hoped to continue the same "tender and affectionate care" of them. With the exception of Edmund they were now all at school, and the education of Henry at Eton was costing him "upwards of sixty pounds" a year. On one point the Colonel was wisely silent. He did not inform the Court that he had just disposed of 153 acres of land, with the buildings thereon, at East and West Stour, which probably included some of the lands which he had purchased of Davidge Gould.* Though not an act deserving special criticism, the sale shows that he was reducing the estate at East Stour to the original dimensions of the trust.

In reply to the insinuation that he was not a fit person to have the custody of his children, he asserted that he was "a Protestant of the Communion of the Church of England"; and denied, hedging somewhat, that he had ever commended "the manner of education of young persons in monasteries if it be meant in respect of religion." He further denied that his present wife was an Italian or had ever kept an eating-house; but he did not say whether she was a Roman Catholic. He had never "threatened" to take his children out of the school at Salisbury; he had merely declared that such was his "design." Should they be restored to him, he would certainly bring them up as Protestants. Incidentally the Court was warned not to regard too seriously Lady Gould's taking a house at Salisbury for their supervision, since she had settled there as much for her own convenience and the desire of "living in a town." It was left to the Lord Chancellor to decide whether the children should remain with their grandmother, now far advanced in age, or be entrusted to himself, who could help them on in the world by means of his kinship with "many noble families." In this manner the Colonel reasoned plausibly; but it does not require a man read in the law to see that his defence was weak, for he admitted or evaded most of the allegations urged against him. He had collected the rents at East Stour and had rendered no

* Miss G. M. Godden, "Henry Fielding," p. 10. See also Mr. J. Paul de Castro, in "Notes and Queries," 12 S. III, 465 (Nov., 1917).

account of them to the trustees. He had married a Roman Catholic and had praised the training to be obtained in Roman Catholic schools, though meaning thereby not religious training. It was clearly his intention to get his children beyond Lady Gould's reach, and then to dispose of them in such ways as he and their stepmother should determine. His distinction between a threat and a design, or between religious and non-religious instruction supplied by monasteries, was altogether too subtle for practical purposes. It must have amused the Lord Chancellor.

The trustees who were named in Lady Gould's Bill of Complaint made no immediate answer to her charge that they had neglected their duty and were acting in league with Edmund Fielding. None was really necessary, for all matters in controversy were well covered by the Colonel as the principal defendant in the suit. Moreover, Lady Gould now persuaded the trustees to come to her aid. At the Lent Assizes, they sought to recover the premises at East Stour by means of a writ of ejectment against the Colonel, who relates that he appeared with counsel in the County court at Dorchester, ready for the fray, but that the case was not tried owing to a defect in the writ. Subsequently a similar action was brought against him on another writ, and this time the Colonel himself prevented the case from coming to trial. While this suit as well as the one in Chancery was still pending, there occurred an incident in which posterity has a much greater interest.

Thus far in the legal proceedings, Henry Fielding had been kept in the background. The quarrel had been over the younger children at Salisbury rather than over him, a boy of fourteen, quietly pursuing his studies at Eton to the apparent satisfaction of all parties concerned. But now something happened, of which we have two versions, both on the authority of his father. According to the story as it was first told, Harry "eloped," that is, ran away,

from Eton on or about the seventh of April, 1721, and fled
to his grandmother. According to a later story, he was
summoned home by Lady Gould and her son Davidge
acting for the trustees. Probably neither account is quite
correct. The boy of course knew of the Chancery suit and
he must have been disturbed by it. There are also indications in the legal documents that he had sided with his
grandmother from the very beginning of the family quarrel
and that he had thereby awakened his father's displeasure
to such an extent as threatened his removal from Eton to
a place nearer at hand. The place settled upon was evidently Westminster School, where his father, who was
living in St. James's parish, would be able to keep a close
watch upon him and prevent him from visiting his grandmother in the vacations. No boy who has spent two years
in a great public school cares to be transferred to another,
even though it have a reputation equally high. Harry, I
take it, suspected his father's design, and simply packed
up and went home to his grandmother for protection, either
on his own initiative or on her advice. He eloped only in
the sense that he left Eton without the knowledge of his
father, who heard the news a week or two after the boy
had safely arrived in Salisbury. Whether the lad made
that journey alone or with his valet, it was a daring
enterprise.

Henceforth the proper regulation of this mettlesome boy
became a question to be decided by the Lord Chancellor as
the Supreme Guardian of the Infants of Great Britain.
Early in May the Colonel sent two servants, Henry Hal-
stead and Frances Barber, down to Salisbury to bring all
his six children up to London. Mary Rookes refused to
surrender the girls to the woman; and Lady Gould, who
had the boys under her own roof, bolted her doors against
the man, who nevertheless succeeded one evening in deliver-
ing a message from the Colonel through the window, accom-

panied with curses of a kind which we do not print in books nowadays. Though this bold attempt to take the children by force completely failed, there was danger that they might be kidnapped at any time by more experienced agents. Fearing this event, Lady Gould on the sixth of June petitioned the Lord Chancellor that the children be allowed to remain where they then were until the cause could be heard. The Court so ordered, and set the eighth of July for the hearing. In the meantime, on a commission issued by the Court for the examination of witnesses, nine distinct affidavits* were taken, of which one bore two and another three signatures. Among the affidavits was one from the Colonel, who insisted upon his militant Protestantism, declaring that as a Dorsetshire justice of the peace at the time of the recent Jacobite insurrection he had dealt severely with all who were in the least suspected of disaffection to his present Majesty. On the day appointed, the Lord Chancellor heard Lady Gould's petition and what was alleged on both sides; and thereupon ordered that Henry be continued at Eton and the other children at Salisbury until Lady Gould's suit should be determined. Thereafter the Court granted two minor petitions preferred jointly by Henry Fielding and Lady Gould. On November 30, 1721, the boy by this means obtained permission to spend the Christmas holidays with his grandmother, and on April 26, 1722, to visit her during the usual recess at Whitsuntide.

There had been some delay in Lady Gould's original suit in Chancery due to the neglect or carelessness of her counsel. Her Bill of Complaint was shown by the Colonel's lawyers to be defective in that it failed to include Henry's

* Affidavit Register. Vol. 37. Trinity Term, 1721. Nos. 14-17, and 402-406. London Record Office. These affidavits were discovered by F. J. Pope, F. R. Hist. S., who gave an account of them in "The Times" (London), Dec. 17, 1913, and in "The British Archivist," Jan., 1914.

younger brother Edmund among the plaintiffs. Accordingly, on October 26, 1721, the Court ordered the Bill to be amended, and at the same time renewed, on the request of Lady Gould's counsel, the commission to examine witnesses. While the case, still incomplete, was thus lagging in Chancery contrary to the desire of the Lord Chancellor, who had urged that it be speeded to a hearing, the Colonel attempted to turn the tables against his prosecutors by filing, on January 30, 1722, a Bill of Complaint* in behalf of his children against the trustees of their estate and against Lady Gould and Mary Rookes, whom he claimed were acting in confederacy. He asked that the trustees be stayed in the action which they had brought against him in the County court and that they be required to convey, in accordance with his understanding of Sir Henry Gould's will, the estate at East Stour directly to the children as tenants in common. He also asked that he be given the custody of his children, who were unlawfully detained by Lady Gould and Mary Rookes, and that his son Henry, who had been with Lady Gould during the Christmas vacation and allowed to "go about in the way of idleness to the irreparable loss of his time, . . . be forthwith returned to Eton School to go on in his learning."

Lady Gould, on the advice of her counsel, paid no attention to this cross-bill, which was directed not so much against her as against the trustees. The Answer of her son Davidge, which took the form of an affidavit executed at Sharpham Park on April 20, 1722, denied any "combination or confederacy" on his part and sought to justify all his acts in connection with the Stour estate. Likewise the Answer of William Day—a similar affidavit dated May 26, 1722—denied the Colonel's main allegation, adding that the defendant was only a "nominal trustee," that he had left

---

* Fielding *v.* Gould. Chancery Proceedings, 1714-1758. Division Reynardson. Bundle 2283. London Record Office.

the entire management of the trust to Davidge Gould, and so knew no more of what had occurred than if he were a stranger. It was a startling revelation.

Two days later, on May 28, 1722, the case was heard by Lord Macclesfield, the Lord High Chancellor. Learned counsel were present on both sides to debate the questions arising out of the Colonel's recent counter suit as well as Lady Gould's original Bill of Complaint. As foreshadowed in the Lord Chancellor's previous orders, the Colonel lost on all the main points at issue. The trust being "well proved," it was ordered and decreed that Edmund Fielding deliver possession of his children's estate to the trustees and render full account of the rents and profits since the death of his wife Sarah Gould, though he might deduct therefrom what he had expended in improvements and in the maintenance and education of the children. William Day, who had failed to perform his duties, must assign his trust to Davidge Gould, and in case the latter should refuse to act, he must in turn assign his trust to such person or persons as the Master in Chancery might appoint. Moreover, until a further order from the Court, the children were to remain in the schools where they had been placed, and were to reside during recesses and holidays with Lady Gould in order that they might not come under the influence of their stepmother, "who appears to be a Papist." The Lord Chancellor also considered at the same time a complaint of Mrs. Cottington, who alleged that the Colonel owed her £700 (presumably lost in gambling), which she would like to have employed for the benefit of her nephews and nieces. She was accordingly directed to sue for this sum, which, if the debt was proved, should be laid out in the purchase of lands for the said children. As the Court anticipated, Davidge Gould was unwilling to take the entire responsibility of the trust; whereupon, as we see by an order dated November 22, 1723, Lady Gould and Catherine

Cottington were appointed trustees in his stead, on the surety of Mistress Mary Bentham.* Subsequently, however, he was persuaded to reassume the trusteeship. Thus terminated the suit in Chancery, with Lady Gould and the other trustees in complete possession of the children and their estate. The blustering and improvident father, really brave and generous at heart, was no match for the aged grandmother, alert and imperious.

The Lord Chancellor's order that Mrs. Cottington obtain judgment for the debt due her from Edmund Fielding explains the curious Bill of Complaint which the Colonel filed a few months later against Robert Midford the gambler for the return of £780 lost at faro. Ordinarily a suit of this kind would have been brought in the Court of Common Pleas or the King's Bench, but in this instance it was very properly made a part of the Chancery proceedings that involved the children. The Colonel seems to have promptly acknowledged his debt to Mrs. Cottington and, having no other means of raising so large a sum, to have attempted to recover what he had paid Midford, on the principle that the money should come from the pocket where it had gone. His suit failed, and so, I fear, the former boundaries of his children's estate were never enlarged by his assistance.

With this defeat, Edmund Fielding drops from our narrative except for an occasional reference. Another family of many children was already growing up about him, among them a son John, blind from his youth—the "dear Jack," to whom Henry became tenderly attached in mature life. Though his grandmother's boy, it would appear that Henry often visited his father and stepmother and liked not only Jack but his other brothers and their sisters, none of whom

* Chancery Decrees and Orders. Trinity Term, 1722. In book for 1721. Vol. 337, fo. 377. London Record Office. For other orders in the case, see Trinity Term, 1721, in book for 1720, fo. 339; Michaelmas Term, 1721, fos. 2 and 70; Easter Term, 1722, in book for 1721, fo. 206; Michaelmas Term, 1722, fo. 5; Michaelmas Term, 1723, fo. 45.

became, so far as is known, Roman Catholics. Certainly there was a complete reconciliation between father and son, if indeed there had ever been any real estrangement. The Colonel of the Invalids was appointed a Brigadier-General in 1727, and a Major-General in 1735. He rose to the rank of Lieutenant-General in 1739 and died two years afterwards, having served, said "The London Magazine" of June, 1741, "in the late wars against France with much bravery." His second wife dying in 1727, he married at least once more. His last (perhaps his fourth) wife survived him for nearly thirty years.* Throughout his later life, General Fielding continued his interest in the education and career of Henry, aiding him, however, rather by promises than by their substance.

* See Mr. J. Paul de Castro in "Notes and Queries," Nov., 1917, p. 465. The dates for the deaths of the second and the last wife are also given in Musgrave's "Obituary" (1900). Perhaps there is a clue to an intermediate wife in the Churchwardens' accounts of St. Martin's Church, Salisbury, for 1739, which contain an entry for fees for the burial of "the wife of Felding," amounting to 2s. 6d.

CHAPTER II

YOUTH AND EDUCATION

It is thought strange that Eton has no record of the boy who came there from East Stour, and after eighteen months ran home to his grandmother. But in the eighteenth century, it was the custom to preserve merely the lists of "collegers," or poor scholars on the foundation, who were provided with wretched food and wretched quarters in the college or school; whereas Henry Fielding, the son of a gentleman, could have entered Eton only as an "oppidan," or independent scholar living at the expense of his family in one of the boarding-houses of the town. Indeed, Fielding later put into the mouth of Parson Adams pleasant banter of the King's Scholars, those young men selected from the collegers to go to King's College, Cambridge, on scholarships and without further examination. Fielding belonged to quite another class. His allowance of nearly £70 a year was very liberal—considerably larger than that of William Pitt, afterwards Lord Chatham, who was at Eton in Fielding's time, coming like him from the West. In after life Pitt formed one of a famous company to whom Fielding read aloud from the manuscript of "Tom Jones." Did the reader include, we wonder, that fine passage wherein the Great Commoner is said to have transferred to his speeches the whole spirit of Demosthenes and Cicero and made "the English senate a rival in eloquence to Greece and Rome"?

Another famous schoolfellow was Charles Hanbury, afterwards Sir Charles Hanbury Williams, wit and diplomatist, to whom Fielding submitted the manuscript of his

41

last comedy, who, rumour once said, took it with him on his embassy to Russia and lost it. But closer to Fielding than either Pitt or Hanbury, was George Lyttelton, destined like Pitt for the peerage, to whose political fortunes the novelist devoted his pen for many years, receiving in return gifts and influence and perhaps periods of leisure for composing his masterpiece. Him Fielding immortalized in the dedication to "Tom Jones." Fielding's near relationship to the Earl of Denbigh naturally made him the associate of boys like these. It is thus a fair inference, though he nowhere, I think, mentions him by name, that he was at least acquainted with another Etonian of the same time— Henry Fox, who became the first Lord Holland and the father of Charles James Fox, the statesman. To Eton came somewhat later Charles Pratt, the first Earl Camden, with whom Fielding afterwards travelled the Western Circuit in pursuit of briefs. Of boys outside this group whom Fielding certainly knew, were Gilbert West, the translator of Pindar; and Thomas Arne, who subsequently wrote the music of Fielding's "Tom Thumb" when that burlesque was turned into a comic opera.

Fielding was sent to Eton, his father declared, in October, 1719, being then in his thirteenth year; his grandmother kept him at Salisbury for a month or two after he ran away in April, 1721; and the Lord Chancellor twice ordered, on July 8, 1721, and May 28, 1722, that he remain in this school. Though these are the only records yet discovered of Fielding's residence at Eton, it is certain that he remained there until 1724 or 1725, when he reached his eighteenth or nineteenth year. Otherwise there is no explanation of the classical knowledge—usually somewhat overestimated—which he showed at the very beginning of his literary career. "At this great seminary of education," it is a tradition handed down from Arthur Murphy, "Henry Fielding gave distinguishing proofs of strong and peculiar parts; and when he left the place, he was said to be uncommonly versed in the Greek authors, and an early master of the Latin classics; for both which he retained a strong admiration in all the subsequent passages of his life.'' Fielding himself, after a sojourn abroad, referred to his classical attainments in more modest terms, saying—

> *Tuscan* and *French* are in my head;
> *Latin* I write, and *Greek* I—read.

The second line of the couplet, despite the exigency of rhyme, probably describes, with a measure of accuracy, Fielding's relative command over the two ancient languages at the time he left school. He was trained to write Latin with ease, and made use of it at a later period in burlesque of the ponderous style then current among classical scholars. But in writing Greek, he never went beyond a few happy phrases and plays upon them for comic effect. From this lack of facility with Greek may be drawn an inference. It is that, owing to one or more interruptions in his stay at Eton, he never passed beyond the fifth form; for boys in the sixth form were then required to write a set of Greek verses once or twice a week.

The curriculum at Eton was very circumscribed when compared with what it is to-day. There was no science, of course; no modern language or modern literature; no mathematics beyond arithmetic and the most elementary algebra; practically nothing except Latin—the main study— and some Greek. But within its limits it was a splendid training for a boy like Harry Fielding. The headmaster under whose instruction he should have come during his last year was Henry Bland, a scholar of moderate attainments, a Whig in politics such as Fielding himself became mainly. Associated with the headmaster were several assistant-masters, two of whom edited excellent selections from the classics for use in the school. To these men who held minor positions at Eton, Fielding was indebted for his love of ancient learning. The first year, if I read the curriculum aright, he was grounded in Latin grammar, ciphered a little, wrote some English for the correct construction of sentences, and drew maps of Greece and Italy, putting in the ancient towns. It was in studies of this kind that Fielding showed "good proficiency." Would that we had the letter from Dr. Bland or one of the assistants to the Colonel, giving the details! In due time came Greek grammar; and then the whole realm of Latin and Greek literature lay open for the boys. They read a few authors regularly and extensively—Homer, Virgil, Ovid, and Horace—and roamed about widely among the rest in the collections prepared by their assistant-masters.

It is interesting for one on the traces of Fielding's knowledge of ancient literature to look into these old collections, to see some of the pieces he read in his youth and to observe his mature comment upon the authors,— occasionally, upon the very passages studied and perhaps memorized at school. The "Scriptores Romani," for example, contained selections from Cicero, Livy, Tacitus, Paterculus, and Pliny. The corresponding Greek collection, called "Scriptores Graeci," contained selections from Herodotus, Thucydides, Xenophon, Plato, Isocrates, and Lucian, with translations into Latin on the opposite pages. In the same manner the boys were aided in their translations from Greek poetry by Latin versions placed side by side with the original Greek. They thus read out of their "Poeti Graeci" famous passages from the Odyssey, much from Hesiod, Pindar, Theocritus, Apollonius Rhodius, and the most beautiful of the Greek lyrics, including the fragments of Sappho. Demosthenes and the Greek dramatists—usually Sophocles and Aristophanes—they studied separately, assisted likewise by Latin versions. The catalogue of ancient writers comprised also Caesar, Nepos, Terence, Seneca, Juvenal, the Latin fabulists,

Plutarch, and many a minor poet or prose writer here and there. Every week the boys recited from memory passages in Latin and Greek—always one from the New Testament on Monday morning; and the upper forms declaimed speeches from Cicero or Sallust or Livy.

All these and other classical authors in the Eton curriculum were afterwards quoted or referred to by Fielding in his own writings; most frequently it was Horace, as was then the fashion, whom from many repetitions he must have known almost by heart. The Odyssey, which was then taken up at Eton only in parts, he never knew very well except in Pope's translation; while of the Iliad, which was read entire, with much memorizing, he sang continued praises. It is of course Fielding who speaks eloquently through Parson Adams of Homer's nice distinctions in character-drawing and of the variety and immensity of his scenes in the Iliad. With equal eloquence the Parson repeats the story of Jason's voyage for the golden fleece, as "sweetly described by Apollonius Rhodius" in the book used at Eton. On the other hand, Aeschylus, who was the Parson's favourite dramatist, Fielding never read at all in the original Greek; and not much of Euripides, only scenes from whom were studied at school. To Fielding, as to all Etonians of that day, Sophocles was "the greatest genius who ever wrote tragedy," and Aristophanes was the earliest of the great humorists. Virgil he praised at times for his restraint, when compared with the exuberance of Homer somewhat overdone. Plutarch and Nepos were long pleasant memories of books read in his youth; and as age crept over him, he turned to the ancient historians again and placed them above the epic poets. "I should have honoured," he then said, "and loved Homer more had he written a true history of his own times in humble prose than those noble poems that have so justly collected the praise of all ages; for, though I read these with more admiration and astonishment, I still read Herodotus, Thucydides, and Xenophon, with more amusement and more satisfaction.'' And to Plutarch he paid the greatest tribute at his command, when he wrote, ''I have not read even Lucian himself with more delight than Plutarch.'' When this mood was upon him, he accused Hesiod as well as Homer of perverting and confusing, perhaps unconsciously, ''the records of antiquity,'' and put the elder Pliny at the head of writers who lie for the lie's sake, attempting ''to impose the most monstrous improbabilities and absurdities upon their readers on their own authority.'' And Aristophanes, whose works he once thought of translating, he eventually classed with Rabelais as two writers whose ''design appears to me very plainly to have been to ridicule all sobriety, modesty, decency, virtue, and religion out of the world.''

Three or four of the ancients whose acquaintance Fielding made at Eton, he never turned against in any mood. Aristotle, whom he was fond of quoting, may have been a later discovery; but Plato, a book of his youth, he took with him on his last voyage. His quotations from Cicero were never ending. The vituperation of Cicero's orations seems to have had no interest for him; but Cicero's critical and philosophical writings became the very warp and woof of his thinking. To cite an instance or two, ''Cicero de Oratore,'' with its disquisitions on wit, humour, and ridicule, contributed directly to his mature views on these subjects; and when sickness and poverty pressed upon him, he sat down and read quietly, says Arthur Murphy, ''Cicero de Consolatione.'' Finally, there was Lucian—''the incomparable Lucian,'' whose dialogues had been in the Eton collections for a century. Lucian he joined with Cervantes and Swift, as ''the great triumvirate''—''the great masters'' who ''sent their satire . . . laughing into the world.'' Lucian, first read in extracts at school, he studied above all

46

other writers. At one time he projected with the Rev. William Young (the original of Parson Adams), a translation of Lucian's complete works; he directly imitated him in the best Lucian dialogue of modern times; and more to the point, formed his style, as Swift had done before him, upon the ancient master of irony.

It is marvellous that Fielding got so much out of Eton. A curriculum such as he was put through often awakens dislike, even hatred, of the authors studied at school, minutely sentence by sentence, line by line. But Fielding possessed that curiosity which distinguishes genius from commonplace minds. A passage from Horace, Virgil, Homer, or the Greek Testament became his own by committing it to memory. An extract from Plato, Cicero, or Lucian led him to read long stretches in these authors, until he found himself in the midst of the "vast, luxuriant stores" of ancient learning. His curiosity then carried him into the modern literatures, into French and Italian, into English from Shakespeare down through Milton to his own times, to Pope, Swift, Addison, and, as we shall see, to the mere scribblers of the age. From childhood onward he also read the fiction, histories, and books of devotion common in country households of the period. He mentions especially "Guy of Warwick," "Argalus and Parthenia," and "The Seven Champions of Christendom,"—all of which then circulated as chapbooks. The "great favourite" of his youth, he said expressly, was Baker's "Chronicle of the Kings of England," which "lay open in the hall window" for children to read. This book he kept by him, and late in life wrote amusing parodies of its wonderful incidents. "The Imitation of Christ" he merely alludes to in one of his many references to the Bible, which he knew thoroughly in the English version, to say nothing of his acquaintance with the New Testament in Latin and Greek by the time he left school. "The Whole Duty of Man," if he had not

47

met with it in his mother's library, he came to know at Eton; for it was then the custom to assemble the boys—both collegers and oppidans—every Sunday afternoon to listen to an hour's reading from this very pious treatise written by a former Provost of Eton.

From all this it should not be inferred that Fielding was one of those boys who are always poring over books away from their fellows. As we know him in mature life, he was the most companionable of men, and there is no reason to suppose that he was different in his youth. He was a full-blooded boy of the kind certain to take an active part in the sports at Eton, such as trapball, swimming, and an occasional cockfight. In one of his rare references to his schooldays, he recalls how, "with true Spartan devotion," he had often sacrificed his blood in the interests of learning upon the "birchen altar" set up by the masters. The "birchen altar," a famous institution at Eton, was an unpretentious pair of movable steps kept in a room off from the library for uses that made the boys shudder. To complete the account of Fielding's schooldays, we must think of him as sometimes kneeling on the lower step of this altar with hands down as Dr. Bland applies the birch and the praeposters stand by as witnesses to the punishment for the young man's neglect of his lessons or his going beyond the bounds fixed by the school. Dr. Bland was so skilled a hand at the birch that the culprit always felt a recurrence of the old tingling sensations along his posteriors whenever he thought of Eton.*

Probably genius should always be allowed to go its own way and take the consequences. But it was very unfortunate for Fielding's subsequent happiness, whatever may have been the gain for literature, that the strong hand which

---

* For Eton in the eighteenth century, see H. C. Maxwell Lyte, "A History of Eton College," London, 1889. Copies of the Latin and Greek collections then in use at Eton are in the Library of Yale University.

had kept him at his books while at Eton was not held over him for a few years more. He ought to have gone at once, prudence says, to the university, as would have happened under the advice of a wise guardian. But owing to the advancing age of his grandmother, he really became his own master, free to follow his own inclinations without the check of practical wisdom. Having satisfied his immediate curiosity about books, he was now curious to know life directly. On the kind of mistake which he then made, he afterwards commented when describing the career of Mr. Wilson in "Joseph Andrews." "Being a forward youth," Mr. Wilson there says, "I was extremely impatient to be in the world: for which I thought my parts, knowledge, and manhood, thoroughly qualified me. And to this early introduction into life, without a guide, I impute all my future misfortunes; for, besides the obvious mischiefs which attend this, there is one which hath not been so generally observed: the first impression which mankind receives of you will be very difficult to eradicate. How unhappy, therefore, must it be to fix your character in life, before you can possibly know its value, or weigh the consequences of those actions which are to establish your future reputation!" When Fielding thus left Eton, not later than the summer of 1725, to mix with the world, he was a very handsome boy of happy temperament, physically perfect like the young men in his novels. In stature he was rising above six feet, with broad shoulders, and strong and well-proportioned arms and legs. His brown hair was doubtless worn long as was then the custom among schoolboys. His forehead was high, his eyes dark, and his nose "a little inclined to the Roman." It was a wonderful face in which brilliant eyes and cheeks radiant with health gave immediate response to the unregulated emotions of love, tenderness, and anger. Despite his large physique, he was graceful in all his move-

ments; he dressed with perfect neatness; and was withal
provided with a valet or man-servant.

For a year or more Fielding and his man—whose name
was Joseph Lewis—probably roamed about in the West,
with perhaps occasional visits to London. In the autumn
of 1725, they were staying at Lyme Regis, a picturesque
little town of West Dorset running down the hills to the
sea—a good distance away from Salisbury and Lady Gould.
Fielding, then in his nineteenth year, the down not yet off
his cheek, had been drawn to Lyme Regis by the wealth and
beauty of Miss Sarah Andrew, a slip of a girl only fifteen
years old. Miss Andrew belonged to a family of successful
merchants in the town, with a seat at Shapwick, "beauti-
fully situated in a sequestered valley," on the Stour, near
Blandford. The estate, once belonging to Newenham
Abbey in the adjoining county of Devon, passed after the
dissolution of the monasteries to the noble family of Petre,
from whom it was purchased by Sarah's great-grandfather,
Solomon Andrew, "three times," says the inscription on
his tombstone, "Mayor of Lyme Regis." Her father, also
named Solomon, was the last in the male line to reach
maturity. And when Fielding entered upon the scene, not
only were Miss Andrew's father and mother both dead,
but by the death of two brothers she had fallen heir to the
family wealth.

Like Fielding's, the estate of Miss Andrew was held in
trust for her by her uncle Andrew Tucker of Lyme Regis
and Ambrose Rhodes of Modbury in South Devon. At that
time Mr. Tucker was a member of the corporation, and soon
became mayor of the town. As one of her guardians, he
took the orphan into his own home where he could watch
over her with a view to her marriage, as soon as she should
reach the proper age, to his son John, a young man twenty-
four years old, destined to become, like his father, mayor
of Lyme Regis. Mr. Rhodes likewise had a son Ambrose,

a student at Oxford, to whom he wished to marry the heiress. In these circumstances, Fielding came to Lyme Regis as Miss Andrew's third suitor, and settled down there with his man in close siege of her heart. There must have been before this some love passages between Henry and Sarah, although the story gives no account of these secret things. If the genealogists speak true, Davidge Gould had married the sister of Miss Andrew's mother. Hence the girl would naturally visit her aunt at Sharpham Park and perhaps Lady Gould at Salisbury, where, at one place or the other, Henry had an opportunity to fall upon his knees before the charming heiress. Very likely she was hurried home to be out of her lover's way and he immediately followed her.

After he reached Lyme Regis, the situation grew more and more desperate owing to the closer guard then kept over Miss Andrew. At last nothing remained but an abduction—a not uncommon way of getting a wife in the eighteenth century,—which was carefully planned by Fielding and his man, probably with the consent of Miss Andrew. So on a Sunday while Miss Andrew was on her way to church towards the eastern edge of the town, Fielding and his man Lewis attempted to carry her off by force. Mr. Tucker rescued her only after a good beating in which he was bruised and perhaps maimed. Thereupon, as recorded in the Registry Book of Lyme Regis under date of November 14, 1725, he summoned Fielding and his man before Mayor John Bowdidge, who bound them over to keep the peace so long as they should remain in the town. Mr. Tucker was in fear, he declared, not merely of bodily harm but of his life from these dangerous men. And that Miss Andrew herself might be safe, she was quietly removed by Mr. Tucker to Modbury and placed under the surveillance of Mr. Rhodes, her other guardian. But Mr. Tucker evidently had not been let into the secret designs of his colleague, who married her the next year to his own son Ambrose, fresh from Oxford. As Mrs. Rhodes, she became the ancestor of a well-known family of physicians and divines. Her portrait as she was in youth long hung, it is said, at Bellair near Exeter, one of the family seats; and was pointed out to visitors as the original of Sophia Western. The identification, as will be seen later, was mistaken, except in so far as Miss Andrew and Miss Western were both beautiful young women of nearly the same age.*

Fielding must have felt some satisfaction when he heard that the Tuckers complained because they had been "tricked out of the heiress." His main feeling, however, was disappointment at the loss of Miss Andrew and her fortune. Assuming the rôle of "an injured lover," he consoled himself by modernizing in burlesque verse a long stretch of Juvenal's "Sixth Satire" on the disloyalties of women. Years afterwards, when Miss Andrew had become a mere memory, he reworked the poem, adding humorous notes in Latin and English, and included it among his "Miscellanies." The poem contains occasional clever lines in Hudibrastic metre, such as—

> What, wilt thou wear the marriage chain,
> While one whole halter doth remain—

but its main interest lies in the fact that it is the earliest extant piece of writing from the pen of Henry Fielding. If married life is so unhappy as it is here made out to be, it is well that Fielding did not wed Miss Andrew, who shut her gate " 'gainst old acquaintance." It is well, too, on

---

* G. Roberts, "The History of Lyme Regis," Sherborne, 1823, pp. 179-180; J. Davidson, "The History of Newenham Abbey," London, 1843, pp. 163-167; J. Hutchins, "History and Antiquities of Dorset," third edition, 1863, II, 37-80; J. Burke, "Landed Gentry" under *Gould*, and "History of the Commoners of Great Britain," 1838, III, 566-571; and A. Dobson, "Henry Fielding," 1900, pp. 277-285.

other grounds, for Fielding, once at Shapwick, would have settled down as a country gentleman; and there would have been no "Tom Jones."

Fielding is not heard of again until late in January, 1728, when he was in London, publishing a poem called "The Masquerade" and preparing his first comedy—"Love in Several Masques"—for the stage. There is evidence in the play that he had not wasted his time since leaving Eton, notwithstanding the escapade at Lyme Regis. It may be that he had been nibbling, as his grandmother would wish, at the law; for he had already acquired a ready knowledge of legal phrases and was familiar with court proceedings. He was still reading the ancient classics—Plato, Aristotle, Cicero, Seneca, and Epictetus; and at the same time he was amused by the satire of Swift, which was reaching its height in "Gulliver's Travels," and he had just discovered Cervantes, the greatest single influence upon him after Lucian. Looking backward, he had not forgotten the dulness, prolixity, and expense of Chancery suits, to which he makes allusion; and the more romantic situation in his comedy reflects with variations the affair with Miss Andrew.

A beautiful heiress named Helena (you see how closely Fielding follows his own experience in this episode of the play) is left a ward to her uncle Sir Positive Trap, a country gentleman proud and surly of temper. She is desperately in love with Merital, against whom her guardian can urge nothing except his small estate. This objection to the match is quite sufficient, however, from Sir Positive's point of view; and every means is taken to keep the lovers apart and to marry Helena off to a suitor in keeping with her comfortable fortune. In a scene of the second Act, Sir Positive and Lady Trap are trying to force upon her Sir Apish Simple:

"*Hel.* Don't teaze me so, dear uncle. I can never like a fool, I abhor a fop.

53

Sir Pos. But there are three thousand pounds a year, and a title. Do you abhor those, hussy?

Hel. His estate I don't want, and his title I despise.

Sir Pos. Very fine! very fine! Despise a title! Hussy, you are no Trap. Oons! I believe you are no woman either. What, wou'd you take a scandalous, sneaking Mister? one who can't make you a lady?

Hel. Since nothing else will do, I am engaged by all the strength of vows and honour.

Sir Pos. Engaged! Why, was not the Widow Jilt engaged to Mr. Goodland, and left him immediately on the arrival of Sir Harry Rich, whom she left again for my Lord Richmore? Never tell me of engagements, contracts, and I don't know what. Mere bug-bears to frighten children with; all women of sense laugh at them. You are no more obliged to stand to your word when you have promised a man than when you have refused him. The law dissolves all contracts without a valuable consideration; or, if it did not, a valuable consideration would dissolve the law."

In the end, Merital wins Helena by a trick; whereupon Sir Positive rushes upon the stage furious, exclaiming, as he points to Merital's neck: "She is an heiress, and you are guilty of felony, and shall be hanged, with the whole company, your abettors."

After this fashion Fielding, by a mere change in the conclusion, adjusted his own romance to the exigencies of the stage. In further memory of Miss Andrew he chose as the motto of his comedy when he published it two lines from the "Sixth Satire" of Juvenal:

> Nec Veneris pharetris macer est, nec lampade fervet;
> Inde faces ardent; veniunt a dote sagittae—

which he had rendered in his burlesque a year or two before:

> Venus ne'er shot at him an arrow,
> Her fortune darted through his marrow.

Finally in closing the play, he made a handsome apology to the ladies for his satire upon their follies, saying through Wisemore as the company advances: "And now, ladies, I think myself bound to a solemn recantation of every slander I have thrown upon your sex: for I am convinced, that our complaints against you flow generally (if not always) more from our want of merit than your want of justice."

In this mood he addressed a very pretty poem, not printed for many years, to Euthalia, someone who had taken the place of Sarah Andrew among the Sapphos and Rosalindas he had met since coming to London:

> Burning with love, tormented with despair,
> Unable to forget or ease his care;
> In vain each practis'd art Alexis tries;
> In vain to books, to wine or women flies;
> Each brings Euthalia's image to his eyes.
> In Lock's or Newton's page her learning glows;
> Dryden the sweetness of her numbers shews;
> In all their various excellence I find
> The various beauties of her perfect mind.
> How vain in wine a short relief I boast!
> Each sparkling glass recalls my charming toast.
> To women then successless I repair,
> Engage the young, the witty, and the fair.
> When Sappho's wit each envious breast alarms,
> And Rosalinda looks ten thousand charms;
> In vain to them my restless thoughts would run;
> Like fairest stars, they show the absent sun.*

In order to bring out his play, it was of course necessary for Fielding to come up to London the previous autumn. Indeed, he refers incidentally to the coronation of George the Second, which occurred on October 11, 1727. He must also have been in London during the dramatic season of 1726-1727, else he could not have acquired the knowledge

* "Miscellanies," 1743, I, 71.

of the town which he was displaying. Clearly the young man had been drifting for some time away from his grandmother to a father who lived amid more exciting scenes than were afforded by Salisbury. The London with which he came into closest contact comprised Covent Garden and its neighbourhood, stretching off to the west through Leicester Square and the Haymarket to the Mall and St. James's Park. This was the theatrical district and the centre of fashion and dissipation. Covent Garden, it ought to be said, was a spacious square sometimes called the Piazza, but this name was more definitely given to the central building with a piazza or arcade running round it as an ornament and a protection to the public and the shopkeepers. The Piazza was the rendezvous of beaus or pretty gentlemen and women of pleasure, who walked the arcades. Here, too, were the auction rooms and china shops in which fashionable ladies and the fine gentlemen of the period met for intrigue under the cover of some slight purchase. In Covent Garden and the streets leading from it were the coffee-houses—the Bedford, Will's, King's, Tom's, Button's, Old Slaughter's, and many others,—where men went to read the newspapers, discuss politics, religion, and current plays, or to talk nonsense or to gamble. At the best of them, like the Bedford, one was sure to meet very good company among wits and scholars. The square was surrounded by taverns and night-houses, in the midst of which lived the theatrical people, sleeping in lodgings, and dining on sixpence or a shilling. The favourite drinks were rack-punch, gin, and champagne if one could pay for it. Needless to say, it was an unmoral world. Within the very precincts of Covent Garden, duels were sometimes fought instead of in Hyde Park. We read of a good one at the Shakespeare's Head between the Honourable Mr. Stanhope (M. P. for Derby and youngest brother of Lord Chesterfield) and Lord Southwell of the kingdom of

Ireland. Mr. Stanhope, said the newspapers, received a thrust in the right side which went through to the back; and yet he managed somehow to live. It was all over a marriage contract. Though the streets of London were elsewhere but poorly provided with lamps, the resorts in Covent Garden were kept ablaze from midnight until morning. Such was the paradise of London when his Majesty George the Second began his reign.

Hovering about this earthly paradise in garrets, along the Strand and Fleet Street, was a vast army of hack-writers, estimated at four thousand. Further away, along the Thames, were the pleasure gardens, famous for their *ridottos al fresco,* or masquerade balls, which broke up at three or four o'clock in the morning. On one occasion "his Royal Highness and several noblemen," we read, went in at ten o'clock, and presumably stayed through it all. Among families in Soho Square and to the west, the most fashionable forms of entertainment were the various sorts of assemblies that passed under the names of drums, drum-majors, routes, and hurricanes, of which the hurricanes, it is said, were "fullest of company, noise, and nonsense," though all were "full of gaming tables." These were the places where women, married and unmarried, met their fate.

It was for this London that Fielding, still a ward in Chancery, left his grandmother at Salisbury. It has often been repeated, on the authority of Arthur Murphy, that he now plunged headlong into the dissipations of the town. This statement is rather misleading. The plunge, so far as it was ever taken, was not yet. At first Fielding entered upon London life as an observer, though in the end he very properly became a part of it. He had formed a serious purpose of making his way in the world through literature and had turned to the drama as the most profitable. To help him on, his father promised him an allowance of £200 a year, "which," Fielding said in his disappointment, "any body might pay that would." Better than that half-fulfilled promise was the patronage of Lady Mary Wortley Montagu, once the friend of Pope, and easily the most intellectual woman of the period. Lady Mary, who was Fielding's second cousin by descent from the third Earl of Denbigh, was captivated by her kinsman as he appeared in his youth—with his magnificent physique, his wit and humour, his high spirits, and his joy of life, which, she said, should have made him immortal. She read the sketch of his comedy in manuscript, suggested changes, and encouraged him to complete it. Largely if not entirely through her influence it reached the stage, where it was "twice honoured" by her presence. The play, laid amid the new life to which Fielding had come fresh from the country, opens on a morning with a conversation under the Piazza between two young gentlemen who have not yet forgotten the champagne of the night before; then the scene shifts to the house of a town lady and afterwards to the house of a country gentleman who has settled in London to marry off his niece. The characters meet in St. James's Park; and the duel, had it come off, would have been fought in Hyde Park. Not knowing very well the life he depicted, Fielding looked upon it with a sort of wonder and hesitancy, contrasting the manners of the town with those of the country in pleasant ridicule of both. He had watched ladies "swim a minuet" and sit at the gaming table all night. They dressed like men, he remarked, "in paduasoy coats and breeches"; whereas the beaus in their smart toupees looked for all the world exactly like women.

The dramatic display which Fielding saw was memorable for the production of "The Beggar's Opera" at the Theatre in Lincoln's Inn Fields, over which presided John Rich, the famous Harlequin. No entertainment on the English stage had ever equalled in popularity Gay's opera. From its first performance on January 29, 1728, it ran for sixty-three nights before the season was over, engrossing, said Fielding, "the whole talk and admiration of the town," and accompanied, according to the newspapers, by a great number of violent crimes such as the robbery of Sir Gilbert Heathcote, the father of the city. For the time being, Gay's "Newgate Pastoral," as it was called, totally eclipsed the Italian opera, which for some years had been the delight of the world of fashion at the Opera House, or the King's Theatre, in the Haymarket. In February Handel brought out there his "Siroe," which was replaced two months later by his "Tolomeo," containing the sentimental echo song— "Dite, che fà, dov'è, l'idolo mio?"—sung by Cuzzoni upon the stage and repeated by Senisino behind the scenes. But artificial love songs in the Italian language, though as beautiful as this one, could not withstand the music of the old English jigs and folksongs which Dr. Pepusch so finely adapted to Gay's words. In the end Italian opera went down to disaster; and Handel's wonderful company of singers was forced to disband and return to Italy. On the other hand, Miss Fenton, the original Polly Peachum in Gay's opera, eloped with the Duke of Bolton and afterwards married his lordship.

On nights when there was no Italian opera, the King's Theatre was given over to masquerades under the direction of Count Heidegger. This man—John James Heidegger— who claimed to be a Swiss by birth, had been long settled in London as the associate of Handel in establishing the Italian opera on the London stage. He enjoyed the reputation of being in features the ugliest person in all England. There is a story that Lord Chesterfield on one occasion betted that he could produce an uglier face. When he confronted Heidegger with a hideous old woman, the bet hung in the balance until the Count snatched off her headdress and threw it over himself; whereupon the spectators agreed that his lordship had lost the wager. All who wish to view that monstrous face, may see it in Hogarth's print of "Heidegger in a Rage." The master of the revels at the Opera House nevertheless possessed a pleasing address and a degree of ready wit which, combined with other qualities, were sufficient to give him the title of "Count" by courtesy and to make him a favourite with the fashionable world, including the King himself. In those days there were masquerades everywhere, but Heidegger's were the most frequented by the upper classes; they were the most notorious and the most scandalous.

Like everybody else who could afford it, Fielding attended Heidegger's masquerades, and found in them what others missed—inspiration for a poem. "The Masquerade," which he then wrote, is an amusing burlesque purporting to come from the pen of "Lemuel Gulliver, Poet Laureat to the King of Lilliput." Much as the author's adaptation of the "Sixth Satire" of Juvenal, the humorous piece is composed in the mock style of Butler or Swift, and is inscribed, in the fashion of the period, to "C---T H--D--G--R." This poem, written under the shadow of the great Swift and published on the initial day of "The Beggar's Opera," was, so far as is known, the first effort of his talent that Fielding gave to the town.* The story which he cleverly tells in verse is of "a young, smart, dapper man of quality" who puts on the shabby dress of a poor poet and takes a chair to the masquerade. While he stands lost in amazement at the strange sight of Quakers dancing and grave churchmen at play for high stakes, and reflects that everybody is masking the face in order to unmask the mind, Calliope in a velvet hood comes up and taps him on the shoulder and tells him what it all means— where those cardinals and judges, nuns and shepherdesses,

* "The Craftsman" for Saturday, Jan. 27, announces that it will be published on the following Monday.

THE
MASQUERADE,
A
POEM.

INSCRIBED TO

C - - - T H - - D - - G - - R.

—— *Velut ægri somnia, vanæ*
—— *Species* —— Hor. Art. Poet.

By LEMUEL GULLIVER,
Poet Laureat to the King of LILLIPUT.

LONDON,
Printed, and sold by J. ROBERTS, in Warwick-lane;
and A. DODD, at the Peacock, without Temple-bar.
MDCCXXVIII.
[Price Six-pence.]

may be found after the masquerade is over. When he sees
Count Heidegger advance, he inquires how it could ever
occur to anyone to devise so horrible a masque; and when
told that Dame Nature gave him that face, he remarks:

> . . . as Mulciber was driv'n
> Headlong, for's ugliness, from heav'n;
> So, for his ugliness more fell,
> Was H-d-g-r toss'd out of hell,
> And, in return, by Satan made
> First minister of's masquerade.

An excellent company was playing every night at the
Theatre-Royal in Drury Lane, then under the skilful
management of Colley Cibber, with whom were associated
Robert Wilks and Barton Booth. For political reasons,
we may surmise, Cibber refused "The Beggar's Opera"
when Gay offered it to him, and proceeded to prepare for
his company "The Provoked Husband," a very brilliant
comedy left incomplete by Vanbrugh. Though the play did
not have the immense run of Gay's opera, it filled the house
owing to the wonderful acting of Mrs. Oldfield in the part
of Lady Townly. In "Tom Jones" Fielding writes as if
he were present on the first night—January 10—when,
according to Macklin, Mrs. Oldfield appeared to rush upon
the stage in full consciousness of her talent and beauty,
and as Wilks in the part of Lord Townly pronounced the
word "prodigious" in the first scene, the audience greeted
the word with a storm of applause as applicable to the
actress herself. So it went on for twenty-eight nights—
with some disturbance on the part of the footmen in the
gallery, who thought the piece "low stuff"—until February
12, when Mrs. Oldfield became exhausted.

Four days later, on Friday, February 16, 1728, the company brought out Fielding's "Love in Several Masques,"*

* The playbill is given in "The Daily Post" for Feb. 16. See also subsequent issues of this newspaper and of "The Country Journal; or, The

and repeated the performance on the following Saturday, Monday, and Tuesday, when it gave way to Congreve's "Old Bachelor." Monday was the author's benefit night. Before the week was over "Mr. Fielding" published his comedy, with a dedication to Lady Mary Wortley Montagu, whose accurate judgment has long been "the glory of her own sex and the wonder of ours," and with a preface giving the circumstances under which the play was produced. He thanked Wilks and Cibber for "their civil and kind behaviour previous to its representation" and especially Mrs. Oldfield, who, though indisposed from the fatigues of Lady Townly, consented to play the part of his Lady Matchless. Both dedication and preface are in admirable style. Very pretty is the author's boast "that none ever appeared so early upon the stage,"—a statement, which, if not precisely true, reminds us that Fielding belongs to the precocious group of Marlowe, Congreve, and Farquhar, who saw their plays performed while they were beardless youths. They were all too wise for their years. Young as he was, Fielding had no illusions about his. first trial for dramatic fame. He called attention, it is true, to the fact that few plays had "ever adventured into the world under greater disadvantages than this," since it followed "The Provok'd Husband" and came into direct competition with "The Beggar's Opera"; but his comedy was well cast; the best actors did all they could for it; and he had the prestige of Mrs. Oldfield's charm and power. All circumstances considered, he felt that his play—the work of "a raw and unexperienced pen"—was as well received as its merits warranted.

"Love in Several Masques" is a comedy of intrigue built on the lines of Congreve, with whose "Love for Love"

Craftsman." The play was published on Feb. 23 by John Watts, who indicated in his advertisements a correction to be made in the preface. There was a Dublin reprint the same year.

Fielding gives evidence of being especially familiar. He was also reading Molière. The various intrigues of the comedy are clever enough, but there are too many of them and they hang together loosely. The play thus hardly fails in structure nor does it quite succeed. The characters were selected from the types then common in artificial comedy, with a view to the parts best adapted to the actors at Drury Lane. In giving final form to his comedy, Fielding was, indeed, considerably influenced by "The Provoked Husband," which they were then playing with great applause. He reproduced, for instance, the town lady, the country gentleman, and ladies in masque. Though Lady Matchless, a young and rich widow, whose assemblies are besieged by many suitors, is a part quite inferior to that of Lady Townly, it nevertheless gave Mrs. Oldfield an opportunity to display her vivacity in smart dialogue. "Who," Lady Matchless says of her dead husband, "would not wish her spouse in heaven, when it was the only way to deliver herself out of hell?" Helena, the girl who has her own way in choosing a husband, was happily suited to Mrs. Booth, who excelled in assuming the air and manners of demure maidens. The part of Wisemore, reflecting perhaps Fielding's reaction against the hypocrisies of the town and his love of books and the country, was taken by John Mills, the actor of the company to whom were assigned the graver rôles of comedy. Fielding had a good Lord Formal, an intriguing maid sufficient for his purposes, and a Rattle, whose part was played by Cibber himself. Less artificial than these characters is Sir Positive Trap, an ignorant and avaricious country squire, who derives his title from Sir Julius Caesar. This man, of the tribe of Squire Western, Fielding knew somewhere in the West. Certain of his characteristics were taken from Andrew Tucker of Lyme Regis. The part fell to John Harper, an actor of fine drollery.

The scene from which I quote is at the house of Lady Matchless. Sir Positive has sworn "by the right hand of the Traps"; whereupon Lord Formal picks him up with the inquiry, "Pray, Sir, who are the Traps?" Then ensues a clash of wit, which we should pronounce excellent, were it found in Congreve:

"*Sir Pos.* Why, Sir, the Traps are a venerable family. We have had, at least, fifty knights of the shire, deputy lieutenants, and colonels of the militia in it. Perhaps the Grand Mogul has not a nobler coat of arms. It is, Sir, a lion rampant, with a wolf couchant, and a cat courant, in a field gules.

L. Form. It wants nothing but supporters to be very noble, truly.

Sir Pos. Supporters, Sir! it has six thousand a year to support its nobility, and six thousand years to support its antiquity.

L. Form. You will give me leave to presume, Sir, with all the deference imaginable to your superiority of judgment, to doubt whether it be practicable to confer the title of noble on any coat of arms that labours under the deplorable deficiency of a coronet.

Sir Pos. How, Sir! do you detract from the nobility of my coat of arms? If you do, Sir, I must tell you, you labour under a deficiency of common sense.

La. Match. O fie, Sir Positive! you are too severe on his lordship.

Sir Pos. He is a lord then! and what of that! An old English baronet is above a lord. A title of yesterday! an innovation! Who were lords, I wonder, in the time of Sir Julius Caesar? And, it is plain, he was a baronet, by his being called by his Christian name.

Vermilia. Christen'd name! I apprehend, Sir, that Caesar lived before the time of Christianity.

Sir Pos. And what then, Madam? He might be a baronet without being a Christian, I hope.''

Notwithstanding the measured success of his first comedy, Fielding showed rare sense in breaking away from London immediately. Within a month—the date is March 16—he was enrolled among the foreign students at the University of Leyden. The reasons that led to this sudden shift of scene from Covent Garden to a Dutch university have been often speculated upon. They lie, however, on the surface. There is nothing unusual in a boy's vacillating over a career. In the case of Fielding, a young gentleman of small estate, the problem of his future was particularly hard to solve. His mother's family had clearly destined him to the law and he had shown inclinations that way. His father's family, closely allied to the nobility, was a call to the church or to the army, both of which the boy's temperament ruled out, or to the life of a gentleman who should do nothing except in so far as he might devote his time to literature. He had failed in an attempt to make secure his means of livelihood by marrying an heiress, as much to the disappointment, doubtless, of the two families as to himself. As to literature, he seems to have known that, though he could write brilliant dialogue, he was not yet really prepared to cope with the contemporary drama. In no other light can we read a passage in ''Tom Jones'' where Fielding insists that all literature is doomed to failure unless it be founded upon direct and intimate acquaintance with the manners depicted. As if thinking of this very period in his own career, he writes: ''Vanbrugh and Congreve copied nature: but they who copy them draw as unlike the present age, as Hogarth would do if he was to paint a rout or a drum in the dresses of Titian and of Vandyke. In short, imitation here will not do the business. The picture must be after nature herself. A true knowledge of the world is gained only by conversation, and the manners of

65

every rank must be seen in order to be known.'' Before adventuring again in the drama, the boy resolved, it is evident, to wait and let his mind mature by experience and discipline.

It is a tradition, based upon the rather general statement of his first biographer, that Fielding went over to the Dutch university to prepare himself for the law. While at Leyden, says Murphy, he "continued to show an eager thirst for knowledge and to study the civilians with a remarkable application for about two years.'' Later times have added the gloss that Fielding was drawn to Leyden by the renown of "the celebrated Vitriarius, Professor of Civil Law in the university; and author of 'Institutiones Juris Naturae et Gentium.' '' Murphy's statement has been questioned by Austin Dobson and others before him; while the gloss rests only upon the authority of Alexander Chalmers, who, discovering in 1806 that Vitriarius was then at Leyden, supplied the interesting detail that Fielding studied under him. There is no evidence whatever that Fielding ever came into contact with Vitriarius or was interested in his "Institutiones.'' Not only did he never quote him, but his library as we know it at the time of his death contained no book by Vitriarius, though it was remarkable for its many treatises on general jurisprudence, among which were the works of Grotius, the Dutch historian and jurist. The fact is, Fielding was enrolled at Leyden not under the faculty of law but under the faculty of letters; the entry in the University Album, under date of March 16, 1728, being "Henricus Fielding, Anglus, Annor. 20. Litt. Stud.''—that is, "Henry Fielding, an Englishman, aged twenty, *litterarum studiosus,* or student of letters.''[*] By

[*] "Album Studiosorum Academiae Lugduno Batavae,'' The Hague, 1775; Edward Peacock, "English Speaking Students at Leyden University,'' in "Index Society Publications,'' 1883, XIII; A. E. H. Swaen, in "Modern Language Review,'' July, 1906, and A. Dobson, "Fresh Facts about Fielding,'' in "Macmillan's Magazine,'' April, 1907.

"letters" was meant at that time Latin and Greek literature. Fielding was thus attracted to Leyden not by
Vitriarius or other civilians but by the great humanists
who had made the university famous ever since the days
of Scaliger and Salmasius. He may, indeed, have worked
at the law while at Leyden; it could have been, however,
only Roman law as a part of his studies in Latin literature,
which included not only literature in its narrow sense and
law besides but also history, philosophy, geography, and
antiquities. No subject ever touched upon by a classical
author, whether trivial or important, could escape a Dutch
dissertation or a Dutch treatise.

When Fielding entered the University of Leyden,
Johannes Wesselius, a learned and eloquent divine, was
Rector Magnificus for the year. Sigbertus Haverkamp and
Petrus Burmannus were then Professors of Greek, though
the latter, except for lectures in Greek poetry, was giving
his time to Latin. All we know points to the conclusion that
Fielding studied mainly if not entirely with Peter Burmann,
to drop the Latin terminations from his name. Burmann
was a typical Dutch grammarian of the period, who, besides
excursions into Greek literature, edited most of the Latin
writers, great and small, in each case with lists of all the
earlier editions, lists of all the manuscripts, with all the
various readings, all the notes of all previous commentators,
supplemented by his own extended comment, both literary
and grammatical, to all of which were usually added several
indexes. Of these editions by Burmann containing an
epitome of everything that had been written or could be
written about a Latin author, Fielding possessed Quintilian,
Petronius Arbiter, Valerius Flaccus, and apparently many
others which cannot be surely identified because of their
scant descriptions in the catalogue of his library. Under
the guidance of Burmann, we may surmise at least, Fielding, who had shown a fondness for the classics while at

Eton, was initiated into that exact and extensive knowledge of Latin literature which appeared so marvellous to his friends and so pedantic to his enemies. He especially loved a Dutch commentator who took up an author line by line and word by word. While in Holland or subsequently he purchased Dutch editions of Lucian, Tacitus, Sallust, Seneca, Aulus Gellius, Paterculus, Silvius Italicus, and Valerius Maximus, to go no further downward among obscure writers. He collected editions of the classics by Scaliger and Salmasius, and had all the works of Lipsius.

His own books are certain evidence that he read diligently the Dutch humanists and scholars, occasionally imitating their style in all seriousness but more often for gentle ridicule or burlesque. When writing fresh from Leyden a preface to one of his editions of "Tom Thumb the Great"—a burlesque tragedy which he calls "The Tragedy of Tragedies"—Fielding playfully informs the reader that "most of the universities in Europe have honoured it with the name of Egregium et maximi pretii opus, tragoediis tam antiquis quam novis longe anteponendum . . . and the great Professor Burman hath styled Tom Thumb Heroum omnium tragicorum facile principem." Thereafter follows in the burlesque annotations to the play an excellent parody of Burmann, who is made to take up laboriously the question of who was "the mighty Thomas Thumb" in real life. "Petrus Burmannus," says Fielding, "makes three Tom Thumbs, one whereof he supposes to have been the same person whom the Greeks call Hercules. . . . Another Tom Thumb he contends to have been no other than the Hermes Trismegistus of the ancients. The third Tom Thumb he places under the reign of King Arthur; to which third Tom Thumb, says he, the actions of the other two were attributed."*

Few details of Fielding's life at Leyden have survived

* "The Tragedy of Tragedies," 1731.

in the records of the university or in the allusions of his own books. In the aggregate, they are, however, more than is generally supposed; and it is worth while to bring some of them together. When he registered at the university, he was staying at a hostelry in the town, called the "Casteel van Antwerpen," which he left before the year was over for lodgings in the house of one Jan Oson. Though living with a Dutchman, he never paid the people the compliment of learning their language beyond a familiarity with the common words and phrases necessary for doing business with them. Even such Dutch expressions as occur here and there in his writings, appear with inaccuracies that cannot always be laid to the printer. Of the Dutch terms in "Tom Jones," a hostile critic remarked with a degree of truth that only "a Dutch commentator" could give "a glimmer of sense to them." There was, of course, no particular reason for his acquiring a knowledge of Dutch, for the medium of instruction in the university, whatever the subject, was invariably the Latin language.

If, as has sometimes been conjectured, Fielding was sent over to Leyden by his relatives in order to remove him from the temptations of Covent Garden, they evidently succeeded; for the Dutch girl as he saw her on the barges or on the streets, stuffed with beef, puddings, and plums, was fat and slatternly, her greasy hair vying in odours with the stench of Dutch coffee-houses. Dutchmen he found jolly, but remarked that they always had uppermost in their mouths the word *gelt,* short for "Pay me"—reminiscent no doubt of cries he had heard from Jan Oson and the tradespeople of Leyden. Outbound or homebound, he encountered a storm at sea; he was annoyed by the profanity and savage behaviour of sailors and wharfmen, perhaps as he landed in Holland; and as he approached The Hague, going or returning, he was greeted by savours from "delicious canals" which he long remembered.

Fielding's main quarrel with the Dutch, however, was the same as Smollett's: it was their lack of imagination and humour. His "Tom Thumb," he says facetiously, "hath . . . been translated into Dutch, and celebrated with great applause at Amsterdam (where burlesque never came) by the title of Mynheer Vander Thumb," and "the burgomasters received it with that reverent and silent attention which becometh an audience at a deep tragedy." As an offset to the dull gravity of the Dutch, Fielding commended the industry with which they cultivated the soil, the solemnity of their public executions, one of which he saw when all the magistrates were in attendance, and most of all their reverence for law and order, on which he remarks: "I long to see the time when here [in England], as in Holland, the traveller may walk unmolested, and carry his riches openly with him."*

Fielding's studies at Leyden were not so serious that he forgot the drama. It is pleasant to find him in the land of windmills reading Cervantes and sketching out "into a few loose scenes" a comedy to be called "Don Quixote in England." But windmills are not an English institution; and English life and character are quite different from Spanish. Fielding quickly discovered that he was imitating Cervantes too closely; and so threw the sketch aside for a time until he should be able to vary the scenes of the romance and fit them more naturally to England. Though that time was to come, it was still several years distant. In the first draft of his play, however, he drew a country squire nearer to life than his Sir Positive Trap of "Love

* "The Coffee-House Politician," Act V, Scene V. For other allusions to Holland, see "The Author's Farce," "The Temple Beau," "The Champion," Aug. 30, 1740, "A Parody from the first Æneid" in the "Miscellanies," "A Journey from this World to the Next," Ch. II, "Tom Jones," Bk. XIII, Ch. I, "The Increase of Robbers," section XI, introduction to "A Provision for the Poor," and "A Voyage to Lisbon," under Sunday, June 30.

in Several Masques.'' Squire Badger of the new comedy has the very language and manners of Squire Western; he takes his kennel of foxhounds with him when he goes a-courting; and when drunk stretches himself out on a table, sleeping there as soundly as if in his feather bed.

Nor did Fielding forget Rosalinda. Once at least he returned to England before finally leaving Leyden. This was during the university vacation of 1728, which extended from the middle of August to the middle of October. On the way between London and Salisbury, he halted for some days at Upton Grey, a small village of thatched houses near Odiham in Hampshire. Perhaps he was on a visit at Hoddington House overlooking the village, the seat of the Sclaters, then an ordinary farmhouse.* Nothing beyond this conjecture is known of Fielding's connection with the Squire Sclater of the time from whom descended the present Lord Basing and to whose family belonged Sterne's Eliza. Whatever the exact place, Fielding renamed it ''New Hog's Norton'' because it was overrun with pigs whose deep organs of sound he found less pleasing than the notes of the nightingale. While at the farmhouse he addressed a poem, called ''A Description of U——n G—,'' to Rosalinda, the young woman of ''ten thousand charms'' whom he had known in London the previous winter. Remembering ''happier days'' and those many charms somewhat exaggerated doubtless in number, Alexis complains in this poem against the ''hard fates'' that have removed him

> From the dear scenes of poetry and love,

to a desolate habitation—half house, half shed, with a neglected garden at the side where flowers never grow— where the ground is kept green the summer through by

---

* T. Keightley, ''The Life and Writings of Henry Fielding,'' edited by F. S. Dickson, Cleveland, 1907, p. 29.

docks and nettles. Alexis is reminded by contrast of another garden, and exclaims—

> Happy for us, had Eve's this garden been;
> She'd found no fruit, and therefore known no sin.*

We may never know the real name of this Rosalinda whose wit and "brilliant eyes" did the business for poor Alexis. She, too, had retired to the country after the season in town; and Fielding had to go back to Holland without seeing her.

It was then, as it is now, the custom at Leyden to register anew every year all students in residence on February 8, which is the birthday of the university. Though a little late, Fielding's name was duly entered again on February 22, 1729. After that date the University Album is silent concerning him. He thus left Leyden for good before the next enrolment in February, 1730, compelled, says Murphy, to cut short his studies, after "about two years" at the university, owing to the failure of remittances from home. From his subsequent movements it is clear that he came home in the summer of 1729, and did not go back to Leyden at the end of the vacation. Accordingly, his residence at the university covered only a year and a half. His father was probably unable rather than unwilling to continue his allowance longer; and Fielding's share in the rents of East Stour was of course too small to support even a poor scholar, much less a gentleman, who must dress well, live well, and buy books. Thus thrown upon his own resources, his choice of a career lay, he used to tell his friends, between being a hackney-writer or a hackney-coachman. He chose the former and took the plunge at the opening of the new year. We are now to follow Fielding through the drama, the newspaper, and the novel, on to very great public services, in the midst of which the curtain will fall. His rare endowments of head and heart are to make for him friends

* "Miscellanies," 1743, I, 38-40.

among all classes from the lowest to the highest; while the open expression of his scorn and hatred of all meanness and hypocrisy is to awaken a swarm of enemies. On the whole, it is to be a stormy career accompanied by great disappointments, pain, and suffering; but Fielding is to preserve through it all his poise and humour, writing even when in distress some of the most brilliant pieces in our language.

CHAPTER III

DRAMATIC CAREER

FARCE AND BURLESQUE

Fielding was still but a boy in his twenty-third year when he broke away from Leyden and returned to London. At first he met with greater difficulties than he anticipated in establishing himself in the theatrical world. For some reason he had lost favour with the managers of Drury Lane. On submitting to them his "Don Quixote in England," Cibber and Booth both told him that it was immature and quite unsuitable for the stage. With their opinion he reluctantly agreed. He then wrote "The Temple Beau," which was probably also rejected. A little later he began another comedy called "The Wedding Day," the leading parts of which were intended for Wilks and Mrs. Oldfield; but being piqued by the conduct of Wilks, he laid aside the play for the present. Where, one may inquire, was Lady Mary with her influence at Drury Lane?

At this juncture Fielding fell in with James Ralph, a young man of some talent belonging to the literary adventurers who haunted the garrets about Covent Garden. This is the James Ralph whom we read of in Franklin's "Autobiography." He had come over to England with Franklin from Philadelphia and had settled in London, assuming for a time Franklin's name as a protection against arrest for his escapades. When Pope came out with "The Dunciad," Ralph published a counterblast called "Sawney," in defence of his Grub Street brethren; and in turn Pope lashed him smartly in the next edition of "The Dunciad," playing upon the word night, the title of one of Ralph's poems:

> Silence, ye wolves! while Ralph to Cynthia howls,
> And makes *night* hideous—Answer him, ye owls!

Ralph was not so wretched a poet as Pope would make out and he possessed many good qualities which appealed to Fielding. He was industrious, had read widely, and was agreeable in his manners. Association with him taught Fielding the ways of Grub Street, of which he soon began to make good use in verse and on the stage. As if he were himself of the tribe, Fielding addressed a facetious poem to Sir Robert Walpole in which he laid claim as a poor bard to all the conventional elements of greatness in a higher degree than had been attained by the Prime Minister, who was becoming known as "the Great Man." Matching Walpole at every point, Fielding says in his poem:

> The family that dines the latest,
> Is in our street esteem'd the greatest;
> But latest hours must surely fall
> Before him who ne'er dines at all.
>
> . . . . .
>
> We're often taught it doth behove us
> To think those greater who're above us.
> Another instance of my glory,
> Who live above you twice two story,
> And from my garret can look down
> On the whole street of *Arlington*.
>
> Greatness by poets still is painted
> With many followers acquainted;
> This too doth in my favour speak,
> Your levee is but twice a week;
> From mine I can exclude but one day,
> My door is quiet on a *Sunday*.*

* "Miscellanies," 1743, I, 41-43.

These verses of course are not to be taken literally. Fielding was not living in a mean garret, where he was so pressed by the tradespeople that he dared not go out on the streets except on Sunday, the only day in the week when he would not be liable to arrest for his debts. He was a young gentleman residing in a fashionable quarter of the town. Probably the only garret from which he ever saw Walpole's mansion in Arlington Street was an upper window of his father's house in or near Piccadilly. The next year, during a most prosperous season, he made Walpole the theme of a similar epistle, again running up a parallel between the Prime Minister's levees and his own doors crowded on a morning with duns, who are turned away by his maid empty-handed just like the suitors that fail to reach the presence of the statesman. Both poems were merely banter of Walpole's lack of interest in letters, with a half-serious hint that the writer would accept a sinecure under him.

The rebuff which Fielding received at Drury Lane did him no harm. It so happened that Thomas Odell, a playwright enjoying a pension from the Government, had just built and opened a theatre in Goodman's Fields, in the East End of London. He formed a good though second-rate company, mostly comedians, under the direction of Henry Giffard, for some time manager of the theatre in Dublin. Better actors than any in the original Irish troupe were William Pinkethman and William Bullock, who were induced to leave Lincoln's Inn Fields for the new theatre. On Monday, January 26, 1730, Giffard brought out Fielding's "Temple Beau," with a prologue by Ralph and an epilogue by "a friend." The play ran almost continuously for nine nights, and was twice revived in February "at the desire of several persons of quality," to say nothing of sporadic performances extending into June. As an attraction for his benefit night on January 28, Fielding added the song in the second Act on the prude and the coquette. Following an old custom, the play was at once published for an audience that wished to read it as well as see it performed.* In his admirable prologue, Ralph lamented the decline of genuine comedy before farce, show, and the tricks of Harlequin; he also complained of the want of patronage among the great, who permitted poor authors to starve; and prayed that the audience of rich merchants might set an example to the fashionable world of the West End by recognizing true merit wherever found and making the stage, as it once was, "the road to fame." And thus it proved to be in Fielding's case. There at Goodman's Fields, among the tradespeople of Whitechapel, Fielding's dramatic career really began. And to link great names, it was there, too, that Garrick a decade later, after being repulsed at Drury Lane, was to make his first appearance in Richard the Third and likewise win his spurs.

"The Temple Beau" follows closely the lines of artificial comedy as established by Congreve, with an occasional reflection of Etherege, Wycherley, and other comic dramatists of a past age. In this general aspect it is "Love in Several Masques" all over again. But since his first play, Fielding had matured greatly. His new comedy is well knit and its leading characters are clear-cut comic types, like Sir Avarice Pedant and his son young Pedant, of whom the former puts money above everything else, and the latter, who has just come from the university, cannot be induced to give up his books for an heiress of £20,000. In remonstrating with his son who has quoted a Dutch logician, the father says: "Logic, indeed! can your logic teach you more than this? two and two make four: take six out of seven, and there remains one. The sum given is twenty thousand pounds; take nought out of twenty, and there remains a

---

* The fortunes of the comedy may be followed in "The Daily Post." The issue for Jan. 26 contains the substance of the playbill.

score. If your great logician, your Aristotle, was alive, take
nought out of his pocket, and there wou'd remain nought.
A complete notion of figures is beyond all the Greek and
Latin in the world. Learning is a fine thing indeed, in an
age when of the few that have it the greater part starve.''
Wilding, the Temple Beau, was a well-known character
about town. Sent up to London from the country to study
law, he squanders his time and allowance on intrigues and
the dissipations of Covent Garden. His father, Sir Harry,
duly appears and discovers in a series of very humorous
scenes what has happened to all the money which the beau
had supposedly spent on books and candles to read them
by. It was all a bit of serious ridicule, for Fielding had
nothing but contempt for beaus in general; while those
living in chambers he described as ''only the shadows of
the others'' or ''the affectation of affectation.'' Pinkethman took the part of Sir Harry, and Giffard that of the
spendthrift son.

All along the proprietor of Goodman's Fields had been
having trouble with his theatre. The better class of people
in the neighbourhood objected to the playhouse on the
ground that it drew away clerks and servants from their
work and brought into the district idle and immoral persons
of both sexes. The crisis came late in April when, on petition of the Lord Mayor and aldermen, the theatre was
temporarily closed by order of the King. Anticipating this
result of the controversy, Fielding had already thrown in
his fortunes with the Little Theatre in the Haymarket,
where, on February 12, 1730,* a ballad-opera entitled ''Love
and Revenge, or the Vintner Trick'd'' was performed for
his benefit, ''at the particular desire of several persons of
quality.'' The Little Theatre, so called to distinguish it
from the large Opera House opposite to it in the same
square, stood near the site of the present theatre in the

* Announced in ''The Daily Post,'' Feb. 9.

FARCE AND BURLESQUE

Haymarket. It was sometimes known as the New Theatre, because it was not erected until 1720. Originally designed for the performance of French comedy by a company of French actors, it had since been given over to the irregular drama—to farce, burlesque opera, and vaudeville—to just what was condemned in the prologue to "The Temple Beau." A young and inexperienced company of English comedians, playing there in 1729, made a lucky hit with a nonsensical performance called "Hurlothrumbo, or the Supernatural," written by Samuel Johnson, not the lexicographer of that name, but a half-mad dancing-master from Cheshire. During its first season, the piece enjoyed a run, it is said, of "above thirty nights"; and late in January, 1730, it was restored to the stage for another run of three weeks. In the meantime it had been printed, with a list of subscribers and two dedications, one of which was to Walpole, who took thirty copies. Neither those who saw the play nor those who read it could form the faintest notion of what it meant, for it was plotless and its scenes were laid nowhere. When a learned bishop, says Fielding, complained to the author that he "could not taste the excellence of his piece," he was told that he should read it with a fiddle in his hand, for it had been composed in that way.* The rôle of Lord Flame, the maddest of all the characters, was taken by Johnson himself, who fiddled and walked the stage on stilts as he uttered his rodomontade. It was "the exquisite badness of the performance,"† says Fielding again, that made "Hurlothrumbo" the talk of the town. When Fielding was forced to turn to the Little Theatre in the Haymarket, it was of course necessary for him to drop for a time comedy for farce and burlesque in order to please his new audience. "Who," asks Luckless in his first play performed at the Haymarket, "would not . . . rather eat

* "Tom Jones," Bk. IV, Ch. I.   † "The Champion," April 15, 1740.

by his nonsense than starve by his wit?'' It was soon apparent, however, that Fielding's talent really lay in farce and burlesque rather than in the regular drama.

His first play at the Haymarket was ''The Author's Farce; and the Pleasures of the Town.'' Interest in ''Hurlothrumbo'' began to fade in February, and another piece by Johnson, called ''The Cheshire Comics, or the Amours of my Lord Flame,'' which displaced it on February 23, was withdrawn after a few nights. The company then returned again to ''Hurlothrumbo'' and tried various burlesques, among which was a revival of ''The Beggar's Opera,'' but with little success. (Performances at the Haymarket were in fact cut down to three a week.) The drooping fortunes of the theatre were immediately revived by ''The Author's Farce,'' which was first performed on Monday, March 30, 1730.* In order to meet the demand for seats, the company added an extra night the next week ''at the particular desire of several ladies of quality,'' and was soon playing the farce, either alone or in connection with other pieces, four or five times a week for the rest of the season. The play was published on the day following its first performance, under the pseudonym of ''Scriblerus Secundus,'' whereby Fielding indicated his satirical design and playfully associated his name with Pope and Swift, the founders of the famous Scriblerus Club for ridiculing social and literary abuses.

As implied by its title, ''The Author's Farce; and the Pleasures of the Town'' consists of two parts. The first part, now the most interesting, is a comic rendering of the life of literary hacks dependent for bread upon theatrical managers and the booksellers. The second part is the rehearsal of a dramatic entertainment ridiculing the amusements of the fashionable world. Though the two parts are so loosely connected that they were sometimes performed,

* ''The Daily Post'' is the source of this and other dates.

one without the other, in conjunction with other plays, they yet form one piece in that Harry Luckless, the poor playwright depicted in the farce proper, is author and manager of the entertainment. It would be going much too far to identify Harry Luckless with Harry Fielding. No farce can be in any true sense autobiographical. As in the epistles to Walpole, Fielding deals in "The Author's Farce" with those phases of the underworld of letters into which he had recently been initiated by Ralph, and obviously follows here and there incidents in his own struggle for recognition, though varying and heightening them for comic effect.

In the first scene, we see Harry in conversation with his landlady, Mrs. Moneywood, who threatens to turn him out of doors for not paying his rent. Three months before this, he knocked at her door, a handsome young man in gold lace, and took lodgings; but in all that time she has never once seen the colour of his coin. During the first weeks he lived like a gentleman, coming in at three or four o'clock every morning and thundering up the stairs. Since then all is changed. Her lodger now keeps to his rooms, and her door is almost beaten down by duns trying to get at him. All his effects have gradually disappeared except a few books and the clothes he wears. For his last dinner he sends his man out to pawn his hat, remarking that in one way or another his head must provide for his belly. Nothing is finally left but his expectations from a play he is writing. But these expectations do not appear as a very tangible asset to his landlady, into whose mouth Fielding puts an observation remarkable alike for its prudence and humour. "I would no more depend on a benefit-night of an unacted play," says Mrs. Moneywood, "than I would on a benefit-ticket in an undrawn lottery."

The play finished, Harry seeks a patron for it, but his lordship "has such a prodigious deal of business" on hand that he must beg to be excused. "Mr. Keyber," that is, Mr. Cibber, of Drury Lane is likewise too busy to bother himself with the production of an unknown poet. Thereupon Luckless summons to his garret Mr. Bookweight, the publisher and bookseller, and tries to obtain from him an advance on his play. Mr. Bookweight tells him bluntly that a play which has not yet reached the stage has no value; and Harry orders his man Jack to kick him downstairs for his insolence. Eventually Marplay and Sparkish (thin disguises for Cibber and Wilks) condescend to let Luckless read his piece to them in a Covent Garden tavern. After listening to a few passages, in which Marplay suggests absurd changes, the play is rejected, not because there is really any fault to be found with it, but solely because "the author has no interest." "Give me interest, and rat the play," says Sparkish. "Rather rat the play which has no interest," adds Marplay in correcting his colleague.

As a last means of escaping starvation, Luckless brings forward a farce and puppet-show that he has been writing. Though spurned by the managers of Drury Lane as too low for their theatre, it is readily accepted at the Haymarket; and Mr. Bookweight, seeing money in it, is eager to undertake its publication. Most amusing is the scene in which Luckless visits the house of Mr. Bookweight to offer him the new piece and describes the sorry literary hacks in a garret, writing poems, pamphlets, and other odds-and-ends for the bookseller. There they all are at separate tables—Dash, Blotpage, and Quibble—and Bookweight standing in the midst and urging them to make their quills move faster. Mr. Index comes in with a handful of Greek and Latin mottoes for the pamphlets, which he supplies for threepence or sixpence apiece. Scarecrow creeps in and is quickly engaged as chief translator, for he possesses the prime qualifications for the position—measureless invention and a lack of knowledge of every language except his own. As Fielding later in the play calls his bookseller Mr. Curry, he evidently wished to suggest him to his audience as a portrait of the notorious Curll, whose shop was close by in Bow Street.

The scene quickly shifts to the Haymarket theatre, where Harry puts into rehearsal "The Pleasures of the Town," which he has called a puppet-show since all its characters— Punch and his wife Joan appearing—are no better than puppets. From this point onward Harry Luckless becomes Fielding's mouthpiece for a burlesque of the follies of the town. As a play within a play, the piece obviously takes its cue from the Duke of Buckingham's famous "Rehearsal"; some devices for its machinery are also appropriated from Pope's "Dunciad"; but in its most interesting aspects it is a break with English tradition. Fielding follows "The Frogs" of Aristophanes and Lucian's "Dialogues of the Dead" in placing his scene in the lower world, whither descend theatrical and other amusements of the day to plead before the throne of Nonsense for a chaplet which she is to bestow upon the person in her train most distinguished for foolishness. The characters are all ghosts. To appreciate the satire, it must be observed that Handel was back at the Opera House with a new troupe of Italian singers; that Cibber's company was playing Thomson's "New Sophonisba," a tragedy full of rant and nonsense, at Drury Lane; and that farces and pantomimes, under the direction of Rich, had long been the rule at Lincoln's Inn Fields. There is some pleasant fooling before the throne of Nonsense, where Signior Opera, Don Tragedio, Sir Farcical, and Monsieur Pantomime in turn cut capers to win her ladyship's heart. The chaplet goes to Signior Opera.

Much other banter is mixed with the puppet-show. Hurlothrumbo arrives at the Styx and requests passage across the river to the court of Nonsense, but Charon hesitates to admit into his boat so mad a man and one bearing a name he cannot pronounce. Mrs. Novel, assuming the airs of a simpering miss, is in the shades also, having died for love of her husband Signior Opera, who deserted her for the Goddess of Nonsense. This is a hit at inane stories such as were written by Mrs. Eliza Haywood, whom Pope had fiercely attacked. But outside dramatic diversions, most attention is given to ridicule of John Henley, the Nonconformist preacher known as Orator Henley, at whose chapel in Lincoln's Inn Fields people were drawn not only on Sundays but also on Wednesday evenings to listen to strange orations and disputes on all sorts of subjects whimsically advertised by the parson in the newspapers.

Henley was a well-educated man of moderate intellect, fanciful wit, and much practical sense, but very pompous and florid in his oratory. In his way he was an actor and as such made his chapel a rival to the theatre as a place of entertainment, where one paid a shilling for the performance, half the price that a good seat cost at the Haymarket. His gorgeous pulpit was covered with velvet embroidered with fleurs-de-lis and trimmed with gold. Pope, who had just put Henley into the "Dunciad," called it a "gilt tub,"—tub being the contemptuous name for a Nonconformist pulpit. Henley captivated many, though exposing himself to the ridicule of others, by what Pope calls his habit of "balancing his hands" while "fluent nonsense trickled from his tongue." In this favourite gesture, the orator leaned over the pulpit and stretched out his hands, each little finger glistening with a diamond ring, as he proved to an entranced audience, for example, how all mankind are fishes of one kind or another—crabs, eels, or pikes. Fielding introduces Henley to the life in his puppet-show and lets him harangue from a tub to the delight of Nonsense, proving to her by a series of conundrums that men are either fiddles or fiddlesticks and then entertaining her with a song—a parody of Aristophanes as well as a burlesque of Henley—on the resemblances between men and birds—kites, owls, swallows, and ravens.

The show closes with a scene advertised as "The Triumphs of the King of Bantam," wherein Harry Luckless turns out to be the son and heir of the deceased King of Bantam. Lost when a child by his tutor in London, he is discovered by the hat he sent to the pawnbroker. Similarly his landlady turns out to be widow of the King of Old Brentford, and her daughter Harriet, with whom Harry is in love, is thus a princess. Harry and Harriet sail away to Bantam to claim the throne, taking with them most of the characters of the play to divert the antipodes. An actress dressed as a cat speaks the prologue, in which it is shown, in the Henley style, that women are nothing but cats.

Fielding's first farce easily won the favour of the town, for people like to see their amusements ridiculed, provided it is done in good humour. There was no bitterness even in the detailed portrait of Orator Henley or in the recurring sport made of "Hurlothrumbo." In fact Fielding's puppet-show was sometimes added as an afterpiece to "Hurlothrumbo," so that the audience on the same evening was presented with a serious piece of nonsense and then watched Fielding consign it to Hades. It was a double-headed performance sure to be enjoyed by anyone endowed with the most rudimentary sense of humour. But "Hurlothrumbo" was not born to last long. On April 24,* Fielding slipped in a new farce called "Tom Thumb. A Tragedy," as an afterpiece to "The Author's Farce; and the Pleasures of the Town." A brief thing in two acts, without prologue or epilogue, it was published the same day or the next.† Its success was immediate. Thereafter

* So announced in "The Daily Post," April 23, 1730.
† See flyleaf of the first edition, and "The Daily Post," April 25.

Fielding's two farces were performed together at the Haymarket almost continuously down to June 22, the fortieth night for "the Author's Farce" and nearly if not quite that for "Tom Thumb."*

"Tom Thumb" is a parody of the heroic drama such as was cultivated by Dryden, Banks, and Lee, their contemporaries and followers. Many of these ranting tragedies still held the stage; and several of them, more or less altered, were being performed that very season. At Lincoln's Inn Fields, the company had been playing Lee's "Rival Queens, or the Death of Alexander the Great"; at Drury Lane there had been a long line of tragedies, including Banks's "Albion Queens" (depicting Elizabeth and Mary), and Thomson's "New Sophonisba," a revamping of Lee's "Sophonisba, or Hannibal's Overthrow." Thomson's tragedy so filled the house that gentlemen were glad to obtain seats even in the footmen's gallery for the first performances, though its run proved to be short. In "Tom Thumb" Fielding was thus really poking fun at the tragedies which his audience had just seen at the other theatres. Ancient tragedy, says Fielding, to paraphrase him, aimed either to awaken terror and compassion or to compose these and all other uneasy sensations by lulling the spectators into slumber; whereas modern tragedy, owing to its absurdities, is frequently greeted by the audience with laughter. Why not, he adds, have a tragedy at which the audience is expected to laugh throughout? "Tom Thumb" is that tragedy.

Fielding accomplished his purpose by taking as his leading characters a Lilliputian victorious over the giants, a sorry King Arthur whom he reduces to the level of a tavern bully, a lickerish Queen whom he calls Lollalolla, and their sentimental daughter Huncamunca; and then letting them

* June 9 was the thirty-third night of "Tom Thumb" ("The Grub-street Journal," June 11).

utter their vulgar sentiments in the lofty language of heroic tragedy. Tom Thumb, just as he is to receive Huncamunca in marriage as a reward for his prowess, is swallowed by a cow in the streets. His ghost, however, rises for the concluding scene, which was quite sufficient to make the fortune of the farce. In memory of the blood-drenched stage of Dryden's "Cleomenes," all the main characters— nine of them—slay one another, except the King who stabs himself. The ghost of Tom Thumb is run through by Lord Grizzle, his rival for the hand of Huncamunca. "No scene, I believe," says Fielding, "ever received greater honours than this. It was applauded by several encores; . . . and it was very difficult for the actors to escape without a second slaughter."

Swift, who attended one performance, is reported to have said years after that he had laughed but twice in his life— once at the trick of a mountebank and the other time when Lord Grizzle killed the ghost of Tom Thumb.* Still, Swift did not at the time quite understand the drift of Fielding's burlesque, for in his "Rapsody" of 1733, he linked Fielding and Welsted as poets proficient in the art of sinking:

> For Instance: When you rashly think,
> No Rhymer can like *Weldsted* sink.
> His Merits ballanc'd you shall find,
> That Feilding leaves him far behind.

Of course Fielding sank lower than Welsted and all other poetasters. That was his aim; that was his jest. For once Swift was caught off his guard. When he saw his mistake, he took Fielding's name out of the passage and made the line to read:

> The Laureat leaves him far behind.

And his Dublin publisher added the footnote: "In the London edition, instead of Laureat, was maliciously in-

---

* Laetitia Pilkington, "Memoirs," 1754, III, 155.

serted Mr. Fielding, for whose ingenious writings the author hath manifested a great esteem.'' There is no good reason to suppose that Swift did not write the line as it originally stood in his poem. The fact is, Fielding not only compelled Swift to laugh but also outwitted him. The great Dean was perplexed by ''Tom Thumb.''*

The Prince of Wales and his party attended the second night;† and so great was the demand for seats from ''persons of quality'' within a week or two that it was necessary to put pit and boxes together in order to accommodate them. A palpable hit was made by two foolish courtiers in the farce—Mr. Noodle and Mr. Doodle; and for keeping them longer on the stage, Fielding inserted two new scenes in the first act, where a bailiff attempts to arrest Noodle at the suit of his tailor, and is at once slain by Tom Thumb, who has resolved to clear the town of bailiffs and render the streets safe for poor gentlemen even at noonday. At the same time‡ Fielding added, besides a few other lines, a prologue and an epilogue, in the latter of which was elaborated further the jest of the concluding scene. The young actress who played the part of Tom Thumb speaks the epilogue, and thus

<blockquote>Tom Thumb, twice dead, is a third time revived.</blockquote>

The enlarged ''Tom Thumb'' was immediately published, with a humorous preface (afterwards discarded), in which Fielding replies to the objections that the critics have brought against the play: its lack of dignity; the destruction of all the characters in the last scene; and the killing of a ghost. With reference to the last two strictures, he

---

* See ''On Poetry: A Rapsody,'' Dublin and London, 1733; and Swift's ''Works,'' Dublin, 1735, II, 451. The alteration—''Laureat'' for ''Feilding''—was first made in the London and Dublin edition of ''A Rapsody,'' dated 1734, though the footnote was not added until 1735.

† ''The Grub-street Journal,'' April 30, 1730.

‡ ''The Daily Post,'' May 1, 5, 7, 1730.

says that in most modern tragedies the characters "drop . . . as soon as they come upon the stage," whereas he keeps his alive to the very end; and that critics who think he exceeds the rules of probability in slaying a ghost should reflect upon such expressions in their favourite tragedies as "kill my soul," "stab my very soul," and "bleeding soul." Facetious as Fielding appears, these criticisms of his farce were real. "The Grub-street Journal" attacked him on June 11, 1730; and eventually, as we shall see, he thought it best to eliminate the ghost of Tom Thumb from the last scene.

The preface has further interest in that it is a burlesque of Cibber's style. When Cibber, back in February, 1728, published "The Provoked Husband," a comedy worked over from the manuscript left by Vanbrugh, he dedicated it to the Queen and addressed the reader in a brief preface, both so curiously absurd in style and substance that the author at once became the butt of the town. In the dedication, "the English theatre," we are told, "throws itself, with this play at Your Majesty's feet, for favour and support"; in the address to the reader, Cibber says he wishes to "give this play a chance to be read when the people of this age shall be ancestors"; and in lauding the actors, he remarks that Mrs. Oldfield in her part "out-did her usual out-doing" and that the ornaments with which she provided herself "seemed in all respects the paraphonalia [*sic*] of a woman of quality." These and other expressions of Cibber's had been ridiculed in an article contributed to "Mist's Weekly Journal" for February 24, 1728. Fielding takes them all up again with added humour in his preface to "Tom Thumb," working them in one by one, as he imitates the very manner of Cibber, answering his critics, praising himself and the actors down to the mutes and the music, and finally throwing "little Tom Thumb on the town'' in the way Cibber had thrown ''The Provoked Husband'' at the feet of her Majesty.

Just as the season was closing, Fielding took advantage of the popularity gained by his farces to bring out at the Haymarket another comedy in the style of ''The Temple Beau.'' He called it at first ''Rape upon Rape; or, the Justice Caught in his own Trap''; but owing to objections against the title, it was changed to ''The Coffee-House Politician; or, the Justice Caught in his own Trap.'' Again he chooses as his background the Covent Garden district, this time the tavern, the roundhouse, and the justice's court for a severe arraignment of the administration of the criminal law. Fielding's Justice Squeezum, a little thin man in amorous dotage, is one of those corrupt justices of the peace about whom one hears a good deal in the literature and the newspapers of the eighteenth century. In the country, the type was known as ''the basket justice,'' because ''for a half dozen of chickens'' he would ''dispense with a whole dozen of penal statutes.'' In the city he was known as ''the trading justice,'' for his court was merely a shop for sharp bargains with the innocent and the guilty alike. Justice Squeezum, as Fielding shows him up, receives money from brothels and gambling-houses, suborns witnesses, and packs jury panels with his creatures. He is in league with the constables, who on his order make arrests whenever there is prospect of gain, and leave unmolested criminals if nothing is to be got out of them. Only the poor and the innocent fear him. His rogueries are at length unmasked by the trick of a clever girl and her accomplices. To make clear that he is not satirizing justices as a class, Fielding gives us the portrait of a Justice Worthy whose court was managed quite differently.

The coffee-house politician, who had been gently ridiculed by Addison in ''The Tatler,'' was likewise a common type; but nowhere do we find him so humorously portrayed as by

FARCE AND BURLESQUE

Fielding. In general he was a tradesman who neglected his business and spent his time at a favourite coffee-house, reading the newspapers and discussing the foreign news as contained in the leading articles, which purported to be letters sent from abroad, though they were really for the most part written by hacks in London garrets. The politician in Fielding's play gives up trade wholly in order to devote himself to various projects such as a scheme for paying off the national debt by inducing the Government to procure a machine for carrying ships across the Isthmus of Suez and thus shortening the route to the East Indies. He has become so absorbed in the newspapers that he is maddened by them as much as Don Quixote was by romances of chivalry, and thinks the world described by them to be the real world, so implicitly does he believe every statement found therein. He is more troubled by rumours of the Dauphin's illness than by the elopement of his own daughter. His sleep is broken by worry over the movements of Don Carlos, the foreign policy of Cardinal Fleury, and fears that the Turks may push their way into Austria, Germany, and France, and finally reach England. In one scene, Fielding very finely parodies the foreign letters in the newspapers. He shows how the hack begins with a rumour in the first sentence, sets up a contradictory rumour in the second sentence, and leaves it to time to settle which rumour will prove correct. Besides the merit of the play as a good comedy verging upon farce, it has another interest in that Fielding himself afterwards became a newspaper man and a justice of the peace. And by a curious coincidence the justice whom he was to succeed got into a quarrel the next year at a coffee-house with another justice, who ran him through the abdomen, though he recovered from the grievous wound and lived nearly long enough to hand on the office to Harry Fielding.*

* "The Craftsman," March 20, 1731.

91

It was in this play that Macklin, the comic actor, received his "first marks of applause" from a London audience. His biographer, reporting a half-remembered conversation with him, says that Macklin was called in to take the part of an actor "who either failed in the representation or was taken ill after the first night," and that his performance more than answered Fielding's expectations, in fact "contributed much to the success of the piece."[*] At that time Macklin was occasionally employed in "trifling parts" at Lincoln's Inn Fields, and when "The Coffee-House Politician" was put on there early the next season, his name occurs against the character of Porer, and it is supposed that he also appeared as Brazencourt later in the play. As neither rôle is of any importance whatever, it is not clear how Macklin could have won applause from them. Porer and Brazencourt together speak no more than ten lines. There are, however, indications that Macklin, then an actor about town, unattached to any company, did take a leading part in "The Coffee-House Politician" when it was first performed at the Haymarket and thereby gained the foothold that was to lead on to fame. For, according to the theatrical news at the time, there was delay over the illness of an actor. The play was announced for Monday, June 15, 1730; but on that night Fielding's two farces were substituted for it "on account of the sudden indisposition of one of the principal performers." It first reached the stage a week later, on Tuesday, June 23, the day on which it was published.[†] After six performances, usually with "Tom Thumb" as an afterpiece, it was again temporarily withdrawn because of the actor's indisposition. Altogether the comedy was acted eight times this season, two of which were for Fielding's benefit.

[*] W. Cooke, "Memoirs of Charles Macklin," second edition, 1806, p. 399.
[†] "The Daily Post," June 12 and 23, 1730.

FARCE AND BURLESQUE

Fielding's plays, with a few others, kept the Little Theatre in the Haymarket running far into the summer, until August at least; and in September the company took the great theatrical booth in Birdcage Alley for the performance of "Tom Thumb" at the time of the Southwark fair. During the summer they tried with slight success an anonymous one-act farce, called "Jack the Gyant-Killer," as an occasional substitute for "Tom Thumb." Though naturally attributed to Fielding, the new farce was only the work of a rather clever imitator—perhaps Thomas Cooke, about whom there is something more to be said soon. The scene is the Palace of Folly, once the seat of "the old Monarch Reason," whom the giants had deposed, putting "the charming Princess Folly" in his place as their Queen. Jack breaks into the palace, kills the giants while they are at coffee and cards with the Queen and her company, and restores Reason to the throne. Though "Jack the Gyant-Killer" contains some fair burlesque of tragedy, it was too poor a replica of "Tom Thumb" to awaken more than passing interest. "Tom Thumb" was the farce that people wished to see and read. In its revised form it was twice printed, making three editions of the farce before its first season was over.

After his last benefit, occurring on July 2, Fielding probably went into the West for the rest of the summer. If he had written no play of the first order, his farces had entertained the town more than any other dramatic pieces since "The Beggar's Opera." They must, too, have enabled him to live like a gentleman. We may wonder what his puritanical grandmother thought of "Tom Thumb" and "The Rape upon Rape." Perhaps she never saw them. Once home in Salisbury, he himself seemed glad to forget that Covent Garden life depicted in these and other plays. Above all the pleasures of London, he now placed conversation with Celia, the reigning beauty of Salisbury, whom he

93

afterwards married. Either this year or the next, he tells Celia:—

> I hate the town and all its ways;
> Ridottos, operas, and plays;
> The ball, the Ring, the Mall, the Court;
> Wherever the beau-monde resort;
>
> . . . .
>
> All coffee-houses, and their praters;
> All courts of justice, and debaters;
> All taverns, and the sots within 'em;
> All bubbles and the rogues that skin 'em.
>
> . . . . .
>
> Ask you then, Celia, if there be
> The thing I love? my charmer, thee.*

* "Miscellanies," 1743, I, 49-50.

94

CHAPTER IV

DRAMATIC CAREER

AN EXPERIMENT IN POLITICAL SATIRE

Fielding appears to have enjoyed the society of Celia through the summer, for there is no sign of his being in London till well on in September, when "The Craftsman" had the following news-item: "We hear that the Town will shortly be diverted by a Comedy of Mr. Fielding's, call'd, 'The Modern Husband,' which is said to bear a great reputation." Whereupon "The Grub-street Journal" remarked: "I don't understand how a Comedy *so* little known *can be* said to bear a great reputation."* For reasons that will eventually become clear enough, the comedy which Fielding's friends were praising was deferred to another season. The Little Theatre in the Haymarket opened on October 21, 1730, with "The Author's Farce" and "Tom Thumb," for which Thomas Cooke, the translator of Hesiod, supplied a general prologue, in which the actors asked the indulgence of the audience on the score of youth and lack of experience.†

As in the previous season, the company's main reliance was the pen of Fielding. While waiting for new farces from him they continued to play the old ones. A novelty in the performance of "The Coffee-House Politician" and "Tom Thumb" on November 30,‡ was the addition of a farce, probably by Cooke, called "The Battle of the Poets; or the Contention for the Laurel," which was adroitly

* "The Grub-street Journal," Sept. 24, 1730.
† Printed with "The Battle of the Poets."
‡ Advertised for this date in "The Daily Post," Nov. 28. Published Dec. 17.

95

worked into the second Act of "Tom Thumb" as a variation and enlargement. Cooke, though Pope had put him into "The Dunciad," was a writer of some ability. The translation he made of Hesiod, whereby he was dubbed "Hesiod Cooke," is still regarded as the best in the language. The farce attributed to Cooke was published under the pseudonym of Scriblerus Tertius. It is a burlesque of the controversy over the appointment of a successor in the laureateship to Eusden, the "drunken parson," who died in September. The three main candidates for the post were Colley Cibber, Lewis Theobald, and Stephen Duck, the peasant poet of Wiltshire, known as "the threshing poet" because of his occupation and a poem on the theme.

Timing his "Contention" to the announcement that the laurel was to go to Cibber, the author introduces the three candidates into the farce under names thinly disguised: Cibber as Fopling Fribble, Theobald as Comment Profund in allusion to his annotations on Shakespeare, and Duck as Flail speaking the broad southern dialect. To make the situation more ridiculous, are added Fielding's friend James Ralph, and John Dennis, the ill-natured critic— who are renamed Noctifer and Sulky Bathos. All five poetasters are permitted to contend in turn for the honour of writing the epithalamium at the marriage of Huncamunca and Tom Thumb. Lord Noodle, Lord Doodle, and other courtiers, acting as judges, decide in favour of Fribble, because he is the poorest poet in the lot. This little farce, forming a genuine addition to the fun of "Tom Thumb," was several times repeated and held the stage for a number of years. It was aimed, of course, especially at Cibber, whose mannerisms and ways of speech on and off the stage were ridiculed in phrases such as "Ay, ay, hum, let me see!" and "Hah! gadso, that's true, strike me speechless!" The rôle was played by Henry Woodward, a boy of sixteen, who afterwards became a famous Mercutio.

EXPERIMENT IN POLITICAL SATIRE

There is a hint that Fielding was annoyed at this engraftment on "Tom Thumb." He could hardly have liked to see Ralph made a fool of on the stage. At any rate, he transferred at this time "The Coffee-House Politician" to the theatre in Lincoln's Inn Fields. The company playing there was much better than the one at the Haymarket. Indeed, John Hippisley, the manager, who had been the creator of Peachum in "The Beggar's Opera," was reckoned near the first comedian of his time; and Elizabeth Younger, who supported him in the leading comic parts, was a charming actress. They brought out Fielding's comedy on December 4, Hippisley taking the rôle of Squeezum, and Mrs. Younger that of Hilaret. According to the newspapers, unusual preparations were made for the author's benefit night, on December 7, when the company performed as an afterpiece Hippisley's own ballad-opera of "Flora" followed by favourite dances—"the Numidian, Fingalian, and Highland." The comedy did not get beyond the fourth night before the Christmas holidays.* Over-frank, though humorous, to begin with, it still remained over-frank despite some revisions on Fielding's part and a reworking of the epilogue at the apparent desire of Mrs. Younger.

The new year saw Fielding back at the Haymarket, where the company continued to perform "Tom Thumb" and added "The Temple Beau" to their scanty repertoire. They also took over W. R. Chetwood's "Generous Freemason" (which had been performed at a theatrical booth the previous summer), containing the "humours of Squire Noodle and his man Doodle." This piece was sometimes played with "Tom Thumb" and "The Contention for the Laurel," so that on the same night the audience had an opportunity of enjoying Noodle and Doodle from three

* "The Daily Journal," Nov. 30, Dec. 4, 7, 17 (when the play was published in its revised form).

different hands and three different points of view. But Fielding put an end to this kind of performance by enlarging his "Tom Thumb" to three Acts. And so thorough was the revision, that he renamed the piece "The Tragedy of Tragedies; or the Life and Death of Tom Thumb the Great." Announced on February 13, by "The Grub-street Journal," the new "Tom Thumb" reached the stage on March 24, 1731, in company with another farce in three Acts by Fielding called "The Letter-Writers: or, a new Way to Keep a Wife at Home." To awaken curiosity in these farces, Fielding published them both just before the first performance. With an eye to business, he evidently wrote his own playbills. In "The Daily Post" for March 23, 1731, we read:

Never Acted before.

By the Company of Comedians,

At the New Theatre in the Haymarket,
To-morrow being Wednesday the 24th
Day of March, will be presented, a new
Play, in three Acts, call'd,

The TRAGEDY of TRAGEDIES,

OR,

The Life and Death of Tom Thumb *the Great.*

Containing,

The Rise, Marriage, Victory and Death of
Tom Thumb; the lawful and unlawful Loves
of King Arthur, Queen Dollallolla; Princess
Huncamunca, Queen Glumdalca, Grizzle, &c.
the Rivalship, Disappointment, and Rebellion
of Grizzle; the memorable Battle between
Grizzle and the Queen of the Giants; with
the terrible Destruction of both Armies;
and the doleful and Tragical Apparition
of Gaffer Thumb. With several other Tragical
and Historical Passages.

EXPERIMENT IN POLITICAL SATIRE

To which will be added, a new Farce of three
Acts (never perform'd before) call'd,

The LETTER WRITERS:

OR,

A New Way to keep a Wife at Home.

Both by SCRIBLERUS SECUNDUS.

Boxes 5s.   Pit 3s.   Gallery 2s.

Places to be taken, and Tickets to be had, at Mr.
Fribourg's, Maker of Rapee Snuff, next Door to the Theatre.

N. B.   Books of the Tragedy, with Notes by Way of
Key, &c. will be sold at the Theatre; as also Books of the Farce.

As Scriblerus Secundus, Fielding displaced the old preface to "Tom Thumb" with a new one, in which Cibber
was dropped for an imitation of the learned style of Dr.
Bentley and Professor Burmann of Leyden.   Adopting
their formal method, he examined his tragedy, in the light
of all that Horace and Cicero had said, with reference to
the fable, the characters, the sentiments, and the diction, to
the conclusion that it excels all other tragedies in every
one of these respects.   Where, he inquires, can you find
more familiar sentiments expressed in sublimer phrases
than here?   Where can you find better inculcated the moral
that "human happiness is exceeding transient, and that
death is the certain end of all men"?—Are not all the
characters killed in the last Act?   In short, is not "Tom
Thumb" the tragedy of tragedies?   The preface contains
incidentally some excellent burlesque of John Dennis, who
was concerned that "a tragical and Christian nation would
permit a representation on its theatre, so visibly designed
to ridicule and extirpate everything that is great and
solemn among us."   The town was divided, says Scriblerus,
on the merits of his play.   "Whilst some publicly affirmed
that no author could produce so fine a piece but Mr. P[ope],

99

others have with as much vehemence insisted that no one could write any thing so bad but Mr. F[ielding]."

The jest of the preface was carried over into annotations with which Scriblerus Secundus buried the text of "Tom Thumb" as if he were editing a tragedy of Sophocles or Seneca after the most approved pattern. The critics—Bentley, Burmann, Dennis, Theobald, and Salmon—are set at loggerheads, with himself as moderator, over a multitude of questions raised by the play: over who the hero was in history, whether there was only one Tom Thumb, or whether there were several Tom Thumbs; over when the giants flourished and who they were; over the differences between ancient and modern tragedy, if "Tom Thumb" be taken as the best tragedy since the Greeks and Romans; and over the correct reading of difficult lines and the beauty or bathos of others, down to the employment of ghosts in tragedy and comedy, with some remarks on "the size of hell." These annotations Fielding called in his playbill "notes by way of key" to the farce, having in mind another characteristic of them. "Tom Thumb," Scriblerus claimed, was written in the time of Queen Elizabeth, and on this assumption he went on to show by parallel passages how Dryden, Lee, Banks, Thomson, and other writers of heroic tragedy had plundered it for their most striking lines; whereas Fielding was of course but parodying the tragedies of or before his time. Thomson's "New Sophonisba"—which was still much talked about, still criticised and defended—continued to be his game. Fielding's parody of one line in the tragedy has become famous. Thomson's

> Oh! Sophonisba, Sophonisba, oh!

was now turned into

> Oh! Huncamunca, Huncamunca, oh!

with the footnote: "This beautiful line ought, says Mr. W[arburton], to be written in gold." The line was certainly gold to Fielding and the players. Lord Grizzle repeated it three times over in a love scene with Huncamunca, who wished another husband besides the little Tom Thumb.

Beyond new lines, Fielding made many larger alterations in the revised "Tom Thumb," some for the better and some, I think, for the worse. Clearly a success was the addition of Glumdalca, the Queen of the giants. Having lost husbands by the score in the battle with Tom Thumb, the giantess inclines her heart towards her captor, and thus comes into rivalry with the Princess Huncamunca for that young hero's affections. A scene in which Huncamunca and Glumdalca meet and pour forth Billingsgate against each other is an exact parody, line by line, of the meeting between Octavia and Cleopatra in Dryden's "All for Love."[*] Just as Octavia in Dryden's tragedy comes close up to Cleopatra to read all the charms of that face which had ruined Mark Antony, so Huncamunca in Fielding's burlesque approaches Glumdalca and holds a candle up to her face, that Tom Thumb, standing by, may see its ugliness when contrasted with her own handsome features. This scene Hogarth chose for a frontispiece to the book of the tragedy which was supplied to the audience at a shilling a copy. Here began, so far as is known, the long friendship between the first novelist and the first painter of the age.

On the other hand, an alteration in the bloody catastrophe was hardly an improvement. Fielding pretended to regard seriously the criticism against slaying a ghost on the ground that when a man becomes a ghost he is already dead. So in the new version the ghost of Tom Thumb does not rise to meet a second death at the hands of Lord Grizzle. The last seen of him is when he is swallowed by the cow. But that there might still be a ghost in the play, Fielding earlier brought in the ghost of Tom's father, Gaffer Thumb, to

[*] J. Nichols, "Literary Anecdotes of the Eighteenth Century," III, 360.

101

warn his Majesty that Lord Grizzle, disappointed in not obtaining Huncamunca in marriage, was raising an insurrection against the throne. The King becomes enraged when the ghost utters a string of similes in the tragic style, and threatens to run him through the body, though he has none, unless he will cease. This amusing scene was followed by a fine burlesque of the single combat, in which Tom Thumb kills Lord Grizzle, sending his soul to hell along with all other traitors. The public was nevertheless loath to give up the old "Tom Thumb" with its exquisite absurdity. While the ghost of Tom Thumb was saved from slaughter at the Haymarket, the company at Goodman's Fields, reviving the old play, continued the practice of stabbing it. And so the two versions were performed, sometimes the one and sometimes the other, for several years thereafter at the various theatres. One might see the tragedy either way, just as he preferred it.

"The Letter-Writers," which Fielding wrote to fill out an evening's entertainment, was received with indifference. Subsequent to the fifth performance its place as an afterpiece to "Tom Thumb" was taken by "The Author's Farce." The new farce turns upon one of the many futile devices employed by old men in facetious literature for keeping their young wives at home away from temptation. In this case each husband by mutual agreement sends to the wife of the other an anonymous letter threatening her with harm if she stirs abroad. Fielding depicts the effect of these letters upon wives of different temperament. Mrs. Softly, in order to display her courage, goes out all the more; while Mrs. Wisdom contrives to manage her intrigues at home. Of course, the farce contains much wit and very funny scenes; but as a whole it was too conventional to arrest attention; it was too detached from those phases of contemporary life that the audience was then demanding of the actors at the Haymarket. "The Author's

Farce'' had presented with uncommon humour the straits of the poor playwright along with ridicule of the amusements of the town. "Tom Thumb the Great," besides being a burlesque of current tragedy, was a hit at Sir Robert Walpole, the Great Man, as he was called in irony by his enemies. Fielding reduced the Prime Minister to a pigmy, to the delight of the audience, making the little man more powerful than men, giants, and the gods combined, and then throwing doubt upon his claims to have killed the giants at all. And yet the political import of the farce was not direct enough to occasion interference on the part of the Government. No one could quite say that Tom Thumb was intended for Walpole, so perfect is the irony. Indeed, had the charge of satirizing the Prime Minister been brought against Fielding, he could have defended himself to the satisfaction of logic. Such is irony in the hands of a master.

Emboldened by success, Fielding and the company at the Haymarket now went too far into politics for safety. Party feeling was running high. Sir Robert Walpole, his place not yet quite secure, had to face a violent and noisy opposition led by Lord Bolingbroke at the head of the Tories, and by William Pulteney at the head of the discontented Whigs. These two politicians formed an alliance, and established a powerful organ, "The Country Journal; or, the Craftsman," for exposing the craft and cheats of Robin (that is, Sir Robert Walpole), who in the elaborate allegory is a dishonest servant of an imaginary Caleb D'Anvers, a bencher of Gray's Inn. This Caleb D'Anvers was the pseudonym of Nicholas Amhurst, whom they placed in charge of their newspaper as conductor (editor, we should now say). He was an able but coarse political writer who had been expelled from Oxford University. During the winter and spring of 1731, "The Craftsman," so called for short, was especially fierce and abusive in its arraignment of the

Government. Its printer, Richard Francklin, was twice taken into custody by his Majesty's messengers for articles written by Bolingbroke, Pulteney, or Amhurst. The political warfare soon spread beyond "The Craftsman" and other newspapers into the most scurrilous pamphlets accompanied by a bloodless duel between Pulteney and Lord Hervey, a close friend of Walpole and the reputed author of a bitter attack on Pulteney and Bolingbroke. In the midst of these political heats, while pamphlets like "Robin's Game, or Seven is the Main" were being hawked about the streets, Fielding ventured to burlesque the political quarrel, throwing the weight of his satire against Walpole. He called his play "The Welsh Opera: or, the Grey Mare the Better Horse." After several delays, the farce was performed at the Haymarket with "Tom Thumb" on April 22, 1731;* and at once made up for any loss in popularity occasioned by the unfortunate "Letter-Writers."

Fielding took his cue from "The Beggar's Opera," the best type of the ballad-opera, in which the dialogue, written in prose, was interspersed with numerous songs for one or more voices. These songs set to popular tunes were the main thing. The plot was of little moment except in so far as the audience might recognize beneath it quite another story, that is, incidents in the social or political scandals of the time. "The Beggar's Opera" was filled with contemporary allusions which everybody well understood. The quarrel, for instance, between Peachum, the receiver of stolen goods, and Lockit, the keeper of Newgate, was perhaps Gay's version of the great quarrel, which had not yet reached its full head, between Walpole and Lord Townshend over their share in political graft. Again, Macheath the highwayman would bring to mind Walpole, who, like his brother on the road, "levies and collects money," said the newspapers, "on people for his own use."

* See "The Daily Post," for April 21, and earlier and later dates.

EXPERIMENT IN POLITICAL SATIRE

It was not Gay's aim to make his satire consistent throughout, to have his characters agree at all points with well-known men in political life; his aim was rather to hit Walpole here and there in two or more characters and wherever else he might wish in the dialogue or the songs. His general thesis was that there is really no difference between the politicians in power and thieves or highwaymen. Let us divest Walpole and the rest of the insignia of office, put them on the road, and then we shall see what admirable highwaymen they would make.

Fielding's "Welsh Opera" wears a very innocent look—so innocent, indeed, that his biographers may be excused for passing it by as merely the title of one of his farces or as "a strange jumble without any intelligible plot or incidents." As if to lead the reader astray, Fielding says naïvely, having in mind two imitations of Gay, that it has been called "The Welsh Opera" because the scene is laid in Wales, just as we have "The Village Opera" or "The Scots Opera," so named because their scenes lie in a village or in Scotland. His piece merely has to do, he might have gone on to say, with a gentleman's household in Wales. There is Squire Ap-Shinken, thoroughly henpecked by his wife, Mrs. Ap-Shinken, who spends her spare time in talking divinity with their chaplain Parson Puzzletext. There is a mischievous son Owen, a thorn in the flesh of both parents, especially the mother, because of his familiarity with the maids and for other reasons. The squire, provided he is left alone with pipe and bottle, is content to let his wife govern the family. She engages and manages all the servants, who, unknown to her, are plundering the household. The worst rogue of them all is Robin the butler. He steals the two great silver spoons, files the plate, "pretending that it wasted in cleaning"; sells the very glasses, "pretending that the frost broke them"; and provides for the brewing of more beer than is needed, in order to give it away to his family, in particular to a brother "who gets drunk twice a day at master's expense." In league with him is John the coachman, who leaves his work undone to whet Robin's knives for him. Incidentally appears Thomas the gardener. And finally there is William the groom, Robin's warmest friend until bitter enmity is stirred up between them by a trick of Owen's with forged letters, one of which purports to have been written by William to Sweetissa, Robin's mistress among the maids. William and Robin meet on the field of honour, and after denouncing each other as liars, proceed to slap and kick each other to the tune of "Britons Strike Home."

What Fielding meant by this fooling must have been as clear as daylight to an audience in 1731. It was a comic version of the political warfare between Walpole and Pulteney, with the Court as background. The humour lies in telling the story in terms appropriate to the disturbances in a Welsh family. King George and Queen Caroline both spoke English with a decided German accent, much as a Welshman would speak the language. Hence the reason for placing the scene in Wales. Both quarrelled with their son Frederick, Prince of Wales, over the question of his marriage, much as do the Welsh squire and his wife over a proper match for Owen. Like Mrs. Ap-Shinken, the Queen ruled the political household while the King was left to his pleasures. No appointments could be made without her sanction; and like Mrs. Ap-Shinken, she dabbled in theology, about which she really knew a good deal, to the amusement of the wits of the reign. All the men-servants in Lady Ap-Shinken's household except William bear the names of the Queen's favourites, and William had been one. Robin the roguish butler is of course Sir Robert Walpole. John, who neglected the coach to whet Robin's knives, is John, Lord Hervey, who was supposed to write the sharp and slashing pamphlets for

Walpole. Thomas is Thomas Pelham-Holles, Duke of Newcastle, a colourless adherent of the Ministry. And William, trying to oust Robin from the Welsh household, is William Pulteney, who struggled hard to win the Queen's favour against Walpole. The variation in the duel as given by Fielding, whereby Robin instead of John fights William, was evidently made for greater dramatic effect. It was better sport to see Walpole and Pulteney, rather than Hervey and Pulteney, slap and kick each other. To proceed further, Robin's brother who drinks the squire's beer as fast as it is brewed, is Sir Robert's younger brother, Horatio, to whom were given many offices near the King. And intermixed with the political satire are social scandals in high life, manipulated on the feminine side under the names of Sweetissa, Susan, Betty, and Margery. The love passages between Robin and Sweetissa reflect Walpole's intrigue with Miss Skerrett, a mistress of several years' standing.

Announced as an afterpiece to "Tom Thumb" for April 7, 1731, "The Welsh Opera" was in fact not performed, as we have seen, for a full fortnight, ostensibly because of its "not being entirely ready" for the stage.* Doubtless the risk involved in its performance had to be considered. There was, however, apparently no opposition as yet from the Ministry. During the next six weeks it was performed ten times or more with other plays, first in its original form and then, beginning with May 19, as revised "with several alterations and additions." Early in May it became an occasional afterpiece to "The Fall of Mortimer," an old historical tragedy by William Mountfort, based upon a fragment left by Ben Jonson, which someone—probably a minor playwright named William Hatchett—worked over so as to fit it exactly to the present political situation from

* "The Grub-street Journal," April 7. See also "The Daily Post," through April, May, and June.

the standpoint of Walpole's enemies. "The Fall of Mortimer" was the boldest attack that the stage had yet made upon the Prime Minister. The Mortimer of history, it will be recalled, was the Earl of March who, conspiring with the Queen-Mother, held Edward the Third in subjection during his minority. With the aid of his creatures he ruled England simply for his own personal aggrandizement, confiscated estates, lived in luxury, and was accused of seeking the throne for himself. Eventually he met a deserved fate on the scaffold. As it stood in the old play, the parallel between Mortimer and Walpole was striking enough for political satire; and when Hatchett had finished his work, it was precise in all essential details. Under the disguise of Mortimer, the audience saw Walpole intriguing with Queen Caroline, rewarding his friends on the basis of their value to him, selling patents, selling places in the army and the navy to the highest bidder—in a word, corrupting, oppressing, and plundering the nation out of his own insatiate greed. That "The Fall of Mortimer" and "The Welsh Opera"—Walpole scourged and Walpole ridiculed— ever got beyond the first night is evidence of the Government's moderation or of its contempt for the Little Theatre in the Haymarket.

Though slow in coming, the blow was struck a month later. In the meantime, Fielding carefully rewrote "The Welsh Opera," retaining the scenes—especially, he says, "the altercative or scolding scenes"—which the town "particularly approved," and extending the play by great additions from two to three acts. He renamed it "The Grub-Street Opera," partly as a retort to Grub Street, which was attacking him, and partly because he regarded the pamphlets which were passing between Walpole's friends and enemies as on the lowest level of the most scurrilous hack-writers. Like Robin and William in the play, these pamphleteers, though gentlemen of quality, merely rapped out the lie to one another. In "you lie," says Fielding, consists "the whole wit of Grub Street." The new version, with new or improved songs, was somewhat severer on Walpole—as in that song where Sweetissa persuades herself into thinking that Robin, though he has robbed everyone else, may yet be honest with her. The Queen's parsimony—"thrift" she called it—was also dwelt upon in a delightful scene between Mrs. Ap-Shinken and Susan the cook, leading up to Susan's praise of old English hospitality against her mistress's denunciation of the same, and to the best-known song that appears in Fielding's plays—"The Roast Beef of Old England":

> When mighty roast beef was the Englishman's food,
> It ennobled our hearts, and enriched our blood,
> Our soldiers were brave, and our courtiers were good.
>   Oh the roast beef of England,
>   And old England's roast beef!
>
> But since we have learnt from all-conquering France,
> To eat their ragouts as well as to dance,
> Oh what a fine figure we make in romance!
>   Oh the roast beef of England,
>   And old England's roast beef!

This song has been attributed to Richard Leveridge, a popular song-writer for the stage, whom Fielding mentions some years later as "my honest friend."[*] But at that time Leveridge was in the employ of Lincoln's Inn Fields and so probably had nothing to do with the words or the music as Fielding gives them. Fielding took the music for songs wherever he could find it, "The Beggar's Opera" being a frequent source. For "The Roast Beef of Old England" he selected the air of "The King's Old Courtier" from the great storehouse of English melodies. But that he appropriated another's words without credit is unlikely. As a

[*] "The Champion," May 24, 1740.

matter of fact, the so-called Leveridge version of the song, which we hear of afterwards, was sung to a different tune from Fielding's.

As thus revised and rechristened, Fielding's opera was advertised in "The Daily Post" for June 11, 1731. The day before, "The Grub-street Journal," to have a little sport with the author, inserted the following notice, signed by Bavius, the pseudonym of the editor:

"Whereas our good friend Mr. SCRIBLERUS SECUNDUS hath composed an Entertainment, called *The Grub-Street Opera,* which he intends to exhibit at our Theatre, in the Haymarket, to-morrow the 11th instant; and as we do presume the said Opera is calculated for the propagation of our Society, we have thought fit to publish these our Orders, strictly charging all our Members to assemble at the sign of the Cock and Bottle, an Alehouse at Charing-Cross, between the hours of three and four, thence to proceed in a body to the said Theatre; and that Mr. SCRIBLERUS do take care, that a great chair be provided for ourself in the Front-box, and do give his attendance to conduct us thereto; and that all our Members be received and placed with that respect which is due to them."

If Grub Street was preparing to attend in a body and hiss down the farce, the society was disappointed. The performance was postponed on a pretext for three days, and then came the announcement from the company that they were "obliged to defer 'The Grub-Street Opera' until further notice.'"* The Government had in some way intervened, presumably in a quiet manner through the Lord Chamberlain, as the newspapers speak of no arrests. Thereupon an enterprising bookseller published "The Welsh Opera," without Fielding's authority, adding a preface to the effect that the town would doubtless find not unacceptable the original of an opera that has "been pre-

* "The Daily Post," June 14, 1731.

vented by a certain influence which has been very prevailing of late years.'' The publication was denounced by ''The Daily Post''* as not a true copy; and subsequently appeared, without any preface, ''The Genuine Grub-Street Opera. As it was intended to be acted, . . . printed and sold for the benefit of the Comedians of the New Theatre in the Hay-Market.'' Still later in the year, Fielding brought out through his own publisher ''The Grub-Street Opera. As it is acted at the Theatre in the Hay-Market.'' With this edition of the opera were bound up the left-over copies of ''The Masquerade,'' that burlesque poem of 1728, for which Fielding now supplied a dedication to Count Heidegger in ironical praise of the gifts that nature had endowed him with. When he wrote these commendatory pages, he was thinking of Wycherley's dedication of ''The Plain Dealer'' to My Lady Bennet, a director of sin and pleasure in the age of Charles the Second.

Despite the statement on the title-page of the authorized edition, it is doubtful whether ''The Grub-Street Opera'' in its final form ever got beyond rehearsal. There may have been a single performance in July as asserted by Genest in his ''Account of the English Stage''; but no record of it has ever been produced. Walpole had clearly determined to suppress open satire and ridicule of himself on the stage as well as in pamphlets and newspapers. Early in July the grand jury for Middlesex delivered into the Court of the King's Bench at Westminster a presentment against several pamphlets, several articles in ''The Craftsman,'' and ''The Fall of Mortimer'' (which had recently appeared in print), as false, infamous, scandalous, seditious, and treasonable libels against his Majesty's Government. In the face of this action, the company at the Haymarket attempted to perform ''The Fall of Mortimer,'' but was prevented by the appearance of the high constable with a

* July 26, 1731. See also ''Fog's Weekly Journal,'' July 31.

warrant for the arrest of the actors, who managed to escape in the confusion. A few weeks later, the actors were again dispersed by the constable and his men while the company was acting "Hurlothrumbo"—a play so harmless in intent as to have been dedicated to Walpole and yet capable of being given a political twist if the actor who took the part of Lord Flame felt disposed to do so. These and subsequent appearances of the constable really broke up the company of young comedians at the Haymarket.* It was triumphantly announced by Orator Henley in his "Hyp Doctor," a newspaper which he had established in the interests of Walpole, that the next performance of these "Hedge-Actors" would take place at Tyburn. The play would be a ballad-opera in one Act by "Doeg Fielding," entitled "Tyburn in Glory, or Thespis in a Cart, tying in one knot the beginning and end of tragedy."†

Thus, so far as Fielding's fortunes were wrapped in the Haymarket theatre, the season of 1730-1731 ended disastrously for him. He had, too, the annoyance of several personal attacks. "The Grub-street Journal," as early as June of 1730, parodied a few lines in the first scene of "Tom Thumb" in gross ridicule of Fielding, and kept up occasional fire at him well into the autumn of the next year, ending with some satirical verses lamenting the decadence of the drama since Shakespeare and Jonson, "names unknown" to Fielding. Nor did he escape the ridicule meted out to contemporary dramatists in a play entitled "The Contrast," which was performed at Lincoln's Inn Fields on April 30, 1731, and ran there for three nights. This satirical piece, the work of the Hoadly brothers—John and Benjamin—was never published owing to the interference of their father, the Bishop of Salisbury, with whom Fielding was doubtless already acquainted. Though "The

* See "The Grub-street Journal," July 15, 29, and Aug. 26, 1731.
† "The Hyp Doctor," June 15 and 22, 1731.

Contrast'' was aimed primarily at Thomson, whom Fielding had also burlesqued, yet the only sentence that has survived from it is a thrust at Fielding, and this comes through ''The Grub-street Journal.'' ''By G—,'' says one of the characters, ''I hate all ghosts, from the bloody ghosts in Richard the Third to that in 'Tom Thumb.' ''*
At the same time there was in circulation a print—purporting to have been painted by ''the famous Mons. Croquinolet, lately arrived from Paris''—called ''The New Grand Triumphal Arch, or the Stage's Glory,'' on which ''The Beggar's Opera,'' ''Hurlothrumbo'' and ''the great dramatic piece of Tom Thumb'' are represented by allegorical figures and described in the annotations as masterpieces of the contemporary drama.†

These attacks on Fielding, arising sometimes from envy, but more often from a love of banter, are an index that he was pleasing a large part of the town. Even ''The Grub-street Journal'' admitted ''the vast encouragement'' that the young author had received from the public. Moreover, Fielding's burlesque of political events hardly passed beyond raillery. Only in a mild degree did he take the side of the disaffected Whigs against the Government. Again, as in the previous year, he could address verses to Walpole in playful irony of the Prime Minister's skill in denying poor authors:

> Great Sir, as on each levee day
> I still attend you—still you say
> I'm busy now, to-morrow come;
> To-morrow, sir, you're not at home.
> So says your porter, and dare I
> Give such a man as him the lie?

* ''The Grub-street Journal,'' May 27, 1731.
† *Ibid.*, April 15, 1731. There is also an attack on Fielding in ''The Candidates for the Bays,'' a poem by a ''Scriblerus Tertius'' (not Thomas Cook), published in Dec., 1730. A footnote says of Fielding: ''This Gentleman is so self-conceited that he quarrels with every one who shows him a Fault.''

CHAPTER V

DRAMATIC CAREER

QUARREL WITH THE GRUB-STREET JOURNAL

Thus far it has been necessary to present Fielding's dramatic history mainly in an indirect manner through his works and the alterations that he made in them. Hitherto the newspapers have furnished little else than dates for the performances of his plays, with an occasional effort at gaiety. For the season of 1731-1732 materials are less scanty. Fielding now drops politics for a time and flirts with the Walpole Administration in the vain hope of winning the Prime Minister as a patron. More interesting still, he becomes involved in a hot controversy with "The Grub-street Journal," which extends to other newspapers. On the one side are the onslaughts from the Grubeans; on the other the denunciations of Grub Street by Fielding and his friends. For the first time we now get a view of Fielding directly in action. How his quarrel with "The Grub-street Journal" arose and incidentally why he modified his attitude towards Walpole find their explanation in certain theatrical changes of the year and in the kind of plays which Fielding wished to produce.

The persecution of the Little Theatre in the Haymarket, which had begun in the summer, was kept up into the autumn and winter. It was no longer safe for the company to continue their performances because of threatened if not actual interference by the Government. We read of the frightened actors refusing to take the parts assigned to them; in a word, of their revolt. By December, plays

114

ceased to be performed at the Haymarket except occasionally; and the theatre reverted to what it had been
before Fielding began to write for it: that is, the chief
attraction there became again a troupe of foreign tumblers
and rope and ground dancers drawn from all nations—
French, German, Italian, and Dutch. In the circumstances
the natural course for Fielding was to make peace with the
managers of Drury Lane—with Wilks and Cibber, both of
whom, it will be remembered, had been treated with dis-
respect in "The Author's Farce." The road to peace was
doubtless easy. The misunderstanding between Wilks and
Fielding had arisen merely from a difference in temperament. Cibber, since his appointment to the laureateship,
had been preparing to quit the stage in favour of his son
Theophilus, to whom he had already delegated his office as
one of the managers of Drury Lane, though he still continued to act in leading rôles in case his son was not
equal to them. As yet Fielding possessed none of the
antipathy for the son that he had felt towards the father.

In other ways, too, the situation had changed since 1730.
At that time Fielding was an unknown quantity; now he
was the most popular of all living playwrights. So, if he
was glad to go over to Drury Lane, the managers must
have been equally glad to obtain him. With him migrated
the best actors of the Haymarket theatre. Apparently they
did not become exactly a part of the company at Drury
Lane, for at first they were employed only to fill out the
rôles in Fielding's farces. The two companies, intermixing
in many plays, went on harmoniously together through the
long and stormy season before them; and the good feeling
that existed between the poet and the players was recorded
in a handsome compliment that Fielding paid the Cibbers in
his preface to "The Mock Doctor," in which Theophilus
performed the leading part admirably. "I shall only con-
gratulate," wrote Fielding, "the town on the lively hope

they may entertain of having the loss, they are one day to suffer in the father, so well supplied in the son."

As the theatre in Drury Lane was under royal patronage, Fielding could no longer indulge in pointed satire against Walpole. "Tom Thumb" was indeed revived there; but the political intent of this burlesque was vague and uncertain. Nor would Fielding's sympathies with Pulteney and "the Patriot Whigs," as they were called, permit him to turn his Muse against the Opposition. Though thus excluded temporarily from the field which he had cultivated the previous year, he still enjoyed great freedom. There still remained for him all the follies of the town, and all the social abuses not too closely connected with politics, though the Government, in the last analysis, might be responsible for some of them. Moreover, the excellent company at Drury Lane, reinforced by the young players of the Haymarket, was ready to take any number of social farces that he might write for them, and—what touched more nearly Fielding's ambition—there was an opportunity to slip in a regular comedy of five Acts, such as the company at the Haymarket had never been able to perform well. Under the stimulus of his new friends, Fielding produced, within six months, five plays and bore a hand in another.

The first of them was "The Lottery," a lively little farce in the form of a ballad-opera—put on at Drury Lane the first night of the new year,* in the wake of the great state lottery whose drawings, extending over forty days, had closed a few weeks before. These lotteries, occurring every year by authority of Parliament as a means of raising revenue, were becoming more and more scandalous. According to the usual scheme, there were 80,000 tickets of which 70,000 were blanks, the prizes running from two of £10,000 down to a large number of £20 only. The big prizes had a way of going to someone connected with the

* So announced in "The Daily Post," Dec. 31, 1731.

Kitty Clive

Court or to "a lady in Germany." The tickets, costing several pounds each, were bought up in the gross by stock-jobbers, who sold them in fractional parts to poor people at immense profits. Particularly bad was their practice of "horsing" the tickets, as the slang of it was; that is, of letting out tickets for hire at so much a day for any one of the forty days of the drawing. Not only were the chances greatly against a man who took a horse; but "the jockies of the alley" often fraudulently horsed again and again blank tickets that had already been drawn. All these abuses Fielding exposed in his farce. The part of Chloe, a girl who comes up to town in the expectation of winning £10,000 in the lottery, was taken by Miss Raftor—afterwards "Kitty" Clive,—an actress for whose talent and character Fielding like everybody else had great admiration. The humour lay in the fact that Chloe conducted herself as if she already had the £10,000 in hand, and got a husband on the strength of her imaginary fortune, who of course resigned her to her true lover as soon as he found himself married to a lottery ticket.

As played on that January night, "The Lottery" was a slight piece of two scenes; but for the performance of February 10, 1732, Fielding added a scene representing the actual drawing in the Guildhall, where all the lotteries were held.* He brought on the stage the great lottery-wheel, with the commissioners, clerks, and spectators, so that everybody might see just how it is done in front and behind the curtains as the wheel is opened and one ticket-holder after another is ruined. No number comes up for more than £20, and most of them are blanks. Chloe's is a blank and she faints. The farce, with its songs set to music by Mr. Seedo, passed through three editions with alterations the first year, and its subsequent performances are unnumbered.

* "The Daily Post," Feb. 10, 1732.

THE HISTORY OF HENRY FIELDING

While "The Lottery" was in its first run, Fielding "stood gossip," in his own phrase, to "The Modish Couple," a comedy by Charles Bodens, a captain in the Foot-Guards and sometime gentleman usher to the King. The play, quite formless and impossible, reached the stage on January 10,* but was withdrawn after the fourth night. Fielding out of kindness to "the Comic Captain" perhaps touched it up here and there and wrote the epilogue, concluding with a doubtful compliment:

> As the first fault, ye critics, spare what's past,
> And spare him, wits, in hopes 'twill be the last.

At the time Fielding had by him a comedy of his own, entitled "The Modern Husband," which, as I have observed, had been circulating in manuscript among his friends for more than a year. He had submitted it to Lady Mary Wortley Montagu, just as was done with his first comedy, "Love in Several Masques," and it was approved by her as well as by many others of the first rank. In her published correspondence appear two rather formal letters† from Fielding to Lady Mary, in one of which he thanks her, on a Wednesday evening, for having read the first three Acts of an unnamed play, and in the other (the beginning of which has been lost) he asks permission to wait upon her at Twickenham with the manuscript of "The Modern Husband":

"I hope your Ladyship will honour the Scenes which I presume to lay before you with your Perusal. As they are written on a Model I never yet attempted, I am exceedingly anxious least they should find less Mercy from you than my lighter Productions. It will be a slight compensation to the modern Husband, that your Ladyship's Censure will

* Genest, "English Stage," III, 329.

† Lord Wharncliffe, "Letters and Works of Lady Mary Wortley Montagu," 1861, II, 19-20.

118

defend him from the Possibility of any other Reproof, since your least Approbation will always give me a Pleasure infinitely superior to the loudest Applauses of a Theatre. For whatever has past your Judgment, may I think without any Imputation of Immodesty refer Want of Success to Want of Judgment in an Audience. I shall do myself the Honour of waiting on your Ladyship at Twickenham next Monday to receive my Sentence and am

Madam, with the most devoted Respect

Your Ladyship's most Obedient

Most humble Servant

London 7^{br} 4   Henry Ffielding''*

The proper date for this letter, though it is not so given by Lady Mary's editors, is probably Friday, September 4, 1730, three weeks before "The Grub-street Journal" announced that Mr. Fielding had completed a comedy to be called "The Modern Husband." The young man, when he told his cousin that it was written on a model which he had never before attempted, meant that it was neither a farce nor a Congreve wit-trap, but a serious comedy representing directly from observation certain phases of contemporary life. What he had really produced, though perhaps he was not aware of it, was a novel in dramatic form running through five Acts to eighty-odd pages of prose. Why the comedy, which was advertised for the stage as far back as the autumn of 1730, had never yet been performed is quite apparent. The company at the Haymarket could have done nothing with it; and its subject was such as to make any theatre, however well disposed to the author, hesitate to take it. Mr. and Mrs. Modern of the play live far beyond their income; and in order to keep pace with the pleasures of the town, the husband persuades

---

* Taken from the MS. in the Athenaeum Library at Boston. Compare with the reproduction of the original letter in "The Works of Lady Mary Wortley Montagu," 1803, I, 106.

119

his wife to sell herself to Lord Richly for £1,500. Though it was not a squeamish age, there were even then limits beyond which the playwright adventured at his peril.

The comedy was hissed on the first night, February 14, 1732;* so the newspapers said and so Fielding later admitted, though he implied that the disturbance came only from clerks and apprentices. Objection was made to the cold-blooded scenes between Mr. and Mrs. Modern and rather strangely to the Lady Charlotte of the play, intended as a type of the harum-scarum young woman of quality, extravagant in speech and in pursuit of pleasure, but quite charming and really sound at heart. That Lady Charlotte should be condemned by anyone as "unnatural" perplexed Fielding, for he had been assured by Lady Mary that she was "the picture of half the young people of her acquaintance."† Despite the interruptions by the audience, the company at Drury Lane went on with the play and actually performed it, somewhat revised, fifteen times, almost continuously. Though never revived, it "had such success," says Fielding, "that I began to think it a good play till the Grub-street Journal assur'd me it was not." With the exception of Miss Raftor, all the best actors took rôles in the comedy. There were the three Cibbers—father, son, and daughter Mrs. Charke,—as well as Wilks, whose Mr. Bellamant in this play was to be his last original character, illness and death being already near at hand. The elder Cibber wrote the epilogue, very moral in tone, for which Fielding substituted one of his own in gayer mood at the fifth performance on February 18. Thereafter the comedy was also followed by dancing to enliven the evening's entertainment. A prologue, which Fielding himself wrote, briefly rehearses the author's dramatic history. He confesses to a

---

* For dates and details, see ''The Daily Post,'' ''The Grub-street Journal,'' and ''Prolegomena'' to ''The Covent-Garden Tragedy.''

† ''Tom Jones,'' Bk. VIII, Ch. I.

want of art in his first plays, apologizes for his monstrous farces, and announces his present aim of restoring true comedy to the stage—

> The stage, which was not for low farce design'd,
> But to divert, instruct, and mend mankind.

There can be no doubt of Fielding's serious purpose in "The Modern Husband," the main situation of which he believed to be common in high life. He may have been mistaken, but Moderns were certainly not unknown in his time. Theophilus Cibber, for example, who had a rôle in this very comedy, subsequently encouraged an intrigue between his wife and a country gentleman, with a view to extorting heavy damages. In all essentials, his case was "The Modern Husband" played over again in real life. And yet, true as the situation may have been to the society of the time, it was not appropriate for comedy. It was appropriate enough, perhaps, for the novel—indeed, we have suggestions of it in "Amelia"—but no audience cares to see actually performed all the sordid incidents involved in a husband's sale of his wife in order to pay their gambling debts. Mr. Modern and Lord Richly, not very unusual characters in novels, are simply unendurable on the stage. The question of morality or immorality, of course, is of little moment. Fielding thought that he was doing right in exposing a shameless vice in society. After all his farces, he would become a censor of the age. Lady Mary approved his design, and Walpole, probably out of friendship to her, accepted the dedication when the comedy was published. The dedication, while containing some general praise of the Prime Minister—his "humanity and sweetness of temper," qualities that impressed all who were acquainted with him,—was in the main an adroitly phrased appeal to him to become a protector of letters.

On the appearance of Fielding's comedy, "The Grub-street Journal'' opened fire. This weekly newspaper, it may be said, had been established in 1730 as the organ of an imaginary Grubean Society having its headquarters at ''the Pegasus (vulgarly called the Flying Horse) in Grub Street.'' According to the jest of the founders, they hoped to do for literature what the Royal Society was doing for science. Mr. Bavius as their secretary was responsible for the leading articles, either writing them himself or procuring them from his friends. Squire Blunderbuss, the historian of the Society, reported its transactions. Mr. Poppy, ''an excellent poet,'' supplied the verse. Mr. Quidnunc collected and digested the news from other newspapers, with satirical comment thereon. If a political article were needed, Mr. Quidnunc was expected to write that too. There appear also a Mr. Maevius as a companion to Mr. Bavius, a Mr. Conundrum, the speculatist, and a variety of correspondents with equally fanciful names, Latin and English. As was then suspected and as is now reasonably certain, the real power behind ''The Grub-street Journal'' was Alexander Pope, who not only contributed, under the signature of Mr. Poppy, numerous epigrams to its columns, but actually planned and maintained the newspaper as a concealed means of praising himself and lashing his enemies. The Mr. Bavius whom Pope employed as his manager or editor was a nonjuring clergyman named Russel, who, being near if not quite a Roman Catholic, was in sympathy with the poet's religious creed. In politics the journal, as well as Pope himself, was on the side of the Tories, who, in union with the disgruntled Whigs, then comprised the Opposition to the Walpole Ministry. Politics and religion, however, were rarely discussed in the abstract by the Grubeans. Men who differed from them in religion and politics were attacked ostensibly on other grounds than their beliefs and opinions. ''The Grub-street Journal'' flourished on personalities, scurrility, and scandal. Within this sphere it was among the most brilliant newspapers ever written. Nothing of its kind could be better, for example, than the scorn and ridicule that it dealt out periodically to Colley Cibber as it took up one by one the odes which he wrote as poet laureate, and reduced them to nonsense and vacuity. Hitherto Fielding had been regarded as fair game by the Grubeans in their lighter mood. Now that he wore the Walpole badge and was associated with Pope's arch-enemy, Colley Cibber, he exposed himself to those heavier shafts of Grub Street wit that were aimed to kill. It is not to be supposed that Pope ordered the attack. He probably instigated and directed the long war on Cibber, against whom he had an ancient grudge. But the case was different with Fielding, who had not yet offended the poet directly. War was doubtless declared against Fielding by the Grubeans on the general principle that all who frequented the camp of Pope's enemies should take their punishment. It was some time after the battle had opened that Pope had reason for hostility towards Fielding.

The attack was begun in "The Grub-street Journal," on February 24, 1732, by a correspondent calling himself Dramaticus, who claimed a grievance against the managers of Drury Lane for rejecting a play that he had submitted to them. Who Dramaticus was it is impossible to determine. The ways of Grub Street were so devious that one may be reasonably sure that he was not an outsider, as he would have it appear, but really one of the Grubeans themselves who assumed a personal grievance as a point of attack, though the play rejected may have been written and sub-mitted by someone else. Nothing more was needed for his article than a copy of a letter accompanying the return of a play. In sending the manuscript back, Wilks wrote the letter for the managers, saying that "the play was a very sensible performance, was really pretty, but not *theatrical;* so that he could not undertake to act it on any account."

This letter was taken by Dramaticus as his text for a sarcastic inquiry into what was meant by *theatrical*. Does the word mean anything more than that an author is a friend of the players? Were the plays that had been damned one after another at Drury Lane that winter *theatrical?* Would it not be well to try now and then a *sensible* and *really pretty* performance and cease playing these *theatrical* pieces?

As yet Dramaticus had not seen "The Modern Husband," then in the midst of its run. Subsequently he visited the theatre, read the book of the play in his closet, and proceeded to cover the first page of "The Grub-street Journal," on March 30, with a belated condemnation of this socalled *theatrical* play by a friend of the managers. Nothing good was found in it at all. Its author, the critic declared, has not the slightest idea of what comedy should be, though he talks about diverting and instructing mankind. There is no unity in the fable; for half the conversations are irrelevant to the business in hand. Several of the characters are old ones purloined from other comedies, and all the rest lie outside of nature. Indeed, whenever the author strives to be original, he produces a Lady Charlotte, vivacious without a glimmer of understanding, or monsters like Lord Richly and Mr. Modern, "the vilest characters that ever yet entered into comedy." Over Lady Charlotte's remark that Gaywit has made her laugh "five hundred hours together," Dramaticus exclaims: "Gods! is't possible! Sure she exaggerates: Oh, Bavius! Oh, Conundrum! Can this be true!" Relenting somewhat at the end, the Grubean conceded a grain of intelligence to Fielding. "I found, indeed," he concludes, "here and there, but very sparingly scattered, a touch that implied good sense and reflection; but like an April sun, it only shows itself, and away; bad weather returns, and we have a great deal of filth to struggle through."

Fielding made no immediate reply to Dramaticus; and when the reply did come, it was mainly concerned with more serious charges. But his friend Thomas Cooke, who established in April a monthly periodical, called "The Comedian, or Philosophical Enquirer," took up in June the case against a "paltry weekly journal." Cooke's retort was sane and dignified. He admitted that "The Modern Husband" has "some scenes independent on the main business of the play"; and yet, taken as a whole, he regarded it as by far the most notable comedy of the season, either at Drury Lane or at Lincoln's Inn Fields. He went so far as to say that it "has wit, humour, satire, and moral reflections not unworthy the pen of the best Stoic." Lady Charlotte, with her foolish alertness and voluble nonsense, was especially commended as the ridicule of a very common type of woman such as anybody conversant with the world of fashionable folly has often seen and heard rattle on over herself and the amusements of the town. Whatever faults the comedy may possess were due, in Cooke's opinion, to the fact that the author "had not leisure to make it otherwise than it now is." Mr. Fielding, we are told in a most interesting passage, feels certain that his aim to make some vices and follies ridiculous and others odious is perfectly legitimate, and so he merely "laughs, without anger, at those who expose themselves by a fruitless endeavour to expose him."

Cooke was, of course, mistaken in supposing that Fielding had been cramped for time in composing "The Modern Husband," which had lain in his desk for many months. Nothing, however, but a desire to keep the theatre going could have induced him to write, as he now did, three more plays in rapid succession for the summer season at Drury Lane. They are "The Old Debauchees," "The Covent-Garden Tragedy," and "The Mock Doctor." As soon as the first two appeared together, Fielding had Dramaticus with Bavius and all the rest at his heels again. Indeed, had he set out on purpose to awaken the ire of "The Grub-street Journal" he could not have chosen a more offensive subject than that of the first of these plays. Everybody was talking about the famous case of Father Girard, Director of the Jesuit Seminary at Toulon in southern France. The priest, it was alleged, had practised sorcery to seduce Catherine Cadière, a beautiful and innocent girl to whom he was confessor. In October, 1731, the Jesuit was brought to trial in the Parliament of Provence and barely escaped conviction and burning at the stake. In fear of his life he fled from the town, and Mlle. Cadière disappeared, none but those who spirited her away knew where. All the details of the seduction during the girl's trances, as brought out by the trial, were spread abroad in the newspapers, in pamphlets, in memoirs, and in an anonymous ballad-opera called "The Wanton Jesuit," which, if the title-page speaks true, was performed at the Haymarket. Fielding here had at hand a theme for quick work. Unlike the author of "The Wanton Jesuit," he did not follow very closely the story of Father Girard. He took just enough of it for an effective play, writing with one eye on the current narrative and the other on the more or less conventional situations and characters of contemporary comedy. He had in mind Molière's Tartuffe almost as much as Father Girard. The Jesuit as Fielding renders him is balked in his attempt at seduction by a ruse of the girl's lover, who substitutes himself for her in her chamber. So "the dirty priest" is exposed and led off the stage to be washed in a horsepond and tossed dry in a blanket. From Fielding's point of view the sorcery carried on at Toulon was all a sham for concealing sexual immorality. Most diverting are the scenes in which several of the characters are represented as possessed by devils, as seeing visions and hearing voices, as receiving messages from saints, which are to be interpreted forwards or backwards, sometimes one way, sometimes the other. And for gaining the proper atmosphere, there is much talk about purgatory, nunneries, and holy water, all of which are keenly ridiculed. How well Fielding enjoyed writing this part of his play may be inferred from the fact that he kept until his death the book from which he derived his most laughable scenes. It was "The History of the Devils of Toulon," and he turned it all into farce.

"The Old Debauchees," having but three Acts, needed another play, of two Acts, to give the required length to an evening's performance. So Fielding wrote "The Covent-Garden Tragedy," interspersed with songs and concluding with a dance. A ballad-opera in form, the afterpiece is in style a burlesque of "The Distrest Mother," a tragedy in blank verse which Ambrose Philips twenty years before had translated, with few alterations, from Racine's "Andromaque." The old tragedy by Philips, which had awakened the wonder of Sir Roger de Coverley, still remained a stock piece at Drury Lane notwithstanding its stilted structure and very narrow interest. Its plot was manipulated mainly by four characters. Pyrrhus, King of Epirus, —long betrothed to Hermione, daughter of Menelaus and Helen,—falls violently in love with Andromache, Hector's widow, whom he has taken captive with her son Astyanax. Orestes, son of Agamemnon, and in love with Hermione, comes to the court of Pyrrhus as ambassador from the Greeks. The plot moves on slowly through long conversations, varied by soliloquies, between Pyrrhus and Andromache, and between Orestes and Hermione, giving the effect altogether of four children at seesaw; when one pair is up the other pair is down. Eventually Andromache consents to marry Pyrrhus in order to save her son from her royal lover, who will otherwise have him put to death. At the instigation of Hermione, Pyrrhus is slain by the Greeks led on by Orestes; Hermione, overcome by remorse, stabs herself and falls upon the corpse of Pyrrhus; Orestes runs mad; but Andromache survives, sound and whole, as a reward for not staining the bed of Hector by a second marriage. Plot, characters, and sentiments, all easily lent themselves to ridicule.

In framing a parallel action necessary to burlesque, Fielding descended lower than he had ever yet gone. He laid the scene of "The Covent-Garden Tragedy" in the back parlour of a brothel near the square whence the tragedy takes its name. The distrest mother in this case is Mother Punchbowl the bawd, whose business, formerly prosperous, has recently declined to a few swaggerers and beaus. Pyrrhus and Andromache are converted into Lovegirlo and Kissinda; Orestes and Hermione become Captain Bilkum and Stormandra. The conversations and soliloquies of "The Distrest Mother" are parodied loosely or exactly, always with the limping and halting of the original tragedy. At the end Bilkum is reported to have run through Lovegirlo with "a cursed thrust," but Lovegirlo soon enters to announce that his coat, not his body, had received the wound; likewise Stormandra is supposed to have hanged herself to "her curtain's rod," but it was her gown, not herself, that had been seen hanging there. The play concludes happily as in comedy; not, however, with marriage, but with the promise of Lovegirlo and Bilkum to remove their mistresses from the street and take them into keeping. The jest of the conclusion—happiness is relative—was derived from a scene in "The Beggar's Opera," which Fielding's farce resembles in general tone and in many other ways also. In fact it was advertised as a rival to Gay's famous piece of social satire.

Into "The Covent-Garden Tragedy" was worked some personal scandal, then clearly understood but now rendered obscure. The scene was associated with a notorious bagnio, and several of the characters with well-known people in the theatrical district. Mother Punchbowl was presumably Mother Needham just off Covent Garden, who, as hinted at in the play, had stood in the pillory not long before, to be pelted by the mob.* Or she may have been the more fashionable Mrs. Haywood, "a useful woman," says Fielding elsewhere, "in the parish of Covent Garden";† or as her obituary notice has it some years later, "a lady well-known to the polite part of the world." According to a story told to Horace Walpole, Fielding had in mind, when describing the mock suicide of Stormandra, Fanny Braddock, who hanged herself at Bath after having gambled away her little fortune; and further reflected in his plot "an amorous discussion" between her brother Edward, afterwards General Braddock, and a Mrs. Upton. Braddock took Mrs. Upton's money by force and left her in the lurch.‡ The character to whom Walpole alludes here is "the mighty Captain Bilkum," a bully who has the reputation at Mother Punchbowl's of bilking his mistresses. Be these allusions as they may, there is no doubt about Fielding's introducing the editor of "The Grub-street Journal" as porter or pimp to Mother Punchbowl. Leathersides—that is the name Fielding gives him—has learned to read well enough to make out the playbills, and so regards himself as fully equipped to write, as he is doing, the dramatic criticisms in "The Grub-street Journal." The character, with amusing additions, was drawn from a real porter at the Rose Tavern, known as "Leathercoat," who for a pot of beer would lie down in the street and let a carriage pass over him. This was Fielding's first retort to the attack on "The Modern Husband."

"The Old Debauchees" and "The Covent-Garden Tragedy" were performed together at Drury Lane on June 1,

---

* "The Grub-street Journal," April 29 and May 6, 1731.
† Annotation to the burlesque of Juvenal's "Sixth Satire."
‡ P. Toynbee, "Letters of Horace Walpole," 1903, III, 334-335.

1732,* at the opening of the summer season, during which the younger members of the company stayed on to play farce and light comedy twice a week, while the older members withdrew for rest. This was the first night for each play. Miss Raftor undertook the rôles of Isabel (Mlle. Cadière) in "The Old Debauchees" and of Kissinda in "The Covent-Garden Tragedy," thus appearing in succession as "a virtuous lady, and a miss confest." In each character she was supported by Theophilus Cibber, first as the Jesuit and then as Lovegirlo. The comedy was endured by the audience—some hissed, more applauded. But the farce even Miss Raftor's acting could not save: it was completely damned. True, there was laughter from the bucks that understood "the secret history" of the piece, but laughter was drowned in whistles and catcalls from the rest of the audience. By consent of author and players "The Covent-Garden Tragedy" was immediately withdrawn; and Fielding proceeded to repair his losses. Stories have ever been current respecting the rapidity with which Fielding worked under pressure; here is an authentic case. He cut from "The Old Debauchees" the passages which displeased the public so that by the next week the comedy was being received with "universal applause"; and within a fortnight he had in rehearsal "The Mock Doctor: or the Dumb Lady Cur'd," as a substitute for "The Covent-Garden Tragedy."

The new masterpiece is sometimes described as a translation of "Le Médecin malgré lui," which, says Fielding, Molière wrote "in a very few days" to accompany and lighten "Le Misanthrope," which was in danger of failing. Fielding's "Mock Doctor" is not exactly a translation, however; it is rather a thorough adaptation, English in setting and in sentiment. The plot is Molière's, but Fielding condenses, expands, modifies in many ways to suit

* "The Daily Post," May 31, June 1 and 5, 1732.

himself. When all is over, Molière's farce of three Acts becomes a ballad-opera of a single Act. No signs of haste are apparent except perhaps that Fielding has fewer songs than usual and that he slightly reworks for "The Mock Doctor" an old song from "The Grub-street Opera." Strangely enough, he made no use of other English versions of "Le Médecin"—Lacy's and Mrs. Centlivre's, for example—but went direct to Molière. The result was most happy. "The Mock Doctor" was put on as the second piece to "The Old Debauchees" for the performance of June 23; and the two pieces ran on together through the rest of the summer.* Miss Raftor and young Cibber in the leading rôles were received with an applause, says Fielding in his preface, that "admits of no addition from my pen." Like Molière before him, he turned threatened disaster into triumph. His enemies, to be sure, told him that it was all due to the acting; that his farce was worthless, or that it was stolen from Molière.

Here as usual Fielding found it difficult to refrain from personal banter. The audience seems to have expected it of him and to have taken delight in it. In this instance his butt was Dr. John Misaubin, a French physician living close by in St. Martin's Lane. Though Misaubin held from the London College of Physicians a licence to practise, he conducted himself as a quack and was so regarded by the public. His foreign manners, his broken speech, and his arrogance were frequent objects of ridicule in the newspapers; he was also caricatured by Hogarth in "The Harlot's Progress" and in other prints of the time. Fielding, who never forgot him, began a chapter in "Tom Jones" with the remark: "The learned Dr. Misaubin used to say, that the proper direction to him was, To Dr. Misaubin, *in the World;* intimating that there were few people in it to whom his great reputation was not known." The physi-

* "The Daily Post," June 23, 1732, and subsequent dates.

cian's "great reputation" rested upon a little pill which he had compounded as a cure for most diseases. In "The Mock Doctor," Gregory, the mock physician, impersonates Dr. Misaubin in speech and gesture and tries to induce his wife to take his "litle peel" for the distemper indicated by her pulse. This very funny scene, not in Molière, Fielding added, it is said, to please Miss Raftor, who wished to have extended her part as the mock doctor's wife. That the public relished the satire on the quack who posed as another Aesculapius is indicated by the fact that Fielding dedicated the farce, when he published it a few weeks later, to Dr. Misaubin, the author not of learned treatises on the art of medicine, but of a little pill which has rendered as many blessings to mankind as were the evils that hopped out of Pandora's box when the lid was lifted.

And where, one may ask, was "The Grub-street Journal" during all this time? Throughout April and May, intermittent shots had been aimed at the management of Drury Lane; and in June the whole artillery of Grub Street was trained on Fielding—by Bavius, Maevius, Dramaticus, Prosaicus, Publicus, Conundrum, and some others in the list of Grubean pseudonyms. The fire came from leading articles, assumed correspondents, satirical verses, and news-items even. No one can say that Pope directed the fire; but he must have consented to it, else it could never had been prolonged, as it was, for three months. Fielding had now surely offended Pope and the staff of his newspaper. In "The Old Debauchees," he had depicted a rascally priest of the Church of Rome, and had given a burlesque account of what one may expect to find in Purgatory. In "The Covent-Garden Tragedy," he had shown his utter contempt for "The Grub-street Journal" by putting editor and contributors in a class with the porters and pimps that bring business to a brothel. Prosaicus and Dramaticus were both present, they said, at the first performance of these plays;

and both were shocked, especially by "The Covent-Garden Tragedy." Prosaicus was induced to go to the theatre that night, he claimed, by a gentleman of the Temple, who told him that he would see as fine a "burlesque piece" as any that had ever appeared on the stage. In fact, nothing had ever excelled it for "pointed satire, true humour, and mock heroic." He was surprised to find so "polite an audience" at that time of the year, and was moderately interested in "the secret history" and "personal scandal" woven into the plot. But he had never before witnessed so dull and obscene a play. It was nothing more than what one might see any night at a notorious bawdy-house, to which indeed several in the audience retired after the play was over. Dramaticus likewise had never before seen "so shameful a piece," and dubbed it "The Common-Garden Tragedy." Fielding, it was insinuated, was really the bully depicted in the farce, and the other characters were his associates.

These attacks on Fielding, which came from "The Grub-street Journal" on June 8 and June 15 respectively, drew a return fire from the players and from the author himself. As the first shot, a correspondent signing himself "Mr. Wm. Hint, Candle-Snuffer" at Drury Lane, published in "The Daily Post" for June 21 a letter addressed to "Dramaticus, alias Prosaicus, alias Bavius, alias &c. &c. &c." It was generally understood that this tart reply was written by Theophilus Cibber, perhaps with aid from Fielding. Dramaticus is accused of attacking Fielding partly because envious of a popular poet and partly because stung by the passage where "the bawd tells her porter (not much, I think, to his honour) that he is one of the authors of 'The Grub-street Journal.'" Dramaticus may be certain that his own play, rejected at Drury Lane, will never reach the stage anywhere. Finally the Grubeans as a whole are challenged to give "some quotations" from "The Covent-Garden Tragedy" or to mention "some particular scene or incidents'' that will substantiate their charge of indecency against a play that goes no further than ''The Beggar's Opera.'' For an instance of the depravity of current taste and morals, one should not look to the theatre but to ''the wretched low stuff'' in ''The Grub-street Journal,'' ''which any person of common sense ought to be more ashamed of reading than women of the first modesty to see any performance ever yet exhibited.''

The next shot was fired by Fielding without disguise. He had published ''The Old Debauchees'' on June 13* as a successful play, though ''The Grub-street Journal'' insisted that it had been damned along with ''The Covent-Garden Tragedy,'' and that on one night the audience had been dismissed because it was not large enough to justify a performance. ''The Covent-Garden Tragedy'' he was content to regard as a failure; but since it had been scandalously misrepresented by his enemies, he now decided to print it. The farce was published on June 24,† with ''Prolegomena'' by way of a preface, cast in the form of a burlesque of the first attack made upon him by Dramaticus in the preceding March. In a mock manner, Fielding utterly condemns ''The Modern Husband,'' ''Tom Thumb,'' and ''The Covent-Garden Tragedy,'' quoting for the purpose ''Horase'' and ''Aristuttle,'' and exclaiming, like Dramaticus: ''Oh! Bavius! Oh! Conundrum, is this true!'' There is a hint, too, in the ''Prolegomena'' that Pope was behind the scurrility of Grub Street. ''I have been long sensible,'' says Fielding, ''that the days of poetry are no more, and that there is but one of the moderns (who shall be nameless) that can write either sense or English, or grammar.'' This was a direct challenge to Pope to come out of his concealment.

Thereupon Pope let loose his array of scribblers who attacked and pommelled Fielding on all sides in the next

* ''The Daily Post,'' June 13, 1732. † *Ibid.*, June 23, 1732.

numbers of "The Grub-street Journal," especially in the issues for June 29, July 13, and July 20. Every play that Fielding had published that year was completely riddled. His pen, it was iterated in varying phrase, "was not only void of wit, manners, and modesty, but likewise of the most common rules of poetry and grammar." His "Mock Doctor" even did not escape censure. That it was taken bodily from Molière, everybody of course knew; but everybody did not know that Fielding had "mangled and misunderstood" Molière's farce "from the very title-page to finis." It ought to have been called, as anyone who could read French should be aware, not "The Mock Doctor," but "The Forc'd Physician." As a jest, "William Hint" was brought out of his seclusion with an affidavit to the effect that the article purporting to come from him was really written by Mr. Cibber and Mr. Fielding; that he had always regarded Mr. Fielding's writings as either above his apprehension or below his notice. The controversy, it is clear, became the talk of the coffee-houses. According to "The Grub-street Journal," Fielding waxed furious, and was prevented only by the intervention of a friend from an actual assault upon one of his enemies.

To nearly all the abuse that Grub Street was pouring upon Fielding the lie was given in a letter signed "Philalethes," which appeared in "The Daily Post" on July 31, 1732. The letter, never since published, was clearly from the pen of Fielding. Not only was it so believed at the time; but there is an almost infallible test of style that may be applied to distinguish Fielding's work from that of the common run of writers in his day. He preferred the verb in *th* where they used *s; hath* instead of *has,* for example. This is what Fielding had to say in answer to his foes; I keep the old style:

"I have read with the detestation it deserves, *an infamous Paper call'd the Grubstreet Journal:* A Paper written by a Set of obscure Scriblers in the true Style and Spirit of Billingsgate, without either Learning, Wit, Decency, or often common Sense, and design'd to vilify and defame the Writings of every Author, except a few, whose Reputation is already too well establish'd for their Attacks, the Characters of whom they have, in the Opinion of all wise Men, blacken'd more with their Applause, than they have the others with their Censures.

"The Love of *Scandal* is so *general an Appetite,* that no one can wonder at the Success of any Nonsense or Ribaldry which hath that to recommend it: To this all the infamous Scriblers of the Age owe a very comfortable Maintenance; and to this, and this only, the *Grubstreet Journal* owes its Being.

"I believe every Man of good Sense and good Nature hath view'd with Abhorrence the scandalous undeserv'd Attacks, which they have lately so often repeated on a Gentleman, to whom the Town hath owed so much Diversion, and to whose Productions it has been so very favourable: An Attack which the Favour of the Town and the good Reception he hath met with from the Players, hath drawn on him.

"The Torrent of Ribaldry hath come abroad under several names, such as *Dramaticus, Prosaicus, Publicus,* &c. Whether these be the same Person is insignificant to determine; however, as they have all said the same Things, or rather call'd the same Names, an Answer to one will serve them all.

"Mr. *Publicus* (whom by the ingenious and cleanly Metaphors he takes from the Streets such as *Nastiness, Dirt, Kennel, Billingsgate, Stews, &c.* one would have imagin'd to have sometime thrown Dirt with other Instruments than a Pen) sets out with a most *notorious Falshood,* where he says *the two Performances* (*the Tragedy and Debauchees*) met with the *universal Detestation of the Town;* whereas the *Debauchees* was received with as *great Applause* as

was ever given on the Theatre: The Audience, which on
most Nights of its Representation, was as numerous as hath
been known at that Season of the Year, seem'd in continual
Good-Humour, and often in the highest Raptures of Approbation; and, except on the first Night, and ev'n then in one
particular Scene, there never was one Hiss in the House.

"He goes on, *Many that were there* (at the Tragedy)
*had neither so much Taste, nor so little Modesty as to sit it
out;* as a Proof of which, three Ladies of the Town made
their Exit in the first Act, while several of the first Rank
and Reputation saw the Curtain fall: And this, had he not
wanted common Sense, or common Honesty, he never had
wonder'd, or pretended to have wonder'd, at; for why
should any Person of Modesty be offended at seeing a Set
of *Rakes* and *Whores* exposed and set in the most *ridiculous
Light?* Sure the Scene of a Bawdy-house may be shewn
on a Stage without shocking the most modest Woman; such
I have seen sit out that Scene in the *Humorous Lieutenant,*
which is quoted and commended by one of the finest Writers
of the last Age.

"The Author is said to recommend *Whoring* and *Drunk-
eness;* how! Why a Rake speaks against Matrimony, and a
Sot against Sobriety: So Moliere in Don Juan recommends
all Manner of Vices, and every Poet (I am sure every good
one) that hath exposed a vicious Character, hath by this
Rule contributed to debauch Mankind.

"After the following excellent Remark, *Methinks the
Writer tho' might as well have left Seas of Sulphur and
Eternal Fire out of the mad Joke, for Fear he should meet
with them in sober Sadness,* he proceeds to *the Epilogue,*
where he says the Author tells the Ladies, without any
Ceremony, *that there's no Difference betwixt the best of
them, and the Bawdy-house Trulls they had been seeing on
the Stage; and that pretend what they would, they were all
a Parcel of Errant Whores:* This is a *most infamous Lye,*

as any one who reads the Epilogue to the Covent Garden
Tragedy must see, where nothing more is asserted, than
that it is natural for one Sex to be fond of the other.

> *In short you* (Men) *are the Business of our Lives,*
> *To be a Mistress kept the Strumpet strives*
> *And all the modest Virgins to be Wives.*

"This is the Compliment for which he hopes the Ladies
will reward him the next benefit Night. I am sorry any
Man so well born as this Author, should be obliged to receive a Benefit Night; but should be much more sorry that
he should depend on such Ladies as this critick's Wife and
Daughter to support it: However, the Wish is human
enough, and shews how void of Malice the Writer is.

"But he is not contented with representing the Poet as
having abus'd the Ladies, (which I believe the Poet is so
much a Gentleman as to think the worst Thing could
be said of him) the critick, after having terribly mangled
the Play by tearing out several Passages, without insert-
ing the whole Speeches, or making the Reader acquainted
with the Character of the Speaker, accuses the Author with
being free with the Bible; how free with the Bible? Why he
has given a ridiculous Description of Purgatory: Well, and
hath Purgatory any thing more to do with the Bible than
a Description of the Infernal Shades or Elisian Fields of
the Heathens, or of the Paradise of the Mahometans. If the
Critick had shewn as much Sense as Malice, I should have
imagin'd the *Popish Priest* had peep'd forth in this Place;
for sure *any Protestant, but a nonjuring Parson, would be
asham'd* to represent a Ridicule on Purgatory as a Ridicule
on the Bible, or the Abuse of *Bigotted Fools* and *Roguish
Jesuits* as an Abuse on Religion and the English Clergy.

"Not having vented enough of his Malice on these two
Pieces, he adds, *Had I either Leisure or Inclination I could
go a little farther with this Writer, and make it appear from
all his Performances, that his Pen is not only void of Wit,*

THE GRUB–STREET JOURNAL

Manners and Modesty, and likewise of the most common Rules of Poetry, but even Grammar: This is a most barbarous Assertion; how true it is I shall leave to the Opinion of the World: As for the strict Rules which some Criticks have laid down, I cannot think an Author obliged to confine himself to them; for the Rules of Grammar, the Education which the Author of the Debauchees is known to have had, makes it unlikely he should err in those, or be able to write such wretched stuff as, *I used to offer in its Behalf, &c.* a Sense wherein that Verb is never found in any good Writer of the English Language; nor indeed will its Derivation from the Latin *Utor* at all admit of it. Again, *Trulls they had been seeing,* Expressions a boy in the second Form at Eaton would have been whipt for: As for the other Part of the Charge, I must tell our Critick, there is a Vein of Good Humour and Pleasantry which runs through all the Works of this Author, and will make him and them amiable to a good-natur'd and sensible Reader, when the low, spiteful, false Criticisms of a *Grub-street Journal* will be forgotten.

Yours
PHILALETHES*

"P.S. Whether his scurrility on the *Mock Doctor* be just or no, I leave to the Determination of the Town, which hath already declared loudly on its Side. Some Particulars of the Original are omitted, which the Elegance of an English Audience would not have endur'd; and which, if the Critick had ever read the Original, would have shewn him that the chaste *Moliere* had introduced greater Indecencies on the Stage than the Author he abuses: I may aver he will find more in *Dryden, Congreve, Wycherly, Vanbrugh, Cibber,* and all our best Writers of *Comedy,* nay in the Writings of almost every Genius from the Days of *Horace,* to those of a most *Witty, Learned, and Reverend Writer* of *our own Age.*"†

* Fielding used this signature at least once in "The Champion." † Swift.

THE HISTORY OF HENRY FIELDING

A letter like this was precisely what Grub Street wished to draw from Squire Fielding, as they now called him because he had put "Esq." after his name on the title-page of "The Modern Husband" instead of using the old pseudonym of Scriblerus Secundus. By self-praise and by reference to his birth and education, the young playwright exposed himself to fresh points of attack. For another month the Grub Street writers buzzed about him like hornets. Publicus replied directly to Philalethes; Prosaicus was delegated to answer the "Prolegomena" to "The Covent-Garden Tragedy"; Maevius contributed the necessary epigrams; and Bavius, as editor of "The Grub-street Journal," gave a résumé of the entire controversy. Of most interest is the "just character of Squire Fielding and his writings" from the pen of Prosaicus in the issue for August 24:

"The Author, from his first appearance in the world as a Poet, has always aimed at humour; which, if founded on a right basis, is the chief support and life of all Comic writing: but as that basis is Nature only, he has often succeeded ill. Humour, when embellished by the assistance of wit, still grows more diverting; and hence it is, that *Congreve* is generally more admired than *Johnson;* a great deal of the Humour of the latter being found in the former, with that charming additional beauty of wit, of which the other was not a master.

"There runs through *The Old Debauchees* a continued *conatus* both at wit and humour: but the poet, like Tantalus in the Fable, is ever aiming at what is ever deceiving him. His wit is nothing but a few forced common place strokes against *Priest-craft;* and the whole character of *Father* Martin is but Dryden's *Gomez* and Shadwell's *Teague o' Divelly* curtailed, and divested of their native beauties.

"As to the *Covent-Garden Tragedy,* I shall pass by the moral part, which has been attacked by other hands, and
140

consider it only in the Author's own way, whether 'tis a piece of just Humour, and as such to be tolerated on the stage. As I lay'd it down before, that Nature must be the basis of *Humour,* Mr. F— may say this is just Humour, as being a just imitation of Nature; and that the characters are drawn from known realities. But *Humour* is to represent the foibles of Nature, not its most shocking deformities; and when any thing becomes indecent, it is no longer Humour, but Ribaldry. Ben Johnson, the greatest Humourist, I believe of any age, never makes any infringement on morals or good manners: That would be only to pretend to an excellence in which a Poet might be equalled, if not excelled, by any Rake or Bawdy house Bully.

"I am ignorant of Mr. F— as to his person; I pay a deference to his birth: but cannot think it a title to wit, any more than it is to a fortune; nor that every man, who has had the honour of being scourged at Eton or Westminster is a man of sense: of which it is no great proof for a Poet to pique himself on his family, or his school."

Fielding remained silent; and so the warfare ended. The last stray shot was fired by his friend Thomas Cooke. It was an epigram in the September number of "The Comedian":

> When *Grubs,* and *Grublings,* censure *Fielding's* Scenes,
> He cannot answer that which Nothing means:
> Scorn'd by the wise, and in their Filth secure,
> How should he damn the damn'd, or soil th' impure?
> When unprovok'd, and envious of his Fame,
> The Wretches strive to blast his honest Name,
> To such, if known, such slander-hurling Men,
> The Cudgel should reply, and not the Pen;
> But from their Holes their Dirt the Vermin throw,
> And to Obscurity their Safety owe.

CHAPTER VI

DRAMATIC CAREER

THE THEATRICAL WAR

When the theatres opened in the autumn of 1732, the glories of Drury Lane were fast fading. For many years its affairs had been shrewdly directed by the great actors— Booth, Wilks, and the elder Cibber, who were the patentees as well as the active managers; that is, they held from the Crown letters patent granting them the sole right to produce plays at the Theatre Royal; and all profits were divided between them. Booth the tragedian, owing to ill health, had long since left the stage, though he still exercised some control over the theatre by passing upon new tragedies submitted to the players. Now came the death of Wilks, in September, 1732, at the very beginning of the season. This was an irreparable loss, for Wilks, though primarily a comedian, was excellent also in tragedy. The elder Cibber, as it has been before related, had ostensibly delegated his powers, with some limitations apparently, to his son Theophilus. Thus it happened that the immediate management of Drury Lane for the season of 1732-1733 fell to young Cibber, except for such occasional advice as he might receive from Booth, and the interference—there may have been a good deal of it—from his father.

His company consisted of the young comedians who had been performing through the summer, with the addition of his father for favourite rôles and of John Mills, a good but not great actor, for tragedy. Mills, assuming the

142

tragic parts of his predecessors, was endured; but when young Cibber, a squat figure with ugly face, attempted Macduff in succession to Wilks, he exposed himself to scorn and ridicule. The only new tragedy that the company tried was Charles Johnson's "Caelia: or, the Perjur'd Lover"—the story of a brutal seduction very like the one employed later by Richardson in "Clarissa Harlowe." The author named it "The Deluded Maid," and Colley Cibber wanted to call it "Maidens Beware"; but Booth protested, and gave it a better title. Much against Booth's advice, the play was accepted, and duly performed on December 11, 1732—only to be hissed and withdrawn after the second night. Particular displeasure was manifested by the audience towards certain comic scenes at the house of a Mother Lupine written in imitation of Fielding's "Covent-Garden Tragedy." Fielding also supplied the epilogue, in which he commented upon the tragic distress of the piece as if it were a farce; and so, his irony being misunderstood, contributed doubly to the tragedy's utter failure.

After this fiasco, the company fell back upon farce and light comedy wherein Miss Raftor shone brilliantly. But in order to compete with Rich, who had just moved from Lincoln's Inn Fields to his new Covent Garden theatre, young Cibber brought out several puerile dramatic entertainments, to the disgust, of course, of "The Grub-street Journal," as well as of that part of the town who went to the theatre to see real plays. The situation was relieved by Fielding's "Miser," which was first performed on February 17, 1733,* and ran, with other plays like "Tom Thumb" and "The Harlot's Progress," for twenty-six nights or more. Elated by the "extraordinary success" of the piece, Fielding dedicated it to Charles, Duke of Richmond and Lennox—a young man of about his own age and a lord of his Majesty's bedchamber. The Duke had in some way

* "The Daily Post," Feb. 17, 1733.

befriended Fielding; and the dedication was a handsome acknowledgment of the favour. Though the two men were subsequently separated at times by differing politics, the novelist late in life referred to his early patron in terms of the highest respect. Fielding seems to have refused to write either prologue or epilogue to his comedy as unnecessary conventions of the stage. The one was contributed by an unknown friend, and the other by Colley Cibber, who worked into it a whimsical conversation with Fielding over the question at issue between Fielding and the managers. Fielding is reported to have cursed the man who invented prologues; and we see here that he felt the same antipathy towards him who invented epilogues. When the play is ended, he said, the time has come to drop the curtain.

In a preface to "The Mock Doctor" the year before, Fielding announced that he intended to transplant other comedies of Molière. "The Miser," based upon "L'Avare," was a partial fulfilment of this promise. In the same preface, Fielding also referred to a translation of the "Select Comedies of Molière" which his publisher, John Watts, was bringing out. It was a fresh rendering of Molière in eight small volumes having the French and English on opposite pages. Among the "several gentlemen who," say the advertisements, "all joined and consulted together about every part of it," was doubtless Fielding. Each play was dedicated to some well-known person, usually of the nobility, with the Prince of Wales at the head. There were the Duchess of Richmond, Lady Mary Wortley Montagu, the Duke of Argyle, the Earl of Chesterfield, and George Dodington, Esq.,—all Fielding's friends. Hogarth designed the frontispiece to the first volume. In this undertaking Fielding had some though an uncertain part. But there are sufficient traces of his hand in the general dedication to the Queen, in the general preface, and in special dedications to the Prince of Wales and to Dr. Mead to warrant the conjecture that Fielding's "Miser" and "Mock Doctor" were adaptations which he made from Molière while engaged upon the laborious task of more literal translations of these very plays. "The Miser" as refashioned by Fielding for the English stage reads like an original comedy; for, though he followed "L'Avare" in some places very closely, he went his own way with incident and character whenever he thought best to do so. The first three scenes of "The Miser," for example, are not in Molière at all. They were added in order to give larger scope to the rôle to be played by Miss Raftor —that of Lappet, "the glory of all chambermaids."

Apart from Miss Raftor's rôle, Fielding was also especially successful with Lovegold the miser. Himself generous to a fault, he detested avarice, and yet took delight in exposing the humorous side of the vice as he had observed it in its varied manifestations. There is in "Tom Jones" the anecdote of the man who "comforted himself . . . on his death-bed by making a crafty and advantageous bargain concerning his ensuing funeral with an undertaker who had married his only child." And there is Lovegold in this play who was caught one night stealing oats from his own horses, and would hang himself to evade the payment of "a poor ten thousand pound" to which he was liable by his breach of a marriage contract. So pleasant was the comedy throughout that even "The Grub-street Journal" had nothing to say against it. The one note of disapproval in the newspapers was raised by a gentleman who thought that Fielding had violated nature in making an old miser in love with a young woman of indifferent fortune. To this lack of knowledge of the heart Belvidera replied with spirit, informing the gentleman that "the heat and force of love would dissolve and melt" avarice and all the other hard vices. The critic, while maintaining his ground against Belvidera in general, admitted that "The Miser" was the only play he had seen for a long time "deserving the name of comedy."*

For the benefit given to Miss Raftor on April 6, 1733, Fielding added to "The Miser" a slight piece called "Deborah, or a Wife for You All."† As the trifle was never published, nothing more is known of it than may be inferred from a stray playbill. There appear to have been only four characters: Justice Mittimus, Lawyer Trouble, Alexander Whittle, and Deborah—the part taken by Miss Raftor. Very likely the afterpiece was a ballad-opera laid in a justice court and mildly burlesquing the libretto of Handel's "Deborah," a new oratorio which was not succeeding very well at the Opera House, though patronized by the King and Queen. Miss Raftor, who had the finest voice of any actress then on the English stage, was very clever in ridiculing Italian music. After playing the artful jade in "The Miser," she needed a musical piece in order to display her full talent; and so, we surmise, Fielding wrote out for her a few scenes with the necessary songs. Having served its purpose, "Deborah" was never again performed.

"The Miser" and "Deborah" were the only plays Fielding produced this season. But his "Tragedy of Tragedies" assumed a new form. The year before, certain scenes of it had been combined with music and dancing for an entertainment in "the long room" at the Opera House.‡ It was now turned into a full-fledged opera by Mrs. Eliza Haywood and William Hatchett, who made large alterations in the text and added songs, which were set to Italian music by Master Arne. After the bloody catastrophe, Merlin appears, and as he waves his wand, the prostrate dead rise one after another and shake hands, happy in the discovery

* "The Gentleman's Magazine," March and April, 1733, III, 138-139, 172.
† Genest, "The English Stage," III, 371.
‡ "The Daily Journal," Feb. 11, 1732.

that they had really never been slain, but only enchanted into the semblance of defunct bodies. There is no record of how Fielding liked the transformation. Still, he and Arne were old friends, and he had been associated with Hatchett at the Haymarket theatre. Mrs. Haywood, the author of scandalous novels, he had ridiculed in "The Author's Farce," and in later life wrote of her with the utmost contempt. The product of these eminent hands, called "The Opera of Operas: or, Tom Thumb the Great," was brought out at the Little Theatre in the Haymarket on May 31, 1733. Four days later it was repeated "at the particular desire of several persons of distinction," and on June 6 the Prince of Wales attended, "with a vast concourse of nobility." There was then no regular company performing at the Haymarket; but Master Arne formed a troupe of singers for the occasion, with himself in the rôle of Tom Thumb. "The crowing of the cock," a playbill promised, would be "attempted by a gentleman for his diversion"; and a dance would be introduced by Mr. Jones "to the fifth concerto of Vivaldi" with his own accompaniment on the violin, "being the first time of his performing it in public." The gay opera kept the Haymarket theatre open for several weeks; it was twice published in book form, and it was revived in the autumn at Drury Lane as well as at the Haymarket.*

In the meantime, the affairs of Drury Lane were becoming desperate. The three patentees of the theatre, it may be repeated, had been Wilks, Booth, and Colley Cibber. Some time after the death of her husband, Mrs. Wilks appointed John Ellys, the portrait painter, as her agent; and Booth, becoming hopelessly ill during the winter, sold half

---

* "The Daily Post," May 28, 31, June 2, Oct. 31, Nov. 7, 1733. "The Grub-street Journal," June 14. The Drury Lane version, for which J. F. Lampe furnished the music, differs somewhat from the opera as performed at the Haymarket.

147

of his share in the patent to an amateur actor named John Highmore, "a gentleman of some money, no judgment, and unbounded vanity." As both Ellys and Highmore were young and inexperienced in theatrical affairs, their interference in the management was naturally resented by Theophilus Cibber, who had begun the season as acting manager in place of his father. The situation became worse on the death of Booth early in May, 1733. Thereupon Mrs. Booth sold the other half-share formerly her husband's to Henry Giffard, the manager of Goodman's Fields; and the elder Cibber, taking advantage of a generous offer from Highmore, sold him his entire share, notwithstanding the fact that he had virtually promised to turn over his patent to his son. As Giffard made his purchase merely as an investment, and with no intention of giving up his own theatre, the result of these changes was to put Highmore into undisputed control of Drury Lane. With him now mainly rested the question whether Theophilus Cibber should continue as acting manager.

Young Cibber was enraged at the conduct of his father and Highmore, who had conspired, he thought, to cheat him out of his birthright. The company, too, did not relish the prospect of being governed—"tyrannized over," they called it—by Highmore, a man who knew nothing of the business he had undertaken. Their temper being thus, young Cibber easily stirred up a revolt among them, with the result that most of them under his leadership left Drury Lane and engaged the Little Theatre in the Haymarket for the ensuing season. No one of importance remained loyal to Highmore except Miss Raftor. Indeed, had not Giffard helped him out with actors from Goodman's Fields, he could not have opened his theatre at all in the autumn of 1733. Fortunately Highmore secured Macklin, but this actor had not yet displayed his wonderful powers. When Fielding came up to London out of the West, he found the maimed

148

company at Drury Lane playing to empty pit and boxes. In accordance with his nature, he took the side of the distressed actors against the mutineers.

It was a bitter warfare. Highmore attempted in various legal ways to suppress the Haymarket theatre on the ground that its managers had no licence. He further claimed that the seceders, as a part of his own company, were infringing upon his patent by performing at another theatre without his permission. But when the case came up for trial, the action was dismissed on some technicality. He next had John Harper, one of the actors at the Haymarket, arrested in the midst of a performance on the charge of vagrancy. The question at issue was whether Harper came within an old Vagrancy Act which classed irregular actors as rogues and vagabonds. The judge, after listening to learned counsel on both sides, discharged Harper on his own recognizance. Having thus failed to break up his rival company by legal means, Highmore encouraged ridicule of them on the boards of Drury Lane, where he brought out, for instance, Vanbrugh's "Aesop," containing a scene which the author once inserted apropos of a similar desertion of actors. The seceders relate their imaginary grievances to old Aesop, who laughs at them for their want of sense and advises the runaway beagles to go back to their former kennel.

At this juncture, Fielding stepped in to aid Highmore by revising "The Author's Farce" with reference to the present theatrical situation. "With great additions, and a new prologue and epilogue," said the playbill, the piece was performed on January 15, 1734, along with an entirely new comedy by Fielding entitled "The Intriguing Chambermaid."* The playbill gives no adequate notion of the very thorough manner in which Fielding reworked the popular farce of four years before. It is in the new version that

* "The Daily Journal," Jan. 15, 1734, has the playbill.

occur his most humorous remarks on the bookseller and the literary hacks as if he had gained more intimate knowledge of their ways during the period. This and all other changes, however, were overtopped by the pointed ridicule of Theophilus Cibber as manager of Drury Lane the previous year under the tutelage of his father, Colley Cibber. As originally performed there had been some banter of Wilks and the elder Cibber. Wilks, as he had since died, was of course eliminated from the play, and young Cibber was substituted for him. Then the scenes in which the managers appear were all expanded. The elder Cibber keeps his old name of Marplay, Senior, and the younger Cibber is called Marplay, Junior, in allusion to their practice of mutilating all plays before they would permit them to be acted. Stopler, a very good comedian, impersonated the father; and Macklin took off to the life the son. Night after night for the rest of January into February, these two actors played the parts of foolish and discredited theatrical managers, making over Shakespeare, accepting poor plays, rejecting good ones, and prattling over their own that had been damned. Here is a short sketch of their conversation in which the father gives directions to his son:

"Mar. jun. What shall be done with that farce which was damn'd last night?

Mar. sen. Give it 'em again to-morrow. I have told some persons of quality that it is a good thing, and I am resolv'd not to be in the wrong: let us see which will be weary first, the town of damning, or we of being damn'd.

Mar. jun. Rat the town, I say.

Mar. sen. That's a good boy; and so say I: but prithee, what didst thou do with the comedy, which I gave thee t'other day, that I thought a good one?

Mar. jun. Did as you order'd me, return'd it to the author, and told him it wou'd not do.

Mar. sen. You did well. If thou writest thyself, and that I know thou art very well qualified to do, it is thy interest to keep back all other authors of any merit, and be as forward to advance those of none.

Mar. jun. But I am a little afraid of writing; for my writings, you know, have far'd but ill hitherto.

Mar. sen. That is because thou hast a little mistaken the method of writing. The art of writing, boy, is the art of stealing old plays, by changing the name of the play, and new ones, by changing the name of the author.

Mar. jun. If it was not for these cursed hisses and catcalls—

Mar. sen. Harmless music, child, very harmless music, and what, when one is well-season'd to it, has no effect at all: for my part, I have been us'd to 'em.

Mar. jun. Ay, and I have been us'd to 'em too, for that matter.

Mar. sen. And stood 'em bravely too. Idle young actors are fond of applause, but, take my word for it, a clap is a mighty silly, empty thing, and does no more good than a hiss; and therefore, if any man loves hissing, he may have his three shillings worth at me whenever he pleases.''

Another scene gives us a conversation between Marplay Junior, Luckless the playwright, and his friend Witmore. Marplay Junior boasts that he has altered Shakespeare even; and then the dialogue proceeds:

''*Mar. jun.* Alack-a-day! Was you to see the plays when they are brought to us, a parcel of crude undigested stuff. We are the persons, Sir, who lick them into form, that mould them into shape—The poet make the play indeed! the colourman might be as well said to make the picture, or the weaver, the coat: my father and I, Sir, are a couple of poetical tailors: when a play is brought us, we consider it as a tailor does his coat; we cut it, Sir, we cut it; and let me tell you, we have the exact measure of the town; we know how to fit their taste. The poets, between you and me, are a pack of ignorant—

Wit. Hold, hold, Sir. This is not quite so civil to Mr. Luckless; besides, as I take it, you have done the town the honour of writing yourself.

Mar. jun. Sir, you are a man of sense, and express yourself well. I did, as you say, once make a small sally into Parnassus, took a sort of flying leap over Helicon: but if ever they catch me there again—Sir, the town have a prejudice to my family; for if any play cou'd have made them ashamed to damn it, mine must. It was all over plot. It wou'd have made half a dozen novels: nor was it cram'd with a pack of wit-traps, like Congreve and Wycherly, where every one knows when the joke was coming. I defy the sharpest critic of 'em all to have known when any jokes of mine were coming. The dialogue was plain, easy, and natural, and not one single joke in it from the beginning to the end: besides, Sir, there was one scene of tender melancholy conversation, enough to have melted a heart of stone: and yet they damn'd it: and they damn'd themselves; for they shall have no more of mine.

Wit. Take pity on the town, Sir.

Mar. jun. I! no, Sir, no. I'll write no more. No more; unless I am forc'd to it.

Luck. That's no easy thing, Marplay.

Mar. jun. Yes, Sir. Odes, odes, a man may be oblig'd to write those you know.''

The play that had "not one single joke in it from the beginning to the end'' was young Cibber's "Lover,'' produced three years before with the playwright in the leading part. As author and actor he was then subjected to a double damnation from the audience. The odes which Fielding refers to with contempt are, of course, those spavined verses that the elder Cibber was writing in the capacity of poet laureate. All this fun with the two Cibbers was prolonged into "The Pleasures of the Town," forming a part of "The Author's Farce." There the father, in allusion to his having just quit the stage, descends into Hades to become the manager of the theatre in the infernal regions; and "his great son" remains on earth to look after the theatrical interests of London.

Equally pertinent and severe was Fielding's renewed burlesque of Italian opera. London had again run opera mad. The native drama was really suffering more this winter from the popularity of Italian opera than from the dissensions among the players. There were now, as never before, two rival operas. Handel's company under the patronage of the King, with Giovanni Carestini as leading voice, was performing at the Opera House in the Haymarket; while a company under the patronage of Frederick, Prince of Wales, with Porpora as composer and director, had taken the theatre in Lincoln's Inn Fields recently abandoned by Rich. It was a bitter contention between the two houses, political in its character as well as artistic: with Handel lined up the Court party; with the Prince of Wales, a determined Opposition. Handel temporarily went down to defeat; and the rival company, intriguing against him, secured the Opera House for the next winter, and drove him into Rich's Covent Garden theatre. He soon had against him some of the finest voices of Italy—Farinelli, Senesino, Cuzzoni, and Montagnana. Thus it happened that the nobility was spending its money upon Italian opera and leaving the regular drama to the support of tradespeople. Fielding protested with his ridicule in "The Pleasures of the Town" and in a new and delightful epilogue on "the soft Italian warblers."

Considering the dramatic situation, the revival of "The Author's Farce" scored a marked degree of success. Better liked even was "The Intriguing Chambermaid," which was added to several other plays after the run of

"The Author's Farce" was over. For this afterpiece, Fielding took the groundwork from Regnard's "Le Retour Imprévu," the plot turning in both comedies upon the unexpected return of a father to find his house overrun with the dissipated companions of a profligate son. But just as in his adaptations of Molière, Fielding here made many departures from the original in order to bring to the front Miss Raftor's rôle as Lettice the chambermaid. In a noble epistle to her as Mrs. Clive (she was now married), he attributed all the success of the comedy to her marvellous performance. He was grieved for the declining fortunes of the stage and looked upon Mrs. Clive as the sole support that prevented an utter collapse. After some introductory paragraphs, Fielding went on to say:

"It is your misfortune to bring the greatest genius for acting on the stage, at a time when the factions and divisions among the players have conspired with the folly, injustice, and barbarity of the town, to finish the ruin of the stage, and sacrifice our own native entertainments to a wanton affected fondness for foreign music; and when our nobility seem eagerly to rival each other in distinguishing themselves in favour of Italian theatres, and in neglect of our own.

"However, the few who have yet so much English taste and good-nature left, as sometimes to visit that stage where you exert your great abilities, never fail to receive you with the approbation you deserve; nay, you extort, by the force of your merit, the applause of those who are languishing for the return of Cuzzoni.

"And here I cannot help reflecting with some pleasure that the town, that part of it, at least, which is not quite Italianized, have one obligation to me, who made the first discovery of your great capacity, and brought you earlier forward on the theatre, than the ignorance of some and the envy of others would have otherwise permitted. I shall not here dwell on anything so well known as your theatrical merit, which one of the finest judges and the greatest man of his age hath acknowledged to exceed in humour that of any of your predecessors in his time.

"But as great a favourite as you at present are with the audience, you would be much more so, were they acquainted with your private character; cou'd they see you laying out great part of the profits, which arise to you from entertaining them so well, in the support of an aged father; did they see you, who can charm them on the stage with personating the foolish and vicious characters of your sex, acting in real life the part of the best wife, the best daughter, the best sister, and the best friend.

"The part you have maintain'd in the present dispute between the players and the patentees, is so full of honour, that had it been in higher life, it would have given you the reputation of the greatest heroine of the age. You looked on the cases of Mr. Highmore and Mrs. Wilks with compassion, nor could any promises or views of interest sway you to desert them; nor have you scrupled any fatigue (particularly the part which at so short a warning you undertook in this farce) to support the cause of those whom you imagin'd injur'd and distress'd; and for this you have been so far from endeavouring to exact an exorbitant reward from persons little able to afford it, that I have known you offer to act for nothing, rather than the patentees should be injur'd by the dismission of the audience."

"Dismission of the audience" when Mrs. Clive was to play the leading rôle! Doubtless there had been instances of this at Drury Lane during the winter. By February, 1734, Highmore gave up the fight against Italian opera and his foes at the Haymarket, and disposed of all his interests in Drury Lane to another gentleman named Charles Fleetwood. Likewise, Mrs. Wilks, tired of playing a losing game, was also glad to find in Fleetwood a purchaser of her share in the patent. Of the former patentees, only Giffard held on with the half-share in the patent that Mrs. Booth had sold him. When Fleetwood made these purchases he had a sort of understanding with Rich of Covent Garden that they should unite their two companies in an attempt to crush the players at the Haymarket. But for some reason, Rich failed him; and a new theatrical war immediately arose. At that time the actors at Drury Lane were rehearsing "Don Quixote in England"—the comedy which Fielding had sketched out while in Leyden and had since completed, turning it into a ballad-opera in accordance with the new dramatic fashion. In order to meet the exigencies of his contest with Rich, Fleetwood never let this comedy reach a public performance, but substituted for it a pantomime entertainment called "Cupid and Psyche," in which the chief attraction was an enormous giant known as Gargantua, or Mynheer Cajanus because he came from Holland or Germany. For "a great number of nights," it is said, the town crowded to Drury Lane to see this "tall man" rise from a trap door.* Though Fleetwood might for a time outdo Rich in monstrosities like this, the victory could not be enduring. He accordingly began negotiations with young Cibber for the return of the disaffected players at the Haymarket. Hard pressed by debts and fearing a permanent alliance between Fleetwood and Rich against them, they were easily persuaded to come back into the fold, with Cibber as the acting manager. The first performance of the united company at Drury Lane took place on March 12, 1734. The war against Rich was kept up with Cajanus, and, when the public grew tired of him, with a giantess and a troupe of tumblers. Then came the benefit nights, and the season ended merrily for all except Fielding, who was apparently piqued by Fleetwood's treatment of "Don Quixote in England," and of course could not at once

* "An Apology for the Life of T— C—," 1740, pp. 103-104.

resume friendly relations with young Cibber, whom he had recently held up to scorn as stage-manager. Not greatly disturbed by his ill fortune, however, Fielding merely remarked that he had been crowded out by "the giant Cajanus."

To say the truth, Fielding was not quite crowded out. Part of the Drury Lane company continued to perform on odd nights at the Haymarket. Tickets sold for one theatre were sometimes accepted at the other. By the middle of April, "Don Quixote in England" was being acted "with great applause" at the Haymarket, together with "The Covent-Garden Tragedy," which—such is the changing temper of audiences—had been hissed out of the theatre two years before. The players sent over to the Haymarket did not comprise the best of the company, if we except Macklin, whom young Cibber feared as a rival and so wished out of the way. In the original cast of "Don Quixote" we miss most of all Mrs. Clive; but with Macklin as Squire Badger the piece was bound to succeed. In itself it is a good comedy; its scenes at the inn of a country borough are new and refreshing by contrast with the London that Fielding had been hitherto depicting; it is really like a chapter out of "Joseph Andrews," of which it may aptly be considered as a foreshadowing. Here occur also an improved version of "The Roast Beef of Old England" and a fine hunting song beginning—

> The dusky night rides down the sky,
>   And ushers in the morn;
> The hounds all join in glorious cry,
>   The huntsman winds his horn:
>   And a hunting we will go.

"Don Quixote" is noteworthy as marking Fielding's return to direct political satire, from which he was compelled to keep clear while writing for Drury Lane. Once back in the Haymarket, he regained his old freedom. The

157

writs for the election of a new Parliament were issued on April 18, the very day on which Fielding published his "Don Quixote."* Adjusting his comedy to the political situation, he introduced three new scenes in the course of which Don Quixote becomes a candidate for Parliament and thereby a means for exposing the bribery in country elections. While the play was acting night after night, the newspapers were giving accounts, some sober, some humorous, of actual or attempted corruption in all parts of England—of a voter, for instance, at Dover, who on coming to the poll produced a letter containing ten guineas which a gentleman had sent him for his vote, not as a bribe, the gentleman declared, but as "an act of charity." As might be expected, Fielding played delightfully with "the humours of mayors and corporations," as he called it. In one of the scenes the mayor of the borough comes to the inn kept by Mr. Guzzle to talk over matters with him and a tradesman named Retail; whereupon takes place the following conversation very like, I daresay, what Fielding had often overheard in the West:

Guz. Mr. Mayor, a good morrow to you, Sir; are you for a whet this morning?

May. With all my heart; but what's become of the gentleman [Don Quixote], the traveller?

Guz. He's laid down to sleep, I believe; pretty well tired with work. What the devil to do with him, I can't tell.

May. My neighbour and I have a strange thought come into our heads; you know, Mr. Guzzle, we are like to have no opposition, and that I believe you will feel the want of, as much as any man. Now, d'ye see, we have taken it into consideration, whether we should not ask this Sir Don to represent us.

．　　　．　　　．　　　．　　　．

Ret. But if you think he intends to offer himself, would

* "The Grub-street Journal," April 18, 1734.

it not be wiser to let him; for then, you know, if he spends never so much, we shall not be oblig'd to choose him.

May. Brother alderman, I have reproved you already for that way of reasoning; it savours too much of bribery. I like an opposition, because otherwise a man may be obliged to vote against his party; therefore, when we invite a gentleman to stand, we invite him to spend his money for the honour of his party; and when both parties have spent as much as they are able, every honest man will vote according to his conscience.

Guz. Mr. Mayor talks like a man of sense and honour, and it does me good to hear him.

May. Ay, ay, Mr. Guzzle, I never gave a vote contrary to my conscience. I have very earnestly recommended the country-interest to all my brethren; but before that I recommended the town-interest, that is, the interest of this corporation; and first of all, I recommended to every particular man to take a particular care of himself. And it is with a certain way of reasoning, that he that serves me best, will serve the town best; and he that serves the town best, will serve the country best.

Guz. See what it is to have been at Oxford; the parson in the parish himself can't out-talk him.

May. Come, landlord, we'll have one bottle, and drink success to the corporation: these times come but seldom, therefore we ought to make the best of them. Come along."

Consistently with scenes of this kind, "Don Quixote" was dedicated to Lord Chesterfield, who had recently been dismissed from his place at Court and was then covertly attacking Walpole in the newspapers by means of anonymous essays on gigantic eyes and gigantic ears, at once bitter and amusing. In his dedication of "The Intriguing Chambermaid" to Mrs. Clive, Fielding, as if acquainted with him, had already alluded to Chesterfield as "one of the finest judges and the greatest man of his age." He now expressed "perfect admiration" for the Earl and just hinted that the stage could do more than the essay in awakening the public to a sense of "the calamities brought on a country by general corruption." In other words, Fielding was offering his aid against the Government in case the Opposition should care for it. Chesterfield understood perfectly what Fielding meant; but the Opposition was not yet ready to make full use of his pen. Two years later, as we shall see, the alliance was formed.

For the present Fielding had to keep up the struggle with slight or no assistance from a patron. His income from the stage, however, must have been at least three hundred pounds a year. A good farce was then valued at forty or fifty pounds, and this sum might be increased by numerous benefit nights in which the author received all the profits after the players were paid. For some reason Fielding was hardly molested this year by "The Grub-street Journal." Bavius even announced that he had refused to publish anonymous letters and epigrams turning to vulgar burlesque Fielding's fine tribute to Mrs. Clive.* Someone must have given the word to the editor to cease his persecution of the young playwright. Was it Pope at the request of his friend Lord Chesterfield? On the other hand, "The Universal Spectator" admitted to its columns a mock testament called "An Author's Will," in which Fielding was taken to task for hasty and careless productions. The burlesque will, which the author writes "From my garret in Grubstreet," ran through two numbers of the newspaper; but the only part of it clearly written with Fielding in mind is the following paragraph in the issue of July 6:

"Item, I give and bequeath to my very *negligent* Friend *Henry Drama,* Esq; all my INDUSTRY. And whereas the World may think this an unnecessary Legacy, forasmuch

* "The Grub-street Journal," Jan. 31, 1734.

as the said *Henry Drama,* Esq, brings on the Stage *four Pieces* every Season; yet as such Pieces are always wrote with uncommon *Rapidity,* and during such fatal Intervals only as the *Stocks* have been on the *Fall,* this Legacy will be of use to him to revise and correct his Works. Furthermore, for fear the said *Henry Drama* should make an ill Use of the said *Industry,* and expend it all on a *Ballad Farce,* it's my Will the said Legacy should be paid him by equal Portions, and as his Necessities may require."

The next month Fielding was so scandalously treated by "Scriblerus Theatricus" in a verse satire called "The Dramatic Sessions; or the Stage Contest of 1734," that even "The Grub-street Journal" protested against his being classed with the blockheads of the age along with playwrights such as James Thomson, Ambrose Philips, Benjamin Martyn, and Philip Froude, of whom the last two were nonentities. The Goddess of Nonsense, missing her favourite son, inquires for "F-ld-ng . . . with his heavy Quixote"; whereupon the young playwright, whose works are dull more by idleness than by nature, steps forward and curses everybody in the company, shouting at last:

> Reach, reach me the chaplet—I'm going to write,
> I'll shew ye the odds, in a crowded ninth-night;
> I alone please the town in the Goddess's vein,
> And if critics damn me—why, I damn them again.

In contrast with this abuse, Fielding received earlier in the season encouragement from an unknown admirer, who sent him a poem of seventy-two lines in appreciation of his talent as displayed especially in "The Author's Farce." Fielding liked the verses well enough to publish them with "The Intriguing Chambermaid." The writer lamented that Fielding was forced into "farce, masque, and opera" in order to earn a living; and yet praised his sense and art and humour even therein. Who wrote the poem, we may

161

never know; but he was no scribbler, and he took a genuine
interest in Fielding's hard career. Witness the lines:

> Long have I seen, with sorrow and surprise,
> Unhelp'd, unheeded, thy strong genius rise,
> To form our manners and amend our laws,
> And aid, with artful hand, the public cause.
>
> Proceed, even thus proceed, bless'd youth! to charm,
> Divert our heats, and civil rage disarm,
> Till fortune, once not blind to merit, smile
> On thy desert, and recompense thy toil:
> Or Walpole, studious still of Britain's fame,
> Protect thy labours, and prescribe the theme,
> On which, in ease and affluence, thou may'st raise
> More noble trophies to thy country's praise.

CHAPTER VII

DRAMATIC CAREER

MARRIAGE AND REST

It is difficult to think of Fielding, the author of sixteen plays, the storm-centre of the English drama, as still only twenty-seven years old. His home, after the death of his mother, had been at Salisbury. As a schoolboy, when away from Eton, he had spent his vacations there with his grandmother and sisters. It is clear, too, that since his return from Leyden he had also visited Salisbury every summer or autumn between the dramatic seasons. The house which Lady Gould took there was in St. Martin's Street, which ran along the eastern rampart of the city to the ancient church from which the street—then an avenue of limes— received its name. Beyond were the Milford hills. By the death of Lady Gould in June, 1733, the family circle was broken, though a Mrs. Fielding,* probably an aunt, dwelt in the house for some years more, doubtless along with Henry's sisters. Fielding became very familiar with the district around Salisbury, which, more or less disguised, is reflected in his novels; and it was but a short walk from Lady Gould's house into the centre of the town, where he made many acquaintances, some of whom may be yet un- covered in "Tom Jones." On his way to the Cathedral Close, he would tramp along St. Ann's Street, just off of which in Friary Lane lived Mrs. Elizabeth Cradock, with

---

* "Mrs." was then applied to unmarried as well as to married women. The Mrs. Fielding, who was assessed in 1734 for "the house late Lady Gould's," may have been Edmund Fielding's unmarried sister Dorothy.

163

her two daughters, Charlotte and Catherine, the reigning belles of Salisbury. Fielding fell desperately in love with Charlotte and married her after a courtship of four years or more.

Nothing is positively known of Mrs. Cradock's husband or of her previous history. But it is to be presumed that she had been left a widow when young, and had settled in Salisbury to educate her daughters or perhaps merely to introduce them into the society of a cathedral town. If Mr. Cradock may be identified with the father of Amelia, "a worthier man . . . never lived," and "he died suddenly when his children were infants." A Mrs. Mary Penelope Cradock, who died in October, 1729, lies buried in Salisbury Cathedral.* The house which the family occupied at the time of Charlotte's marriage is evidence of a comfortable income, unless they were living far beyond their means. Still standing, it is now known, as it was then, as "the Friary House" from its adjoining an old Friary. It is a remodelled Elizabethan mansion having commodious rooms and chambers in oak panels and facing a large inner garden. Except for some later additions, including a Georgian front,

* The inscription gives her age at the time of her death, Oct. 28, 1729, as twenty-four. Lawrence ("Life of Fielding," p. 68) says there were "three sisters named Cradock," one of whom Fielding married. Mr. J. Paul de Castro ("Notes and Queries," Nov., 1917, p. 467) thinks that Mary Penelope may have been a sister of Charlotte and Catherine. If this be so, she was incorrectly described in the burials register as "of the Close," for the house where the Cradocks who concern us lived, was outside the Cathedral Close—not, as Mr. de Castro assumes, within the gates. My own opinion that there were but two Cradock sisters is supported by the fact that Henry Price, in a poem to be described, mentions only Charlotte and Kitty. Apparently his poem was written before the death of Mary Penelope Cradock. The late Mr. Thomas H. Baker of Salisbury was the first to identify the Cradock house from the assessments. In the summer of 1911, I went over his notes with him and verified the most important of them. From these notes I find that in 1734 Mrs. Cradock was assessed in St. Martin's parish for 3s. 8d.,—presumably the monthly rate. The entry comes for the house at the lower end of St. Ann's Street. There can be no mistake in Mr. Baker's identification of the house. No evidence has been produced to show that the Cradocks ever lived within the Close.

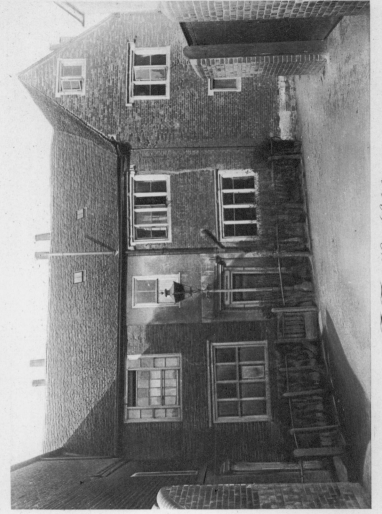

The Friary House. Salisbury

the house remains much as it was in Fielding's time. Its finest room was the great hall, now a dining-room, with flowered ceiling, an immense fireplace in ancient tiling, and a superb Jacobean mantel representing Joseph with a Lamb in his Arms, the Virgin with Child, St. Matthew with open Book, and several smaller figures, all grouped around the York rose. Here the young Romeo, having failed to abduct Miss Andrew, found his wife.

The house was in the parish of St. Martin's, and the Cradocks had to pass Lady Gould's on their way to the church, where perhaps Fielding first saw them on his return from Leyden. Of that we do not know; but by 1730, he was celebrating their charms in verses, which he gave to the public in his "Miscellanies" of 1743. In one of these poems, Venus is represented as holding a Court of Beauty in the Elysian Fields for the appointment of her vice-regents upon earth; and before her Jove appears to plead the cause of the Miss Cradocks above all the other "nymphs" of New Sarum:

> And can you, daughter, doubt to whom
> (He cry'd) belongs the happy doom,
> While C———cks yet make bless'd the earth,
> C———cks, who long before their birth,
> I, by your own petition mov'd,
> Decreed to be by all belov'd.
> C———cks, to whose celestial dower
> I gave all beauties in my power;
> To form whose lovely minds and faces,
> I stript half heaven of its graces.
> Oh let them bear an equal sway,
> So shall mankind well-pleas'd obey.

The fame of their beauty spread over the West and reached London even. Down at Poole on the coast, there was a young man named Henry Price, who, as a relief to his occupation as port-master, wrote many poems in imitation of greater poets than himself. He translated from the Greek "The Battle of the Frogs and the Mice," that mock-heroic once attributed to Homer, and turned into verse the story of Shalum and Hilpa from "The Spectator." Among his short facetious poems on local themes is one—in Latin and English, side by side—addressed to "Charlotte and Kitty Cradock," which eventually found its way into "The London Magazine."* From this poem, written not in very good taste, it would appear that "the dear charmers" had graced Poole with their presence and that the poet was lamenting their departure. Kitty is described as the more sprightly, but Charlotte as the more lovely—"Sit noctis Charlotta regina!" Far-off London knew of them simply as "the pretty Miss Cradocks of Salisbury."†

If in the first flush of youthful desire Fielding vacillated between the two girls, his doubt was resolved as soon as he came to know them better. Catherine then had to give way to Charlotte as the special favourite of Venus. Under the name of Celia he sent Charlotte all manner of verses— some were love allegories, others merely rhymes and epigrams—extolling her beauty, tender heart, and understanding. He is glad to exchange, he tells her, all the distractions of London for her company in the quiet cathedral town, and he bids the envious nymphs of New Sarum to cease contending with her for the prize of beauty. On her remarking that she would like a Lilliputian to play with, he puts it into a poem that he would like to be that pigmy, or guardian sprite, dancing upon her hand, or lying in a fold of her gown, or sitting astride upon the steeple of her hat. When she is perplexed at Gay's severity on her sex, he replies that if the women whom Gay knew had possessed her "tenderness" and "accomplished mind," there would be no point in the poet's satire. In lighter vein he composes

---

* April, 1744.

† "Advertisement" at end of "The Tryal of Colley Cibber," 1740.

a riddle on her name and finds occasion for a poem in the humorous circumstance that one night, when the Cradocks feared their house would be broken open, Charlotte placed on guard an old man "with a gun without any ammunition." Supposing the harmless gun to be loaded, the faithful servant kept up the watch till morning. The year of her marriage, Fielding also paid Charlotte a compliment by giving her name to the beautiful and amiable young lady in "The Intriguing Chambermaid," who bestows herself and her little fortune on Valentine. Perhaps there are other correspondences between the play and Fielding's courtship. Certainly some of Valentine's songs, as the one in praise of "Charlotte's charming form," were intended for the real Charlotte away in Salisbury.

At the moment Fielding was too absorbed in his passion to give many details of Charlotte's appearance. His poems rather describe, with a lover's exaggeration, the effect of her beauty upon those who had seen her. In the Salisbury Assembly Rooms, she outshines all the rest in the dance; none are "half so fair." At church, the priest forgets his text at sight of her; and her lover, entranced by her lips, her neck, her eyes, her dimple (it was in her right cheek), declares she "was made of an angel in heaven." This vision of Charlotte haunted Fielding to the end of life. When the romance and the marriage had become but a memory, he drew her portrait in "Tom Jones" as she was in her youth. With some variations, she is the Sophia Western of that novel. She was, as we may see in that portrait, a rather tall, graceful brunette, with large eyes, and black hair so luxuriant that it fell below her waist, until in compliance with a new fashion she cut it and let it curl gracefully in her neck. "Her eyebrows were full, even, and arched beyond the power of art to imitate." Her nose was "exactly regular," but there was "a little scar," we are told elsewhere, on one side of it, which Fielding thought rather added to than diminished her beauty. It was an oval face with a neck "long and finely turned," and a complexion of a delicate whiteness easily changing with exercise or emotion to a colour which "no vermilion could equal." It was a face like this, says Fielding, that moved Dr. Donne to cry out:

> ——Her pure and eloquent blood
> Spoke in her cheeks, and so distinctly wrought,
> That one might almost say her body thought.

"Such," adds Fielding in summary, "was the outside of Sophia; nor was this beautiful frame disgraced by an inhabitant unworthy of it. Her mind was every way equal to her person; nay, the latter borrowed some charms from the former; for when she smiled, the sweetness of her temper diffused that glory over her countenance which no regularity of features can give." Not that she was learned; for we know from that other portrait of her in Amelia that her reading was confined mostly to plays and poems and a few excellent books in divinity. Making due allowance for a lover's eyes, there still remains "a most charming woman"—Fielding's own phrase when in a sober mood. Miss Cradock, one easily sees, was of a rather delicate constitution, ill adapted for the hard life before her.

The circumstances concerning the marriage are not fully known. It is agreed that Fielding in depicting the career of Mr. Wilson in "Joseph Andrews" recoloured here and there incidents in his own life, though opinion has always differed on which are purely fictitious and which have a basis in fact. The Harriet whom Mr. Wilson marries certainly has some of the characteristics of Charlotte as Fielding drew her—the easy blush, the sweet smile, the sweet voice, and perfect amiability. One is tempted to go a step further and find in Mr. Wilson's long-delayed proposal of marriage (owing to his ill fortunes) and Harriet's answer, "I believe you cannot ask me what I will deny," a reflection of what occurred at the Friary House in Salisbury. At any rate, Fielding's marriage, like Wilson's, was the result of a sudden impulse after a protracted courtship, and seems to have been an elopement. The secret came out a decade ago when a gentleman of Bath discovered the entry of the marriage in the registry of St. Mary's Church at Charlcombe, a secluded parish nearly two miles north of Bath. The record runs: "November ye 28, 1734.—Henry Fielding of ye Parish of St. James, in Bath, Esq., and Charlotte Cradock, of ye same Parish, spinster, were married by virtue of a licence from ye Court of Wells."* There may be several inferences from the entry and none quite certain. One inference is that Fielding and Miss Cradock fled from Salisbury to Bath, obtained a licence there under the fiction of their residence in the parish of St. James, and then hurried over to the friendly Vicar of Charlcombe. The scene where the romance ended is a pretty stone church with embattled tower, at that time—it has since been enlarged—one of the smallest churches in England. Situated high on the slope of Lansdown, it overlooks a deep ravine and a few scattered cottages, with an extensive view across Bath to Hampton Down in the distance. If, as seems most probable, Fielding and Miss Cradock had eloped thither, there is an imaginative rendering of it in "Amelia." Booth and Amelia escaped from the pursuit of a distracted mother to be married by their friend Dr. Harrison. When all was over, she became quickly reconciled to the marriage, and, as she came to know her son-in-law better, expressed "great fondness for him." Amelia's unkind sister, however, never forgave the lovers; she quarrelled with them, and with her mother, who in consequence disinherited her. All this is in general harmony with the events which immediately suc-

---

* "Notes and Queries," 10 S. VI, 47 (July 21, 1906). An engraving of Charlcombe Church, showing the north and west sides, is given by F. Grose in "The Antiquities of England and Wales," new edition, V, 1786, p. 38.

ceeded the marriage of Henry Fielding and Charlotte Cradock.

Soon after his marriage, Fielding settled with his wife in London for the winter, taking lodgings in Buckingham Street,* near the theatres. As a Mr. Thomas Cradock was then a householder in this street, which runs from the Strand to the river, it has been surmised by Miss Godden that the Fieldings lived with him, presumably a brother or cousin of Mrs. Cradock's deceased husband. On January 17, 1735,† Fielding brought out a farce at Drury Lane called "An Old Man Taught Wisdom: or, the Virgin Unmask'd." A country squire, "with a good ten thousand pound," resolves to marry his only daughter—possessing no knowledge of the world, he thinks—to the most worthy of his poor relations, who are summoned for her to pass upon, one by one—an apothecary, a dancing-master, a singing-master, a lawyer, and a student from Oxford. Lucy proves to know more of the world than her father suspected, and marries a footman with whom she has been long in love. The piece gave Mrs. Clive, who took the part of Lucy, an opportunity to display her talent in smart comment on different types of young men as they appeared one after another to sue for her hand. The audience, however, hissed Bookish, the Oxford student, being especially displeased with a scene between him and Lucy, where he says: "I shall throw myself at no woman's feet, for I look on myself as the superior of the two." The remark was regarded as an insult not only to Lucy but to all the women in the audience. In a note to the farce when published a week later, Fielding announced that the objectionable character, as well as several songs and speeches in other places, had since been omitted by the players. Thus curtailed, the farce became very popular and continued to be acted through the rest of

* Dedication of "The Universal Gallant."
† "The London Evening Post," Jan. 16-18, 1735.

the century. Near the end of its first season, Hogarth designed a benefit ticket for John Laguerre, who played the rôle of the beau or dancing-master.

This farce, cast in the mould of the ballad-opera, was succeeded, on February 10,* by a regular comedy in five long Acts, bearing the title of "The Universal Gallant: or, the Different Husbands." Like "The Modern Husband," the new play resembled too much a novel. Captain Spark, the universal gallant, boasts that he has had intrigues with most of the ladies in town. The different husbands are Sir Simon Raffler and his brother the Colonel—the one inordinately jealous of his wife, and the other so confident of his wife's virtue as to expose her to the solicitations of his friends. The comedy met with instant condemnation, despite the excellent players, among whom were James Quin and young Cibber as the universal gallant. No one except the author had a good word to say for it; not even Fielding's friends. In the preceding November, Aaron Hill and William Popple, brother playwrights very well disposed towards him, began a semi-weekly periodical called "The Prompter," dealing with the drama and other literary topics. In an article on the stage appearing in the number for February 18, one of the editors remarks of the behaviour of the audience on the first night of "The Universal Gallant": "Till almost the third Act was over, they sat very quiet, in hopes it would mend, till finding it grew still worse and worse, they at length lost all patience, and not an expression or sentiment afterwards passed without its deserved censure." The actors nevertheless persisted for two nights more before giving up the fight. In Fielding's brief phrase, the play was "condemn'd unheard." Each performance seems to have ended in a tumult of groans, catcalls, whistles, and horse-laughs. Remembering the scene, "The Prompter," when describing later a riot at Orator Henley's chapel, says

* "Fog's Weekly Journal," Feb. 8, 1735.

there were "such hissings and clappings, that I thought myself, for a long time, at a representation of a new piece of
Mr. F—l—g."*

The reasons for the hostility of the audience were quite
sufficient. Never before had Fielding been so dull; never
before had he put into the mouths of his characters so
caustic remarks on the frailties of women; no scene until
the fifth Act was really dramatic, and even there he was but
reworking scenes from his "Love in Several Masques."
The author, however, was surprised and grieved at his
treatment, and so appealed to the town by publishing the
play a week after its failure. A prologue and an epilogue,
evidently retouched if not written after the first performance, scored the audience, given over to "soft Italian airs
and French buffoons," for killing his comedy, and urged
the ladies to assist by their applause "the satire of the
stage." A pathetic advertisement complained of the barbarous usage to which he had been subjected by a set of
"young gentlemen about this town, who make a jest of
damning plays," though the author "be so unfortunate
[as] to depend on the success of his labours for his bread."
"He must be," Fielding concludes, "an inhuman creature,
indeed, who would out of sport and wantonness prevent a
man from getting a livelihood in an honest and inoffensive
way, and make a jest of starving him and his family. . . .
Of all persons, I am the last they should attack, as I have
often endeavoured to procure the success of others, but
never assisted at the condemnation of any one." There was
also a dedication to Charles, Duke of Marlborough, who had
recently come into his title and was taking sides with the
opponents of Walpole. In his distress Fielding besought
his lordship's favour and protection, saying: "Poverty
has imposed chains on mankind equal with tyranny."

Fielding's distress, though temporary, was real. For

* "The Prompter," No. 82. Aug. 22, 1735.

himself alone the theatre had provided a precarious living. Now there was a wife to support also; and his second play after marriage had been hissed from the stage by an impartial audience ready, I think, to applaud, had there been anything in the piece worthy of approval. At this time an anonymous maker of verses took Fielding as an example of the violent changes to which fortune subjects those dependent upon her. In "Seasonable Reproof, a Satire in the Manner of Horace," which was published the following November, he was described as he looked before and after a successful play:

> F......g who *yesterday* appear'd so rough,
> Clad in *coarse Frize*, and plaister'd down with *Snuff*.
> See how his *Instant* gaudy Trappings shine;
> What *Play-house* Bard was ever seen so fine!
> But this, not from his *Humour* flows, you'll say,
> But mere *Necessity*;—for last Night lay
> In *Pawn*, the *Velvet* which he wears to Day.*

These lines, which have no bitterness, should not be taken literally; for it was not necessary for Fielding this year, if ever, to pawn his coat. They are only Grub Street's vivid way of saying that he could buy a new suit when a play succeeded, but must wear his old clothes if it met with disaster.

On other occasions when a play failed, Fielding had quickly substituted another; but he was prevented from doing so this year by the death of his wife's mother and the evident desire of Mrs. Fielding to quit London. Mrs. Cradock, by her will executed on February 8 and proved on February 25, 1735,† left her entire estate—except "one shilling" for Catherine—to her "dearly beloved daughter Charlott Ffeilding wife of Henry Ffeilding of East Stour." Mrs. Fielding was named in the will as "sole executrix,"

* Written by James Miller, parson, playwright, and satirist.
† The will is at Somerset House—"P. C. C. 27. Ducie."

and as such presented the will for probate in London, taking the usual oaths. No bond was required of her; no inventory of goods was ever exhibited; nothing is, therefore, positively known of the value and specific character of the estate, except that the will mentions "ready money, plate, and jewels." According to Arthur Murphy, writing many years afterwards, Mrs. Fielding's fortune "did not exceed fifteen hundred pounds." That estimate is a safe guess, for it may mean any sum up to fifteen hundred pounds, and there is no reason for believing that the so-called fortune was larger. Small as it was, it was enough to relieve a family in need of assistance. Why Catherine was cut off with a shilling still remains a mystery. Perhaps, like the envious sister of Amelia, she had intrigued against Charlotte and so displeased her mother. Something very wicked must have happened. Nor has it been ascertained what became of Catherine. Did Fielding have her in mind when he wrote the epigram?—

> That Kate weds a fool what wonder can be,
> Her husband has married a fool great as she.*

Mrs. Cradock's will properly described Fielding as belonging to the parish of East Stour, which had been his legal residence since his coming of age. The family estate there still remained in trust for the six children, awaiting the majority of his brother Edmund, born in 1716. The rents, then estimated at £200 a year, had been divided equally among them. Naturally, Henry as the eldest son had for some time kept an eye on the management of the property much as his father had tried to do before him, going to East Stour at least every autumn to hunt and to talk over affairs with the man in immediate charge of the farm. Events as well as tradition point to Fielding's retirement to East Stour this spring after a visit to Salisbury in connection with the estate which his wife had inherited

* "Miscellanies," 1743, I, 63.

from her mother. If Murphy is to be trusted, it was now his intention "to bid adieu to all the follies and intemperances" of the town and to turn gentleman farmer. However this may be, Fielding stayed with his wife in the country through the summer and autumn. It was the longest rest he had taken since he began his dramatic career. Here the months went by in quiet and comfort amid the scenes of his childhood. The huge locust tree was still standing; and at a short distance were the orchards and gardens with high walls through the holes of which, it is said, he used to shoot rabbits and other small game. A massive oak table purporting to be the one from which he dined now reposes in the Museum of Taunton Castle.

There were old and new faces in the neighbourhood. Fielding's former tutor, the Rev. Mr. Oliver, lived on at Motcombe; while over the parish of East Stour presided the Rev. William Young, who had been appointed to the curacy only four years before. A poor Wiltshire boy, Young had somehow managed to go to Oxford, where he matriculated at the advanced age of twenty-five and duly obtained his degree. In 1735 he was thirty-three years old. His odd personality, compounded of rustic manners and university culture, was a source of perennial interest to Fielding. He had a strong and awkward frame such as one would expect in a cudgel-player rather than in a student of the ancient classics who always carried in his coat pocket a copy of Aeschylus. Absorbed in his books, he was absent-minded to an absurd degree; and when pleased or embarrassed, he had the habit of snapping his huge fingers loud enough to echo through the hall. Withal he was an inveterate smoker and he loved the home-brewed ale. Doubtless Fielding and the parson wore down many a night in the old stone house at East Stour over their pipes and mugs and anecdotes of London and Oxford.

Four miles down the river Stour was Stalbridge Park,

the seat of a notorious London attorney named Peter Walter. Then an old man, he had amassed a fortune—estimated at £40,000 or more—as steward to the Duke of Newcastle and other noblemen and gentlemen. He was very shrewd and perhaps equally dishonest. When Fielding knew him, he owned not only Stalbridge but several other estates in Dorset and Somerset, often acquired, it was claimed, by loans at exorbitant rates of interest. His greed for land was satirized by Pope, who charged him with a desire to purchase the nation just as Didius, the Roman lawyer, had bid for and obtained the Roman Empire on the death of Pertinax. Fielding was amused by this hoary miser and sinner who denied himself the comforts of life and spent all in the purchase of dirt. He subsequently referred to him in irony as "My worthy friend," and as "Mynheer Petrus Gualterus." According to Fielding, Walter regarded "rows of fine oaks" as an expensive ornament to the landscape, and so cut them down and sold them; and guineas so tenaciously stuck to his hand that no force could make them let go. Of this man it is unnecessary to say more in this place; for he will appear in "Joseph Andrews" under the alias of Mr. Peter Pounce in the company of the Rev. William Young, renamed the Rev. Abraham Adams.

CHAPTER VIII

DRAMATIC CAREER

PASQUIN

If Fielding, as has been alleged, was disposed at this time to renounce the stage for the life of a country squire, the old longing for the town soon returned to him. The quiet of East Stour gave him an opportunity to take a comprehensive view of his dramatic talent—to see that it lay, not in depicting the irregular sex relations of fashionable society, but in farce, burlesque, and political satire. On mature consideration, he must have known why "The Universal Gallant" had failed, and that to regain his audience he had but to produce another play in the manner of "Tom Thumb" or "The Author's Farce." Perhaps while at East Stour, he sketched out "Pasquin," and went up to London with it early in 1736. He took lodgings or a house for himself and wife near the theatres, in the parish of St. Martin's in the Fields, where their first child, Charlotte, was born on April 27, and baptized on May 19, 1736. So Mrs. Fielding, who had shared in her husband's chagrin over "The Universal Gallant," was now to see him retrieve his fortunes handsomely.

The theatrical situation had not greatly changed since I last described it. Drury Lane was still under the direction of Fleetwood as the chief patentee, with young Cibber and Mrs. Clive among the leading players. Rich's company at Covent Garden was amusing the town with "dramatic entertainments," varied by light comedy and an occasional tragedy. Giffard began the season at Goodman's Fields but in April he closed this house except for occasional performances, and removed to Lincoln's Inn Fields, thus bringing together in close rivalry three theatres. The fierce war between the two operas also continued. Farinelli, under the patronage of the Prince of Wales and his friends, was singing at the Opera House in the Haymarket; while Handel, belonging to the King's party, was giving operas and oratorios at Rich's theatre in Covent Garden. There remained the Little Theatre in the Haymarket where Fielding had brought out his "Don Quixote in England." Since that time this theatre had been in the hands of a company of French comedians until the summer of 1735, when it was taken by the younger members of Drury Lane for comedy and farce, twice a week. These young players, some of whom were in the original cast of "Don Quixote," kept up a loose organization into the winter of 1735-1736, their last play being Vanbrugh's "Aesop," which was performed on February 20, 1736. It was at this time that Fielding appeared and reorganized them into "The Great Mogul's Company of Comedians." Immediately before taking this step he had had a play—doubtless "Pasquin"—rejected by Rich and probably by Fleetwood also. According to Thomas Davies the bookseller, who was then associated with the actors of the Haymarket, Fielding was assisted in the management by his old friend James Ralph. The facetious title that Fielding chose for his company, was suggested by the fact that a theatrical manager, owing to his absolute power to accept or reject plays, was known as the Great Mogul. Disgruntled aspirants for the stage were then applying the name to Theophilus Cibber in succession to his father. By way of jest Fielding would claim for himself the honour of being the Great Mogul in the theatrical world.

Free to put upon the stage such plays as he wished without the interference of a Cibber, Fielding resumed political satire and burlesque where he had left it in his "Don

Quixote." That play, it will be remembered, was inscribed
to Lord Chesterfield, who, in Fielding's phrase, had "so
gloriously distinguished himself in the cause of liberty."
Since that time the war against Walpole had drifted on
languidly, with occasional flashes of fierceness; but by 1736,
fresh blood was being infused into the Opposition, or the
Country Party, as it was then commonly called. In the
House of Lords, Chesterfield found an able supporter in the
young Duke of Bedford, who had taken his seat a few years
before. In the House of Commons, the position of Pulteney
and the "Patriots" was greatly strengthened by George
Lyttelton and William Pitt, subsequently Earl of Chatham,
both of whom were returned in the by-elections of 1735.
These five men, uniting round the Prince of Wales as a
figurehead against the King and Walpole, were for the time
being the conspicuous leaders of the Country Party. With
these Patriots, mostly young men near his own age, Fielding joined hands, and made the Little Theatre in the Haymarket an organ of the Opposition. His relations with
Pitt and Chesterfield became most friendly, with Bedford
and Lyttelton in particular they became intimate.

As political satirist, Fielding assumed the name of Pasquin in place of Scriblerus Secundus, which he had used in
the earlier days. It was an old tale that there had formerly
been at Rome, in opposite quarters of the city, statues called
Pasquin and Marforio, to which people by way of thrust
and parry were accustomed to fasten epigrams. Pasquin
brought the charge, and Marforio made the reply in kind.
In Fielding's time the names of these two statues were
common pseudonyms among political pamphleteers. A
few years previously, a London newspaper bore the name
of Pasquin, and during the spring of 1736 appeared the
anonymous "Political Dialogues between the Statues of
Pasquin and Marforio," dedicated to "the most renowned
modern equilibrist," that is, to Walpole. In his new rôle,

179

Fielding announced in the newspapers for Friday, March 5, 1736, the first performance of "Pasquin. A Dramatick Satire on the Times: Being the Rehearsal of two Plays, *viz.* A Comedy call'd, The Election; and a Tragedy call'd, The Life and Death of Common-Sense." The advertisement concluded with several facetious notices:

"N. B. Mr. Pasquin intending to lay about him with great Impartiality, hopes the Town will all attend, and very civilly give their neighbours what the [*sic*] find belongs to 'em.

"N. B. The Cloaths are old, but the Jokes intirely new.

"N. B. All Ladies that intend to be present during the first Run, cannot take Places too early.

"To prevent any Interruption in the Movement of the Persons in the Drama (some of whom are Machines) no Person whatever can possibly be admitted behind the scenes."*

The scene of "Pasquin" is a playhouse. The poet Trapwit first puts into rehearsal a burlesque of comedy, and Fustian follows with a mock-tragedy. It is as if an audience were entertained with "The Author's Farce" and "Tom Thumb" on the same evening. For his election scenes Trapwit seats the Mayor and Aldermen of a provincial town round a table in deep consultation over the proper representatives of the borough. So far as they have any political principles, they are in favour of Sir Harry Fox-Chace and Squire Tankard, their neighbours and the candidates of the Country Party; but they cannot help reflecting that "a man who lives an hundred miles off may be as honest as him who lives but three." While they are in this mood the candidates of the Court Party—Lord Place and Colonel Promise—appear, and his lordship easily wins them over by a civil squeeze of the hand:

"*Mayor.* My Lord, we are sensible of your great power

* "The London Daily Post," Feb. 24, 1736.

PASQUIN.

A DRAMATICK

SATIRE on the TIMES:

BEING THE

REHEARSAL of Two PLAYS, *viz.*

A COMEDY call'd,

THE ELECTION;

And a TRAGEDY call'd,

The LIFE *and* DE.ATH *of*

COMMON-SENSE.

As it is Acted at the THEATRE in the
HAY-MARKET.

By *HENRY FIELDING,* Efq;

LONDON:

Printed for J. WATTS at the Printing-Office in
Wild-Court near *Lincoln's-Inn Fields,*

MDCCXXXVI.
[Price One Shilling and Six Pence.]

to serve this corporation; and we do not doubt but we shall feel the effect on't.

Lord Place. Gentlemen, you may depend on me; I shall do all in my power. I shall do you some services which are not proper at present to mention to you; in the mean time, Mr. Mayor, give me leave to squeeze you by the hand, in assurance of my sincerity.

Trapwit. You, Mr. that act my Lord, bribe a little more openly if you please, or the audience will lose that joke, and it's one of the strongest in my whole play.

Lord Place. Sir, I cannot possibly do it better at the table.

Trapwit. Then get all up, and come forward to the front of the stage. Now, you gentlemen that act the Mayor and Aldermen, range yourselves in a line; and you, my Lord, and the Colonel, come to one end, and bribe away with right and left.

Fustian. Is this wit, Mr. Trapwit?

Trapwit. Yes, Sir, it is wit; and such wit as will run all over the kingdom.''

This incident of direct bribery over, Trapwit clears the stage of the gentlemen from the Court in order to make room for the candidates of the Country Party, who are skilled in giving the indirect bribe. Sir Harry, suspecting what has just happened, persuades the Mayor and Aldermen that it will be for their best interests in the long run to stick to the Country Party. He tells them that he is going to pull down his old house and build a new one; that he must have his bricks of the Mayor, his iron of one of the Aldermen, and his timber of another; while of still another he orders a hundred yards of silk for his wife to hang her rooms with. In anticipation of the time when Sir Harry will be deep in their books, they all drink to ''liberty and property and no excise'' until they are as drunk as they are hoarse. The election at length takes place; and, though the Mayor votes the other way, Sir Harry Fox-Chace and Colonel Tankard are elected by a clear majority. Thereupon the Mayor is in a dreadful state of mind, knowing that he will never be forgiven by Sir Harry for voting against him, and that he can now expect nothing from the Court. His wife, however, saves the day by persuading him to return the defeated candidates as duly elected. Lord Place is overwhelmed by the favour of the Mayoress, and Colonel Promise in gratitude marries her daughter. The comedy thus ends pleasantly in the prospect of a contested election, which will take half the electors and their wives up to London at the expense of the candidates. Whatever the result of the contest, there will be a chance to see once more the sights of the town.

With less strict reference to party politics, "The Election" contains also several stretches of most brilliant dialogue. There is an amusing semi-political quarrel between Miss Mayoress and Miss Stitch, who derive their politics respectively from "The Daily Gazetteer" and "The Craftsman"—the first the organ of Walpole, and the second the organ of the Opposition. In her passion Miss Stitch by accident tears her fan and is appeased by the promise of a new one from Miss Mayoress on condition that she shall bring her sweetheart over to vote for the candidates of the Court Party. As indicated by the context, this incident of the fan had reference to the disaffection of Lord Hervey, popularly known as Lord Fanny, who had been persuaded by the Queen to desert Pulteney for Walpole. The scene gave Fielding an opportunity to pay his compliments to "The Gazetteer," which, he says, the Government was sending through the kingdom "every week for nothing"; and the garrulous editor in the pay of Walpole, he called "an old woman." On the other hand, Fielding incidentally praised the newspapers of his own party, and referred particularly to a contribution of Chesterfield's to "Fog's

Weekly Journal'' for January 17, 1736, wherein his lordship had recently described the King's army as ''An Army in Waxwork.'' An ignorant elector takes literally Chesterfield's irony and offers to supply the Court with ''a most delicate piece of black wax'' for a chaplain in his Majesty's regiment.

Neither is Colley Cibber forgotten. In publishing his ''Caesar in Egypt'' some years back, Cibber had prefixed to each Act a motto from Lucan as a summary of what the Act was intended to teach. So Fielding, in burlesque of him, pretends to have for his successive scenes a moral such as ''we are all under petticoat government.'' The current ridicule of the laureate's odes had become perhaps a trifle stale; but no one else ever did it so well as Fielding in the scene where a rural voter asks Lord Place for a position at Court. Here is the conversation:

''*Second Voter.* My Lord, I should like a place at court too; I don't much care what it is, provided I wear fine clothes, and have something to do in the kitchen, or the cellar; I own I should like the cellar, for I am a devilish lover of sack.

Lord Place. Sack, say you? Odso, you shall be poet-laureat.

Second Voter. Poet! no, my Lord, I am no poet, I can't make verses.

Lord Place. No matter for that,—you'll be able to make odes.

Second Voter. Odes, my Lord! what are those?

Lord Place. Faith, Sir, I can't tell well what they are; but I know you may be qualified for the place without being a poet.''

With scarce an interruption, Trapwit's comedy passes into Fustian's tragedy, partially written in the blank verse of Cibber's ''Caesar in Egypt,'' and fitted up with a dedication, mock prologue and epilogue, and the necessary machinery for ghosts, thunder, and lightning. Fielding here develops a rather severe arraignment of contemporary society by means of an allegory representing a contention between Queen Common-Sense and Queen Ignorance, which ends in an open fight between the adherents of each. Almost everybody is now on the side of Ignorance, though nearly all were formerly the friends of Common-Sense. This is especially true of the professions. Common-Sense says:

> Religion, law and physic, were design'd
> By heaven the greatest blessings on mankind;
> But priests, and lawyers, and physicians made
> These general goods to each a private trade;
> With each they rob, with each they fill their purses,
> And turn our benefits into our curses.

The clergy, forgetting their duties, "groan for power, and cry out after honour"; the lawyers interpret the law only for the benefit of gentlemen able to pay large fees; while physicians are enraged at Common-Sense because she recommends water gruel instead of their drops and pills. Thus deserted by her supporters of old, Common-Sense is stabbed to death by Firebrand, the priest of the play; but her ghost soon afterwards "rises to soft music" and frightens Ignorance and her train from the stage. While they are running helter-skelter, the ghost advances to proclaim the moral:

> Here, tho' a ghost, I will my power maintain,
> And all the friends of Ignorance shall find,
> My ghost, at least, they cannot banish hence.
> And all henceforth, who murder Common-Sense,
> Learn from these scenes that tho' success you boast,
> You shall at last be haunted with her ghost.

Here the play concludes with a brief conversation between a critic at the rehearsal and the author:

"*Sneerwell.* I am glad you make Common-Sense get the

better at last; I was under terrible apprehensions for your moral.

Fustian. Faith, Sir, this is almost the only play where she has got the better lately. . . .''

Fustian's satire was aimed in part at the kind of plays that were being produced at the rival theatres, especially by John Rich at his theatre in Covent Garden. It is in the open square near this playhouse that Ignorance marshals her forces, and Common-Sense is given her quietus, though her ghost survives the dagger; for we may kill the substance but not the spirit or the shadow of common sense. On the same spot, too, Tragedy and Comedy were slain earlier in the play, but their ghosts rise to tell the tale. They had been forced to give way to the favourites of Ignorance—the pantomimes and vaudeville performances which Rich and other theatrical managers had introduced as afterpieces to the regular drama. Sneerwell the critic asks Fustian why "pantomimical farces" came to be called "entertainments," and receives the ironical reply:

"Faith, Sir, out of their peculiar modesty; intimating that after the audience have been tired with the dull works of Shakespear, Johnson, Vanbrugh, and others, they are to be entertain'd with one of these pantomimes, of which the master of the play-house, two or three painters, and half a score dancing-masters are the compilers: what these entertainments are, I need not inform you who have seen 'em; but I have often wond'red how it was possible for any creature of human understanding, after having been diverted for three hours with the productions of a great genius, to sit for three more, and see a set of people running about the stage after one another, without speaking one syllable."

The satire becomes most direct when Harlequin, dressed perhaps to impersonate Rich, enters to swear allegiance to Ignorance, bringing with him a catalogue of his choicest treasures as hostages—"a tall man," "a tall woman," "two dogs that walk on their hind legs only," "two human cats," and other grotesque substitutes for great actors.

Finally, "Pasquin" depicts in both its parts the humorous incidents connected with the rehearsal of a play. The rehearsal of the comedy is threatened with delay because "the author was arrested as he was going home from King's Coffee-house . . . for upwards of four pound"; and a player remarks, "I suppose he will hardly get bail." Similarly the prompter has fears for the gentleman who is to play the first ghost in the tragedy because he has such "a church-yard cough" that he cannot be heard to the middle of the pit. Again, the ghost of Common-Sense enters in the wrong place, even before she has been killed; and the flour must be wiped from her face, and she must go back to make ready for the dagger scene. The tragedy is interrupted by the arrest of Law, and Fustian gets into a quarrel with one of the actors. All this fooling leads up to Fustian's summary of an author's troubles in bringing out a play:

"These little things, Mr. Sneerwell, will sometimes happen. Indeed a poet undergoes a great deal before he comes to his third night; first with the Muses, who are humorous ladies, and must be attended; for if they take it into their head at any time to go abroad and leave you, you will pump your brain in vain: then, Sir, with the master of a play-house to get it acted, whom you generally follow a quarter of a year before you know whether he will receive it or no; and then perhaps he tells you it won't do, and returns it you again, reserving the subject, and perhaps the name, which he brings out in his next pantomime; but if he should receive the play, then you must attend again to get it writ out into parts, and rehears'd. Well, Sir, at last the rehearsals begin; then, Sir, begins another scene of trouble with the actors, some of whom don't like their parts, and all are continually plaguing you with alterations: at length, after having waded thro' all these difficulties, his play appears on the stage, where one man hisses out of resentment to the author; a second out of dislike to the house; a third out of dislike to the actor; a fourth out of dislike to the play; a fifth for the joke sake; a sixth to keep all the rest in company. Enemies abuse him, friends give him up, the play is damn'd, and the author goes to the devil, so ends the farce.''

This account of a play's hard journey to a third night is a sort of version of what happened to ''The Universal Gallant'' the year before. Trapwit professes to fear that the same fate will befall the new play. And so for a guinea in the hand, he offers Sneerwell a crown a night for ''Pasquin'' as long as it runs. If Fielding made that bet he lost. By the time ''Pasquin'' was published, early in April,* it had been performed for thirty nights, ''to crowded audiences, with universal applause''; and it went on continuously for twenty nights more. It reached its sixtieth night, the author's benefit, on May 26, and was thereafter frequently performed during the summer. The rôles of ''the contrasted poets,'' Trapwit and Fustian, were taken by John Roberts, then reckoned Fielding's best man, and James Lacy, who later became associated with Garrick as patentee and manager of Drury Lane. From time to time, as the playbills announced, Fielding made minor alterations in the speeches, and secured for the twelfth night (Friday, March 19) an important addition to his company. Up to that night, the rôle of Lord Place had been assigned to Richard Yates, who also took the part of Law. Ostensibly to relieve Yates of a double rôle but really to give éclat to the performance, Fielding enticed from Drury Lane, on the promise of four guineas a week, the notorious Mrs. Charlotte Charke, an exceedingly clever impersonator of mas-

* Dates and playbills are given in ''The London Daily Post.''

culine characters—and, to add to the piquancy of the incident, a daughter of Colley Cibber. She was not on very
good terms with either her father or her brother, and she
had recently quarrelled with Fleetwood. Fielding knew
the situation and made the most of it. "Pasquin" would
have had its long run without Mrs. Charke, but her presence
contributed to its vast success. The climax in her performance of Lord Place was, of course, the scene from which
I have quoted, where she ridicules the odes of her father.
There was never an audience able to withstand the jest of
that incident.

No play since "The Beggar's Opera" had enjoyed an
immediate run of sixty-odd nights. Performances at the
other theatres—Italian opera even—all fell into the background, and managers became alarmed at the severe blow
dealt them by "Pasquin." "When I went out of town last
autumn," Mrs. Pendarves wrote to Swift over in Ireland,
"the reigning madness was Farinelli; I find it now turned
on 'Pasquin,' a dramatic satire on the times.''* "The
Prompter''† said the same thing, but added: "Farinelli's
benefit has pass'd, without an article mentioned in any
paper, of a single present made him," whereas in other
years he had received great sums. The audience that deserted the other houses for the Little Theatre in the Haymarket was vividly described four years later in "An
Apology for the Life of Mr. Theophilus C[ibber]." Who
was the author of this burlesque autobiography has never
been determined. Perhaps it was written in irony by Fielding himself. With an air of hostility, it is said of Fielding: "He drew the *mob* [the mob of fashion] after him
from Grosvenor, Cavendish, Hanover, and all the other
fashionable squares, as also from Pall Mall, and the Inns

* "Autobiography and Correspondence of Mary Granville, Mrs. Delany,"
1861, I, 554.
† April 2, 1736.

of Court. . . . It could not but regret me to see some
noble peers and gentlemen I had entertain'd a very good
opinion of, as to their parts and capacities, sitting in the
side-boxes, and seemingly delighted with the performance.''* From the context it is clear that among those
peers and gentlemen were the leaders of the Opposition,
who came not only for the wit and humour of the play but
to encourage a burlesque of the Walpole Government.

For the first month interest centred on the political
scenes, which were regarded as a comic version of what had
taken place at the last general election. As an aid to those
curious of the exact correspondences between the play and
real life, someone prepared and published in March ''A
Key to Pasquin.'' This sixpenny pamphlet, of which no
copy seems to have survived, was likely a humorous rather
than a serious undertaking. Critics who found fault with
''Pasquin'' as a whole, usually excepted the bribery passages. Fielding's old enemy, ''The Grub-street Journal,''
for example, though still inclining to censure and abuse,
praised his unmasking of corrupt politicians. ''The surest
way,'' wrote one of the editors, ''to render all such persons
ridiculous, and consequently despised, is to introduce them
personated upon the stage, and there openly acting those
vile parts, which they daily act in a more clandestine manner
upon the stage of the world. This the Author of 'Pasquin'
has done; and if success be a certain sign of the goodness of
a dramatic piece, as it is generally taken to be; the prodigious success of this has fixed it secure beyond the attaques
of any malicious critic.''† The impartial ''Prompter''
put the case clearly for the audience by saying that for a
time Mr. Trapwit's comedy supported Mr. Fustian's tragedy, which was not fully understood at first, some calling
it ''stupid, dull, nonsensical.'' But by April people began

* Edition of 1740, p. 92.

† ''The Grub-street Journal,'' April 22, 1736. See also the issue for May 6.

to see what was meant by the mock-tragedy—"much the finer performance of the two"—so that now "it supports the comedy, at least it loses nothing by coming after it."*

This change in the attitude of the public was occasioned, according to "The Prompter," by "a short, humorous advertisement" which attracted general attention. Of Pasquin's many facetious playbills, "The Prompter" perhaps referred to the one for the benefit of the actor playing the part of Fustian—which occurred on April 6. Hitherto Fielding had kept the comedy to the front, but in that playbill he brought forward the tragedy—Mr. Fustian against Mr. Trapwit. The last paragraphs of the playbill show with what ready humour it was done:

"Mr. Fustian desires the Audience (notwithstanding his Brother Trapwit's unfair Advertisement to the contrary) to take particular Notice of the Tragedy, there being several New and very deep Things to be spoke by the Ghost of Tragedy, if the Cock does not crow him away too soon.

"N. B. *As Mr. Fustian is the first Poet that ever cared to own, that he brought Ignorance upon the Stage, he hopes all her Friends will excuse his calling in particular upon them, and favour him with their Company along with the Friends of Common Sense, which he hopes will be the Foundation of a Coalition of Parties.*

"N. B. As Mr. Fustian is in great expectation of a vast Demand for Places, all Ladies and Gentleman, who design to do him the Honour of their company, cannot send too soon; he hopes the Town will not be so particular, as to break thro' a custom for one Night only, but take the whole House at least a Fortnight beforehand.

"Particular Care will be taken to get the Thunder and Lightning in Order."†

An advertisement in this style was well adapted to tickle the ears of the public and so make them consider more

* "The Prompter," April 2. † "The London Daily Post," March 29, 1736.

closely Mr. Fustian's satire on the stage. But this was not all. Without doubt "Pasquin" underwent many alterations during the first weeks of its performance. Fielding gave, I daresay, a sharper and more personal sting to his denunciation of pantomimes and entertainments, and so awakened the anger of Rich, whose theatre mainly depended upon these spurious dramatic pieces. Accepting the challenge to a quarrel, the manager of Covent Garden brought out, on April 10, "Marforio, A Theatrical Satyr, being a Comi-Tragical Farce call'd The Critick of Taste; or, A Tale of a Tub." It was an afterpiece to Dryden's "All for Love." In this way, as if writing a political satire, Marforio replied to Pasquin, his "witty brother." Though Rich's play was never printed, its nature may be inferred from the title and advertisements in the newspapers. Among the characters was the Great Mogul—clearly an impersonation of Fielding himself, who was charged with stealing his best things from Rich, especially the idea of contrasting the two poets, Trapwit and Fustian; and the playbill was a close parody on the first playbill to "Pasquin" down to notices like this:

"Mr. Marforio hopes those who have paid a Visit to his Brother Pasquin, will not refuse him the same Favour.

"His Clothes are as Old, and the Jokes somewhat more New.

"All Ladies who intend to be present during the first Run, are desired to take Places for the first Night, lest they never may have such another Opportunity."*

Incidentally, the satire included some of Fielding's friends. The sub-title, "The Critick of Taste," for instance, was levelled at Aaron Hill, the principal editor of "The Prompter," who was brought into the play itself under the name of his periodical, along with Singlewit and Drawcansir, Tweedledum and Tweedledee, the Embryo of Common-Sense and a chorus of ghosts.

* "The London Daily Post," April 10, 1736.

"Marforio" did not survive the first night. One performance and the rumours of the previous fortnight were, however, enough to arouse Fielding and his supporter Aaron Hill. On April 8,* Fielding published "Pasquin" in anticipation of the attack upon it; and the following day "The Prompter" protested against the forthcoming satire of so excellent a play and the ridicule of a periodical whose purpose was to cultivate good taste in actors and the audience. The next morning Rich replied with spirit in "The Daily Post," disclaiming any intention of doing injustice to the author of "Pasquin" that night, though he would perhaps take "a little liberty with him." Already, we see by "The Prompter" of April 2, Fielding had begun a new farce, which, doubtless aimed at Rich from the first, he now turned hotly against him. Since the beginning of March, the company at Drury Lane had been frequently playing as an afterpiece a pantomime entertainment in which Rich bore a hand, called "The Fall of Phaeton." It was a poor thing founded upon the old Greek myth, but had succeeded very well owing to novel machinery invented by Mr. Pritchard, some good music by Master Arne, and the charm of Mrs. Clive as Clymene. Fielding seized upon the piece for a slight but very funny parody, which he named "Tumble-Down Dick: or, Phaeton in the Suds. A Dramatick Entertainment of Walking, in Serious and Foolish Characters: Interlarded with Burlesque, Grotesque, Comick Interludes, Call'd, Harlequin A Pick-Pocket . . . Being ('tis hop'd) the last Entertainment that will ever be exhibited on any Stage." The parody followed exactly the current type of pantomime, in which scenes among the Greek gods alternated with the tricks of Harlequin—a sort of seesaw between the serious and the comic, or, in Fielding's phrase, between "the duller" and "the dullest."

Fielding got his burlesque effects in the so-called serious

* "The Grub-street Journal," April 8, 1736.

parts by reducing the divinities to the state of vulgar mortals. Phoebus becomes the leader of the London watch, with his throne in a roundhouse instead of a temple; while Clymene is an oyster-wench who has had an intrigue with him. Their son Phaeton obtains permission of his father to carry a lantern for one night; and, like some other watchmen, falls asleep in a wheelbarrow, tumbles out and leaves the town in darkness. For a dance of the Hours and the Seasons in the Drury Lane play, is substituted a jig by a group of rakes and loose women at King's Coffee-House. In the comic parts, Harlequin—that is, Rich himself—is transformed into a thief, who picks a play out of a poet's pocket, in allusion to the charge sometimes brought against Rich of rejecting a comedy and afterwards appropriating the plot for an entertainment of his own. Rich is elsewhere many times hit hard, as when Fielding accuses him of cutting out the first and fifth Acts of "Othello" in order to make room for a pantomime as afterpiece, or when Jupiter describes him as the grandson of an ass, who has "turned all nature topsy-turvy." The curtain falls upon a scene representing the stages of Covent Garden and Drury Lane side by side; the managers, Rich and Fleetwood, appear along with young Cibber and the rest of the players, all of whom mount a cart and sing the praises of pantomime to the tune of "The Abbot of Canterbury."

"Tumble-Down Dick" was cleverly adjusted to "Pasquin" as a rehearsal in continuation of that double play. Here again appear Mr. Fustian and Mr. Sneerwell the critic, to whom the composer, called Mr. Machine, explains the significance of the action scene by scene. A characteristic touch of humour is where Machine corrects the Drury Lane pronunciation of Clymene, saying that they call her, as they actually did, Clymène over there, whereas it should be Clymĕne; and again where an old schoolmistress is teaching a justice of the peace, who afterwards plays

Harlequin, how to spell. "Sir," remarks Machine to Fustian, "the Justice is a very ingenious man, and a very great scholar, but happen'd to have the misfortune in his youth never to learn to read." The jest lay in the fact that Rich was notoriously illiterate.

It took Fielding a full month to write, rehearse, and bring out "Tumble-Down Dick." Definitely announced a day or two after the performance of "Marforio," it did not reach the stage until April 29,* when it formed the afterpiece to "Pasquin." The delay was caused by the excitement and celebrations connected with the marriage of the Prince of Wales to Princess Augusta of Saxe-Gotha, which occurred on April 26. In fact Fielding had to close his theatre on several nights, while for two weeks "people of quality" crowded Drury Lane, where their Royal Highnesses twice occupied a box ornamented with great splendour. The afterpiece at Drury Lane was "The Fall of Phaeton," which, in the concluding speeches of Jupiter and Phaeton, clearly pointed to the reconciliation between King George and his rash and undutiful son. At the first opportunity, Fielding thrust in his "Tumble-Down Dick," with Mrs. Charke in the rôle of Clymĕne, in rivalry with Mrs. Clive's Clymēne at the royal theatre. The royal marriage over, the farce had a good run, with "Pasquin" and other plays, to the end of the season. On the day of its first performance, it was published with a mock dedication to "Mr. John Lun, vulgarly call'd Esquire"—Lun being the name under which Rich played Harlequin and "the Squire" being his familiar title about town. As a piece of ironical invective it would be hard to surpass this dedication to a great man who, owing to his "heels" or his "head," had invented or brought into fashion pantomime entertainments without any aid from common sense. Fielding thanks him for rejecting a play of his last winter and for bringing out "Mar-

* "The London Daily Post," April 28, 1736.

forio,'' which served only to confirm the town in its applause of "Pasquin." He enlarges upon Lun's "wit and other perfections," best known to those best acquainted with them; and concludes abruptly, lest the dedicator, in pleasing himself, should offend by expatiating further upon the "great endowments" of a genius distinguished above all others for his modesty.

In the war on Rich and the harlequinades which under his influence had invaded the other theatres, Fielding received assistance from his friends. First, as we have seen, there was "The Prompter," disguising Aaron Hill, and to a less degree William Popple, afterwards Governor of the Bermudas. Their neatest compliment I have passed by. Early in the previous dramatic season they had inserted in their periodical an advertisement offering a reward to anyone who should seize and deliver into the hands of a justice of the peace "a lean, ragged, uncurried, creature, call'd Common Sense," who had been hunted out of the London theatres and was then "lurking in some private and remote part of the country." Subsequently an assumed correspondent calling himself "Verax" informed the editors that he had discovered Common Sense straying about the country, but that he was resolved to keep her out of town until the theatres were once more worthy to receive her. After seeing "Pasquin" Mr. Prompter became convinced that "Verax" was none other than "Mr. F—d—g," who, after a year in the country, had come up to London, bringing with him the said stray, Common Sense, and restoring her to her former glories. "A gentleman, under the disadvantage of a very bad house, with scarce an actor, and at a very little expense, by the single power of satire, wit, and common sense," it was said, "has been able to run a play on for twenty-four nights, which is now but beginning to rise in the opinion of the town."*

* "The Prompter," Nov. 29, 1734, and April 2, 1736.

THE HISTORY OF HENRY FIELDING

At the same time Hogarth supplied a ticket for the benefit given to John Roberts as Trapwit on April 5. He chose for his scene the murder of Common Sense in the fifth Act of "Pasquin." This, however, is not half the story; and all of it is worth telling. A rumour became current that "the great Mr. Pope" attended that benefit. A gentleman who claimed that he saw him there sent some verses on the occasion to "The Grub-street Journal" for April 8, prefaced by a sentence or two in which Fielding or Common Sense—it is left ambiguous—is made to say: "I was mightily pleased to see the greatest poet of this age applaud me there." Subsequently the editor twice denied the rumour on the authority, it was implied, of Pope himself.* The author of the verses, the editor went on to say, was probably some scribbler who does not know Mr. Pope when he sees him. So it remains uncertain whether Pope ever honoured "Pasquin" with his presence. The rumour nevertheless persisted and was accepted by an unknown but rather clever artist, who redrew Hogarth's benefit ticket to "Pasquin," putting in many new figures and among them Pope as a spectator. This print, often erroneously attributed to Hogarth himself, represents the interior of the Little Theatre in the Haymarket just before the curtain falls on the last scene of "Pasquin." The stage is crowded with the characters of the play intermixed with the dancers, singers, rope-walkers, jugglers, and contortionists of popular entertainments. In the centre of the group stands Queen Ignorance in fool's cap and ass's ears, singing or declaiming; and by her side stands "the tall man," near whom a knock-kneed singer—Farinelli perhaps—is falling backward as if fainting or expiring at the conclusion of his song. In front are three dogs walking on their hind legs and two cats quarrelling, while down in one corner Punch, resting on one knee with bellows between his hands, is

* "The Grub-street Journal," April 15 and 29, 1736.

PASQUIN

blowing into flame the works of Ben Jonson, Shakespeare, Rowe, Congreve, and Pasquin. Common Sense, in disgust with it all, is just leaving the stage when the Priest of the Sun stabs her over the shoulder. In the side-boxes ladies and gentlemen are all standing ready to depart but taking a last look at the strange performance. Among them, a little, high-shouldered man in cocked hat—Pope surely— with his back to the stage remarks, as he is leaving, to his companion, supposed to be Lord Chesterfield: ''There is no whitewashing this stuff.'' A ribbon over the stage bears the motto, ''Vivetur Stultitia''; and below the design are verses quoted from ''Pasquin.''*

The immense success of ''Pasquin'' kept Fielding in high spirits, as may be seen from his playbills and advertisements. Pit and front boxes he often announced would be put together at five shillings a seat by ''the particular desire of several ladies of quality,'' and although the capacity of his theatre was unequal to the crowds asking admission, he could insert in the newspapers a notice like this concerning a benefit night:

''As there is little Hope of a great Demand of Tickets, or Places for that Evening, the Doors will be open'd by Six o'Clock in the Morning, and constant Attendance the whole

* F. G. Stephens and E. Hawkins, ''Catalogue of Prints and Drawings in the British Museum,'' No. 2466. Two or three remarks on this paragraph have become necessary owing to an attack on the genuineness of the Hogarth ticket by Mr. Paul de Castro in ''Notes and Queries'' for March 10, 1917. Samuel Ireland, in his ''Graphic Illustrations of Hogarth'' (London, 1794, I, 130), says that the original ticket had in Fielding's own hand the inscription: ''Tuesday, April 25, Boxes.'' The inscription may be set down at once as a forgery. The handwriting does not resemble Fielding's. April 25 fell upon a Sunday. The ticket was engraved for Roberts's (*not* Fielding's) benefit on Monday, April 5. In announcing the benefit, ''The London Daily Post'' for April 3 described the ticket ''representing the Murder of Common Sense,'' but did not give the name of the artist. Still he was probably Hogarth. See H. B. Wheatley, ''Hogarth's London,'' 1905, p. 335. The second print, though ascribed to Hogarth by Ireland, is only an imitation.

Day given, for fear any Application shou'd be made for either.''

At other times his audience was gravely warned against the cheats of dishonest doorkeepers; and full directions were given to the ladies, that they might avoid waiting at the entrance of his theatre and easily reach their seats without disturbance. When summer approached, the public was informed that his theatre ''is much the coolest house in town.'' His generosity—and how fine it is!—appears in several benefits at the Haymarket for persons in distress, one of which was for a young woman ''of virtue and of family,'' whose father, an officer in the army, had lost his life at Gibraltar and whose mother had subsequently died. This gentlewoman in unhappy circumstances was the daughter of General Nugent, who had commanded a regiment in Flanders at the time Edmund Fielding was serving there as a captain.*

As the season advanced, Fielding occasionally brought out other pieces than his own, though there was rarely a night when ''Pasquin'' or ''Tumble-Down Dick'' did not form one of the two plays acted. Late in March, he put in rehearsal a play by Ralph called ''The Astrologer,'' but owing to ''the prodigious run of 'Pasquin,' '' it was indefinitely deferred, and Ralph had to accept in place of its performance a benefit with ''Pasquin'' as the sole play. Once Fielding revived ''Tom Thumb''; and once Henry Carey's imitation of it—''Chrononhotonthologos,'' sometimes erroneously ascribed to Fielding—along with the same author's ''Wonder, or an Honest Yorkshireman,'' a popular ballad-opera. There were also several new plays, such as Elizabeth Cooper's ''The Nobleman''; the anonymous ''Sailor's Wife, or the Deferred Wedding,'' a ballad-opera; Robert Drury's ''Temple Rake, or the Rival Mil-

* ''The London Daily Post,'' May 25, 1736. See also issues for March 8, 15, April 3, and May 27.

· liners," which had been tried the year before; the anonymous "Female Rake, or Modern Fine Lady," taking its cue from Pope's well-known line—"But every woman is at heart a rake"; and "The Rival Captains, or the Imposter Unmasked," written, it seems, by Thomas Phillips, a young "gentleman," whose masque "Love and Glory" had been performed at Drury Lane two years before. Of these new plays none but "The Rival Milliners" and "The Female Rake" was ever printed. Something, however, is also known of "The Rival Captains" from the playbills. It was a short ballad-opera containing a number of songs by the author of "Bacchus one day gayly striding," and "When Fanny blooming fair."

Quite different from these trifles was Lillo's "Fatal Curiosity," which Fielding's company performed just as the season was closing. In 1731 George Lillo, a London jeweller, had suddenly come into fame with a bourgeois tragedy at Drury Lane entitled "The London Merchant; or, the History of George Barnwell," which tells the story of the temptation, fall, and ultimate fate of a London apprentice on the gallows. Before the play was printed, the Queen sent to the theatre for a copy of the manuscript, which Mr. Wilks carried out to her at Hampton Court. Subsequently "Their Majesties and the entire royal family" attended a performance.* "The London Merchant" was not only a great dramatic success, but it marked an epoch in English dramatic history in that it brought tragedy down to common life. But Lillo's second serious venture, "The Christian Hero," performed at Drury Lane in 1735, had nearly failed. He now came forward with a third tragedy, more in line with his first. A poor old man and his wife living at Penryn in Cornwall murder for his wealth their guest, who turns out to be their son, whom they did not recognize, just back from India after a long absence.

* "The Grub-street Journal," July 8 and Nov. 4, 1731.

While the son is sleeping, his mother opens a casket of jewels which he has entrusted to her. That is "the fatal curiosity" which leads to murder, remorse, and suicide. Evidently repulsed at the other theatres owing to the failure of "The Christian Hero," Lillo made advances to Fielding, who took "the plain and simple" tradesman under his protection and became greatly interested in him. When Lillo died, Fielding paid him a fine tribute in "The Champion":

"His *Fatal Curiosity,* which is a Masterpiece in its Kind, and inferior only to Shakspeare's best Pieces, gives him a Title to be call'd the best Tragic Poet of his Age; but this was the least of his Praise, he had the gentlest and honestest Manners, and at the same Time, the most friendly and obliging. . . . He had the Spirit of an old Roman, joined to the innocence of a primitive Christian; he was content with his little State of Life, in which his excellent Temper of Mind, gave him an Happiness beyond the Power of Riches. . . . In short he was one of the best of Men."[*]

Lillo's new tragedy, then called "Guilt its own Punishment; or Fatal Curiosity," was first performed at the Haymarket on May 27, 1736,[†] with "Tumble-Down Dick" as the second piece. Mrs. Charke and John Roberts appeared in the rôles of the curious old woman and her husband, while Thomas Davies, ambitious to become an actor, took the part of the murdered son. Davies, who afterwards edited Lillo's works, commented in his biographical sketch upon "the great politeness and friendship" with which Fielding treated Lillo, so far beneath him in rank. The manager not only instructed "the actors how to do justice to their parts," but he revised the tragedy and wrote the prologue.[‡] If it would be too hazardous to select from the

[*] "Index to the Times," in "The Champion," Feb. 26, 1739-40.

[†] "The London Daily Post," May 27, 1736.

[‡] "The Life of George Lillo," prefixed to his "Works," 2 vols., London, 1775, I, xv-xviii.

PASQUIN

play lines or passages which Fielding may have written, we may quote the prologue, all Fielding's own, which is most interesting for his view of tragedy and the reference to his little theatre:

> The tragic Muse has long forgot to please
> With Shakespear's nature, or with Fletcher's ease:
> No passion mov'd, thro' five long Acts you sit,
> Charm'd with the poet's language, or his wit.
> Fine things are said, no matter whence they fall;
> Each single character might speak them all.
>
> But from this modern fashionable way,
> To night, our author begs your leave to stray.
> No fustian hero rages here to night;
> No armies fall, to fix a tyrant's right:
> From lower life we draw our scene's distress:
> —Let not your equals move your pity less!
> Virtue distrest in humble state support;
> Nor think, she never lives without the Court.
>
> Tho' to our scenes no royal robes belong,
> And tho' our little stage as yet be young,
> Throw both your scorn and prejudice aside;
> Let us with favour, not contempt be try'd;
> Thro' the first Acts a kind attention lend,
> The growing scene shall force you to attend;
> Shall catch the eyes of every tender fair,
> And make them charm their lovers with a tear.
> The lover too by pity shall impart
> His tender passion to his fair one's heart:
> The breast which others anguish cannot move,
> Was ne'er the seat of friendship, or of love.

"Fatal Curiosity"—the tragedy is commonly known by this title—ran continuously, omitting of course a Sunday, for six nights, with either "Tumble-Down Dick" or "The Rival Captains" for a comic afterpiece. With the sixth

201

performance, on June 2, the season closed. Fielding, however, remained in London for some weeks, long enough to see his company well on into the summer season, which opened at the Haymarket on June 7 with "Pasquin." From this time on until the first part of August, the Great Mogul's Company gave performances two or three times a week. The plays most often acted were "Pasquin," "Fatal Curiosity," and "The Rival Captains." On July 30 were performed Aaron Hill's "Fatal Extravagance" and Drury's "Temple Rake" for the benefit of Thomas Odell, playwright and formerly proprietor of the theatre in Goodman's Fields. "The Beggar's Opera" was revived for two or more nights—first on June 26 with "The Mock Doctor," and again on August 2 with a new farce entitled "The Deposing and Death of Queen Gin, with the Ruin of Duke Rum, Marquee de Nantz, and the Lord Sugarcane." Mrs. Charke played the Captain Macheath of Gay's opera— a part in which she must have succeeded as well as in Lord Place.

"The Deposing and Death of Queen Gin" is a rather slight but very funny piece in blank verse—there are only two scenes of it—occasioned by the so-called Gin Act which Parliament had passed at the last session, imposing a duty of twenty shillings a gallon on spirituous liquors and requiring a licence of fifty pounds to sell them. Though the law was not to go into effect until Michaelmas, the poorer classes of London were agitated over the measure and were preparing to resist the attempt to raise the price of their favourite beverage. In the midst of this excitement, the farce was put on at the Haymarket and published as a sixpenny pamphlet. In a brandy-shop, Queen Gin takes her last drop and expires amid a crowd of men and women noisy over their cups. This "heroic-comi-tragical farce," as it was called, purports to have been written by "Jack Juniper, a distiller's apprentice, just turn'd poet," who adds a preface, saying that he sees no reason why a distiller's apprentice may not succeed in the drama, since learning, knowledge, and genius are no longer necessary to success, but only the approval of "a Certain Gentleman in Power"—Sir Robert Walpole. The farce is of interest not only as an echo of "The Life and Death of Tom Thumb the Great," but as an intimation that the manager of the Haymarket lent assistance to other friends besides Lillo.

Fielding's first year as manager was a signal triumph. His wares scorned at the royal playhouses, he took the smallest theatre in London, formed and trained his own company, and in brilliant war against political corruption, pantomime, and Italian opera, drew the town away from his rivals. That the enterprise was profitable is implied in his dedication of "Tumble-Down Dick"; and Mrs. Charke long looked back to her engagement with Fielding as her fat season. "At my benefit," she says, "I cleared sixty guineas; and walked with my purse in my hand 'till my stock was exhausted, . . . squandering what might have made many a decayed family truly happy."* Fielding's benefits were numerous, and there were also his profits as manager. As "Pasquin" rose in popularity, he raised the price of tickets, so that a full house, when boxes and pit were thrown together, meant much more than sixty guineas a night from the entire sale. To the outsider it looked as if guineas rained upon him, and he had but to stretch out his hands for them. This view was depicted in an anonymous print which appeared when "Pasquin" was running at its height. The friendly cartoon bears the title: "The Judgment of the Queen o' Common Sense. Address'd to Henry Fielding Esq." On a dais in the centre of the stage stands Common Sense, who is pouring from a bag in her right hand gold into the lap of Harry Fielding who kneels before her. Behind him stand an actor and actress—

* "Narrative of the Life of Mrs. Charlotte Charke," 1755, pp. 63-66.

Mr. Roberts and Mrs. Charke—watching the scene; while Shakespeare, long and lank, sits at a table in front with the manuscript of "Hamlet" before him, one of his feet close to the tail of a cock, which a ghost, descending through a trap-door, is trying to keep from crowing as long as he can. To the left of Common Sense are three figures representing the lawyer, priest, and doctor satirized in "Pasquin"; and in front of them is an acrobat with heels in the air, a clown, and Rich as Harlequin; to the last of whom Common Sense is handing a halter that he may hang himself. Verses beneath announce that the Queen is bestowing "showers of gold" upon the author of "Pasquin," who has just arrived from the Court of the Great Mogul, with three "benighted exiles"—Wit, Humour, and Satire.*

* Stephens and Hawkins, "Catalogue of Prints and Drawings in the British Museum," No. 2283.

CHAPTER IX

DRAMATIC CAREER

THE LICENSING ACT

I

One more brief season at the Haymarket, and the Great Mogul's Company of Comedians went down to irretrievable disaster. "Like another Erostratus," said Colley Cibber picturesquely, Fielding "set fire to his stage, by writing up to an Act of Parliament to demolish it."[*] This is the mixed metaphor of an enemy; but the words are essentially true. Fielding's attacks on the Ministry, becoming more and more unrestrained, were the cause, if not the immediate occasion, of the Licensing Act of 1737, which closed his theatre and rendered impossible the performance of a "Pasquin" elsewhere. How Fielding thus wrote up to an Act of Parliament that placed the theatres under the direct control of the Government, is the subject of this chapter.

As usual, Fielding probably passed the late summer and autumn of 1736 on his farm at East Stour and returned to London after the Christmas holidays. The extraordinary run of "Pasquin" the previous season had evidently led the manager of Drury Lane to look upon the Great Mogul as a factor in the dramatic world to be reckoned with; for Fielding's first play of the new year—"Euridice, or the Devil Henpeck'd"—was rehearsed by Fleetwood for Satur-

[*] "An Apology for the Life of Colley Cibber," edited by R. W. Lowe, 1889, I, 287.

day, February 19, 1737, as an afterpiece to Addison's
"Cato."* A farce in one Act, "Euridice" burlesques the
story of Orpheus and Eurydice, ridiculing through them the
obvious foibles of fashionable society. The scene lies in
the lower world at the Court of Pluto and Proserpine, and
the characters are ghosts or shadows. Euridice is a fine
lady who has left her husband and gone to the deuce; while
Proserpine remains faithful to Pluto only in order to retain
her power over him and thus have her say in all affairs of
the infernal regions. Orpheus, who descends into Hades to
recover his wayward wife, is a flabby, doting husband with
the voice and bearing of Farinelli, whom he was intended to
ridicule. There is also a Captain Weazel, who went to the
devil long ago and now welcomes across the Styx a brother
beau from the Court who, "thanks to a little fever and a
great doctor," has just "shaken off a bad constitution."
As the action progresses, the author, seated with a critic
between the scenes, explains the behaviour of his characters,
and tells Mr. Chetwood, the prompter of Drury Lane, when
to ring his bell and let loose "the devil and the ghosts"
upon the stage. The farce in the printed form fails to give
the cast; but Captain Weazel, it is said, was performed by
Macklin, and the rôle of Euridice was especially adapted
to Mrs. Clive.

The night set for "Euridice" proved most unlucky. At
that time, the performance of a play, whatever its merits
might be, was exposed to interruptions by footmen, who were
admitted *gratis* to the gallery or allowed to occupy places
in the boxes until their masters or mistresses appeared
for the later Acts. This was a time-honoured concession to
ladies and gentlemen, who wished to have immediate attendance at the conclusion of a play. These footmen, sitting
in the boxes with their hats on, conversing aloud, applauding
and hissing, became an intolerable nuisance to people in the

* "The London Daily Post," Feb. 19, 1737.

pit as well as to actors, manager, and author. With footmen
as judges, no play was certain of a fair hearing; and ticket-
holders were in danger of being cheated out of an evening's
entertainment for which they had paid three shillings. On
the night of February 19, the pit rose against the footmen
in the boxes and drove them out of the theatre. The footmen, however, raised a disturbance outside, broke down a
door, and rushed into their gallery. In the midst of the
hubbub, young Cibber harangued the audience from the
stage; and, failing to quell the gallery, summoned the High
Sheriff of Westminster, who read the Riot Act, and with the
aid of his posse made several arrests. After a fashion, the
actors went through "Cato," but seem to have been unable
to complete "Euridice," which was drowned in hisses,
whistles, and catcalls.* Apart from the angry mood of the
audience ready to condemn any new play, there was genuine
resentment at Captain Weazel, the ghost of a military beau,
who was regarded as an affront to the army. A second performance of "Euridice" was attempted on the following
Monday; again there was a disturbance; and the piece was
withdrawn. When Fielding published it long afterwards in
his "Miscellanies," he put on the title-page: "Eurydice, a
Farce: As it was d-mned at the Theatre-Royal in Drury-
Lane."

Fielding took his failure in good humour, and fell back
upon the Great Mogul's Company at the Haymarket, which
for variety's sake he sometimes called after Kuli Khan, the
reigning Shah of Persia, whose exploits were bringing con-
sternation to the minds of coffee-house politicians lest he
should invade and conquer all Europe as well as Asia. To
add to the jest, the name of Kuli Khan was coupled with
that of King Theodore of Corsica, a military adventurer
who was also frightening these same politicians. A curious
advertisement in "The Grub-street Journal" for February

* "The Daily Journal," Feb. 22, 1737.

24, 1737, announced perhaps the first performance of the company under its new name:

"Never Acted before, *By a Company of Comedians dropt from the Clouds, late Servants to their thrice renown'd Majesties* Kouli Kan *and* Theodore. At the NEW THEATRE in the HAY-MARKET, Wednesday the 9th of March, will be presented a New Dramatic Comi-Tragical Satire of three Acts, entitled, A Rehearsal of KINGS; or The Projecting Gingerbread BAKER, with the unheard of Catastrophe of *Macplunderkan,* King of Roguomania, and the ignoble Fall of Baron *Tromperland,* King of Clouts . . . To which will be added a new Farce of one Act, call'd Sir PEEVY PET . . . Considering the extraordinary Expence that must necessarily attend the equipping so many Monarchs of different Nations, the proprietor hopes that the Town will not take Umbrage at the Prices being raised . . . The Proprietor begs leave to enter his Caveat against all . . . who may *hire* or *be hired* to do the Drudgery of *Hissing, Catcalling* &c. and entreats the Town would discourage, as much as in them lies, a practice at once so scandalous and prejudicial to Author, Player, and every fair Theatric Adventurer."

The advertisement further promised for the main piece of the evening six kings besides two wandering kings, two queens, and two ghosts, including the ghost of a Dutch statesman, "with new scenes, habits, and proper decorations." Mrs. Eliza Haywood had the part of the First King, or Macplunderkan, who was travelling incognito; and Roberts took the rôle of the King of Clouts. To Mrs. Charke was assigned Don Resinando; and to Lacy fell Mynheer Wiserman. Another character bore the name of Mynheer Maggot, and still another the name of Crimcrowky.[*]

Who wrote the two plays, never published, with which

[*] "The Grub-street Journal," March 3, 1737.

Fielding thus adorned the Haymarket theatre? Were they by Fielding or by another hand? These are questions that may be asked but not definitely answered. Of "Sir Peevy Pet" nothing is known except that it was a farce in one Act, such as Mrs. Haywood might have written. "A Rehearsal of Kings" is the title of an anonymous farce performed, it is said by Baker in his "Biographia Dramatica," back in 1692, but never printed. The chances are that the old play was worked over by Fielding, and given a political turn with Walpole disguised as Macplunderkan, King of Roguomania. The ghosts and the reckless political satire are sufficient warrant for the surmise. Perhaps Mrs. Haywood, who afterwards broke with Fielding, had his kings especially in mind when she wrote of the Little Theatre in the Haymarket as "F—g's scandal shop," where he exhibited "certain drolls, or, more properly, invectives against the Ministry."*

After a second advertisement, in which "the late Servants of Kouli Khan and Theodore" gave notice that they would endeavour to entertain the town for the remaining part of the season, ".A Rehearsal of Kings" passed into oblivion except for an occasional use of the name of Macplunderkan in the newspapers. The farce seems to have run for a week or two; but by April, at the latest, it was swept from the stage by Fielding's "Historical Register for 1736," containing "freshest advices, foreign and domestic." The first playbill of this "dramatic satire" has never been discovered; but its date may be determined within narrow limits. According to the newspapers, the eleventh performance of "The Historical Register" occurred on April 13, the twenty-first on April 25, and the twenty-fifth on April 29.† Assuming that it had run con-

* "The History of Miss Betsy Thoughtless," 1751, I, 76-77.
† "London Evening Post," April 7-9; "The Grub-street Journal," April 7 and 21; and "The Daily Advertiser," April 29, 1737.

tinuously, Sundays excepted, from the beginning, as it was then doing, its first night would be the first of April. This is the latest date to which the first performance of "The Historical Register" may be assigned. Were there a break or two, as is probable, in the run, the true date for the play should be towards the end of March. A reference within the play to Monday, March 21, as the day on which Christopher Hen will sell his parcel of curiosities at auction, points to that date as the very night when the mock auction scene was first represented on the stage. Again, an obscure allusion to "A Rehearsal of Kings" would suggest that "The Historical Register" closely followed this play, along with a revival of "The Fatal Curiosity." It passed through the ordeal of a first night, unscathed except for the hissing of one scene which was afterwards eliminated, and began a career rivalling that of "Pasquin."

Fielding's title, requiring explanation now, was excellent banter for those who then understood it. For some time there had been appearing every year a summary of the events of the previous twelvemonth, bearing the title, to give the one for 1736:

"The Historical Register, Containing An Impartial Relation of all Transactions, Foreign and Domestick. With A Chronological Diary of All The remarkable Occurrences, viz. Births, Marriages, Deaths, Removals, Promotions, &c. that happen'd in this Year: Together with the Characters and Parentage of Persons deceas'd, of eminent Rank."

Fielding, as it were, burlesques this enlarged newspaper. The events therein chronicled, he would say, are not the most interesting or the most important ones of the past year; and he will relate what has really been going on behind the scenes in the theatrical and political worlds. This can all be done in the rehearsal of a farce in three Acts. "Mr. Medley," the author of the piece, will comment on the scenes for the benefit of "Lord Dapper" and "Mr. Sowrwit,'' of whom the latter belongs to that class of critics who write elaborate treatises ''to prove that a farce of three Acts is not a regular play of five.'' By way of proper prologue, Fielding opens his play with an ''Ode to the New Year'' in parody of the odes with which Colley Cibber greeted every new year, and then launches out into banter and satire. For a benefit night early in May the tickets bore Fielding's parody beginning

> This is a day, in days of yore,
> Our fathers never saw before—

along with the music, from a copper engraving so that both words and music might be eternal.

Two theatrical incidents of the winter concerned the author most. In December there had been a violent contention at Drury Lane over who should have the rôle of Polly Peachum in ''The Beggar's Opera.'' The part belonged by right to Mrs. Clive; but Theophilus Cibber wanted it for his new wife, the young and handsome daughter of Master Arne. The affair went so far that Mrs. Cibber was actually cast for Polly, while Mrs. Clive was relegated to the rôle of Lucy. Thereupon arose a rough storm in which the two actresses came near if not quite to blows in the greenroom of Drury Lane. The friends of each appealed to the public in letters and squibs sent to the newspapers, Cibber defending his wife and outrageously attacking her rival.* In the end Mrs. Clive won; and the ignoble strife was burlesqued at Lincoln's Inn Fields in an entertainment by Henry Woodward, called ''The Beggar's Pantomime; or, the Contending Columbines,'' in which two actresses quarrel and scold until they are out of breath over who shall be the first Columbine. Fielding, it is so implied, also put the two Pollys into ''The Historical Register,'' but cut them out after the first performance, as the audience

* See ''The Grub-street Journal,'' Dec. 9 and 16, 1736.

thought the jest rather stale. Naturally taking the side of Mrs. Clive, he represents young Cibber as a mad Pistol, his nickname in contemporary farce, running about town and collecting, with the aid of friends, drum, and fiddles, a mob who follow and hiss at his heels when he asks them whether it is their will that the rôle of Polly Peachum be taken from Mrs. Clive and given to his "great consort."

The second dramatic incident that had engaged the wits during the past winter was Colley Cibber's attempt to make over Shakespeare's "King John." According to Cibber, Shakespeare had splendid opportunities in the material of this tragedy, but for some reason missed most of them; especially did he fail to "inspirit" John with the resentment proper to an English monarch against "the intoxicated tyranny" of the Church of Rome. So Cibber stepped in and rewrote the play, doing his will upon it. To bring to the front his point of view, he even renamed it "Papal Tyranny in the Reign of King John." The wretched piece was put to rehearsal at Drury Lane, but the actors, knowing that it would be damned, refused to go on with it, and it had to be withdrawn. At one of the rehearsals Cibber, incensed by the conduct of the company, put the play into his pocket and walked off with it. The press and the coffee-houses were still rallying Cibber on his failure, when Fielding took it up in "The Historical Register." In one of the scenes Apollo, a theatrical manager, is represented as casting the parts for the original "King John" when Cibber under the name of Ground-Ivy appears, and thus remonstrates with him:

"Ground-Ivy. What are you doing here?

Apollo. I am casting the parts in the Tragedy of King John.

Ground-Ivy. Then you are casting the parts in a tragedy that won't do.

Apollo. How, Sir! Was it not written by Shakespear,

and was not Shakespear one of the greatest geniuses that ever liv'd?

Ground-Ivy. No, Sir, Shakespear was a pretty fellow, and said some things which only want a little of my licking to do well enough; King John, as now writ, will not do— But a word in your ear, I will make him do.

Apollo. How?

Ground-Ivy. By alteration, Sir; it was a maxim of mine, when I was at the head of theatrical affairs, that no play, tho' ever so good, would do without alteration—for instance, in the play before us, the bastard Faulconbridge is a most effeminate character, for which reason I would cut him out, and put all his sentiments in the mouth of Constance, who is so much properer to speak them."

Fielding goes on much further in ridiculing the presumption of Cibber, who, uttering his favourite "damn me," declares himself the equal of all actors and authors, living or dead. Mr. Medley, who is here the mouthpiece of Fielding, quietly remarks that if Shakespeare is to be altered, no man is better able "to alter him for the worse." As for himself, he says finely, "I have too great an honour for Shakespear to think of burlesquing him, and to be sure of not burlesquing him, I will never attempt to alter him, for fear of burlesquing him by accident, as perhaps some others have done."

From the affairs of Drury Lane, Fielding passes pleasantly to the affairs of state, with the remark that the management of each is equally damned by the public. Midway in his course, he introduces an auction scene which must have awakened great mirth. At that time, London had an "eloquent auctioneer" named Christopher Cock, whose rooms, first near Golden Square and afterwards in the Grand Piazza of Covent Garden, were a fashionable resort for the purchase of old china and useless but expensive furniture. Taking a hint from this institution,

213

Fielding works up an allegorical auction for the amusement of his audience. Mr. Cock is converted into Mr. Hen—and very appropriately, for the auctioneer's rôle was played by Mrs. Charke, whose forte was male characters. Most of the curiosities which Mr. Hen puts up for sale before a group of "gentlemen and ladies," either nobody wants or they go cheap; for they include such old-fashioned articles as "a most curious remnant of political honesty," "a most delicate piece of patriotism," and "a very clear conscience, which has been worn by a judge and a bishop." The bidding, however, becomes spirited for "a very considerable interest at Court," which is knocked down at a thousand pounds. As a climax to the jest, a gentleman gets "all the cardinal virtues" for eighteen pence; but on looking them over and discovering among them such stuff as temperance and chastity, he refuses to take them on the ground that he misunderstood the auctioneer and supposed he was purchasing not the cardinal virtues, but "a cardinal's virtues," which were what he wanted.

There are only two outright political scenes; but they created a sensation, for nothing so daring as the second of them had ever been seen on the English stage. To escape prosecution by the Government, it is stated by Mr. Medley that the transactions which he is about to represent occurred not in England but in Corsica. Then he gives the signal for the entrance of five politicians of the party in power—"the ablest heads in the kingdom"—who meet to talk over the state of Europe, about which they know nothing, and to devise means for getting more money, concerning which they are not quite so ignorant. They have just intelligence enough to see that the surest way to obtain more money is to impose a fresh tax on the people; but as nearly everything is now taxed, they are confronted with difficulties. Learning, they conclude, will not yield a sufficient revenue, since it is so rare a commodity and is found mostly among the poor. So they hit upon ignorance, which they think will take in most people of the kingdom, though they seem unaware that they are thereby taxing themselves. Throughout the conversation, one of the politicians—a "little gentleman" sitting in a chair—keeps silent. It is explained that he knows it all, for in these days a politician, to be thought wise, need give no instance of his wisdom. To lay a new tax and then collect it, Fielding means to say, has been the main business of the Walpole Government.

To show how some of the money obtained in this way is expended, is the object of the second political scene, with which the farce closes. The scene was known as "The Dance of Patriots." Four "shabby fellows" who claim allegiance to the Opposition, are seated at a table, drinking to prosperity, liberty, and trade, and complaining of the hard times that have fallen upon Corsica. Just as one of them declares that they are "a set of miserable poor dogs," "a poor impudent fellow," called "Quidam," who has stood laughing at them behind the scenes, enters and tells them that they are mistaken. As he says this, he pours on the table a purse of gold, which they snatch up, convinced that they are indeed rich and are living under the best possible Government. Quidam picks up a fiddle and dances the patriots off the stage, to the perplexity of the audience, until Mr. Medley explains the allegory to them. "Every one of these patriots," we are told, "have a hole in their pockets, as Mr. Quidam the fiddler there knows, so that he intends to make them dance till all the money is fall'n through, which he will pick up again, and so not lose one halfpenny by his generosity; so far from it, that he will get his wine for nothing, and the poor people, alas! out of their own pockets, pay the whole reckoning." By the patriots, Fielding meant men like Lord Hervey, whom Walpole had induced by money and place to desert the

Opposition. Whatever Walpole had given them, Fielding would say, had come from the taxes which a corrupt Parliament had laid upon the nation. There was no mistaking the satire of this farce. Under the disguise of Quidam, Fielding here represented Walpole engaged in open bribery.

For his own benefit night on April 13,* Fielding extended "The Historical Register," which was much shorter than "Pasquin," into the rehearsal of "a very merry tragedy," as a companion piece to the rehearsal of his political farce. The mock tragedy, standing by itself, was called "Eurydice Hiss'd, or, a Word to the Wise," and gives, said the playbills, "an account of the rise, progress, greatness, and downfall of Mr. Pillage, the author"; that is, with some reservations and embellishments, the dramatic career of Fielding himself up to the appearance of "Pasquin," when he was "followed, flattered, and adored," and then downward to the utter failure of "Euridice," when he was "deserted and abandoned" by all who had previously coveted his favour. The piece is filled with playful personal references—half true, half false. A scene especially advertised in the newspapers was one between the poet and the Muse who inspired him to write "Pasquin"—"nine scenes with spirit in one day"—and now chides him for deserting her for the strumpet that inspired "Euridice." Then, not very consistently, he tells the audience that there was never a better farce than "Euridice." At first, he says, the pit applauded "Euridice" vigorously; but as the plot began to open more, the applause grew faint and subsided altogether; then a hiss was heard here and there, then a catcall from the gallery, and finally all was lost in a chorus of halloos, hisses, and groans. How little Fielding was disturbed by the fate of "Euridice" is indicated by the fact that he could take it as the subject of a farce. The humour with which in "Eurydice Hiss'd" he turned the tables

* "The London Evening Post," April 7-9, 1737.

THE
HISTORICAL REGISTER
For the Year 1736.

As it is Acted at the

NEW THEATRE
In the HAY-MARKET.

To which is added a very merry TRAGEDY, called,

EURYDICE HISS'D,
OR,
A Word *to the* Wife.

Both written by the Author of *Pasquin.*

To thefe are prefixed a long *Dedication to the Publick,* and a *Preface* to that *Dedication.*

LONDON,

Printed: And fold by *J. Roberts,* near the *Ox-ford-Arms-Inn* in *Warwick-Lane.*

against the town must have been greatly relished. You damned my play, he says to them; now I, too, will damn it before your eyes, and you cannot damn the damnation of it without damning yourselves. Withal, the audience was quick to see the political significance of the farce. In the downfall of Mr. Pillage, put to sleep by two bottles, was a prophecy of the downfall of Walpole, which the Opposition was also then predicting.

The two farces together still made a scant evening's performance; and they were sometimes tagged, on benefit nights, with what Fielding described in his advertisements as "an additional Addition of a new entertaining Scene, call'd 'The Female Free Mason,' in which the whole Art and Mystery of Free Masonry is delineated, by the Admission of a Lady.''* This little farce, probably burlesquing the exposures of freemasonry then common in the newspapers, was never published; but it was the kind of thing that Mrs. Haywood would write. On many occasions, "The Historical Register" with or without "Eurydice Hiss'd," formed the afterpiece to Lillo's "Fatal Curiosity," which "had a fresh run" throughout the season with Mrs. Charke and Mr. Roberts again playing the leading rôles. "Roberts, a very judicious speaker," wrote Mrs. Charke, "discovered a mastership in the character of the husband." With the possible exception of Drury's "Rival Milliners," which went into a second edition, the plays thus far mentioned in this chapter mainly comprise the Great Mogul's repertoire for the spring of 1737. There were but two or three others. It is rather surprising that Fielding did not try "Pasquin" once more, a few performances of which were given in January by Giffard at Lincoln's Inn Fields. More surprising still, while Fielding was laughing at the Cibbers in "The Historical Register," the company at Drury Lane was playing his "Mock Doctor" and "Virgin Unmask'd."

* "The Grub-street Journal," April 21, 1737.

II

For two years Fielding had done brilliant work for the Opposition. He was par excellence his party's humorist and satirist. His "squibs and crackers," we read, were carried away by the audiences at the Haymarket and "let off in the country and sometimes at Court." A suggestion was made that "Pasquin" should be acted in every borough of England before the elections as a caution to people against "the artifices of those who come to corrupt their honesty with adulterate wine and more adulterate promises." That Fielding's assistance was fully appreciated by the leaders of his party, there is adequate contemporary evidence. An enemy meant it as a charge against him when he said that "The Historical Register" appeared "under the patronage of the great, the sensible, and the witty, in the Opposition." To the flattering impeachment, Fielding replied: "I shall not be industrious to deny what you are so good to declare, that I am buoy'd up by the greatest wits, and finest gentleman of the age. . . . Of such patrons I shall be always proud, and to such I shall be always glad of the honour of owing an obligation." The insinuation that he was but the hireling of a party, he passed by in silence.*

Two of the gentlemen who then most encouraged Fielding paid him a high compliment. On February 5, 1737, Chesterfield and Lyttelton established a new weekly newspaper to supplement "The Craftsman" as an organ of their party. They called it "Common Sense: or, the Englishman's Journal." Chesterfield, who wrote the first "leader," made it clear, without exactly saying so, that they took the name from Fielding—from "an ingenious Dramatick Author [who] has consider'd Common Sense as so extraordinary a thing, that he has lately, with great wit and humour, not only personified it, but dignified it too

* See "Common Sense," May 21, 1737, April 1 and Oct. 28, 1738.

with the title of a *Queen.*" And just as in "Pasquin" also, Chesterfield's design, as set forth in the first paper, was to erect a Court of Common Sense, before whom were to be tried the various vices, follies, and corruptions of the time. Broadly speaking, the aim of the newspaper was to carry to a larger audience than could be reached by a London play the social and political ridicule which had been so effective on the stage of the Little Theatre in the Haymarket.

Naturally, Fielding's apparent alliance with the leaders of the Opposition embittered the attacks upon him in the newspapers conducted in the interest of the Ministry. On May 7, 1737, the Government's leading organ, "The Daily Gazetteer," went so far as to warn him of danger and much else, if he continued in his political satire. The author of the article, who styled himself "An Adventurer in Politicks," is not known; but Fielding surmised that he was a person of rank—Lord Hervey of the Privy Council, perhaps, who had left the Patriots and was then writing for "The Gazetteer" under the direction of Walpole. Whoever he may have been, he assumed greater authority than would be expected of an ordinary correspondent. He begins with a pretty contrast between the indulgence of the English Ministry and the situation across the Channel where *lettres de cachet* and the Bastille await such as dare inquire into the state of affairs "in a manner different from the sense of the Court." While he hopes that England will never be compelled to imitate France in suppressing free speech, yet everyone must know that there is a point at which liberty must be restrained in order to be preserved. He would place no obstacle in the way of a sober discussion of public affairs or even of a Minister's conduct in the press; but "no argument whatever, can be alledged to support the bringing of politicks on the stage." Fielding is held responsible not merely for his own political satires, but for setting an example to other playwrights. "Pasquin," from the critic's point of view, was open to less censure than the plays that followed, inasmuch as its satire, rather general in character, did not come "so near, as to point any person out"; but even in that piece, Fielding was guilty of "making light of one of the gravest evils our Constitution is subject to." He ought to know that a humorous treatment of corruption will increase, not suppress, the evil, just as Gay's turning highwaymen and lewd women into heroes and heroines "served only to increase the number of those corrupt wretches." Then came "The Historical Register," in which the author, spurred on by the wits of his party, insinuated "ignorance in the Ministry" and exhibited an "impudent fellow" to the hisses of the audience.

The critic admits that there is "something most ridiculously pleasant" in the conception that nothing of consequence has happened for a year outside of Corsica; only it is not true. As everybody knows, "events, as great as any recorded in history, have come to a definitive crisis" within the last year. Genuine humour, Mr. Fielding must be aware, is based upon fact, not falsehood. In thus misrepresenting the Government, Fielding, it is declared, has done his country incalculable harm both at home and abroad. "Will the exposing the Ministry," he is asked, "before the eyes of the representatives of all the princes of Europe, give their masters a higher idea of the Court of England?" As if Fielding cared. In conclusion the gentlemen of the Opposition are warned that Fielding may some day turn against them, should they ever come into power; and are asked what they will then do with a "witty writer" who derides patriotism and proclaims "that all Government is but a farce (perhaps a damned one too)."

These sober charges were gaily met by Fielding in an open letter published two weeks later as the leading article in "Common Sense" for May 21, 1737. I do not know that this "leader," signed "Pasquin," has even been attributed to Fielding by his biographers; but it is his beyond a doubt. He takes notice, he says, of the attack upon him, not because he has any regard for the ideas and opinions of the author, but merely out of respect to the person whom he supposes him to be. He denies that he has ever asserted "all Government to be a farce," though he is unterrified by power, and regards "greatness in mean hands" as a proper subject for burlesque. He denies that he has ever ridiculed patriotism, and explains that in his bribery scenes it has been his clear purpose to show what obstacles against a proper exercise of "this noble principle" have been laid by the hands of corruption. He is surprised that anyone should think that the ridicule of corruption or of any other vice serves its cause; for this was not the opinion of Hobbes and Horace—one of whom tells us that "laughter is a sign of contempt," and the other that a laugh against vice inflicts a sorer wound than "can be produced by the gravest and bitterest satire." He retorts that the drama is as legitimate a means as the newspaper for canvassing the acts of the Government and that any arguments for the freedom of the one will hold for the other. Surely no one will be frightened by the threat to introduce into England *lettres de cachet,* the Inquisition, or any of the other "damned engines of tyranny."

As to the effect of political satire or ridicule on other nations in lowering the prestige of the British Empire, Fielding remarks humorously: "I do not believe foreign Ministers to be so weak, as to remain in an entire stupid ignorance of what we are doing; nor do I think, if well considered, a more ridiculous image can enter into the mind of man, than that of all the Ambassadors of Europe assembling at the Hay-Market Play-house to learn the character of our Ministry." And in reply to the insinuation that he will exhibit to derision the leaders of his own party, if it ever becomes his advantage to do so, he adds a clever

THE HISTORY OF HENRY FIELDING

paragraph in conclusion: "I must beg leave to say, without any reflection on our present Ministry, that, I believe, there are now amongst those gentlemen who are stiled the Opposition, men in genius, learning, and knowledge so infinitely superior to the rest of their countrymen, and of integrity so eminent, that should they, in process of time, be in the possession of power, they will be able to triumph over, and trample upon all the ridicule which any wit or humour could level at them."

That the candid reader might weigh for himself the full charges against him, Fielding had already published "The Historical Register" and "Eurydice Hiss'd" in a single volume, which was advertised for May 12,* only five days after the onslaught by the "Adventurer in Politicks." The great haste with which "The Historical Register" was prepared for the press is shown by numerous misprints, which were partially corrected in a new impression made a few weeks later. The two plays were introduced with a "Dedication to the Publick" preceded by a "Preface to the Dedication"; in the first of which Fielding says he chose the public as his patron for two reasons: first because they have honoured his performance "every night of its exhibition" and "never failed shewing the greatest delight and approbation"; and secondly because he has something which he really wishes to say to them. So he talks rather seriously about the state of theatrical affairs,—the rivalry between managers, who bid against one another for the best actors (he had lost Yates, who went over to Giffard), the high prices of seats in consequence, and the difficulties that confront a new playwright in getting his pieces, however excellent, properly performed unless they happen to suit the taste of the manager, that is, Mr. Fleetwood, possessing the largest purse. All this serves as an introduction to the power of the purse in affairs of state and to a mock appeal

* "The Grub-street Journal," May 12, 1737.

to the public to defend him against "the iniquitous surmises" of "The Gazetteer" with reference to the import
of "The Historical Register." He maintains—ironically,
of course—that this farce, as anyone "not very blind or
very dishonest" may see, is "a ministerial pamphlet, calculated to infuse into the minds of the people a great
opinion of their Ministry, and thereby procure an employment for the author, who has been often promised one,
whenever he would write on that side."

No one should suppose, he says blandly, that his "politicians" were intended to represent the present Ministry,
for they are nothing but "a set of blundering blockheads,"
incapable of "aiming at being at the head of a great
people"; they are "too low even for a conversation at an
alehouse." Clearly the politicians were only meant "to ridicule the absurd and inadequate notions persons among us,
who have not the honour to know 'em, have of the Ministry
and their measures." Again, his "patriots" he thought
would have made his fortune, for just like other ministerial
advocates, he represented them as "a set of cunning, self-
interested fellows, who for a little paltry bribe would give
up the liberties and properties of their country." Granting
that there was some slight reason for misapprehension here,
Fielding is amazed that anyone should not know who was
intended by Quidam, who bribes the patriots out of their
honesty. The readiness of "The Gazetteer" to identify so
evil a character with its patron reminds him, he says, of the
story of the near-sighted gentleman who was enraged because an innkeeper had hung out his portrait as a sign, until
he saw, on closer view, that it was not his portrait at all, but
the portrait of an ass. It ought not to be necessary to
explain that Quidam has the salient attributes of the devil
as he is "described in Scripture, and the writings of our
best divines," wherein we are informed that gold has
always been his favourite bait when he goes fishing for

sinners, and that he laughs in his sleeve at the poor wretches when he has once caught them. "Indeed, it is so plain who is meant by this Quidam, that he who maketh any wrong application thereof, might as well mistake the name of Thomas for John, or old Nick for old Bob."

After he has thus shown his contempt for Sir Robert, calling him by indirection "old Bob," and ass, and the devil, Fielding thanks the town for their patronage of his little theatre during the last two years and promises them, for the next season, new decorations, an enlarged house, and a better company of actors, if a proposal of a subscription for these purposes should meet with their favour. He hopes to entertain them next year in a cheaper and better manner than the other theatres, and assures them: "If nature hath given me any talents at ridiculing vice and imposture, I shall not be indolent, nor afraid of exerting them, while the liberty of the press and stage subsists, that is to say, while we have any liberty left amongst us."

When Fielding wrote these words, he was not very apprehensive that his theatre would be suppressed. In his mind the freedom of the theatre was so involved with that of the press as to be inseparable. The Government, he believed, would not dare to raise again the question of a free press, which had been settled a half century before; and for this reason the theatre would escape a special statute. Affairs would go on, he seemed to think, just as they had been doing since he came to London. From time to time, the printer of a newspaper would be arrested on the charge of libel against his Majesty's Government, and a play would be prohibited by the Lord Chamberlain ostensibly in the interest of public morals, but really because of its political innuendoes. He knew, of course, that many people were writing and speaking against the licence (licentiousness they called it) of the stage; and that the managers of the two patent theatres—Drury Lane and Covent Garden—would like to see the Government silence the irregular theatres such as his own in the Haymarket, and thereby confirm their monopoly over all dramatic performances. But he evidently did not regard these forces as potent enough to overcome the widespread belief in the Englishman's inalienable right to free speech. Indeed, he had seen two abortive attempts to regulate the stage. In 1733, a bill was introduced for this purpose into the House of Commons; it was debated for two hours, and that was the end of it. Two years later Sir John Barnard brought in another bill, which, with the active support of Walpole, progressed further; but that, too, was eventually withdrawn because of the violence of the opposition to its rigid provisions for a censorship. Neither bill was very seriously regarded.*

But since 1735, the situation had changed. Fielding was, it is true, strictly correct in claiming that he was not the first to bring political satire on the stage. There was Aristophanes, whom he cited; but an appeal to the Greek dramatist could not have been very effective. There were Gay and several imitators of him besides Fielding; but their satirical strokes were incidental or by way of allegory. Going far beyond Gay, Fielding threw off the disguise altogether, or made the political allegory thin enough for the intelligence of the most stupid in his audience. His satires on the Government were so successful that the managers of the patent theatres took the alarm; and to compete with him they were forced to provide plays of a decided political cast. Such, for instance, was Robert Dodsley's "The King and the Miller of Mansfield," performed at Drury Lane on February 1, 1737, containing in the songs and dialogue remarks on the bribe as the courtier's instrument for obtaining what he wants. And this at the Theatre Royal! No wonder that Fielding's influence was looked upon by the Ministry as

* W. Nicholson, "The Struggle for a Free Stage in London," Boston, 1906, pp. 55-59.

thoroughly dangerous. Moreover, he was making his theatre, in appearance if not in reality, an adjunct of an aggressive Opposition.

It may be, however, that the Government would have taken no action at this time but for an untoward incident which quickly brought matters to a crisis. In the preceding March, "Common Sense" published a scurrilous attack on Walpole and his associates entitled "The Vision of the Golden Rump"—descriptive of a god worshipped, not in England, but in far-off India. He is a huge idol of human shape, except that his legs are those of a goat terminating in the cloven feet of the devil. His head is of wood, his trunk is of silver, and his monstrous posteriors, whence he derives his name, are of pure gold. It is quite unnecessary to describe here the scene in the eastern temple as the god stands with his back to the congregation; and the worshippers, with strict respect to their rank and position, fall prostrate before him and perform, under the guidance of the chief magician, the rites expected of them. They are all there—Walpole with his subordinates in the Ministry, the Privy Council, the Knights of the Bath, a horde of placemen, and less patently the King and Queen. "The Vision" ran through two numbers of "Common Sense"* and was extensively reproduced in other periodicals; while from the description someone immediately drew a gross caricature which circulated as a shilling print bearing the title: "The Festival of the Golden Rump. *Rumpatur, quisquis Rumpitur invidiâ.* Designed by the Author of Common Sense. Published according to Act of Parliament."† The current translation of the Latin motto was: "Whoever envies me, or whoever is not on my side, let him be *rumped,*"—the slang for disregarded or snubbed.

The next step was to turn the popular satire into a

* March 19 and 26.

† British Museum, "Political and Social Satires," No. 2327.

dramatic exhibition. This was done some time in May by an unknown wit who sent a two-act farce, called "The Golden Rump," to Giffard for his theatre in Lincoln's Inn Fields. Giffard, so the story goes, wishing to win the favour of the Ministry, took the manuscript to Walpole who, in order to keep the piece from the stage, paid the manager his price for it, then made extracts of its "most treasonable and profane" passages and laid them before the King. As the farce was thus bought off and never reached a printer, it cannot be determined how near its satire came to the person of the King; but Walpole, it would seem, was introduced as an indecent Harlequin marshalling the worshippers around the golden rump. Naturally, too, the author of so scandalous a production concealed his name and never afterwards claimed the honour due to him. It was hinted that Walpole himself had the farce written by one of his scribblers as a cunning device for bringing to an end political satire on the stage. This view, though accepted by several recent writers on Fielding and the period,* is preposterous. The idea was first set forth as a jest with no expectation that it would ever be taken seriously by sober historians. Some years later, Walpole's son Horace, who found "an imperfect copy" of the piece among his father's papers, attributed the authorship definitely to Fielding.† With reference to this statement, it is a safe remark that Fielding would never have given to another theatre a political farce certain to draw away from his own house the very audience on which he was depending for the support of his company. He must be credited with sufficient business sense to have avoided that. Others besides himself were then writing and submitting to the

* W. Nicholson, for example. See his "Struggle for a Free Stage" for the literature on the Licensing Act.

† H. Walpole, "Memoirs of the Reign of King George the Second," second edition, 1846, I, 13-14.

theatres these "masques drawn to the life." So many of them, says Fielding playfully, were sent in to the Haymarket that "a large buck-basket" had to be provided to hold them. "The Golden Rump" was one of these many allegorical masques, coming no one knew whence, which Giffard probably picked out of his basket at Lincoln's Inn Fields, and turned over to the Prime Minister for a consideration. Had he known who the author was, he could not have thus sold it. Surely not, had the farce been submitted to him by Fielding.

And yet the positive statement of Horace Walpole that Fielding wrote "The Golden Rump" cannot be set aside without the courtesy of an explanation. It is not enough to say that Horace Walpole, the scandal-monger, was notoriously inexact in what he wrote or that he always displayed special hostility towards Fielding. His assertion, if not his hostility, clearly had its source in family tradition. Naturally the suspicions of his father would have pointed to Fielding as the author of the farce in question; for Fielding above all other playwrights had most openly ridiculed him. If Sir Robert ever read "The Historical Register," he saw himself portrayed there in a manner not very remote from that in "The Golden Rump." In fact, there was no essential difference between representing Walpole, fiddle in hand, dancing a jig with the patriots, and representing him dressed as Harlequin and dancing around the golden rump. His suspicions must have been strengthened two years later when Fielding, as editor of "The Champion," reproduced in that newspaper the old print of "The Festival of the Golden Rump," accompanied by an article having the frank indecency of the original. Here were grounds quite sufficient for fixing, in Walpole's mind, "The Golden Rump" upon Fielding.

Once in possession of the farce, Walpole made immediate use of it for the enactment of a law placing the stage under strict censorship. On May 20, the House of Commons ordered the preparation of a bill for this purpose by way of an amendment to the Vagrant Act of Queen Anne's time "relative to common players of interludes." In pursuance of this order the so-called Licensing Act—really Sir John Barnard's bill of 1735 revamped—was introduced on May 24, and pushed rapidly through both houses. Its design was "the regulation of theatrical entertainments, which, from their excess, fill both town and country with idleness and debauchery; and, from being under no restraint, exhibit to the publick encomiums on vice, and laugh away the sober principles of modesty and virtue." As a means for thus protecting the morals in both town and country, the bill prohibited, under a penalty of £50, the acting for "hire, gain, or reward" of any play or dramatic performance whatever unless previously sanctioned by letters patent from the Crown or licensed by the Lord Chamberlain. By further provisions of the bill, copies of all plays had to be submitted to the Lord Chamberlain two weeks before their performance, and all theatres, not within the verge of the Court, were to be restricted to the city of Westminster and the liberties thereof.

Against the drastic measure, Pulteney led the Opposition in the House of Commons. He "roasted" Walpole for bringing in so important a bill near the close of the session, when many members were absent and there was no time for adequate debate, and charged him with concealing the real intent of the measure, which, under the pretext of administering to the public welfare, was aimed at silencing criticisms of the Ministry. The next step, he declared, would be a law to squelch the newspapers also. He was reminded, he said, of the old story concerning Charles the Second, who, seeing a man in the pillory, asked the crime, and was informed that " 'twas libelling Lord Clarendon." "Odds fish," cried the King, "why did not the fool go on libelling

229

of me! He must now suffer for libelling this great man."
In reply Walpole read to the House parts of "The Golden
Rump," saying that he was indifferent to personal ridicule,
and expressed an opinion that those gentlemen of the Opposition who were away on their estates were better employed
there than they would be in speaking against the present
measure. Except for this passage at arms, in which some
other members took part, the bill moved easily through its
third reading.

During its progress through the House of Lords, the
bill met with the opposition of Lord Chesterfield, who there
spoke for his party as Pulteney had done in the Commons.
His carefully prepared speech has been often praised as an
eloquent and well-tempered summary of the arguments for
a free press and a free stage. Lord Hervey, who was present, said that it was "one of the most lively and ingenious
speeches" he had ever heard in Parliament, "full of wit,
of the genteelest satire, and in the most polished, classical
style that the Petronius of any time ever wrote."* The
speech is thought to rise so far above Chesterfield's other
efforts, that there have been surmises that he was aided in
its composition by Fielding. Any direct assistance from
Fielding, however, was impossible. Chesterfield's views
were mainly those of his party; and where he deviated from
them, he displayed no intelligence so extraordinary that it
may not be credited to him as his own. If the desire of the
Government was to prevent the appearance on the stage of
anything held to be "blasphemous, seditious, or immoral,"
then, he argued, the proposed measure was unnecessary,
since the existing laws, if enforced, would accomplish that
end. Why, he asked in irony, did not the Government pros-
ecute the author of "Pasquin"—a farce wherein "the
three great professions, religion, physic, and law," were

* Lord John Hervey, "Memoirs of the Reign of George the Second," 1884,
III, 143.

represented "as inconsistent with common sense." Just as Pulteney had done, he went on to insinuate that the real design of the measure might be quite different from what it professed to be. In this connection, he would remark that when a man in public life "has the misfortune to incur the hatred or contempt of the people," an audience will often apply to him some unlucky phrase in a play never intended for ridicule. Again, a man "conscious of the wickedness or weakness" of his conduct sometimes feels uneasy when any disgraceful act whatever becomes the object of satire. Likewise "a public thief is as apt to take the satire, as he is apt to take the money, which was never designed for him." Human nature being what it is, an innocent drama- tist may be punished for the sins of others.

In this way, Chesterfield meandered on through banter, irony, and innuendo to the conclusion that the purpose of the bill was not at all the restraint of immorality, but the restraint of the liberty of the stage in criticising public men and their measures—a function of the theatre that had proved most useful in all countries. In one notable passage, written clearly with Fielding in mind, he went further than this and claimed that the bill was "an encroachment upon property." "Wit, my Lords," he said, "is a sort of prop- erty; it is the property of those who have it, and too often the only property they have to depend on. It is indeed but a precarious dependence. Thank God! we, my Lords, have a dependence of another kind; we have a much less pre- carious support, and therefore cannot feel the inconvenience of the bill now before us; but it is our duty to encourage and protect wit, whosoever's property it may be. Those gentle- men who have any such property, are all, I hope, our friends. Do not let us subject them to any unnecessary or arbitrary restraint. I must own, I cannot easily agree to the laying of any tax upon wit; but by this bill it is to be heavily taxed, it is to be excised; for, if this bill passes, it cannot be retailed in a proper way without a permit, and the Lord Chamberlain is to have the honour of being chief-gauger, supervisor, commissioner, judge, and jury. . . . As the stage has always been the proper channel for wit and humour, therefore, my Lords, when I speak against this bill, I must think, I plead the cause of wit, I plead the cause of humour, I plead the cause of the British stage, and of every gentleman of taste in the kingdom.''[*]

Chesterfield's eloquence was of no avail. The Licensing Act passed its third reading in the House of Lords on June 6, 1737, and duly received the royal assent on the twenty-first of the month. By its provisions were closed, on June 24, the three unlicensed theatres—Fielding's Little Theatre in the Haymarket and the two houses where Giffard's company was playing. Nothing remained but the two royal theatres—Drury Lane and Covent Garden—whose patentees, now in possession of a complete monopoly, were able, they thought, to maintain their prices for seats and to keep down the salaries of actors. They had, however, a public somewhat disaffected to deal with, and they were subjected to the interference of a licenser of plays appointed under the Act as a subordinate to the Lord Chamberlain. It was suggested by a writer in "Common Sense" that the clause in the law imposing a fine of £50 upon the performance of an unlicensed play for "hire," might be evaded by making no charge for seats. A rather impracticable idea, it would seem; but Giffard, letting his mind work upon it, eventually opened his theatre in Goodman's Fields for "concerts of vocal and instrumental music," between the parts of which were presented *gratis* his usual repertoire of plays. The Government winked at Giffard's clever evasion perhaps as a reward for services rendered in running to Downing Street with "The Golden Rump."

[*] "Letters and Works of Lord Chesterfield," edited by Lord Mahon. 1853, V, 15-16.

But the situation was quite different with Fielding. He could hope for no consideration from the Government, for the Licensing Act was aimed directly at him. On this point there is evidence of the most positive sort. While the bill was still pending in the House of Lords, the "Adventurer in Politicks" published in "The Daily Gazetteer" for the fourth of June a full rejoinder to all that Fielding had said in his dedication to "The Historical Register" and in the letter he had sent to "Common Sense." It was a prosecutor's final summary of the case. In a personal address to Fielding, the spokesman of the Ministry asserted: "I believe, and am confident, the Government had no thought of vesting any power in any great officer's hands for this purpose, had not you pav'd the way for the subversion of the stage, by introducing on it matters quite foreign to its true object; and by making yourself a tool to the indiscreet mirth of some great men, put others upon keeping the stage within its proper bounds." And in more vigorous phrases, Chesterfield or one of his subordinates declared the next year that Walpole "resolved, since he could not damn the poet, to ruin him, and send the players [at the Haymarket] a begging.'"* Though Fielding survived the blow, and several of his company found employment at the royal theatres, most of them were indeed broken. Lacy, who had played the part of Fustian in "Pasquin," supported himself for several years as lecturer and conductor of musical entertainments before becoming, by a turn of good fortune, a patentee of Drury Lane. Others were reduced to vagabondage and drifted to debtors' prisons. Fielding, be it said to his credit, submitted quietly to the law. He did not act upon a hint that "Pasquin" be performed *gratis;* nor did he, like several other playwrights of his party, write and publish by subscription further dramatic satires, such as could never have passed

* "Common Sense," Oct. 28, 1738.

233

the licenser and reached the stage. He obeyed the law in its spirit as well as in its letter.

The resentment of the public towards a measure which deprived them of "a poet whose little pieces" were for two years "the delight of the town," was expressed in a theatrical riot which occurred a year later. At the opening of the dramatic season in October, 1738, the Lord Chamberlain issued a permit to a company of French players to act at Fielding's theatre. No sooner was the announcement made in the newspapers than all the coffee-houses from the East to the West rang with indignation. The Lord Chamberlain, they declared, was granting to foreign strollers concessions which he refused to English actors who were starving or lying in prison. It was even charged by the Patriots that the Government had brought over the French comedians as a means of flaunting its power; and the charge seems to have been true. So loud were the clamours at what was regarded as an insult to the nation, that the Government took extraordinary steps for the protection of the French actors on the night set for their first performance, which was the ninth of October. Two files of Grenadiers, with fixed bayonets, were placed on the stage; two justices of the peace took seats in the pit; and a full company of the Guards was stationed outside the theatre. At the first sign of disturbance, one of the justices informed the audience that the play must be acted, for such was "the King's command." A spokesman for an angry house replied that by common custom and ancient usage an audience had the right to show its dislike to any play or actor, and that the right would be exercised despite the presence of soldiers. A terrible uproar followed; a justice began to read the Riot Act, but the candle was snatched from his hand, and he was forced to order the Grenadiers from the stage. Whenever members of the troupe attempted to dance, peas in great quantities were thrown upon the stage; whenever they attempted to speak their parts, they were greeted with cat-calls and the noise of every screeching instrument known to the theatre. At one point in the riot, the audience by previous arrangement rose and sang all together Fielding's "Roast Beef of Old England," ending with three huzzas! The play was over. The town could not force the Lord Chamberlain to grant a licence to Fielding's company, but it could prevent a performance by another company at his theatre.*

The loss of the Little Theatre in the Haymarket was also a keener disappointment to Fielding himself than the world knows. For seven years, his main support had been his plays. While dependent upon other theatres, he usually received, as became the custom, only the receipts on his benefit nights after the payment of the actors.† There were short periods in the first years when his purse was empty, but except for the lean months his numerous benefits enabled him to live easily as a gentleman. And when sub-sequent to his marriage he opened, in order to increase his income, a theatre of his own, he displayed unusual skill in adapting his art to the temper of his audience, while main-taining his wit and humour at their highest pitch. But he had hardly more than discovered where his talent lay before his dramatic career was ended. As he used to say, "he left off writing for the stage when he ought to have begun." But for the Licensing Act he would have rebuilt or enlarged his theatre and continued to delight London audiences for another decade or more. On Fielding's stage rather than Giffard's, Garrick would have won his spurs. Fielding and Garrick, working together, would have given the British theatre a fame unequalled since the days of Shakespeare.

The drama, I have tried to make clear, was to Fielding much more than a means of support; it was his soul; it was his life. Underlying all his plays—farce as well as comedy

* "Common Sense," Oct. 21, 1738.   † "The Champion," Dec. 11, 1739.

—was a serious intent. The young man thought that he was performing a public service in exposing folly, vice, and corruption. As he afterwards looked back upon the events of 1737 and their consequences, and on the men and women whom he had drawn from the very life during the years of his apprenticeship, they all seemed to him incomprehensible, and he believed that they would thus appear to posterity. Sane and unembittered, he so expressed himself in a striking passage that has barely survived to these later times:

"Several Characters which were receiv'd with great Applause at the *Haymarket* a few Years since, will be very little relished by future Ages, who will probably look on them only as absurd Creatures of the Poet's own Brain. They may possibly doubt whether there ever existed an impudent Bookseller, who kept *Grub-street* Scriblers at his own Expence in a Garret, to traduce the Reputations of the best Men, and the Writings of the greatest Authors of his Time; whether such a Contempt was ever laid on the Muses as the Preferment of a Man to be Poet *Laureate,* who could not write either Metre, Grammar, or *English;* whether the Theatres were permitted to be under the Government of such as did not know a Tragedy from a Comedy; whether the Publick Taste was ever suffer'd to be debauch'd at a Time when the Stage was under a Licencer, by introducing the meanest, absurdest, childish Entertainments, and banishing and mangling the best Plays of all our *English* Poets on their Account; whether Libels on the greatest Men in the Kingdom, only because they disdain'd to fall in with the Corruption of the Times, were spread abroad *Gratis* for a long Continuance over the whole Nation. . . . They may perhaps doubt whether universal Corruption was ever publickly or professedly maintain'd and practiced by all Degrees of Men; whether by means of such Corruption, those Persons whom the whole Kingdom despise and detest, should be able to shew their Faces, and retain the Power of undermining the *British* Liberties. Lastly, whether the hundredth Part of what hath been thrown on one Man, be true, or was indeed possible to be so."*

* "The Patriot," Edinburgh, July 11, 1740; quoted from "The Champion," apparently for July 1, 1740.

CHAPTER X

LAW AND JOURNALISM

I

A month before the passage of the Licensing Act, Fielding intimated in his dedication to "The Historical Register" that, should his theatre be suppressed, he would carry the war against "vice and imposture" over into the newspapers. A week later it was in his mind that he might establish a new organ of the Opposition, as is evident from an introductory note to his Pasquin letter to "Common Sense" for May 21, 1737. "As I have yet no vehicle of my own, I shall be obliged to you," he writes to the editor, "if you will give the following a place in the next stage." But on further consideration Fielding must have seen that it was not an opportune moment to carry out his design. There were already half a dozen anti-ministerial newspapers in London, the best of which—"Common Sense"— had been running only a few months, and they were all being watched closely by a Government determined to enforce the laws against libel. During June several men connected with a most violent Opposition journal called "The Alchymist," were arrested, and one of the writers was sent to Newgate. The next month various contributors to "The Craftsman" and the printer and publisher of "Fog's Weekly Journal" were taken into custody. On these occasions, it was usual for the King's messenger to search all papers in the office of a newspaper and to break up the printing press. It was a time of fear and trembling.

Probably Fielding could find no supporters for his project, though he himself may have been ready to risk imprisonment in the cause of free speech.

Why, one may ask, was not Fielding taken on the staff of "Common Sense"? He may, indeed, have contributed a few articles to this newspaper on general subjects relative to the theatre and the nature of wit and humour; but in the absence of direct evidence, there are none—except the one already described—that can be attributed definitely to him. At best his articles could have been but occasional, much as Chesterfield and Lyttelton may have wished to make use of his talent; for they had placed the immediate management of "Common Sense" in the hands of one of the best informed and most spirited newspaper writers of the period—Charles Molloy, an Irishman who had had long experience in aggressive journalism against Walpole. Molloy, of course, could not be displaced even for Fielding. There was nothing for Fielding to do except to retire to his farm at East Stour, and make plans for a new turn in his career. Sometime during the year had been born a second daughter named Harriot or Harriet, and it behooved him to find an occupation.

Since his last summer at East Stour, provision had been made for dividing the property there, which had remained in trust ever since the death of his mother, Sarah Fielding. The division was now rendered necessary by the fact that his brother Edmund, the youngest member of the family, had reached his majority. Two indentures,* forming a part of the transaction, have recently come to light. Both are dated February 3, 1737. In the first of them, the original trustees—Davidge Gould and William Day—were relieved of their trust by the Fielding children—Henry,

---

* Sold at Sotheby's, London, July 20, 1916. See Sotheby's Catalogue, 1916 (pp. 135-136), for a brief description. Copied by permission of the former owner of the documents.

Catherine, Ursula, Sarah, Beatrice, and Edmund. In the second indenture, the estate was conveyed, by Peter Davies of Wells (in whose name it had been held), the two trustees, Henry Fielding, and his brother and sisters, to Robert Stillingfleet, a lawyer and land agent who appears occasionally in the local records of Salisbury. These documents do not mean a sale of the property. By them the original trust was dissolved and Robert Stillingfleet took the place of Peter Davies "to attend," in legal phrase, "the fee simple and inheritance of the said premises." The conveyance of the estate was but a preliminary step to its division into six equal parts for the six children of Edmund and Sarah Fielding. And if, as tradition has it, Stillingfleet be the original of Dowling, "the attorney from Salisbury" who plays a part in "Tom Jones," he turned out to be a scoundrel.

No further details of the transaction have yet been discovered; but that the estate was immediately divided may be inferred from a deed of the next year. During the Trinity Term of 1738, Henry Fielding and his wife Charlotte conveyed to "Thomas Hayter, Gentleman," for the sum of £260, "two messuages, two dovehouses, three gardens, three orchards, fifty acres of land, eighty acres of meadow, one hundred and forty acres of pasture, ten acres of wood, and common of pasture for all manner of cattle with the appurtenances in East Stour."* If these lands represented Fielding's entire share in the estate, they were sold for half what was paid for them. Owing to neglect, the farm had doubtless depreciated greatly in value; and Fielding, in need of money, must have been glad of a purchaser. Fielding's days at East Stour were now over, though certain legal matters with reference to the estate required, as we shall see, his attention a few years later. His brother and sisters, it would appear, did not dispose of their shares

* London Record Office. "Feet of Fines, Dorset. Trinity, 11-12 George II."

in the property for at least two years. Eventually, it is said, the entire farm—house, closes, lands, and meadows where Henry Fielding passed his boyhood—fell into the hands of Peter Walter,* the rogue who figures in "Joseph Andrews" as Peter Pounce.

As an offset to such depreciation as there may have been in the value of the farm at East Stour, the Fieldings had in prospect legacies from the estate of their uncle George Fielding, Lieutenant-Colonel of the Royal Horse Guards, who died at Windsor in the summer of 1738. By his will, proved on September 28, he left to them and other members of the Fielding family the reversion of three annuities, of fifty, thirty, and twenty pounds respectively, after the death of his aunt Mary Cockayn of Richmond, and the reversion of a very handsome annuity of two hundred and ten pounds on the death of Captain John Hawkins, perhaps the husband of one of his sisters. By the terms of the will Henry Fielding should have received as much as fifty pounds a year, his wife Charlotte sixty pounds a year, and his brother Edmund and each of his four sisters—Catherine, Ursula, Sarah, and Beatrice—twenty pounds a year. There was litigation over the will, and a part of the annuities may have been sold in order to satisfy certain notes and bonds of George Fielding. It is probable also that Charlotte Fielding never came into possession of her annuity, for she died before the case was finally settled. The same is true of Edmund, whose career was cut short by death. Entering the army, Edmund received when a mere boy his commission as ensign in 1733, and subsequently, on March 22, 1740, another commission in the Royal Inniskilling Fusiliers. In 1743 he was a first lieutenant in Colonel Cochran's Regiment of Marines. For a time he was stationed at Minorca. After the contest over

---

* "Salisbury and Winchester Journal," Sept. 11, 1780.

his uncle's will, the young man disappears from view.* Nor is it positively known that the others ever obtained their annuities. The chances, however, are that Henry Fielding and his four sisters received theirs, though there may have been some decrease in their value. A legacy of fifty pounds a year to Henry Fielding with his growing family must have been most welcome; and twenty pounds a year to each of his sisters besides their other income enabled them to live together as poor gentlewomen, not quite on the verge of distress.†

In the meantime, Fielding, despite his full thirty years, had decided to become a lawyer—a profession for which he had been destined by his mother's family and towards which he had long had an inclination, as is shown by his fondness for legal phrases. Almost at the outset of his career there had been the call to law and the call to literature. The immediate necessities of his purse then as always determined for him which of the two voices he should heed. At the moment he could see no opening in literature —the royal theatres were closed against him and the newspapers of the Opposition were full-manned. In the circumstances he might better risk the law, in the hope that his own and his wife's small income, eked out by occasional hack-writing, would carry him through to the bar. Accordingly, at the close of the hunting season of 1737, he returned to London and enrolled as a student at the Middle Temple, where his cousin Henry Gould had been admitted to the

---

* Mr. J. Paul de Castro in ''Notes and Queries,'' 12 S. III, 217 (March 17, 1917).

† The will of George Fielding is at Somerset House, P. C. C. 213 Brodrepp. To the original will, dated Aug. 16, 1733, was added a codicil on Jan. 19, 1735, and another on March 1, 1737. Charlotte was called Catherine by mistake in the first codicil. Her name, which of course does not appear in the original will, was corrected in the second codicil. For the litigation over the will, see Feet of Fines, 1745, Book A, at the Record Office. The case was heard on March 15, 1745.

bar three years before. The entry in the books of the society reads:

1 Nov^{ris} 1737

Henricus Fielding, de East Stour in Com Dorset Ar, filius et haeres apparens Brig: Gen^{lis}: Edmundi Fielding admissus est in Societatem Medii Templi Lond specialiter et obligatur una cum etc.

Et dat pro fine 4.0.0.

To men unacquainted with Fielding's antecedents and character, the playwright turned into a law student was a curious sight. One "among the many" who were unable to understand the transformation, made the incident the occasion of a poem in heroic couplets running to seventy-seven lines. It bore the title "An Epistle to Mr. Fielding, on His Studying the Law."* Who the anonymous author was it would be vain to inquire, for he says that Fielding himself could "scarce guess." A reader can only wish that the gentleman's skill in verse were equal to his admiration of Fielding:

> While Others feel the drowsy Pow'r of *Coke,*
> Thy Antidote shall be some well-tim'd Joke;
> And what to some shall seem *Herculean* Pain,
> Shall only be th' Amusement of thy Brain.

And the hope was expressed that Fielding might become a Lord Chancellor of Great Britain:

> Accept the Hearty *Wish,* nor take it ill,
> Plainness is Elegance with pure Good Will.
> O! may the plural Fee so fertile rise,
> *Briareus'* Hands to take shall scarce suffice:
> May the vast Toil be paid with vast Reward;
> May Furry Honours crown the Muse-lost Bard:
> May to the *Orator* the *Member* follow,
> And yield at last a *Talbot* from *Apollo.*

---

* "London: Printed in the Year M.DCC.XXXVIII." The poem is in the Library of Harvard University.

243

THE HISTORY OF HENRY FIELDING

For two years after paying his fee of four pounds, Fielding applied himself to the study of law without the interruption, so far as is known, of other work save for a possible contribution now and then to "Common Sense." Though much older than his fellow students, he easily fell into their ways of life, and they became strongly attached to him. On these points, his first biographer has left a crimson passage, from which I must clip the closing phrases and keep them until I have told the real story of Fielding's life. "The friendships," says Murphy, "he met with in the course of his studies, and, indeed, through the remainder of his life, from the gentlemen of that profession in general, and particularly from some, who have since risen to be the first ornaments of the law, will for ever do honour to his memory. His application, while he was a student in the Temple, was remarkably intense; and though it happened that the early taste he had taken of pleasure would occasionally return upon him, and conspire with his spirit and vivacity to carry him into the wild enjoyments of the town, yet it was particular in him, that, amidst all his dissipations, nothing could suppress the thirst he had for knowledge, and the delight he felt in reading."

Though what Murphy loosely asserts of Fielding's dissipations, as if they were unusual in young men of the time, should be taken with some abatement, all the rest is confirmed by the array of lawyers and judges who subscribed to Fielding's "Miscellanies" in 1743. They number more than two hundred. Of the men with whom Fielding associated at the Middle Temple, was Charles Pratt, an old Etonian, who long afterwards rose to the Lord Chancellorship and died as Earl Camden. He is remembered in the United States for the stand he took against the Stamp Act and other measures for the direct taxation of the Colonies. His meeting with Fielding is specifically mentioned in certain memoranda which his nephew George Hardinge, a

Welsh judge and one time member of Parliament for Old Sarum, left towards a biography of the Lord Chancellor. The note reads: "Fond of convivial habits and convivial talents—but abstaining from vice . . . formed an acquaintance with Hawkins Brown and with Henry Fielding . . . became intimate with Lord Northington . . . called to the bar—very little business—hated it —was often going to leave it."* As Pratt was admitted to the bar at the Middle Temple in 1738, he should have met Fielding there soon after the latter's entrance upon his legal studies. Isaac Hawkins Browne, wit and poet, was a barrister of Lincoln's Inn. He subsequently became a Member of Parliament; he wrote a poem on a pipe of tobacco, and in a more serious mood another on the immortality of the soul. The three men, all Patriots, all lovers of wine and conversation, all quite uncertain of the future, may well have sat together in London taverns till far into the night, talking over their prospects in a profession concerning which they had profound misgivings. With them was probably Lord Northington. He was the Robert Henley who subscribed to Fielding's "Miscellanies." Like Pratt he drank freely and became a Lord Chancellor. There is a story that, when suffering from the gout in later life as a result of early indiscretions, he was heard to mutter to himself in the House of Lords: "If I had known that these legs were one day to carry a Chancellor, I'd have taken better care of them when a lad."

But there is the other side of the picture. The zeal with which Fielding entered upon his new studies may be inferred from the large library of law books which he is known to have possessed at a later period. These books, numbering several hundred, he began to collect at the very beginning, as may be seen by quotations from them in "The Champion." He had all the statutes at large, with various

* John Lord Campbell, "Lives of the Lord Chancellors," 1846, V, 356.

abridgments and readings thereon, nearly all the reports in law, cases in Chancery, treatises on Roman law, Crown law, conveyancing, poor laws, parish laws, forest laws, and so on through the catalogue of books necessary to a well-equipped lawyer down to the handbooks and dictionaries which he liked to ridicule. He was particularly interested, says Murphy, in Crown law. His copy of Hawkins's "Pleas of the Crown," when it emerged from his library, was indeed annotated "with a great number of manuscript notes" in his own hand; and his copy of Wood's "Institute of the Laws of England" was "interleaved with manuscript notes," likewise of his own making. In line with these lost manuscripts, have survived two undated pages of notes perhaps to be identified with leaves once inserted in Wood's treatise, containing three lists of offences against the King —"offences against the King and his State immediately, which the law terms High Treason," "offences against him in a general light as touching the Commonwealth at large, as Trade, etc.," "offences against him as supreme Magistrate, etc."* These fragments, long preserved in the Morrison Collection of Manuscripts, may carry us directly back to Fielding at the Middle Temple.

It has usually been taken for granted that Fielding lived alone in lodgings, apart from his family, while studying law. This seems fairly certain only for the first year and somewhat more. Where in the meantime were Mrs. Fielding and the children? By 1738 at the latest they left the farm at East Stour. The probability is that they were settled as early as the winter of 1737-1738 at Salisbury, and that Fielding thereafter made this town his home for several years when away from London. According to local tradition, the Fieldings lived for a time in a gabled house within the Cathedral Close belonging to the Minor Canons.

* "Catalogue of the Collection of Autograph Letters and Historical Documents . . . by Alfred Morrison," II, London, 1883.

It is the first house to the left, much altered in exterior, as one enters through St. Ann's Gate. Nearly opposite, next to the Gate, lived James Harris, author of the once famous "Hermes." Some years later Fielding referred to him approvingly as "my friend";* and Harris wrote of Fielding as "a witty friend of mine," whose "uninterrupted pleasantry" flowed from a most fertile genius.† It was in conversation with Harris that Fielding cursed the inventor of fifth Acts. Of the relations between the two men we shall hear more.

Another tradition connects Fielding with a larger house, now gone, near Salisbury—a mansion of red brick with Gothic roof, at the foot of Milford Hill, and within the parish of St. Martin's, where his grandmother Gould and the Cradocks had lived. A fine mantel-piece and some of the panelling—nothing more—were used in the modern Gothic structure that has displaced the old manor house of Fielding's time. In a large and beautiful rear garden a stream has been let in from the river with overhanging limes, and a little way down the stream is a garden house where, they say, Fielding used to sit and write. That Fielding did at some time live there for a few months is quite likely. The property then belonged to the Swayne family, the last of whom—Bennet Swayne—died unmarried at Epsom, Surrey, in 1748, and to whose memory a monument was erected in St. Martin's Church. Being a bachelor who spent his time in London and at watering-places, he would have had no use for the house of his ancestors and would have been glad to let it to a gentleman whom he had known since boyhood. But it seems more appropriate to think of Fielding as leaving his wife and children at first within the quiet and protection of the Cathedral Close, and to regard the red brick mansion with extensive grounds as a second residence of uncertain date. Though beyond reasonable

* "Miscellanies," 1743, I, 122.　† "Philological Inquiries," 1781, p. 163.

247

doubt Fielding's family remained for a time at Salisbury and he visited them often, it must be admitted in conclusion that the statement rests upon no positive evidence. An examination of the Corporation records fails to reveal any taxes levied against him in Salisbury. Hence he held no formal lease of a house there.

One certain glimpse, however, we get of Fielding at this time in a note, dated July 9, 1739, but without name of place, which he sent up to a London bookseller—John Nourse without Temple Bar. It runs as follows:
"Mr. Nourse,

Disappointments have hitherto prevented my paying y^r Bill, which, I shall certainly do on my coming to Town which will be next Month. I desire the favour of y^u to look for a House for me near the Temple. I must have one large eating Parlour in it for the rest shall not be very nice. Rent not upwards of £40 p. an: and as much cheaper as may be. I will take a Lease for Seven years. Y^r Answer to this within a fortnight will much oblige

Y^r Humble Servt

HENRY FFIELDING.

I have got Cro: Eliz.
July 9th 1739.''*

Between the lines of this letter, brief as it is, much may be read. Fielding is in the country—at Salisbury probably—with his family. He is unable to pay for the law books with which Mr. Nourse has been supplying him; and when he next comes to London, he will bring his wife and daughters with him and take a house within easy reach of the Temple. There will be no more living by himself in lodgings. Where, we may wonder, were the forty pounds rent to come from? The book—"Cro: Eliz."—which he had obtained

---

* Taken from the original in the Huth Library.—Miss G. M. Godden, ''Henry Fielding,'' pp. 94-95.

without Mr. Nourse's help, was Sir George Croke's Reports covering the years 1580-1640 and written in Norman-French. It was rather crabbed reading, one would think, for the summer. Croke's Reports, however, amused Fielding and he parodied the style a few months later in "The Champion."

Perhaps it was the expense of maintaining a house in London that drove Fielding, on coming to town, to revive the project of a newspaper. What he received for his lands at East Stour could not have lasted long. The time was more favourable for a new periodical than it had been two years before. Since then "The Alchymist" had disappeared; "Common Sense" had suffered from a revolt of several writers, so that "Common Sense" and "Old Common Sense" ran for a time as rivals; and "The Craftsman," long the leading organ of the Opposition, had been so badly managed that its circulation had shrunk a full half—from 4,500 copies at an issue to only 2,000.* Walpole, growing older and infirm, was weakening under the impassioned assaults of Pitt; and Bolingbroke had returned from France as adviser of the Opposition. The great question before the people was now Spain's interference with British trade in her American colonies, her claim of the right to search British vessels on the high seas, and the barbarities which, it was alleged, she had inflicted on British seamen. A certain Captain Jenkins appeared before a committee of the House of Commons, bringing with him one of his ears in a box, which he said had been cut off seven years before by a Spanish coastguard. The young leaders of the Opposition were for immediate war with Spain; and the Ministry, though opposed to war, was soon forced to give way to the passions of the people. War was declared in October, 1739. Young men everywhere lined up with the war party, which was

* "The Patriot," Oct. 24, 1740.

especially strong in London and in the coast towns where the merchant class predominated. They regarded Walpole as a traitor, bent upon the enrichment of himself and family, and caring nothing for the general prosperity of the country. Like the rest, Fielding was stirred by the war spirit and felt the patriotic impulse. He knew, too, that newspapers thrive on war. London printers and booksellers were aware of that also.

Accordingly, a partnership was formed for publishing "The Champion," Fielding's first newspaper. There were at least seven partners, probably eight, with Fielding at the head. His associates were a group of six or seven London booksellers, including Henry Chappelle, Lawton Gilliver (formerly printer of "The Grub-street Journal"), and John Nourse, to whom he was in debt for books. The printing was undertaken by "J. Huggonson in Sword and Buckler Court, over-against the Crown-Tavern on Ludgate Hill." To Fielding were assigned "two sixteenth shares" in the partnership.* As an assistant editor, he engaged James Ralph, who had aided him in the management of the Little Theatre in the Haymarket, and was then directing "The Universal Spectator." The two men soon received from the ministerial press the facetious names of Sir Hudibras and Squire Ralpho. Behind the undertaking were doubtless Fielding's friends in Parliament. He became effusive in praises of Argyle, Chesterfield, Lyttelton, and Carteret. In honor of the Duke of Richmond, to whom he had dedicated "The Miser," he began and afterwards completed a poem called "Of Good Nature,"† placing above all other titles of the Duke his generosity and goodness. And a new friend was found in George Bubb Dod-

* For details of the partnership, see Miss G. M. Godden, "Henry Fielding," pp. 100, 115, 138-139.

† "The Champion," Nov. 27, 1739. See J. E. Wells, "Modern Language Review," Jan., 1912.

ington, a clever and witty gentleman, who had left Walpole for the Patriots. For some time Dodington had been employing Ralph to write bitter denunciations of the Ministry in the newspapers; and Fielding, in the heat of party zeal, addressed to him a poem "On True Greatness" wherein Dodington is styled the Maecenas of the age. Dodington was indeed a generous patron of literature; and the indications are that Fielding received substantial support from him in the new enterprise.

The first number of Fielding's periodical made its appearance on Thursday, November 15, 1739, bearing the title of "The Champion; or, British Mercury" with the announcement that it would be continued every Tuesday, Thursday, and Saturday morning at three halfpence a copy.* Like most newspapers of the time it had four pages—thirteen and a half inches in length and ten inches in width, including margins. It professed to have as author (editor we should now call him) "the celebrated Capt. Hercules Vinegar, of Hockley in the Hole"; and a design depicting Hercules slaying the Hydra with a huge club divided the two parts of the title. In the background were Westminster bridge and the dome of St. Paul's.

The military name which Fielding assumed was derived from one adopted by a cudgel-player who was performing, back in 1731, at the bear-garden in Hockley in the Hole, Clerkenwell, and in other rings such as the one at Tottenham. He was known in fact all over London and became the manager of a company that entertained the public with a series of boxing matches or prize fights, ending with the appearance of the great champion himself, who had discovered an "easy and concise way of breaking loggerheads." In July, 1731, was published a sixpenny pamphlet, no copy of which seems to be extant, purporting to be a

* "The London Daily Post," Nov. 12, 1739.

vindication of the champion's character and conduct as a gentleman. It was entitled: "An Answer to one Part of a late infamous Libel, reflecting on Captain Vinegar and the late worthy Jonathan Wilde. . . . In a Letter to Mr. James F—gg, the supposed Author thereof." The pamphlet may have been what it claimed to be, but it was probably a mere skit aimed at James Figg, another prize-ring champion. Captain Vinegar survived this facetious use of his pseudonym and lived to see it employed by Aaron Hill in explaining why he gave the name of "The Prompter" to the semi-weekly periodical which he established three years later. In the fourteenth number of that publication, Hill wrote: "There is a Prompter, of athletic abilities, commonly known in the Fields of Mars, about this city, under the military title of Captain Vinegar; whose task it is, to clear the ring, from trumpery, in order to make way for entrance of those Patriot Champions, who devote their heads, in combat, to the publick renown of their country." Hill thus likened himself to Captain Vinegar, the bear-garden manager, who drove from the ring all but the real fighters, such as the Patriots, who were there to break their heads. Fielding announced himself as the very Captain Hercules Vinegar who had formerly been the terror of the ring, and was now resolved to strike down with his club every abuse that came in his way, while protecting always the innocent. He proclaimed himself the Censor of Great Britain, and the Champion of Virtue, Honour, and Patriotism. Sometimes dropping the figure, he would say that he had decided to lay aside the sword for the pen and would tickle rather than bruise mankind into good manners.*

Developing the fiction whimsically, Fielding drew sketches, in the first numbers of "The Champion," of other members of the Vinegar family who were to aid

* For the literature on Captain Vinegar, see J. E. Wells, "Modern Language Review," April, 1913.

the bear-garden hero in conducting the newspaper. The
Captain's father, Mr. Nehemiah Vinegar, who was so
thoroughly versed in affairs at home and abroad that he
could foretell long beforehand what was going to happen,
consented to supply the politics, though not always under
his own name. His brother William, a Counsellor of the
Middle Temple, would deal with all matters relating to
the laws of the kingdom. The Counsellor's son John,
having degrees from Oxford, promised to look after the
medical part of the paper and to "publish some prescrip-
tions of great use." The Captain's brother Nol, a profound classical scholar, a great admirer of Dr. Bentley,
whose notes on Milton he thought worth their weight in
gold, would undertake to criticise the critics of the age;
while the Captain's two sons about town—Tom and Jack—
were ordered to report on the theatres, assemblies, and
amusements of all kinds; the former being an adept in
damning the best plays on the first night, and the latter
being skilled in living like a gentleman without an allowance from his father or other visible means of support.

The Captain was provided with a wife Joan, very loqua-
cious and inclining to a scold, and yet extremely tender-
hearted, who, as she was everywhere well received in polite
families, would be able to give the readers some domestic
"particulars of an higher nature than can possibly reach
the ears of vulgar news-writers." The Captain himself,
who had resigned the sword for the pen, reserved as his
own particular field all affairs relating to the army. His
great club, which had "a very strange and almost incred-
ible quality" of falling, of its own accord, upon knaves of
every sort, he promised to keep chained over the mantel-
piece unless some uncommon vice or folly required that it
be taken down; and the ladies were assured that in their
presence the magic club rarely made any threatening movements of its own volition, either because they were all

virtuous or because it had acquired, by long association, the gallant behaviour that characterized the owner. The Captain further announced that at times he would erect a Court of Judicature, with himself as sole judge, before whom might be summoned, tried, and sentenced grave offenders whom the imperfect laws of the kingdom never reach. There was to be no capital punishment, but he intended so to deal with the guilty that they would be willing to hang themselves. Such punishments as should be necessary were to be executed on the stage of Drury Lane theatre "between the second and third music." This would enable people of fashion, who are great lovers of executions, to view the spectacle at their ease, and would also draw "larger audiences, than at present frequent our theatres."

These imaginary Vinegars, in line with Steele's imaginary Bickerstaffs in "The Tatler," formed a pleasant device for multiplying the very few writers of "The Champion"—Fielding, Ralph, and stray correspondents, with perhaps an occasional contribution from Lyttelton or another light of the Opposition. A typical number of the paper consisted of a leader (or two or three shorter pieces taking its place), often a literary article, home and foreign news, a "Journal of the War," and advertisements. Sometimes the foreign news was burlesqued under the head of "Political Amusements"; and the department of "Home News" usually contained one or more hits at Walpole and his "Gazetteer." Occasionally appeared a list of "Rumours," followed by lists of the "Married" and of the "Dead," concluding with "Puffs" on the living extracted from other newspapers. The share that Fielding had in this entertaining medley has never been critically determined. Murphy thought the problem impossible of solution, and Fielding's recent biographer, Miss Godden, seems to agree with him. But Professor Wells has shown that the

NUMB. 91.

THE CHAMPION;
OR, THE EVENING ADVERTISER.

By Capt. HERCULES VINEGAR, *of Pall-mall.*

THURSDAY, JUNE 12, 1740.

(*To be continued every* Tuesday, Thursday, *and* Saturday *Evening.*)

Per varios Casus, per tot Discrimina Rerum.
VIRG.

WHEN first I communicated my Design of taking up the Pen to my Bookseller, who is a Man of much Knowledge in his Profession, he shook his Head, and answer'd me, *Ah! Sir, there are a great many Papers in the World already.* He is a close Person, and of very few Words: For which Reason, all who know him catch eagerly hold of every Thing he delivers, which, as it is often as obscure, so we treat it with the Reverence of an Oracle.

In the same Manner I behaved to him on this Occasion, I ask'd him " If he thought there was " any extraordinary Merit in any, he answer'd, " *No.* Do you imagine it impossible to excel " them? *No.* Is there so much Weight in Pre- " possession and Favour? And are some of them " so well establish'd in the Opinions of the Peo- " ple? *You have it.*"

Indeed, I have had Reason to admire the Sagacity of his Observation; for we were a long Time in the World before we were taken much Notice of, and the *London and General Evening Post,* two Papers of most extraordinary Merit, were read in many Coffee-Houses where the *Champion's* Name was never heard of.

However, notwithstanding this Prejudice, and notwithstanding an Opposition which was carried on in the most unprecedented, and by the meanest Methods, such as desiring Coffee-Houses not to take our Paper in, *dealing with* Hawkers not to spread it through the Town, and if asked, to deny there was any such Paper extant, of which we have many Proofs, with many other excellent Devices known only to the Adepts of the present Age; notwithstanding all these, we have at length arrived at a Success and Reputation which may justly make us vain, and which (after returning Thanks to our Readers for it) we do assure them we shall endeavour more and more to deserve.

When I look back on the Precipice of Oblivion (if I may so call it) whence this Paper so narrowly escaped, (our little Stock being at one Time almost exhausted) I must own myself in a more than ordinary Manner elated with my present good Fortune: For besides the Discouragements I have before-mention'd, the Difficulty of pleasing all Palates will be easily acknowledged, not only by those who have attempted it, but even by such sensible Persons as will give themselves the Trouble of reflecting on it: For first a cursed Spirit of Indignation, rages against every Writer before he hath established a Reputation. Another Obstruction is, the great Difference of Opinion concerning all Works of Wit and Humour, so that there is nothing truer than Shakespear's Observation in his *Love's Labours lost,*

*A Jest's Prosperity lies in the Ear
Of him that hears it, never in the Tongue
Of him that makes it.*

Thus we often hear one Gentleman expressing himself with a most *exquisitely good, most inimitably fine indeed;* and another presently after, laying down the same Treatise, and crying out *what cursed Stuff is here?* Thus the Audience at a Play-House are sometimes divided about what is *low* *, and the Criticks on *Homer, Virgil, Milton,* and *Pope,* have been at variance concerning what is *high.* Thus the Characters of several Authors, and of particular Works, have been controverted thro' Ages, and I have heard the divine Translation of the Iliad which I have lately with *no Disadvantage to the Translator* COMPARED with the Original, censured for too much Deviation, by some good Scholars, whose Knowledge in the *Greek* hath been unluckily a little deficient in the Alphabet of that Language.

But the greatest Difficulty with which a miscellaneous Author must struggle, is the Variety of his Reader's Palates. If he is serious, one half of his Readers cry he is dull; if ludicrous, the other half call him ridiculous, foolish, farcical.

All Persons moreover are desirous to be entertained with what they are most conversant with and best understand. I believe, I have, since my undertaking this Province, received Advertisements from every Order and Profession among us, requesting me for not taking more Notice of them. From all which, I have the Pleasure of observing the particular Bent which at present governs among them. Thus the Ladies, who reprehend me for not sufficiently inspecting the several Assemblies (most of them at present *sub Dio*) of the polite Persons of both Sexes; all wonder I do not censure the Men for making so much Noise about a Woman, who hath no other Charms, at first Sight, than the most beautiful Face, and one of the finest Persons in the World. Letters in a military Stile and Spelling accuse me of taking too little Notice of Cockades, Lace and Hats and Feathers. Several Intimations are likewise received, (from what Corner I know not, nor from a religious one, for there is not a Word of Religion mention'd) that the Land-Tax falls too heavy on the Clergy. Nor can I omit a Letter from a Country Gentleman, who sends me word he is busy in making Interest against the next Election, and wonders, I never take an Opportunity of informing the Country of the Number of Employments in the Court and Revenue, with their several Sallaries and Perquisites,

I have two Epistles by the same Post, the one dated from *Oxford,* the other from *Cambridge,* which when I opened and saw the Word Greek written in a very distinguishable Manner, I apprehended I should be desired to insert frequent Quotations from that Language; but to my Surprize, I was only earnestly intreated never to put any

* A Word much used in the Theatre, but of such uncertain Signification, that I could never understand the Meaning of it.

[Price THREE HALF-PENCE.]

Greek Words in my Paper without translating them, kindly assuring me in a Postscript, which I had well nigh overlooked, that those learned Bodies did not require me to sacrifice my whole Paper to their Use.

If my Reader already should think me exposed to some Hardship, what Opinion will he be of, when he considers that as all Professions seldom talk, so they seldom desire to hear of any Thing besides themselves; and at the same time are all so involved in Mysteries, that what we write of each particular Profession will be unintelligible to all besides the Members thereof. For Instance in Physick † " The Solids (which concentred, " consolidated and condensed, into their real " or first Formation Star, would not equal a " Grain of Sand) are permanent and durable, " and continue pretty much in that State of " Elasticity and Firmness, they were first cre- " ated with; and they are strong or weak, small or " coarse, firm or lax, loose or elastick, blunt or " sharp, as they were first made by the Supreme " Artificer, or are altered somewhat by the ori- " ginal Dyscrasy or Distempers of the Parents. " (The Mother can only mend or spoil their Jui- " ces, which might be easily perfected by long " continuance of a sweetening Diet, during their " younger Days; which if they survive, they ge- " nerally grow stronger as they grow older, be- " come the Genii and the Governors of the World; " because the Solids thus purified come from the " Father alone) and continue much the same till " the Time of their Duration on this Globe, ex- " cept so far as the small temporary and toge- " ther Alteration that Diet, Exercise, or Evacuations, " or mild, ponderous Medicines, long continued, " may make on them, &c." ‡ Now all this may be Sense for ought I know, but it can be only understood by a Physician. Again, in natural for as our Author calls it *conjectural*) Philosophy, " This spiritual animal Body, at first divinely " organized, may be rolled up, folded up there " and contracted in this present State of this Dura- " tion, into an infinitely small *Punctum Saliens* " into a *Miniature of a Miniature,* to *Infinitum* " lodged in the Loins of the Male of all Animals, " (so it is highly probable the Female was but a " SECONDARY INTENTION OR A BUTTRESS TO A " FALLING EDIFICE) and proceeding in a diverging Series, and progressive Gradation, that " in due Time it may be fit to be nourished, and " increased by the Juices of the proper Female, " and thereby enabled to bear the Coarseness and " Injuries of this ruinous Globe, and gross ele- " ment to which it is condemned for a certain " Period." ‖ This is a Tid-bit for a philosophical Palate only. I could give other Instances in other Sciences; but I believe it already appears,

† This is not the Beginning of the Sentence, nor can we well tell which it, there being almost two Pages from one full Stop to the next.
‡ Cheyney's practical Essay on the Regimen of Diet, Page.
‖ Id. Philos. Conject. on the original animal Body. Pag. 7.

A Title Page of the Champion

longer essays by Fielding may be easily picked out. Beginning with the fifth number, nearly all the leading articles and some others were marked at the end, partly that each author might claim his own, and partly that he might not be held responsible for the opinions of another. In June, 1741, these articles, with some miscellaneous paragraphs, down to June 19 of the previous year, were collected in two volumes; and the publisher's "Advertisement" expressly stated that "all papers distinguish'd with a C or an L" were the work of one hand; while those having double stars or signed "Lilbourne" came from another. It was added that this other hand was also responsible, except in a few instances, for the "Index to the Times" (the head under which were reprinted selections from the home and foreign news and rumours); but it was not said to whose account should be placed the many other miscellaneous paragraphs. Beyond question the signatures of C and L were Fielding's; and the two stars and Lilbourne belonged to Ralph. With regard to these distinguishing marks, Fielding said playfully, in the issue for March 1, 1740, that he had adorned his papers with a capital letter at the end, as well as with a motto at the beginning, in order to pacify his bookseller, who wished "The Champion" to look like "The Spectator." And curiously enough, it has been pointed out by Professor Wells that C and L are the first letters of Clio, the word from which Addison took by turn a capital letter for his four signatures in "The Spectator."* Fielding employed C down to March 4, 1740, when he moved on to L; and after that either was used, perhaps indifferently. In course of time he might have gone on to I and O. The two volumes of "The Champion," as republished, contain ninety-four issues. Sixty-two articles and two paragraphs—one an Index to the Times, and the

* J. E. Wells, "Englische Studien," 46 Band, 3 Heft, pp. 355-366; and "Modern Language Review," July, 1912.

other a letter from Adam Double on the disenchantment of marriage—are intended to be covered by Fielding's marks. Forty-eight have the C, and sixteen have the L.

But these sixty-four articles and paragraphs (all of which except the paper of December 8, followed by Adam Double on his wife, have now been reprinted in the Henley edition of Fielding) by no means comprise his whole contribution to "The Champion" during this period. For various reasons Fielding left several long articles and many shorter ones without his usual marks. Until Ralph appeared with a leader in the fifth number, none, of course, was necessary; while in other places "Captain Hercules Vinegar" or another fictitious name served Fielding's purpose and at the same time gave the impression of a variety of contributors. Paragraphs here and there were not of sufficient importance to receive a signature; and withal there was the usual carelessness on the part of the printer as well as of Fielding himself. No one can doubt, for example, that the unsigned essays in the first four issues were written by Fielding. They are all in his style; they have the *hath* and they contain quotations—some of them used elsewhere —from his favourite authors. Just as clearly Fielding's are the account given by Captain Vinegar of his magic club (December 8); a letter to "the ten thousand Authors of the Gazetteer" (December 25); Timothy Drugget on his talkative wife (January 12); a "literary article" on the occasional essay (February 9); a tribute to the character and dramatic talent of Lillo in the Index to the Times (February 26); the "proposals" of Nicodemus Bungle for "a course of lectures on the elements of Prime-Ministry," together with the comment thereon (February 28); an address to "all the ideots of Great Britain" (March 1); a series of letters to Captain Hercules Vinegar in criticism and approval of "The Champion" (March 25); an attack on Colley Cibber (May 6); a letter to Mrs. Joan Vinegar from

A Fourth Page of the Champion

Belinda on the rights of women, along with the "literary article" on Gravelot's prints (May 15); a letter from H. Bottle on the delights of drinking (May 20); and the parallel between Walpole and a quack doctor (June 17). Beyond this the list may be safely extended somewhat; but increasing caution is necessary as one proceeds, since Ralph adopted more and more the technique of Fielding's style. Now and then a humorous advertisement also bears Fielding's unmistakable stamp.

. If we take these assignments as approximately correct, Fielding contributed above seventy long essays to "The Champion" during the first seven months of its existence. Nor is this the whole tally. Minor pieces from Fielding's pen were not included in the two-volume collection. How many they comprise cannot be determined, for no complete file of the original numbers of "The Champion" has yet been discovered. But in such stray issues as may be found, there are several contributions by Fielding which have never been reprinted. Obviously, for example, a full statement of the policy of his periodical, which appeared in the number for April 10, 1740, was written by Fielding. Again, on May 27, he put into the form of a letter to Captain Vinegar some conjectures about the meaning of "that little picture" at the head of his paper, and about the personality of the editor—"a tall man with a grey coat and a long chin." And along with this fanciful communication, he published verses "writ some years ago by one of the family of the Vinegars, on a half-penny; which a young lady gave to a beggar, and the author purchased at the price of half a crown." This poem, having then only sixteen lines, was afterwards reworked, with additions and altered phrasing, for the "Miscellanies" of 1743. The more we learn of "The Champion," the more dominant seems Fielding's hand.

Signs of his waning interest in the periodical, however, began to appear in the spring of 1740, due doubtless to a closer attention to his legal studies. On June 20, he was called to the bar at the Middle Temple. Henceforth the barrister became known, especially by the wits, as "Counsellor Fielding." The Benchers of the Inn assigned for his use, during "the term of his natural life," chambers at No. 4 Pump Court, up three pair of stairs; but on the twenty-eighth of the following November he surrendered these chambers overlooking Brick Court with its beautiful buildings. In the meantime, he attended the summer session of the Dorset assizes, as we know from a brief correspondence with his uncle Davidge Gould over a question which still remained unsettled concerning the conveyance of the East Stour property to Robert Stillingfleet. Fielding wrote to his uncle:

"Basingstoke 15 July 1740

"Dear S^r

I beg y^o would without fail send me the Conveyance I mentioned to y^o to Dorsetshire Assizes, as I am advised my Success will greatly depend thereon, whatever y^o please to mention in a Letter to me by the Messenger I will satisfie him and am

S^r

y^r affect Nephew
and obliged humble Servt
HEN: FFIELDING

"To Davidge Gould Esqre
   at Sharpham Park
      by Bridgewater Bagg
         Somerset"

His uncle replied:

"D^r S^r

I have sent the deeds as you desired they have received Damage by the Water, that it may be difficult to read some part of y^m but I believe there's nothing in them that will be

serviceable to y^r point you told me was in question. I have
cursorily cast my Eye on all the other old deeds & I can
see nothing of use to you—I have attested copy's of them
all. However accord^s to your Letter I thought myself
obliged to send to you. Mr Blake requires to Guineas for
his trouble and Expenses if he is detain'd at Dorchester till
Saturday, but if dispatch'd Fryday one Guinea & Half,
but you may agree with him as cheap as you can—I am

y^r affection^t Humble Servt

DAVIDGE GOULD

"Sharpham: park
　July 23^d 1740.
"To Henry Fielding at Dorchester
　　　　Dorsetshr"*

With this case of his own, Fielding began his career on
the Western Circuit. Pratt, who rode the same circuit, may
have been in his company.

Despite the demands of his profession, Fielding continued to guide "The Champion," even when out of town.
For several numbers appearing while he was in the West,
he must have left with Ralph the satirical voyages of Job
Vinegar, an ancestor of Captain Hercules Vinegar, which
were doled out piecemeal to the public; and altogether,
during the three months beginning with June 21, no less
than a score of long articles appeared in the periodical
with Fielding's specific marks. These and subsequent
papers have never been assembled. Perhaps they have not
quite the interest of the earlier ones, though many of those
which I have seen deserve preservation for their humour.
But as time went on, Fielding wrote less and less for "The
Champion" and in June, 1741, ceased altogether.† On the

---

* These two letters, copied by permission of their former owner, were sold
at Sotheby's, July 20, 1916.

† Preface to the "Miscellanies," 1743, xxxiv and xxxvi.

twenty-ninth of that month, the partners of "The Champion" met at Feathers Tavern, and sold at auction among themselves their reprint of the articles covering the first seven months. The purchaser was Henry Chappelle, who paid the partners £110 for an edition of a thousand copies. Fielding, it is clear from the minutes of the meeting, disapproved of the sale, either because he thought the price too low or because he thought the reprint inadvisable; and thereupon withdrew from the business as well as the literary management of "The Champion," flatly refusing to write any longer for it or to have anything more to do with it. In the following March the partners assigned his "two sixteenth shares" to Ralph, who had already succeeded him as chief writer and sole editorial manager. From Ralph came the fierce denunciation of Walpole that was prefixed to the two-volume reprint as an address to the Members of the new Parliament. In his hands "The Champion" was immediately transformed into a rather dull and narrow political organ, which nevertheless survived for several years under the title of "The British Champion; or, The Impartial Advertiser."

II

While Fielding conducted "The Champion," it was the scene of a merry warfare with his old antagonisms—Walpole, the Cibbers, the stage, the press, lotteries, and quacks of all kinds. A periodical such as he conceived it—a cross between "The Tatler" or "The Spectator" and "The Grub-street Journal"—gave him, of course, much wider sweep for social satire than was afforded by the drama. In his plays he could but strike a blow and pass on; in his "leaders," he could lay about with his club on all sides, and return again to the attack whenever he saw an exposed place which had not been already hit. Everywhere Captain Hercules Vinegar was recognized as Pasquin fighting in a larger ring. A facetious gentleman in one of the coffee-houses, while reading a copy kept exclaiming, as overheard by Fielding: "Ha! ha! old Truepenny!—art thou there-abouts, my boy? . . . Well said, well done, old boy!"*

Many difficulties, however, were encountered at first in getting "The Champion" before the public. The whole story is lightly told by Fielding here and there in various numbers. Publishers of other newspapers tried to per-suade the coffee-houses not to take it in; booksellers, in league with them, refused to put it on sale; hawkers were paid not to spread it about town and to say, when inquiry was made for it, that they had never heard of any paper bearing its name; and the Government would not permit it to pass through the post-office; so it had to go into the country by stage or wagon. More than once "The Cham-pion" was declared "defunct," "dead." Then, when it began to make its way, other newspapers of Fielding's own party in town and country enriched themselves with its spoils; and to prevent these piracies, so far as they con-cerned news-items, Fielding was compelled to alter the time of publication from morning to evening. On April 10, 1740, his periodical appeared with the title "The Cham-pion; or, Evening Advertiser." Huggonson's name as printer now disappeared; and an announcement was made that hereafter the paper would be distributed by James Graham, bookseller, under the Inner Temple Gate, where all advertisements and letters to the author were to be left.

Long before this, Captain Hercules Vinegar changed his imaginary residence from Hockley in the Hole to Pall Mall, in order to be, he said, nearer the Court, and also to quiet the remonstrances of many subscribers who were averse to reading articles emanating from a prize-ring. So there-after the title-page of "The Champion" gave the Captain lodgings in Pall Mall. At length all obstacles were over-

* "The Champion," Sept. 16, 1740 (not reprinted).

come. Patrons of coffee-houses demanded the new periodical; booksellers and hawkers found it to their advantage to take copies, and it reached the country despite "the clerks of the road." Two months after it had been turned into an evening newspaper, Fielding announced that "The Champion" had arrived at a success which made the editors "vain." He said nothing precise of its circulation; but if it sold two or three thousand copies at an issue, it did well and brought to Fielding several guineas a week. Already "The Champion" was being extensively quoted in the magazines; and a periodical much like it in appearance, called "The Patriot," was established at Edinburgh, mainly for the purpose of reprinting its articles, with or without credit, as the case might be, for a Scotch audience. The two little volumes of "The Champion," which appeared in London, were reissued in 1743 with an index and a new title-page.

Fielding professed to have no skill in politics. "It is true," he said, "I have read most of the ancient and modern historians, as well as the most celebrated writers on government, but alas, *non omnia possumus omnes*. . . . A man must be born a politician as well as a poet, or else *omnis effusus labor*. Mr. Bayle tells us that some of the Rabbi's, who agree that Adam, at his creation, contained all the other learning and knowledge of the world, assert that he was no politician. I know some have thought that Eve was the first vers'd in this art, which she is thought to have learnt of the devil; an opinion confirm'd by Dr. South. . . ."* So it was Ralph that wrote most of the articles in "The Champion" dealing with the measures before Parliament, with ministerial appointments, and with the movements of the army and navy. Perhaps from Ralph rather than Fielding would come an announcement like the following:

"The Right Hon. Sir Robert Walpole, being *Chancellor*

* Feb. 14, 1740.

of the Exchequer, the Right Hon. Lord Walpole, *Auditor,* and Edward Walpole, Esq; *Clerk of the Pells;* 'tis presum'd, the *Teller's Place,* lately vacated by the Death of Lord *Onslow,* will be given to *Horatio Walpole,* Esq; Jun. that the *Virtues,* not the *Iniquities* of the *Father,* may be rewarded in the Children to the *Third* and *Fourth Generation.''*

Likewise came from Ralph the continuous hounding of the Ministry for want of vigour in prosecuting the war with Spain—verses and paragraphs on one Forage, who, forced to arm, delays the fight, and ruins his country, as if he were in league with the enemy. When the news reached England that Admiral Vernon, who belonged to the anti-ministerial party, had captured Porto Bello with only six ships, that exploit was hailed as showing what could be done by a man whose heart was in the fight. Walpole, it was intimated, held aloof from the public rejoicing over the victory. ''The said great Colossus,'' runs a paragraph, ''being ask'd by a gentleman of distinction, whether he was pleas'd with Admiral Vernon's conduct, and answering in the affirmative, the querist reply'd, 'Then there is not a man in England dissatisfied.' '' When great disasters subsequently befell the English fleet, they were all laid to Walpole. Throughout this period ''The Champion'' maintained its satirical ''Journal of the War,'' in which was given a list of the merchant ships ''taken by the Spaniards'' and directly beneath it another list enumerating the ships ''taken by the English.'' In the first list there were usually several captured immediately off the coast of England; while the second list was almost always comprised in the word NONE, written in large capitals.

Though Fielding directed these detailed attacks upon Walpole, his own articles proceeded, like his political plays, more by allegory, irony, and ridicule. He adopted the in-

* June 14, 1740.

263

direct method, suppressing names, he said, because of his fears of the pillory—because there was no part of his body for which he had greater respect than his ears. He asks why "a certain great man," whose policies are set forth and praised by paid scribblers, has been overlooked by the real men of letters—by Pope, Swift, Young, Gay, Thomson.* He expatiates on the ingredients of the successful politician, which are found to be deceit, impudence, and ingratitude; and in another place describes the salient qualities of "Jonathan Wild and his confederates," leaving it to the reader to fit the parallel. Similarly he has, much like Sterne after him, a whimsical disquisition on good and bad names, in which it is discovered that Robert was anciently borne by "the leader of a gang of thieves" infesting England, and that the name had since become general for liar, robber, and plunderer. He retells the story of the wolf in sheep's clothing, with its obvious application, or relates the history of wicked advisers who, without birth, virtues, or abilities to recommend them, have by some accident gained an ascendancy over kings to the great harm of the nation. The evil days are approaching when the people will turn to God as their sole protector, and add to the litany: "From the Prime Minister, good Lord deliver us."

The long "Voyages of Mr. Job Vinegar," running through many numbers, carry the reader to the land of the "Ptfghsiumgski, or the Inconstants," where the chief deity of the people is Money, and the high priest of the cult a certain Humclum, who tries to get all the money into his own pocket or into the pockets of his friends. Humclum himself is advanced to a sort of god worshipped by the Humclumists, whose creed, given in detail, ends with "The wretch that licks thy feet, thou liftest up, and the Great Man who scorns thee hast thou cast down. . . . There will

---

* Sept. 6, 1740 (not reprinted).

never be any thing like thee, O Humclum!''* In a vision imitated from Lucian, ''a very fat gentleman'' on the road to Hades attempts, when reaching the ferry, to pass Charon and Mercury with a bank-bill in his fist wherewith to bribe the devil. A day of solemn fast, set apart by the King to implore the blessings of heaven upon the fleet, becomes the occasion for an essay on the custom among ancient nations, in times of great public calamities, of asking for a voluntary victim to appease the wrath of the gods. Wherefore if any of his Majesty's subjects is convinced in his own mind ''that he ought to be hanged, tho' the law cannot reach him,'' he should now step forth and pass under the gallows with the glad heart of a Horatius Cocles, ''lest his country should pay the forfeiture of his crime.'' ''It is not being hanged, but deserving to be hanged,'' remarks Fielding, ''that is infamous.'' Indeed,

> . . . What a pity is it
> We can be hanged but once to serve our country?

There were times when Fielding dropped his vein of wit and spoke out in full seriousness. Such was his stirring address to the citizens of London in ''The Champion'' of December 18, 1739, just before a municipal election which engaged Walpole and his opponents in a bitter struggle. Fielding exhorted the citizens not to be bribed and drunk and laughed out of their integrity by a set of rascals. The Opposition won the election; and Fielding overwhelmed ''the glorious city of London'' with praise for defying, to its eternal renown, ''the devil and all his works.'' Becoming bolder in the use of Walpole's name as the Prime Minister's resignation seemed imminent, he printed, evidently writing it himself, an illiterate letter to Sir Robert, purporting to come from his ''lovin cosen John W'llp'le,'' condemned to death and awaiting execution in Chelmsford

---

* June 28, 1740 (not reprinted).

jail. Both John and Robert, it is related, had set out in life
together and both were approaching similar ends. He
republished that old print of the Golden Rump which had
been put into circulation just before the Licensing Act, and
explained in detail the worship of the obscene monster. To
Fielding was attributed, though the pen was probably held
by another hand, a powerful arraignment of Walpole that
appeared under the signature of "B. T.," in "The Champion" for June 14, 1740, and was reprinted on the seventh
of the following October. The two parties were already
preparing for a general election, which was to take place the
next spring. "The Champion" looked forward to that election drawing near, as "a Tryal between the whole *Nation
Plaintiff*, and one *single Man Defendant*"; and prophesied,
what was to come true, that it would be the last hearing and
that the judgment then given would be without appeal.
Twenty-seven queries were put to the electors of Great
Britain, involving the conduct and measures of a Prime
Minister who had managed the affairs of state for the sole
benefit of himself, his relations, dependants, and satellites—
who, within a space of twenty years, had acquired, out of an
employment of five thousand pounds per annum, an estate
in land of ten thousand pounds a year besides spending
twenty thousand pounds annually and laying out two hundred and fifty thousand pounds in a house and gardens.
This and other scathing denunciations of Walpole put "The
Champion" in the forefront of the Opposition newspapers.

Upon Walpole's organ, "The Daily Gazetteer," fell the
burden of meeting the attacks of "The Champion." Its
principal writer—one of a "legion" which included Theophilus Cibber—signed himself "Ralph Freeman." Without much doubt, he was one Thomas Pitt alluded to in "Pasquin," who was then writing under the name of "Mr.
Osborne."* According to "The Champion," this man had

* E. Budgell, "The Bee," Feb. 3-10, 1733, p. 14.

formerly been arrested for "virulent libels" on the Walpole Government, and had afterwards changed his politics, becoming an advocate of the Minister, in order to escape with unmaimed body. Freeman was a master of vituperation. For a time he ignored "The Champion," but one sting after another—one or more in almost every issue—at length irritated him into reply. He could not forever remain silent while "The Champion" was calling him a dull and scurrilous fellow, a gnat, a garrulous old maid, a thing void of common sense, long since frightened out of the little wit he ever had, a political hack just learning to spell, who, when facts and rumours fail, flings about scandal "as a madman would firebrands, on all he meets." Such was the mouthpiece, if "The Champion" is to be believed, of the Administration. In this wretch lay its chief defence before the people.

Freeman retaliated in the same kind of abuse. One or both of the writers of "The Champion," it was asserted, had done their best to get on the staff of "The Gazetteer," but had been rejected as soon as their "character and morals were known." And there did actually appear in "The Gazetteer" articles and letters signed Hercules Vinegar, burlesquing Fielding's style and opinions.* There were also verses addressed to Fielding, epigrams upon him, and fictitious interviews at the Globe Tavern with the man who "scandal prints for bread." Over against Fielding's account of the Vinegars, Freeman set his own story of the family; which originated, he said, in Homer's Thersites and was now terminating in Captain Hercules, a quarrelsome fellow, who, after breaking heads in a country parish, had come up to London with the intention of turning solicitor, but all of a sudden took up his present occupation of mountebank, thinking that he might earn a living by bantering "the good people of Great Britain not only out of

* "The Daily Gazetteer," March 30, and Sept. 18, 1741.

their senses, but their affection to the best modell'd Constitution in the world, and obedience to the mildest Government that ever was.''* Especially was Freeman's ire aroused by the attack on Walpole repeated in ''The Champion'' of October 7, 1740. Two days later he came out with a terrible onslaught on Fielding as a small cur yelping in favour of faction. Fielding was thoroughly incompetent, Freeman declared, to discuss the great questions of state then before the people—the use or abuse of power, the conduct of the war, or the freedom and independence of Parliaments. For he was merely ''a little, low creature, whose utmost extent of politicks has been employ'd in over reaching managers of play-houses and actors''; and in this low sphere even, he had not succeeded as a politician, but had brought upon himself the contempt of all who had ever dealt with him. This Hercules Vinegar, who poses as the champion of virtue, honour, and patriotism, is ''a contemptible, abject thing,'' whose private character cannot be touched upon lest the rehearsal make the reader blush with shame. Like the bear-garden hero whom he assumes, he drinks with anybody. He is ''a hireling, and a mercenary,'' ''a parrot'' taught to utter the resentments of his party. Some years ago, his satirical plays against ''all government and all religion whatever'' resulted in a restraint upon the stage; and his present conduct, he is warned, will surely lead to a curtailment of the freedom of the press. Such is the fellow, when his masque is off, who presumes to address the nation, to set forth its wrongs, and ''to harangue like a Demosthenes.''

The arraignment of the Ministry in ''The Champion'' of October 7, however, could not be dismissed by personal abuse or by inquiring what right its author had to set himself up as ''the attorney-general'' of his party. The

* ''The Daily Gazetteer,'' July 24, 1740. Also July 4, 29, 30, Sept. 3, 12, 17, 19, Oct. 9, 17, 20, 1740; July 31, Aug. 5, 7, Sept. 2, 7, 23, 30, Oct. 30, 1741.

twenty-seven articles in the indictment demanded an answer; and in order to answer them, it was necessary to reprint them in "The Gazetteer." Fielding was amused to see the editor in a dilemma. In Freeman's view, "The Champion" had "outstripped all vehicles of sedition in the service of the Opposition." Other writers had hinted at similar accusations against an "Honourable Person," whispering them about; but only "Counsellor F—d—g" had ventured to put them into print, leaving no doubt as to what the leaders of the Opposition were secretly aiming at—which was nothing short of "a thorough change and a general censure of his Majesty's Administration and its measures." On October 16, 1740, Fielding returned Freeman's fire by advertising for speedy publication:

PROPOSALS for printing, by Subscription, an Apology for the Life, Actions, and Writings of RALPH FREEMAN, alias, COURT EVIL, Esq; containing an authentic History of the several wonderful Stages, thro' which he *hath* passed in the World; together with the successful Progress of *Corruption, Baseness,* and *Treachery,* during his Time.

Written by HIMSELF.

In a mock account of what the reader might expect to find in the Apology, Fielding enumerated eight heads, the first three of which he felt constrained not to enlarge upon since they were "entirely of a private nature." Still, enough was left to satisfy the curious; for the book would tell how Freeman wrote "a most ingenious comedy, called, *The Old Maid,*" which the capricious Mr. Rich rejected; how, "all other trades failing," he turned political writer to the surprise of his acquaintances, who apprehended that he had not yet learned to spell; how at first he wrote upon the "miserable state of the nation," and was quieted by his Majesty's messengers, who took possession of his "precious carcase"; how he thereupon deserted his party out of fear, and has since set up "a splendid equipage. . . . To which will be added, a penitential Hymn upon his *late Mockings and Revilings of the* MAN, *whom the* KING *delighteth to honour;* and a new *Te Deum,* upon his happy Conversion to the *ministerial Faith.* To be sung by the Charity Children of St. James's Parish, and accompanied with the Organ, by *Himself.*"

It is unnecessary to descend further into the political billingsgate of Freeman *versus* Fielding. "The Champion's" bill of complaint against the entire policy of Walpole, foreign and domestic, by whomsoever drawn up, was the Opposition's announcement of open and direct war to the finish. During the following winter similar assaults were made in Parliament by Argyle, Carteret, and Sandys, culminating in February, when a motion was introduced into the Lords and Commons for an address to the Crown that Walpole be removed from "his Majesty's presence and counsels for ever." Though the motion was lost, the Ministry went down to defeat in the next Parliament, and Walpole was forced to resign. While the ministerial party was jubilant over the failure of the motion, Fielding figured in two political prints quickly placed on sale by the artists of Grub Street. The first of them, appearing in February, was called "The Political Libertines, or Motion upon Motion." The leaders of the Opposition, having been defeated, are setting out in a coach from Westminster Hall for Yorkshire, with the Duke of Argyle in the forebox, and the lean Lyttelton following on Rosinante. In the foreground stands Pulteney piercing with drawn sword, held in his right hand, the last number of "The Gazetteer," and leading with his left hand the editors of "The Champion" and "Common Sense" by a string attached to their noses. Fielding, who is celebrated in doggerel verses beneath as "the Champion of the agee," to rhyme with "Being witty, wise, and sagee," is dressed in barrister's wig and gown, and holds in his right hand a scroll inscribed *Pasquin.* A gentleman in black remarks to him: "Z—ns it's over."

The second print, issued in March, depicts the burial of "faction," which had "died of a disappointment" on February 13. A long funeral procession is led by five standard-bearers representing the five anti-ministerial newspapers and holding aloft inscribed banners. Then comes the bier on which lies concealed the dead motion, followed by a line of mourners bringing up the rear and uttering their grief in conventional phrases. By the tomb of faction, where long ago were buried Jack Cade and Wat Tyler, stand, awaiting the procession, Sandys, who had introduced the motion in the Commons, and the poet Glover, who had taken an active part against the ministerial candidates in the recent municipal election. Sandys is pronouncing a funeral oration, and Glover is reciting an elegy. In front, Walpole and a group of his followers are holding their sides with laughter at the motion-makers, towards whom a merry devil is advancing with the hangman's rope noosed for immediate use. Among the standard-bearers—his banner emblazoned with the club of Captain Hercules Vinegar—Fielding occupies the third place. It is a rather tall and vigorous figure with prominent nose and chin, in harmony with his description of himself in "The Champion."*

Next to the Prime Minister, the poet laureate engaged Fielding's attention most. Early in April, 1740, Cibber published an autobiography, giving it the absurd title of "An Apology for the Life of Mr. Colley Cibber, Comedian, and late Patentee of the Theatre Royal . . . Written by Himself"; hence the point in Fielding's announcement, as we have just seen, of "An Apology for the Life, Actions, and Writings of Ralph Freeman." Both men had lived

* The two cartoons are reproduced by Miss Godden from copies in the print room of the British Museum. See Stephens and Hawkins, "Catalogue of Prints and Drawings in the British Museum," Nos. 2479 and 2487.

lives for which they owed an apology to the public. Cibber's book is still interesting, and most valuable for details concerning the stage. But it is a formless narrative, beginning and ending nowhere, verbose, and at times running into nonsense through a strange and forced usage of words and phrases which the author thought elegant or sublime. At many points, book and author exposed themselves to ridicule. The old quarrel between Cibber and Fielding had never been patched up. Fielding's last word on Cibber, except for an incidental thrust here and there, had been the scene in "The Historical Register," where the actor and stage-manager make over Shakespeare's "King John" into a better play. In his "Apology," Cibber had his revenge. He there referred to Fielding under various opprobrious names, but most exasperatingly as "a broken wit," who a few years ago collected a company of comedians "who for some time acted plays in the Haymarket." These pieces were mostly "frank and free farces that seem'd to knock all distinctions of mankind on the head; religion, laws, government, priests, judges, and ministers, were all laid flat at the feet of this Herculean satyrist." Cibber refrained, he said, from describing these farces further and from giving their titles or the real name of the author, lest by mentioning them in his book he should cause them to be remembered. The inference was that "Pasquin," even the memory of it, was already dead, while the "Apology" would be immortal.*

It is not pleasant to be called "a broken wit" if the descriptive title have a grain of truth in it. Still, Fielding was as little piqued by the appellation as a man could be. In any case the "Apology" would not have escaped his ridicule. Indeed, he condemned the book of the laureate before he could have read much of it, remarking equivocally that, "however the illustrious person may wind up as a

* "Apology," edited by R. W. Lowe, 1889, I, 285-288.

man, he will certainly end as an author with a very bad Life." This was anticipatory of the sport that was to begin in "The Champion" as soon as the "Apology" was generally in the hands of the public. Fielding announced for the next issue of his paper the performance of "a farce call'd the *Apology*"; which proved to be a brief sketch of Cibber's life made up of absurd shreds from the autobiography. The author of the "Apology," instead of being *born,* as one usually writes, in 1671, "made his first forward step into nature" during that year, so that "the fate of King James, the Prince of Orange, and himself, were all at once on the anvil." In course of time he fell in love with "the Emanation of Beauty," etc. Fielding also picked out pages of detached sentences and phrases which failed in grammar or meant nothing, such as the use of "shine" and "regret" as transitive verbs and of the noun "adept" in the sense of "novice." In one mood, he thought the "Apology" worth translating into English; in another he proved against cavillers that, if logic is to be trusted, it was already English and so stood in no need of translation. "Whatever book," he said, "is writ in no other language, is writ in English. This book is writ in no other language, *ergo,* it is writ in English."*

In continuation of the jest, Fielding summoned, on May 17, 1740, Cibber before the Court of Censorial Enquiry set up by Captain Hercules Vinegar, on an indictment for murdering the English Language. This number of "The Champion" became so popular that the pirate Curll two months later republished it with other Cibberian passages, in a pamphlet called "The Tryal of Colley Cibber, Comedian . . . for writing a Book intitled An Apology for his Life . . . being a thorough Examination thereof; wherein he is proved guilty of High Crimes and Misdemeanors against the English Language, and in characterising many

* See numbers for April 1, 15, 22, 29, May 3, 6, 10, 17, 24, 1740.

273

Persons of Distinction.'' It was dedicated by its compiler, ''T. Johnson,'' to Ralph, and it ended with an ''advertisement'' in which Fielding (who had married ''one of the pretty Miss Cradocks of Salisbury'') was assured of being mentioned in capitals in the third edition—the second was already out—of the ''Apology,'' provided he would acknowledge himself the author of ''eighteen strange things called tragical comedies and comical tragedies'' lately advertised by his publisher.

It was a busy day when Cibber appeared before Captain Hercules Vinegar. A complaint had been lodged against ''A. P. Esq.'' (short for Alexander Pope, Esq.) for abetting the rogueries of ''one Forage, alias Brass, alias his Honour'' (otherwise Walpole), because, though knowing them, he had not exposed them. On the plea of Pope's lawyer that no one could be punished in one court for not doing the thing for which he would surely be punished in another, the prisoner was discharged; and Mr. Pope's conduct of remaining silent, in view of the Ministry's control of the higher courts, was fully approved. Brass himself was also brought to the bar; but, as the indictment against him was very long, reaching indeed ''from Westminster to the Tower,'' the Captain deferred the hearing until the next day. As an incident of the proceedings, T. P. (Theophilus Pistol alias Theophilus Cibber) was called to the bar, but the jailer announced that he could not produce the prisoner, for he had been ''that morning taken out of his custody by the officer of another court.'' Young Cibber was then suing a country gentleman for detaining his wife.

As soon as other business was out of the way, Colley Cibber stepped to the bar and was asked to hold up his right hand. The prisoner hesitated, uncertain which was his right hand. The ludicrous incident might be interpreted in two ways. The actor was, as the town all knew, left-handed; and the inability to distinguish between the right and the left hand is, according to the proverb, the mark of a fool. The equivocation was left to the reader's sense of humour. It was brought out by various witnesses who had seen Cibber composing his book or who had read it, that the defendant had made a grievous assault upon the English language with a goose quill, but that he had not actually murdered it. The prisoner himself, on addressing the court, pleaded that such wounds as he may have inflicted proceeded not from enmity but from accident only; and called a critic to show that the real murderer was Dr. George Cheyne, physician of Bath, whose ''Philosophical Conjectures'' was simply a congregation of sentences without any meaning at all; whereas in Cibber's ''Apology'' for his life the meaning was merely obscured by slips in grammar and orthography. The Court, after hearing a passage read from Dr. Cheyne's late book, ''ordered it to be immediately taken into custody,'' and pronounced sentence upon Cibber. From all that he had heard, the Captain said, in summing up the evidence, the ''Apology'' was ''a very entertaining'' book, and ''several parts of it were really excellent.'' The trouble was that the author's warmth of imagination often led him into nonsense, while at the same time the coldness of his principles led him into the expression of political opinions that could never come from the head or heart of a true Englishman. At this point, the Captain's wife Joan whispered into her husband's ear that Cibber had promised to advertise the ''Apology'' twice in ''The Champion''; whereupon the Captain, ''not from the motive of a bribe, but of the prisoner's submission to his correction,'' directed the jury to bring in a verdict of chance-medley.

As if in accordance with the author's promise, two advertisements of the ''Apology'' appeared in ''The Champion.'' Were they genuine or were they inserted by Fielding to complete the jest? They were notices of the second edition at five shillings; the first had cost a guinea, which Fielding thought might interfere with that eternity of fame the modest laureate felt so certain of. Fielding kept up the fun with Cibber as long as it interested the public. Perhaps his best stroke is in a Lucian vision, where the laureate is sent to Hades. All who pass Charon's ferry are stripped by Mercury of clothes and belongings. "An elderly gentleman with a piece of wither'd laurel on his head," however, slipped into the boat with the laurel on, though otherwise dismantled, for it was so small that it escaped the notice of the clear-eyed Mercury.

Burlesque, satire, and politics gave zest to "The Champion" and made secure its circulation. Fielding was fearless and reckless in the style of the old "Grub-street Journal," which he affected to despise; but "The Champion" was much more than a newspaper of the smart type. Like "The Tatler" and "The Spectator," it professed rather to give the news, as it were, of the moral world—to deal with the follies of society and with the virtues and vices inherent in human nature. Fielding's touch was rarely so light as either Steele's or Addison's. His character-sketches, few in number outside the Vinegars, never had the vividness of a Sir Roger de Coverley or a Will Wimple even. This seems strange when one considers that Fielding's hand had been long practised in the drama. His dreams and visions, too, after the manner of Addison's "Vision of Mirza," seem mostly forced and unnatural. Likewise his direct imitations of Swift lack the invention and fancy of the Dean of St. Patrick's. His "Voyages of Mr. Job Vinegar," lying hidden in "The Champion," ought perhaps to be reprinted as a curiosity, but the book would have little of the charm of "The Voyages of Mr. Lemuel Gulliver"; boys would not read it. The fact is, one is apt to feel that there is a man of rare talent behind the Champion papers, but that he has not adequately expressed himself, that he has written in haste, that he has had no time to revise and mould his essays into the perfect form of which he is capable.

"The Champion" nevertheless must have been a revelation to Fielding's contemporaries, who had hitherto known him only as the author of clever farces. The man who had written "Pasquin" and "Tom Thumb," was strangely familiar with the great essayists like Montaigne and Bacon; his mind was saturated with the ideas of several of the great moralists and philosophers—Plato, Cicero, Horace, Locke, and Shaftesbury; he had read innumerable sermons, preferring because of their wit those of Dr. South; his knowledge of the New Testament, which he read in the Greek, seemed as intimate as if he had been bred to the church; and for the deism and atheism of the time he had all the abhorrence of the most orthodox bishop. So, apart from his political allegories and his sport with Cibber and Freeman, his most characteristic essays became, from the very first, moral disquisitions. He liked to show, expanding Horace, how narrow is the boundary between the virtues and the vices—that certain endowments of nature or acquired characteristics, like valour and wit, though admired by the world, are really dependent, for the good or the harm they do, upon the disposition of the possessor. Again, the world judges, we are told by Fielding as well as by Montaigne, mostly by appearances; so that a good man, in order to preserve his reputation, must always wear a decent behaviour; while a rogue—a Jonathan Wild, for instance— may assume all the trappings of the cardinal virtues and pass for one of the best men in the kingdom. The conclusion is, after the subject has been examined in many aspects, that not much can be determined of a man's character by his outward practice of the ancient virtues. The hypocrite is most ostentatious of them.

Above all else Fielding places "good nature," which he

defends against the charge that it is but the passive attitude of a fool or a coward, ready to accept an affront and averse to the punishment of vice and villainy. On the contrary, he maintains that it is a most active impetus of the heart, and so contributes to the welfare and happiness of all who come within its sphere. "This is that amiable quality," he says in an eloquent paragraph, "which, like the sun, gilds over all our other virtues; this it is, which enables us to pass through all the offices and stations of life with real merit. This only makes the dutiful son, the affectionate brother, the tender husband, the indulgent father, the kind master, the faithful friend, and the firm patriot. This makes us gentle without fear, humble without hopes, and charitable without ostentation, and extends the power, knowledge, strength, and riches of individuals to the good of the whole. It is (as Shakspeare calls it) the milk, or rather the cream of human nature, and whoever is possessed of this perfection should be pitied, not hated for the want of any other. Whereas all other virtues without some tincture of this, may be well called *splendida peccata;* for the richer, stronger, more powerful, or more knowing an ill-natured man is, the greater mischief he will perpetrate."*

There are, too, impressive essays on charity and poverty, ending with a description of the debtors' prison, which Fielding aptly calls "a prototype of hell." He writes a paper against cruelty to horses as he has seen it along Fleet Street by the Temple,—animals that contribute so much "to health, business, and diversion"; and another paper against "roasting," or making sport of some mental or physical blemish of a good but awkward man in company. As for himself, Fielding says that he can never forget that he is a son of the "great and general mother," and feels pity rather than contempt for the misfortunes and

* "The Champion," March 27, 1740.

miseries of others. So when he sees an ill-natured jester at this kind of play, it is his custom to protect the gentleman ridiculed and to turn "the current of laughter" upon the sorry buffoon. No less than five papers are given to "An Apology for the Clergy" against the infidelity of the age, in the course of which are enumerated all the good qualities that should be possessed by the country parson if he would follow in the footsteps of his Master, as distinguished from the inherent meanness of another type of parson who makes use of his religion as a screen to a malevolent temper, "not grieving at, but triumphing over the sins of men, and rejoicing, like the devil, that they will be punished for them." The people are warned against philosophic atheism, the acceptance of which, whether true or false, will put an end to happiness on earth; and, if false, will lead to dreadful consequences hereafter. This is the Fielding that could not have been surmised from his farces.

Several of his moral essays proceed by irony, in which he was fast becoming skilled. Fielding argues, for example, that learning—Greek and Latin—is no longer necessary to success in law, medicine, divinity—or in poetry. True, in this contention, he differs from Cicero; but times have changed since then, and London now has many men eminent in the professions who are outspoken in their contempt for the classical literatures,—and a poet laureate who pretends to nothing more than an ability to read. On the oft-repeated saying that the use of speech is the essential mark dividing man from the brutes, Fielding expresses some doubt, contrary to the opinions of Cicero and Locke, as to the universal advantages of speech, in view of man's misuse of language in many current words and phrases that contain no more ideas than the unintelligible sounds of the brute creation. The old maxim that "the force of example is infinitely stronger, as well as quicker, than precept" in its action on the young, which has the authority of Terence,

279

he would not question, but he would go a step further and assert that "we are much better and easier taught by the examples of what we are to shun, than by those which would instruct us what to pursue." Accordingly he would advocate the establishment of a school, of which the master "should get drunk twice or thrice a week . . . and expose himself to the scholars," and the usher should place the blockheads at the head of the class to the discouragement of learning and the ridicule of virtue. This was a deserved satire on the ordinary grammar-school of the period, such as Laurence Sterne had attended only a few years before.

There is also a vision imitated from Lucian, in which Fielding assembles on the hither side of the Styx a crowd of his contemporaries who are not suffered to enter Charon's boat unless they consent to be shorn by Mercury of their gewgaws, affectations, and honours. One of the company thought the ceremony of undressing was carried too far, and so had to return to the earth. He was, says Fielding, "a tall man, . . . who stripp'd off an old grey coat with great readiness, but as he was stepping into the boat, Mercury demanded half his chin, which he utterly refused to comply with, insisting on it that it was all his own. On enquiry, I was told that he had been sent hither once or twice before by the pit. After a long dispute, Mercury bid him go back and be d—mn'd again; to which he answer'd, he would see him d—mn'd first."* That tall man in grey coat and long chin London audiences had in truth sent across the Styx more than once.

The importance of "The Champion" as the link between Fielding's plays and his approaching work in prose fiction should be apparent. In his contributions to this periodical lie imbedded the first draft of "A Journey from this World to the Next," indications of the ironic point of view elaborated in "Jonathan Wild," the first sketches, though

* "The Champion," May 24, 1740.

lacking in narrative, for a Parson Adams and a Parson Trulliber, and the ethics on which was built the young man named Tom Jones. For nearly two years Fielding's mind thus luxuriated in all those moral considerations necessary to the serious novel of character. The pressure of circumstance had made an essayist out of a playwright, and Fielding thereby gained that same facility in continuous prose which he had shown in writing dialogue. Without his experience on "The Champion," the novel would not have come so easily to him—if, indeed, it would have come at all.

CHAPTER XI

SHAMELA AND STRAY PAPERS

While writing essays for "The Champion"—one, two, and sometimes three a week—Fielding also put forth, as occasion arose, "a large number of fugitive political tracts," says Murphy without mentioning any one of them by title. For this reason, the truth of Murphy's statement has been often questioned; but search has brought to light Fielding's definite or probable connection with several anonymous productions lying partly within this period, not all of which are political. At the same time re-examination of one or two minor pieces formerly thought to be his has made the ascription doubtful. It will be interesting to state here the results.

Fielding was once suspected of having a hand in a mock autobiography of Theophilus Cibber, which was published in July, 1740,* by J. Mechell of Fleet Street. It was a two-shilling pamphlet entitled "An Apology for the Life of Mr. T........ C....., Comedian. Being a Proper Sequel to the Apology for the Life of Mr. Colley Cibber, Comedian. . . . Supposed to be written by Himself." As this apology for the misdeeds of the son followed closely upon the sport that "The Champion" was having with the father, the wits naturally regarded it as Fielding's completion of the jest. Who else, it might be asked, possessed the intimate knowledge of the stage displayed in the pamphlet, or the ability to write in a style which everybody at once recognized as a burlesque of both father and son? It was the style of a

* "The Gentleman's Magazine," July, 1740.

madman who had a fool for a father. Subsequent papers in "The Champion," not included in the reprint, rather deepened the suspicion of Fielding's authorship of the pamphlet. On September 6, he ironically praised the Cibbers as two great writers, hitherto overlooked, who had aided Freeman of "The Gazetteer" in rendering Walpole that justice which was denied him by Pope, Swift, and Young, who seem never to have been warmed by his glorious deeds. The shrillness of the son's style he likened to a trumpet; while the father's style, he thought, resembled more a lute or rather a jew's-harp. "The father lulls you to sleep, the son awakens you out of it; the father sets your teeth on edge: the son makes your head ache. To sum up their merits in two words: the father writes as no one ever wrote before, the son as none will ever write again." Then came, on October 16, Fielding's proposal for printing by subscription "An Apology for the Life . . . of Ralph Freeman Esq.," which he said would appear under the auspices of "T[heophilus] C[ibber], Publisher-General of the Ministerial Society." In line with this jest is an ironical dedication of young Cibber's "Apology" to "a certain gentleman," that is, to Walpole, in which the author, burlesquing Colley Cibber's dedication of his book to another "certain gentleman," hints that he is ready, on proper encouragement, to write an apology for the life of the Prime Minister also. This all sounds very much like Fielding. So, too, the facetious chapter headings and sometimes the concluding sentence of a chapter, like "As I have given you, reader, the bill of fare of the next chapter, it is in your own option whether you will set [sic] down to the meal."

The technical features of the style, however, are not Fielding's; nor do any books known to be his bear the imprint of Mechell. Accordingly, without positive external evidence, it is impossible to fix upon Fielding this piece of mischief. "Who the low rogue of an author was," said young Cibber a decade later, "I could never learn." The "low rogue" was someone connected with the Opposition. So much is certain. Although Fielding, I think, did not actually write the book, he was doubtless in the secret, and may have lent his aid here and there. A passage in the seventh chapter, apparently hostile to him, does not militate against this conclusion, for the passage is clearly ironical. By whomsoever written, it was framed as it is in order to give the impression of a genuine autobiography.

Not long ago it was discovered, almost by accident, that Fielding had some part in an extensive piece of translation—three octavo volumes of it, covering more than a thousand pages. The evidence is a receipt that Fielding gave to John Nourse, the bookseller, for an advance payment on the work. It is a narrow slip of paper running as follows:

> Recᵈ March the 10 1739 of Mʳ John
> Nourse the sum of forty five Pound in
> Part of Payment for the Translation of the
> History of Charles the twelfth by me
> > Hen: Ffielding.

On the reverse side of the slip are curious reckonings in pounds, shillings, and pence, amounting to seventy pounds or more. The date March 10, 1739, means in the present usage March 10, 1740. According to the story, this old receipt, long hidden away in a scrapbook owned by Mr. John Dillon of Kensington, was overlooked when the larger part of the collector's books and manuscripts were sold half a century ago. It was but a yellow strip of paper among the remnants of Mr. Dillon's library, having little consequence. The supposed autograph is now valued at several guineas a word.*

* The history of the receipt as given here was derived in June, 1911, from Mr. James Tregaskis, 232 High Holborn, London, who had then recently purchased the manuscript. The receipt was sold at Sotheby's, July 20, 1916.

SHAMELA AND STRAY PAPERS

The book of which Fielding agreed to supply a translation was the "Histoire Militaire de Charles XII Roi de Suede . . . par Mr. Gustave Adlerfeld, Chambellan du Roi." Adlerfeld, as royal historiographer, had accompanied Charles on several of his campaigns down to the disastrous battle of Poltava, where he was slain. A very full and complete diary of military events which he kept for the King, was translated from the Swedish manuscript into French by his son, C. M. E. Adlerfeld, and published at Amsterdam, with some additions, under the title as given above. A dedication to the Duke of Schleswig-Holstein is dated July 6, 1739; while the title-page bears the date of 1740. So intimate a biography as this of the man who had been the terror of Europe within the memory of men still living, called for immediate translation into English; and Fielding was selected to do the work. On October 16, 1740, "The Champion" announced, as this day published, "The Military History of Charles XII. King of Sweden, Written by the express Order of his Majesty, By M. Gustavus Adlerfeld, Chamberlain to the King. To which is added, An exact Account of the Battle of Pultowa, with a Journal of the King's Retreat to Bender. Illustrated with Plans of the Battles and Sieges. Translated into English. . . . Printed for J. and P. Knapton in Ludgate-street; J. Hodges upon London-Bridge; A. Millar opposite to St. Clement's Church in the Strand; and J. Nourse without Temple-Bar." The booksellers among whom was divided the expense of the undertaking were all Fielding's friends. Nourse and Hodges were partners in "The Champion"; the Knaptons, as well as Nourse, received much free advertising from the newspaper in the way of puffs for their books;* and Millar

Copied by permission. On the question whether Fielding actually translated the book, see J. E. Wells, "Journal of English and Germanic Philology," Oct., 1912, Vol. XI, No. 4, pp. 603-613. See also "The London Times," Sept. 3 and 4, 1913.

* For example, on June 17 and Oct. 16, 1740.

was soon to publish "Joseph Andrews." It is to be surmised that the Knaptons were also shareholders in "The Champion," though their name does not appear in the list so far as it has been published. But that list is incomplete, lacking, it would seem, just one name. At any rate the translation was mainly an enterprise of those booksellers who were interested in "The Champion."

It is not quite certain that the translation was made by Fielding. There have been intimations that the receipt may be a forgery. Fielding's name does not appear on the title-page; nor is the style marked by his favourite phrases or peculiar usages, like *hath* for *has*. Further perplexity has arisen with the discovery of an abridgment of the translation in one volume which appeared in 1742, having the name of "James Ford, Esq." on the title-page as translator. Hence the inference that this gentleman, otherwise unknown in the world of letters, was really the translator of the complete work and that he afterwards abridged it in order to secure a wider sale. Notwithstanding these considerations, the first translation was probably Fielding's either in whole or in part. No good reason has ever been offered for questioning the genuineness of the receipt, the signature of which corresponds, though assertions have been made to the contrary, with other signatures of Fielding. Naturally Fielding, who often published anonymously, would not care to put his name to a piece of hack-work. Aiming to be faithful to the French, his style would of necessity lack its usual freedom, and his publishers might well request him to discard the antiquated verb forms which he loved. The abridgment of 1742, be it observed, has on its title-page no name of publisher, but instead of it the phrase: "Printed and Sold by the Book-sellers in Town and Country." This was a common imprint of the pirate. Without doubt the pirate in this instance was R. Walker, a small bookseller in Fleet Lane, who advertised his wares at the end of the volume. The poor drudge in his employ may or may not have been named James Ford; may or may not have had the right to place "Esq." after his name; for a fictitious author with a fictitious title was then regarded as a profitable adjunct to literary piracy. Very likely Fielding began the work on Adlerfeld, became tired of it, and turned it over to Ralph or to his friend Parson Young, who was then in London, seeking employment of this kind.

The English of the translation, especially through the first of the three volumes, is reasonably exact as well as beautiful, rarely giving, except for some purpose, the impression that there was a French original. At times an unnecessary footnote is omitted, or a new one is added as an aid to the English reader. This is the manner in which Fielding would have proceeded. It cannot be said, however, that the translation is all of a piece; its quality is more uneven in the later volumes, indicating either haste on Fielding's part or the appearance of another writer less familiar with the French. Whatever may have been Fielding's share in the translation—whether it be all his own or whether he farmed out a part of it—the task proved most uncongenial to him. He could not have been beyond the first volume when he stopped, in a paper on true and false greatness published in "The Champion" of May 3, 1740, to vent his impatience at the praise commonly bestowed upon an engineer who blows up "a rotten redoubt" or successfully defends "a sound and strong rampart," or upon a world-conqueror who out of sheer vanity has occasioned the death of men by the hundred thousand, and should have been hanged at the outset. He there expressed a hope that Charles the Twelfth of Sweden and Kuli Khan of Persia would be the last of these heroes and madmen to "infest the earth."

In the mood that prompted this outburst, Fielding composed two poems, which a Fleet Street bookseller, Charles

Corbett, brought out for him separately in January, 1741. They were mentioned by Fielding in a note requesting one of the partners in "The Champion" to place them on sale with another:

"Mr Nourse

Please to deliver Mr Chapell 50 of ~~my~~
True Greatness and 50 of the Vernoniad.

Y^{rs}

"Ap! 20 1741.   Hen: Ffielding"*

The first of these poems—"Of True Greatness. An Epistle to The Right Honourable George Dodington, Esq."†—was announced as by "Henry Fielding, Esq.," and was afterwards included in his "Miscellanies." It is a poem of two hundred and eighty-two lines written in the heroic couplets and general style of Pope's Epistles. Fielding expresses surprise that, though everybody pays homage to greatness, few know what true greatness really is. It is not to be sought in an Alexander, who reached, not a "hero's glory," but a "robber's shame" through "ravag'd fields," "burning towns" and "o'er heaps of murder'd men," but rather in a Marlborough,

> Whose conquests, cheap at all the blood they cost,
> Sav'd millions by each noble life they lost.

It is not to be found in the mock state of a Minister who lets learning go unrewarded. See, says Fielding,

> . . . the great tatter'd bard, as thro' the streets
> He cautious treads, least [sic] any bailiff meets.

Nor does true greatness reside in the hermit or cynic who rails at the world of men; nor in the pedant who writes folios of dulness on the beauties or blemishes he discovers

---

* From the autograph in the collection of W. K. Bixby, Esq., of St. Louis. A facsimile reproduction of the note was published by Thomas Roscoe in his edition of "The Works of Henry Fielding," London, 1840.

† Published Jan. 7, 1741 ("The London Daily Post" of same date).

288

in Milton or Virgil, and thus soars to fame. No: true greatness, confined to no profession, party, or place, "lives but in the noble mind." It shines in men like the Duke of Argyle, Bishop Hoadly of Winchester and formerly of Salisbury, in Sir William Lee, chief justice of the King's Bench, and most of all in Chesterfield, Lyttelton, Carteret, and Dodington—all Fielding's friends. If the list strikes one as an anticlimax, it must be remembered that Dodington was the last of the literary patrons; that he had befriended Young, Thomson, Whitehead, and Glover. As the successor of Lord Halifax of the past age, Dodington was worthy of the neatly turned character-sketch, modelled upon Pope's Atticus, with which Fielding concluded his poem.

Of greater interest than the poem itself is a preface which has never been reprinted or mentioned by editor or biographer, though its tone is more personal than anything that Fielding had hitherto published. In 1740 Dodington, who had been a Lord of the Treasury under Walpole, went over to the Opposition and became the Duke of Argyle's man. For this act he was flayed in the ministerial press, in pamphlets and cartoons, as a turncoat, a renegade, and a traitor. The very month Fielding published his poem, Hanbury Williams discussed his "damn'd behaviour" in a verse dialogue between Giles Earle and George Bubb Dodington. With "True Greatness," Fielding came to the rescue of his friend against "the most pernicious vermin that ever infected a common-wealth," by which he meant the scurrilous writers in the pay of Sir Robert Walpole. His poem, he says, "was writ several years ago, and comes forth now with a very few additions or alterations . . . almost against the consent of him to whom it is addressed." For Dodington, whose "conduct" he has observed and whose "conversation" he has enjoyed, he expresses perfect respect and admiration. The ruffians who are now waylaying this "illustrious person" in the dark are the very ones who have persisted in attacking himself because he refused to be of their number. Of the scurrility heaped upon him, he says:

"For my own Part, I may truly say, I have had more . . . than my Share, or than I believe was ever before applied to one of my very little Consequence in the World. Indeed, I have been often so little conscious of the Merit, that if they had not laid violent Hands on some Letters of my Name; I should not have known for whom the Picture was designed; for besides the Imputation of Vices (particularly Ingratitude) which my Nature abhors, as much at lest [sic] as any one Man breathing, I have been often censured for Writings which I never saw till published, and which if I had known them, and could have prevented it, never should have been published. I can truly say I have not to my Knowledge, ever personally reflected on any Man breathing, not even One, who has basely injured me, by misrepresenting an Affair which he himself knows, if thoroughly disclosed, would shew him in a meaner Light than he hath been yet exposed in."

It is not clear to what base personal injury, quite different from the ridicule and satire of political warfare, Fielding here refers. He may have in mind Walpole's report on "The Golden Rump" or a passage in Colley Cibber's "Apology," or one of the many charges against him in "The Daily Gazetteer," or some transaction of which no account has survived. Following this obscurity, the preface concludes with a paragraph which tells the story of Fielding's flirtation with the Walpole Government. Walpole was ready to take him over if Fielding would pay the price, which was the betrayal of all his former political friends—Argyle, Pulteney, Chesterfield, and Lyttelton. How Fielding spurned the dishonourable proposal is related in these words:

"But to talk of himself is rarely excusable in a Writer, and never but in one, who is otherwise a Man of Consequence; and, tho' I have been obliged with Money to silence my Productions, professedly and by Way of Bargain given me for that Purpose, tho' I have been offered my own Terms to exert my Talent of Ridicule (as it was called) against some Persons (dead and living) whom I shall never mention but with Honour, tho' I have drawn my Pen in Defence of my Country, have sacrificed to it the Interest of myself and Family, and have been the standing Mark of honourable Abuse for so doing; I cannot yield to all these Persuasions to arrogate to myself a Character of more Consequence than (what in spite of the whole World I shall ever enjoy in my own Conscience) of a Man who hath readily done all the Good in his little Power to Mankind, and never did, or had even the least Propensity to do, an Injury to any one Person."

"The Vernoniad,"* another poem in heroic couplets, was issued as an anonymous pamphlet of thirty-seven pages, costing a shilling and sixpence; whereas "True Greatness" sold for only a shilling. Fielding never reprinted "The Vernoniad," and except for the slip of his pen in the letter to Nourse, nowhere in his published works acknowledged it as his own; but his authorship is open to no question. A long title-page, partly in Greek, informs the purchaser that "The Vernoniad" is the first book of a poem foreshadowing the exploits of Admiral Vernon, originally written by Homer and now done into English from a Greek manuscript "lately found at Constantinople," with all notes necessary for a complete understanding of it. One of these notes states that the translator believes the poem to be the lost epic of Homer's about which Pope wrote in his essay on that bard—"a satirical work, levelled against the vices of men, and founded on the old fable of the Cercopes,

* Published Jan. 22, 1741 ("The London Daily Post" of same date).

a nation, who were turn'd into monkies for their frauds and impostures." "These Cercopes," says Fielding further, "were the inhabitants of an island called Inarime; Suidas records two brothers among them, who were particularly eminent for their impostures, and were call'd Candidus and Atlas." Inarime means, in the allegory, England; and Atlas and Candidus stand for Sir Robert Walpole and his brother Horatio. Another note points out that Homer had Admiral Vernon in mind when writing a passage in the fifth book of the Iliad where it is said that Hercules once took Ilium "with six ships only." Did not Vernon boast that he could take Porto Bello "with six ships only," and did he not do it? Where the original Greek text is obscure or corrupt, a footnote gives the line, phrase, or word as it stands in the manuscript, so that the reader may be his own judge of the meaning of the passage, accepting or rejecting it as "cured" by the translator. "Judices, lector erudite." Parallel passages from the Iliad and the Odyssey prove conclusively that Homer wrote the poem in question. Lines quoted from Virgil, Horace, Claudian, and Lucan show that they were all acquainted with it; and hence that the manuscript was not lost until after their time. Whether Milton's eyes ever fell upon "The Vernoniad" is left in doubt. This burlesque of learned pedantry, resembling the annotations on "Tom Thumb," was aimed partly at Dr. Trapp, who had encumbered a translation of Virgil with absurd notes, and partly at Dr. Bentley, who had purged the text of "Paradise Lost" and various ancient classics of false readings. "If Dr. Bentley," says Fielding, "had never given us his comment on Milton, it is more than possible few of us would have understood that poet in the same surprizingly fine manner with that great crick."

Admiral Vernon had easily captured Porto Bello in the manner foretold by Homer, for the Spanish town was

wholly unprepared to resist an attack. The garrison consisted of few men; most of the guns were not in place; and
there was little ammunition. A brief bombardment, and
the English marines climbed into deserted fortifications
through embrasures where cannon should have been. But
after this glorious exploit, which sent a thrill through all
England, Admiral Vernon was able to make little headway
with his six ships against other Spanish settlements in the
West Indies. He insulted several Spanish towns, but they
mostly refused to be destroyed; and for these failures the
Government was blamed. It was giving, said the Opposition, only lukewarm support to a brave admiral. And when
Walpole, impelled by popular clamour, prepared to send
out twenty-five ships to reinforce Vernon, there were many
necessary delays at which the people became impatient.

More delays ensued when the fleet was ready to set forth,
due ostensibly to contrary winds and bad weather; so that
for one reason or another a year elapsed after the fall of
Porto Bello without the news of another great victory over
the Spaniards, while English shipping was not safe even
in the Channel. Then it was that Fielding wrote "The
Vernoniad," drawing for his machinery upon the "Aeneid"
and "Paradise Lost." In this mock epic Satan is represented as being angry at the success of Vernon; for he
sees—now that Louis the Fourteenth and Charles the
Twelfth are gone and can plague the world no more—his
control over Europe slipping away from him everywhere
except in Iberia, or Spain. His "deadliest foe" is the hero
of Porto Bello, who is proving himself a Marlborough of
the sea; and as a means of squelching him, the infernal
fiend instigates Mammon to go to the cave of Aeolus and
bribe him to let forth all the violent winds from the north
and the west upon the fleet ploughing the waves to reinforce
him. Swift come the hurricanes, for even they cannot withstand the power of gold. Sails are struck, and refuge is

sought in a peaceful bay, where men and ships must lie idle indefinitely.

The Mammon who appears in the poem is a full-length portrait of Walpole, whom Fielding clothes anew with the many vices and crimes attributed to him in "The Champion." They are all enumerated in an ironical panegyric that Aeolus—any one of Walpole's miserable placemen—pronounces upon his master:

> All things in colours, as you bid them, glow,
> Virtue looks black, and vice resembles snow.
> Pale honour sickens with a yellow mien,
> And infamy in scarlet robes is seen.
>
> . . . . .
>
> Dulness and ignorance through thee preserve,
> Their faint weak works, while wit and learning starve.
> Nor things inanimate alone obey,
> Submissive men yield to thy sway.
> The world's thy puppet-shew, and human things
> Dance, or hang by, as thou dost touch the strings.
> In gay and solemn characters they shine,
> In robes or rags: for all the skill is thine.
> Behind the curtain, in a various note,
> Thou bawlest or thou squeakest through each throat.

Walpole is also charged with opposing the progress of the war out of regard to Spain, which he loves better than his own country; and by the allegory it is to be understood that all his policies, foreign and domestic, are derived from Satan. Text and footnotes describe, under the guise of Mammon's palace, Walpole's magnificent house at Houghton, with its "heaps of ill-got pictures" hiding the walls, at which the great man looks up and stares like the "stupid fellow" in Virgil, with wonder and astonishment, not knowing wherein their merit lies. Of the Minister's retirement to his country seat every November for a three weeks' hunt, Fielding writes:

SHAMELA AND STRAY PAPERS

Mammon returns to hell, with transports blest
And in his palace keeps a three weeks feast
With roaring fiends the vaulted roofs rebound,
And in each cup Augusta's curse goes round.

A few weeks after "The Vernoniad," on the approach of a general election, both political parties poured forth from their mills numerous sixpenny addresses to the electors of Great Britain; and in this hot debate overflowing from the newspapers, Fielding took a hand, outdoing all the rest. A hundred years ago Nichols in his "Literary Anecdotes"* said that he then had in his possession a pamphlet called "The Crisis: A Sermon, on Revel. XIV. 9, 10, 11. Necessary to be preached in all the Churches in England, Wales, and Berwick upon Tweed, at or before the next General Election. Humbly inscribed to the Right Reverend the Bench of Bishops. By a Lover of his Country. *Vendidit hic auro Patriam.* Virg. London: Printed for A. Dodd, without Temple-Bar; E. Nutt, at the Royal-Exchange, and H. Chappelle, in Grosvenor-Street, MDCCXLI." On the title-page, Nichols added, a former owner had remarked: "This sermon was written by the late Mr. Fielding, author of Tom Jones, &c., as the printer of it assured me.—R. B." The man who signed himself R. B. has never been identified; nor after the publication of the "Literary Anecdotes" was anything more definite heard about "The Crisis" until a copy of the pamphlet was procured in 1914 by Mr. Frederick S. Dickson of New York City for the library of Yale University. Before that time my own knowledge of "The Crisis" had been confined to a résumé published in "Common Sense" on May 9, 1741.

No one can read this passionate appeal to the electors, which was issued in April,† without declaring at once that

* J. Nichols, "Literary Anecdotes of the Eighteenth Century," 1814, VIII, 446.

† "The Gentleman's Magazine," April, 1741, XI, 224. There was also a second edition, which sold at threepence.

it came from Fielding. Aside from its content, it is marked by Fielding's extreme mannerisms; and of the booksellers who distributed the tract, Chappelle was one of Fielding's partners in "The Champion"; and Dodd, just without Temple Bar, where Fielding passed every day, had been connected with the publication of "The Masquerade." Always a good deal of a preacher, this is the first time that Fielding ever cast an address in the form of a sermon. With perfect ease he moved through firstly, secondly, and thirdly for twenty pages as if he were in the pulpit of his grandfather. He took as his text the cry of the angel in the Apocalypse—"If any man worship the beast and his image, and receive his mark in his forehead, or in his hand, the same shall drink of the wine of the wrath of God,"—and exhorted the electors to put no trust in a Minister working, like the Mammon of "The Vernoniad," in league with Satan and dependent upon the bribe—the mark in the hand—for his power:

"Let us be true and honest to one another, let us faithfully and justly discharge this great and important Duty, which we owe to our selves, our Wives, our Children, our Neighbours, and our Country; by committing the Care and Guardianship of their Liberties and Properties to Men, who, we have Reason to be most confident, will, to their utmost Power, preserve and defend them. This is the Day God hath once more committed our Freedom to our Hands, let us rejoice and be wise in it. No Man, who would not direct a Knife to his own Throat; who would not administer Poison to his Friend, or apply a Firebrand to his City; no such Man can hesitate a moment, whether he shall refuse his Vote, notwithstanding any Consideration, to a Representative whom he suspects, much less knows by Experience, will betray his Trust, and deliver up his Country to that Enemy, which the Devil hath raised up against us; and this at a Season too, when the Gates of Hell are open, when the Devices of the Evil One are ripe, and when it is the last time we shall have an Opportunity of struggling against them.''

And in conclusion:

''Now may the great God who searches all Hearts, and in his own good Time restrains, and directs the perverse Will of Man, lead you all into the Ways of Truth and Righteousness, and put a timely Stop to that Torrent of Corruption, which the Devil and his Angels have let loose over this Land, and which God only can prevent from overwhelming us: to him therefore who bestoweth Freedom, and delighteth in it, may Freedom lift up her Voice, and ascribe, as is most due, all Honour, Praise, Glory, Might, Majesty and Dominion for evermore. *Amen.*''

It was a quick intelligence that could compose at will a farce or a mock trial of Colley Cibber or a sermon in the rhythm of the Prayer Book.

Still another anonymous political pamphlet, of twenty-four pages, though it has never been mentioned in connection with Fielding, perhaps came from his pen in the following month. The title-page runs: ''The Plain Truth: A Dialogue between Sir Courtly Jobber, Candidate for the Borough of Guzzledown, and Tom Telltruth, School-Master and Freeman in the said Borough. By the Author of the Remarkable Queries in the Champion, October 7. London: Printed for J. Huggonson in Sword and Buckler Court, on Ludgate Hill. M.DCCXLI. (Price Six-Pence).''* Huggonson will be recognized as the first printer of ''The Champion''; and ''The Remarkable Queries'' as a reference to the vigorous indictment against Walpole's conduct that had appeared in ''The Champion,'' without Fielding's or Ralph's mark. As it is not known who drew up the indictment—whether Fielding, Ralph, or someone else—so it cannot be determined who wrote the pamphlet. All that

* Advertised in ''The Champion,'' May 19, 1741.

can be said is that it is too good for Ralph and that it reads somewhat like Fielding. Sir Courtly asks Tom for his vote; and Tom, in refusing it, tells the candidate why he cannot let him have it. A stretch of dialogue opens like this:

"*Sir Courtly.* Come begin then, produce your Accusations, I'll hold *up* my hand.

Tom. No Offence to your Honour, I believe you are more us'd to hold *out* your Hand.

Sir Courtly. Thou'rt smart, Tom. . . ."

Thereupon Tom launches out into denunciation of the tribe of placemen to which Sir Courtly belongs, and of Walpole for using the Civil List as a means of corruption. "I think," Tom tells him, "robbing upon the highway a much honester thing than selling one's vote; which I think is the greatest crime a man can commit." Parallels to these sentiments may be pointed out in Fielding's contributions to "The Champion"; but such sentiments were not his exclusive property. Here the question of authorship must be left in uncertainty.

Fielding took a rest from politics in the following December, after writing one more sixpenny pamphlet called "The Opposition. A Vision."* It is a sort of newspaper leader arraigning his party, stretched out to twenty-five pages and issued as a pamphlet in order to keep concealed beyond surmise the hand whence it came. The publisher was Thomas Cooper in Paternoster Row. Had not Fielding later mentioned "The Opposition" in the list of his recent works given in the preface to his "Miscellanies" of 1743, no one would have dared assign the pamphlet to him from internal evidence; for, on the assumption that he was the author, it would seem as if he had changed his politics. Such, however, was not really the case. "The Opposition" was a good-natured rebuke of the leaders of his party like

* "The Gentleman's Magazine," Dec., 1741, p. 669.

298

what had occurred in briefer form in "Pasquin." In the election of the preceding summer, the Opposition had made great gains almost everywhere, and especially in Scotland and Cornwall; but on the face of the returns Walpole still had a majority of sixteen or more in the House of Commons. Whether he could hold that majority would depend upon how the many contested elections should be settled. The new Parliament met on December 1, 1741, and at once took up the election petitions. Though some of them were decided in favour of the Patriots, it looked as if Walpole could hold on with a few votes. Rumours were afloat that members prominent in the Opposition—Carteret and several others—were trying to make peace with Walpole; while the leaders in general, expecting the downfall of the Ministry, were forgetting their patriotism and the welfare of the country in their hungry dreams of office. More or less disgusted with their conduct, Fielding thereupon described for them what he had just seen in a vision.

He was reading, he says, one evening "An Apology for the Life of Mr. Colley Cibber, Comedian," and soon came upon the remarkable expression, "Here I met the Revolution," the meaning of which he could not comprehend, or even guess at. In this perplexity he retired to his chamber, and fell asleep, when his fancy, always livelier in sleep than when one is awake, helped him out. By a quick succession of ideas common in dreams, his mind ran from the comedian's book to that company of strolling comedians described by Scarron in the "Roman Comique." He recalled the scene of those French strollers, just as they were entering the town of Mans, walking by the side of a cart piled high with their luggage and drawn by lean and hungry oxen. Then Cibber and Scarron coalesced, and he had his own vision in which all was harmonized. He fancied himself out on the highway leading to London, where he met the Opposition on the way to town for the opening of Parliament. It was a heavy wagon loaded with immense trunks and boxes labelled "Grievances," "Public Spirit," and "Motions for 1741-2." There was a horde of passengers climbing up or leaping down as the vehicle moved slowly on through the mud, hauled, not by oxen or horses, but by ill-matched asses of all colours and sizes, driven by a gentleman—perhaps the Earl of Wilmington—who scarce knew whither he was going. A great mob surrounded and followed the wagon, huzzaing, haranguing, and giving advice to the passengers, who in turn were shouting to the driver to go this way or that way. All the time the asses also kept up a terrible braying. "They appear to me," remarks a sly fellow, "to be the worst fed asses I ever beheld; why there's that long-sided ass they call Vinegar, which the drivers call upon so often to gee up, and pull lustily, I never saw an ass with a worse mane, or a more shagged coat; and that grave ass yoked to him, which they name Ralph, who pulls and brays like the devil, sir, he does not seem to have ate since the hard frost. Surely, considering the wretched work they are employed in, they deserve better meat." Though the asses were aided, when the road became very bad, by a herd from Cornwall and another from the North, the wagon eventually got stuck fast in the mud—perhaps for another seven years. At this moment, the wagon was met by a coach and six headed for the country and bearing "a fat gentleman"—Walpole—who appeared to have "one of the pleasantest, best-natured countenances I had ever beheld." After a brief parley, the wagon was ditched, many of its passengers climbed up behind the coach, and the poor asses were unharnessed and turned into "a delicious meadow, where they all instantly fell to grazing."

This is the way that the political situation looked to a Patriot during and after the election. Fielding felt that the leaders of the Opposition had not been sincere in their motions in censure of the Prime Minister and in their talk about public spirit and grievances. He saw that what some of them were really after was office, which they were ready to accept, if it could not be obtained otherwise, even from Walpole. Men like himself and Ralph, who had been doing the dirty work in newspapers and pamphlets, were but ill-fed asses. He would have no more of it. He resigned from "The Champion" and told the public why in his vision. Fielding's prophecy proved only in part true. Walpole was unable to purchase a majority in the new Parliament, and so went down to defeat. Then began the scramble for office. As foretold in the vision, the Opposition wagon left the great country road which it had professed to follow for the public good and turned the asses directly towards St. James's, where all the passengers wished to be set down.

Ridicule of Cibber's "Apology," like that at the opening of this vision, supplied perennial amusement to Fielding and his contemporaries. It was well-nigh impossible for Fielding to write a pamphlet without giving the player a hit somewhere. In "The Vernoniad," the hit came by way of a footnote in which it was proved—Cibber being the example—that the modern writers greatly excel the ancients. True, most of the beauties of the laureate were for a time hidden and so needed a commentator; but they have now been explained and set forth by "the Herculean labours of Captain Vinegar." Fun with Cibber's style was, however, reaching the danger point of monotony. It surely lacked variety. Soon Fielding scented larger game; perhaps he had scented it already. Cibber dropped to second place; and Richardson came to the front as Fielding's butt.

On November 6, 1740, "The Champion" announced the publication of "Pamela: or, Virtue Rewarded. In a Series of Familiar Letters from a beautiful Young Damsel, to her

Parents. Now first published in order to cultivate the Principles of Virtue and Religion in the Minds of the Youth of both Sexes." This novel, in two volumes, appeared anonymously; but the author, as known to a few friends, was Samuel Richardson, a prosperous London printer, fifty years old, living in Salisbury Court, just off Fleet Street. He had printed the Journals of the House of Commons and for a time "The Daily Gazetteer," then conducted by Fielding's arch-enemy. The story that Richardson wove into his letters is of a young waiting-maid of low degree, named Pamela Andrews, who on the death of her mistress remains in the household under the protection of her lady-ship's son, Mr. B——. It was a well-to-do family belonging to the squirearchy, with estates in two counties. Mr. B——, a rather stupid young fellow, attempts by many clumsy devices to seduce the innocent and beautiful girl; but she easily outwits him and so gains him for a husband. Thus virtue is rewarded on both sides. Mr. B——, casting aside sensual folly, is put into possession of an amiable wife, though she is really nothing more than a servant who had hitherto looked after his linen; and Pamela, somewhat unfortunate on the score of birth, overcomes by her prudent conduct the barriers of rank.

"Pamela" created a furore. As many as six editions were called for within a year; and the novel through trans-lations almost immediately began its journey into Euro-pean fame. A play was made of it, in which Garrick, new to London, took a part besides writing the prologue. It was also adapted to the French and the Italian stage—by Voltaire and Goldoni. Richardson's friends, who were in the secret of the authorship, overwhelmed him with letters of congratulation. Aaron Hill read the book aloud by the fireside to his family and guests, who were so overcome by the pathetic passages, he told Richardson, that they were often compelled to retire to separate rooms to compose themselves. But they always returned; Hill added, to hear the reading go on. At Slough, the villagers gathered round the local blacksmith to listen to the story; and after being assured of Pamela's ultimate victory and marriage to a gentleman, they ran off to ring the church bells. It was a wonderful triumph for the little fat printer of Salisbury Court.

But success in literature, as Richardson discovered, has its woes as well as its pleasures. Booksellers, seeing a chance to turn a penny, set their literary hacks upon Richardson's heels to retell the story in briefer form or to carry it forward from the period where the author had left off. A spurious sequel called "Pamela's Conduct in High Life" compelled Richardson in self-defence to add two more volumes to his own "Pamela," descriptive of the heroine's "behaviour in married life, her correspondencies with new and more genteel friends, her conversations at table and elsewhere. . . ." He was also greatly annoyed by the wits who could not resist the temptation to ridicule his bedchamber scenes and his fussy and wire-drawn style spun out into an endless series of letters. A gentleman in one of the coffee-houses was overheard to remark, says the anonymous author of a humorous "Life of Pamela," that he wondered why Richardson did not tell the exact number of pins that Pamela had about her when she set out on a journey to one of her master's estates, and how many rows of them she bought for a penny.

Of these "scandalous engraftments" on the original novel, there were, Richardson complained, sixteen; and he did not have a record of them all. The one that concerns us here made its appearance on April 4, 1741,* immediately after the third edition of the genuine "Pamela" in two volumes. It has for its title-page: "An Apology for the Life of Mrs. Shamela Andrews. In which, the many no-

* "The Craftsman," April 4, 1741.

torious Falshoods and Misrepresentations of a Book called Pamela, Are exposed and refuted; and all the matchless Arts of that young Politician, set in a true and just Light. Together with A full Account of all that passed between her and Parson Arthur Williams; whose Character is represented in a manner something different from what he bears in Pamela. The whole being exact Copies of authentick Papers delivered to the Editor. Necessary to be had in all Families. By Mr. Conny Keyber. London: Printed for A. Dodd, at the Peacock, without Temple-bar. M.DCC.XLI." With some variations in the title-page and elsewhere, the pamphlet was reset and reissued in the following November.* In its first form it runs to fifty-nine pages, exclusive of introductory matter, and sold for a shilling and sixpence. The pseudonym "Conny Keyber," which appears likewise at the end of a dedication, is so transparent as to be hardly a disguise for "Colley Cibber." But Colley Cibber, of course, did not write this burlesque of "Pamela." The real author lurking behind the pseudonym was certainly Fielding. "Shamela" consequently assumes an importance quite apart from its literary merits, as the point where Fielding first collided with Richardson and was turned by the impact from the essay to the novel.

The evidence for Fielding's hand in "Shamela" is almost as strong as it can be in the face of his own silence. True, his biographers have not listed the pamphlet in Fielding's works—either because they have not had the evidence or because they have wished to save him from the authorship of a burlesque thought to do him no credit. On the other hand, the recent biographers of Richardson—Miss Clara L. Thomson especially—have rather inclined to father "Shamela" upon Fielding. Mr. Austin Dobson, who has had by him more of the evidence than anyone else, did not mention "Shamela" in his life of Fielding, but brought

* "The Champion," Nov. 3, 1741.

forward in his life of Richardson some circumstances that make for Fielding's authorship, and then left the question hanging in the air. It remains to present the evidence more at length.* Richardson himself, as pointed out by Mr. Dobson, became fixed in the opinion that Fielding was the author of the burlesque. In a letter to Mrs. Belfour towards the end of 1749, he says that "Pamela," which Fielding "abused in his 'Shamela,'" first taught the rogue "how to write to please." And in his old age his trembling hand appended to a letter mentioning "Shamela" the note: "Written by Mr. H. Fielding." Richardson should have known whereof he was speaking, for at that time he had become acquainted with Fielding's four sisters, one of whom—Sarah, the novelist—was a frequent visitor at his house for days or weeks, and when absent kept up a correspondence with him on general topics and mutual flatteries.

But if Richardson had nothing certain on which to base his conviction, he was justified in it by common report. At the time "Shamela" came out, there was a colony of young English gentlemen settled at Geneva for study and pleasure. They explored the Mer de Glace in the valley of Chamouni, and, standing on the ice, drank a health to Admiral Vernon. In the numerous company were Lord Haddington; Richard Aldworth, afterwards statesman and diplomat; William Windham, a future supporter of Pitt; and their tutor, Benjamin Stillingfleet the naturalist. Home news was supplied them by Thomas Dampier, one of their Eton friends, who lived to be sub-master of his college and Dean of Durham. In a letter full of political and literary gossip, dated Mitcham, July 30, 1741, Dampier wrote in reply to an inquiry on "the state of learning in England":

* Since I wrote this, Mr. J. Paul de Castro has published some of the evidence. See "Notes and Queries," 12 S. II, 24-26 (Jan. 8, 1916). See also Barbauld, "Correspondence of Richardson," IV, 286; and Dobson, "Samuel Richardson," New York, 1902, pp. 42-45.

THE HISTORY OF HENRY FIELDING

"The book that has made the greatest noise lately in the polite world is 'Pamela,' a romance in low life. It is thought to contain such excellent precepts, that a learned divine at London recommended it very strongly from the pulpit. You desired Still[ingfleet], to have some account of Dr. Middleton's book ['Life of Cicero']. People are much divided about it, but in general 'tis thought inferior to what was expected: 'tis very much so in my humble opinion. The dedication to Lord Hervey has been very justly and prettily ridiculed by Fielding in a dedication to a pamphlet called 'Shamela' which he wrote to burlesque the forementioned romance."*

The statement of this young man not long out of Eton is at least two thirds true. Dr. Benjamin Slocock† of St. Saviour's, Southwark, had exhorted his congregation to read "Pamela"; and Dr. Middleton's dedication to his "Life of Cicero," which appeared in February, 1741, was ridiculed, as we shall see, in the dedication to "Shamela." The presumption is that the rest of Dampier's statement is true also—that Fielding was the man who burlesqued at one stroke both Middleton and Richardson, whose books people were talking about everywhere. This was the view of Horace Walpole, who read "Shamela" in the second edition. In his copy, happily preserved, he explained several of the allusions, and wrote on the title-page "By Fielding."‡

* "Historical MSS. Commission. Twelfth Report, Appendix, Part IX," p. 204.

† Mr. Dobson (in his "Henry Fielding," New York, 1900, p. 101) says that "Dr. Slocock," the name of the clergyman as given by Mrs. Barbauld, is a strange misprint for "Dr. Sherlock." The Richardson correspondence at the South Kensington Museum shows that neither Mrs. Barbauld nor the printer made a mistake in reading the name. It is "Dr. Slocock."

‡ Walpole's copy of "Shamela," the title-page of which is reproduced here, is in the collection of Mr. A. S. W. Rosenbach, of Philadelphia. In agreement with Dampier, Walpole wrote on the margin of the dedication near the head: "Burlesque on Dr Middleton's Dedication of the Life of Cicero to Lord Hervey."

AN
APOLOGY
FOR THE
LIFE
OF
Mrs. SHAMELA ANDREWS.

In which, the many notorious FALSHOODS and
MISREPRSENTATIONS of a Book called

PAMELA,

Are expofed and refuted ; and all the matchlefs
ARTS of that young Politician, fet in a true and
juft Light.

Together with

A full Account of all that paffed between her
and Parfon *Arthur Williams* ; whofe Character is
reprefented in a manner fomething different from
that which he bears in *PAMELA*. The
whole being exact Copies of authentick Papers
delivered to the Editor. *By Fielding.*

Neceffary to be had in all FAMILIES.

By Mr. *CONNY KEYBER.*

LONDON:
Printed for A. DODD, at the *Peacock*, without *Temple-bar.*
M. DCC. XLI.

SHAMELA AND STRAY PAPERS

The ascription of "Shamela" to Fielding—whether founded on direct knowledge or on general opinion—is supported by the book itself. The "A. Dodd," whose imprint the book bears, was one of the three booksellers for whom "The Crisis" was printed later in the same month. "Mr. Keyber" had been one of Fielding's names for "Mr. Cibber" as far back as the first performance of "The Author's Farce." Fielding, however, did not then displace "Colley" for "Conny," since the occasion had not yet come for that. "Conny," now first used by the author of "Shamela" to complete Cibber's nickname, is a parody on "Conyers," Middleton's Christian name, and was drawn from the slang of the street, in which the word "conny" had come to mean, not a rabbit, but the dupe of a sharper— that is, easy game to hit and kill. It is the sort of addition that one would expect from Fielding in his fun with Cibber.*

The style, too, of "Shamela" everywhere displays those mannerisms of Fielding which were so obvious to his contemporaries that pamphleteers later adopted them when burlesquing his essays and novels. Throughout "Shamela" appear, for example, the almost inevitable *hath* and *doth,* and the transitional phrase that Fielding liked to use so well—"To say the truth." So, too, occur very often his favourite "whereas" and "apprehend," and the "vartue" which we have in "Joseph Andrews." Just as in that novel also, the heroine becomes the "lady" rather than the "wife" of the hero; and she has Parson Adams's habit of snapping her fingers. Again, attention has been drawn by Mr. Dobson to a few specific parallels between "Shamela" and "Joseph Andrews" of the next year. First, there are the similar comic word-blunders. Mrs. Malaprop was not

* Although "Conny" for "Colley" appears to have been Fielding's own jest, "Keyber" for "Cibber" had long been common among the wits. See, for example, "Mist's Weekly Journal," Feb. 23 and March 9, 1723.

yet born, and characters dependent for piquancy upon mistakes in speech were not common in the literature of 1740. But Fielding had been playing in this way with language ever since he began the ridicule of Cibber's style in his first preface to "Tom Thumb." Though we have in Shakespeare the employment of word-confusions as a source of humour, it was Fielding who set the fashion for the eighteenth century in the Mrs. Slipslop of "Joseph Andrews." These word-blunders—usually arising from the use of a wrong word for the right one of similar sound—occur also in "Shamela." Both the heroine and Mrs. Jewkes the housekeeper stumble in their speech. The former refers, for instance, to the "Statue of Lamentations" when she means the "Statute of Limitations"; and the latter, just like Mrs. Slipslop, talks of her "sect" when she intends to say her "sex." Among other comic slips resulting from ignorance are "Pallament," "pollitricks," "syllabub," and "monysyllable"—the last of which Shamela says she does not understand, but believes "it is bawdy."

Moreover, it was asserted by Arthur Murphy that Parson Trulliber of "Joseph Andrews" had an original in the humorist's first tutor—a Parson Oliver, whom we have identified with the Rev. Mr. Oliver of Motcombe. By a curious coincidence if nothing more, a country parson playing a leading part in "Shamela," bears the name of Oliver also. Finally, in "Joseph Andrews," Fielding fills out the dash of Richardson's "Mr. B——" into "Mr. Booby," a name then applied, as Fielding remarks elsewhere, to a country squire, who, whatever his own morals may be, insists that the woman he marries shall be chaste. But this transformation, which has tickled the humorous sense of a multitude of readers, had already taken place in "Shamela," where the young gentleman is always called "Mr. Booby" or "Squire Booby." It is unnecessary to proceed further. Fielding held it as a principle and reiterated it again and again that, whereas the ancients are common property, no one is at liberty to take directly from a living writer without due acknowledgment. Had not "Shamela" been his own, he would never have silently transferred Mr. Booby to "Joseph Andrews." There would have been in the process some remark about the facetious author of "Shamela," for that was Fielding's way in similar cases.

Fielding did not ridicule Richardson out of any personal dislike or misunderstanding. There was no old quarrel with him as with Cibber. In fact, Fielding was probably then unacquainted with Richardson. He may have passed by the printer's shop, or noticed his name at the foot of "The Gazetteer." Nothing beyond that. Such conversation as ever existed between the two men belongs to a later date, when Sarah Fielding had become one of Richardson's visitors. Moreover, the author of "Shamela" seems to have been unaware that he was hurting the feelings of an obscure printer in Salisbury Court. "Pamela" was an anonymous publication. Outside of Richardson's circle, the authorship was a mystery. Dampier, it will be noticed, did not give the novelist's name in the letter to his Eton friends at Geneva. As the year rolled by, Richardson was drawn out of his shell by a sequel to "Pamela," purporting to have been written by the original author or with his sanction. Even then Richardson's claims were disputed, and he had to fight for his own. The novel was thus to Fielding as to many others but an anonymous production open to ridicule because of its affected style, formal morality, and the unreality of its characters. Pamela herself was a sham; hence her new name, Shamela. Fielding was amused by the fuss made about her; by the excessive praise lavished upon her and the author in two commendatory letters that Richardson added to the second edition; and by the way she was being taken up in the pulpit as a model for a young woman's conduct. Nor did Fielding have any long-standing grudge against Middleton. He simply did not regard the new "Life of Cicero" as the masterpiece of fine writing that it was proclaimed to be. On this score, he expressed himself humorously in "Joseph Andrews," declaring that the Muse of Biography had no hand in that work, and would have struck out, had she been consulted, the dedication, preface, and translations. The case was different with Lord Hervey, whom Fielding had already satirized for his shifty politics and character. All three men, whether known or unknown to him, now became, along with Cibber, Fielding's game.

"Shamela" was to "Pamela" what "Tom Thumb" had been to the heroic drama; it was a dirèct parody. It moves, however, on a lower plane than "Tom Thumb," resembling in this respect that other parody called "The Covent-Garden Tragedy," in which all the characters are disreputable. By way of introduction, "Mr. Conny Keyber," the reputed author, dedicates his book to "Miss Fanny," a girl who was carried, when very young, into "the ball-room at the Bath, by the discerning Mr. Nash," and has since become Mr. Conny Keyber's mistress and the inspirer of the present romance. Miss Fanny was at once recognized by Dampier and the wits as the effeminate Lord Hervey who had been unsexed by Pope several years before. Beginning with the substitution of names, the dedication of "Shamela" to Miss Fanny follows very closely Middleton's dedication of his "Cicero" to Lord Hervey through laboured sentences of involved panegyric down to the signature, "Conny Keyber," in place of "Conyers Middleton." "It was Cicero," Middleton tells Hervey, "who instructed me to write; your Lordship who rewards me for writing." "It was Euclid," says the author of "Shamela" to Fanny, "who taught me to write. It is you, madam, who pay me for writing." There are also similar

310

parodies of the two commendatory letters that adorned the second edition of "Pamela." One is from the author (called "the editor") to himself, and the other is from "John Puff, Esq.," who finds everything in the book drawn to perfection except virtue. A note adds that further commendatory letters, and verses also, will be prepared for the next edition. Then comes the story.

Parson Tickletext writes a letter from town to Parson Oliver in the country, lauding "Pamela" and sending him a copy of the book. He begins and goes on:

"Herewith I transmit you a Copy of sweet, dear, pretty *Pamela*. . . . The Pulpit, as well as the Coffee-house, hath resounded with its Praise, and it is expected shortly, that his L[ordshi]p* will recommend it in a [Pastoral] Letter to our whole Body. . . . This Book is the 'Soul of *Religion*, Good-Breeding, Discretion, Good-Nature, Wit, Fancy, Fine Thought, and Morality. There is an Ease, a natural Air, a dignified Simplicity, and MEASURED FULLNESS in it, that RESEMBLING LIFE, OUT-GLOWS IT. . . .' As soon as you have read this your self five or six Times over (which may possibly happen within a Week) I desire you would give it to my little God-Daughter, as a present from me. This being the only Education we intend henceforth to give our Daughters. And pray let your Servant-Maids read it over, or read it to them. Both your self and the neighbouring Clergy, will supply yourselves for the Pulpit from the Booksellers, as soon as the fourth Edition is published."

In reply Parson Oliver, after reading the novel, expresses amazement that Tickletext and the town should run mad over such wretched stuff, saying:

"If I had not known your Hand, I should, from the Sentiments and Stile of the Letter, have imagined it to have come from the Author of the famous Apology, which was sent me last Summer; and on my reading the remarkable

* Edmund Gibson, Bishop of London, noted for numerous pastoral letters.

THE HISTORY OF HENRY FIELDING

Paragraph of *measured Fulness, that resembling Life out-glows it,* to a young Baronet, he cry'd out, C—ly C—b—r by God—. But I have since observed, that this, as well as many other expressions in your Letter, was borrowed from those remarkable Epistles, which the Author, or the Editor hath prefix'd to the second Edition which you send me of his Book.''

Not only are several scenes, Oliver declares, unfit for the perusal of his daughter and the servants, but the entire story is a misrepresentation of facts and a perversion of truth, for he knows intimately the history of Pamela who lives in his neighbourhood. Her name should be Shamela. And that Tickletext may see for himself just what and who the "sweet, dear, pretty Pamela" was in real life, Oliver sends him a bundle of the genuine letters which passed between her and her friends. These letters are very gross but very clever parodies of Richardson. Shamela's father, setting out in the world as a drummer in a Scotch regiment, became an informer against his friends after the late Gin Act, and now has in consequence a snug place in the Customs. Her mother was an orange woman at the playhouse. It is uncertain whether her parents were ever married. The girl had an intrigue with Parson Williams, a hypocrite of the worst sort, who not long ago preached a sermon on the text, "Be not righteous over-much," showing us "that the Bible doth not require too much goodness of us . . . that those people who talk of vartue and morality, are the wickedest of all persons; that 'tis not what we do, but what we believe, that must save us." By feigning innocence, Shamela alias Pamela got Mr. Booby for a husband; but the squire, catching her with her lover, afterwards turned her off and prosecuted Mr. Williams in the spiritual court.

In conclusion, Parson Oliver, dropping the fiction of a Shamela, brings a series of sober charges against Richardson's "Pamela" as if he were gathering up the points of a sermon in order to thrust them home. All the characters in Richardson's novel are declared to be either unreal or not at all what they were intended to be. Pamela, despite her frights and moralizing, is a scheming politician actuated only by motives of self-interest. Mr. B—— is a booby caught by her wiles. Parson Williams, whom the author regards as a faultless character, is at best a busybody. And as for Lady Davers and other ladies who come into the novel, they do not exist at all; "there is not the least foundation for any thing which is said" of them. Of the story as a whole, the obvious moral is that young gentlemen should marry their mothers' chambermaids if they would be happy; and that the chambermaids should in turn look out for husbands in their masters. It is not virtue that is rewarded; it is cunning. The final inference is left to the reader. It is either that the author of "Pamela"—a parson, probably—has romanced a very low intrigue, or that he knows nothing of the life he attempts to describe. Whichever the inference, he should be ridiculed off the stage. No wonder Richardson winced and could never forgive the man whom he supposed to be the author of "Shamela." His first act was to withdraw from "Pamela" the commendatory letters which had been subjected to ruthless parody.

CHAPTER XII

JOSEPH ANDREWS

I

The success of Richardson made a novelist of Fielding. Without a "Pamela" there would have been no "Joseph Andrews." For this new turn in his art Fielding was equipped at all points. It was as easy for him to write a novel as to write a play. There was but little worth while in the realistic fiction of his own or earlier times with which he was not well acquainted. He had read "The Golden Ass" of Apuleius, and presumably "The Satyricon" of Petronius, a copy of which was in his library. Ever since his school days, he had taken supreme delight in "The Dialogues" of Lucian, which had led him into the way of irony and burlesque. Antiquity could supply him with little else bearing directly upon the novel as distinguished from romance and wild adventure. As a boy, too, he had met with a translation of "Don Quixote"—it must have been the one made by Motteux—and he had adapted, while at Leyden, the Knight of La Mancha to the English stage for a contrast between the noble idealism of a Spanish gentleman and the hypocrisies and sordid motives of a group of English men and women gathered at a country inn. He may never have seen a Spanish rogue story, depicting, in the form of an autobiography, the seamy side of life with a comic or farcical intent; but this type of novel as adjusted to French manners he was familiar with, and he praised it again and again for its truth to human nature. The French line, so far as it concerns Fielding, began with

314

JOSEPH ANDREWS

Scarron's "Roman Comique," passed through Lesage's "Gil Blas," and ended with Marivaux's "Le Paysan Parvenu," in the last of which it is related how an obscure country boy made his way in Paris against poverty and the temptations of women. "Don Quixote" and "Le Paysan Parvenu" gave Fielding the hint for a great novel which should be incidentally a burlesque of "Pamela."

Fielding named his novel after the pair of characters that were to divide the reader's interest: "The History of the Adventures of Joseph Andrews, and of his Friend Mr. Abraham Adams." He did not place his own name on the title-page, but instead of it the descriptive phrase: "Written in Imitation of The Manner of Cervantes, Author of Don Quixote." The date of publication of the two neat duodecimo volumes, as given in "The Champion" and elsewhere, was February 22, 1742; and the price for them was six shillings. They were printed for Andrew Millar, the bookseller. A story once current said that Fielding first submitted his manuscript to another publisher and was at the point of letting him have it for twenty-five pounds, when his friend James Thomson intervened and persuaded him to try Millar for a larger sum. Millar turned the manuscript over to his wife, who told him, after reading it, that he must not let it slip through his fingers. Subsequently Millar, Thomson, and Fielding retired to a tavern to make the bargain. After the second bottle of port, Fielding asked the bookseller, with some trepidation, what he would give for the novel. "I am a man," said Millar, "of few words, and fond of coming to the point, but I don't think I can afford to give more than £200." "Two hundred pounds!" said Fielding, in amazement, "are *you serious?*" "Never more so," replied Millar. "Then," said the delighted author, "give me your hand, the book's yours."* The details of this tavern scene are

* F. Lawrence, "Life of Henry Fielding," 1855, p. 164.

doubtless apocryphal, but an essential truth lies behind them. Happily the original assignment* of the copyright in "Joseph Andrews" to Millar still exists. It is throughout in Fielding's own hand, and bears the date of April 13, 1742, when negotiations had begun for a second edition. According to this document "Henry Fielding of the Middle Temple, Esqr" received one hundred and ninety-nine pounds and six shillings for "Joseph Andrews" and two minor publications of the year ("Miss Lucy in Town, a Farce" and "A Full Vindication of the Dutchess Dowager of Marlborough"). On the back of the assignment is a note by Millar, which shows he was to pay one hundred and eighty-three pounds and eleven shillings for "Joseph Andrews," ten pounds and ten shillings for "Miss Lucy," and five pounds and five shillings for "A Full Vindication." The name of James Thomson does not appear among the witnesses to the agreement. They were the author's friend William Young and a certain William Hawkes. The printer of "Joseph Andrews," we now know, was Henry Woodfall of Paternoster Row, whose ledger, under date of February 15, 1741-1742, gives the information that the first edition of the novel ran to fifteen hundred sets.† With two hundred pounds in his pocket, Fielding must have felt that the prosperous days of "Pasquin" were returning.

There is, Fielding would say in "Joseph Andrews," a good deal of shamming in the biographies, real and fictitious, which claim to depict contemporary life and manners. This was the point in "Shamela" also. Colley Cibber has written an autobiography in which he meant to attribute to himself all the virtues except chastity; but he left that one out, rather posing as unchaste, because he thought unchastity really a virtue. He set himself up as a pattern to

* Now in the Forster Collection of MSS. at South Kensington.
† "Notes and Queries," 1 S. XI, 419 (June 2, 1855). See also 7 S. II, 186 (Sept. 4, 1886).

THE
HISTORY
OF THE
ADVENTURES
OF
JOSEPH ANDREWS,
And of his FRIEND
Mr. *ABRAHAM ADAMS.*

Written in Imitation of
The *Manner* of CERVANTES,
Author of *Don Quixote.*

IN TWO VOLUMES.
VOL. I.

LONDON:
Printed for A. MILLAR, over-againſt
St. Clement's Church, in the *Strand.*
M.DCC.XLII.

the male sex, quite unaware that his vanity drew for him a ridiculous portrait. Indeed, there are those who think that the life recorded in his book was lived by the great man in order that he might write an apology for it. Now comes the autobiography of Miss Pamĕla, or Pamēla, Andrews—some pronouncing it one way, some the other. Though this young woman, unlike Colley Cibber, did not actually live the life related of her, the narrative purports to be founded upon "authentic papers and records." She is supposed to be—the author and the laudatory epistles say so—a model for her sex as much as Cibber is for his. She possesses in equal degree all the virtues, including the one which the great apologist omitted in describing himself. In distinction from him, her prime characteristic is chastity; that is her stock in trade for rising in the world. Now, real men and women are not these made-up figures that appear in Cibber and Richardson. Let us remove their masques and look at them as they are, as anyone may see them in town or country, or on a journey from London to Bath or Salisbury.

To this end Fielding takes all the Boobys over into his novel, enlarging the family considerably, and assigns them to two adjoining parishes in his own Somersetshire. To Richardson's Mr. B— are given an uncle and an aunt— Sir Thomas Booby and Lady Booby—in whose service has been bred a reputed brother of Pamela, named Joseph. A lad just reaching his majority, wonderfully strong and perfect in physique, Joey has risen from the stable to the post of my lady's footman. In the same household has grown up also a wonderfully beautiful girl known as Fanny Goodwill, two years younger than Joseph Andrews; but just before the story opens, Mrs. Slipslop, my lady's house-keeper and waiting-maid, turns Fanny off, in order to nip in the bud the love becoming apparent between the boy and the girl. The curate of the parish is Parson Adams, who has made the acquaintance of Fanny and Joseph in the servants' hall, and acts as a check and counsellor in the desperate situation. At this point, Lady Booby, who likes the town better than the country, goes up to London with several members of her household—Mrs. Slipslop, Joseph, and her husband. But hardly has she entered upon the gaieties of the season before Sir Thomas dies, and for six days the poor lady is forced to confine herself to her house with no other companions than Mrs. Slipslop and a few female friends, who make a quiet party at cards. Unable to endure the monotony longer than the seventh day, she then orders Joseph to bring up the tea-kettle for her relief. Thereupon begin her attempts, running from cajolery to threats, to break down the virtue of her handsome footman. But all in vain; for Joseph has been well grounded in morality by Parson Adams, has read several good books besides the Bible, and—more than all else—has got by heart the letters that his sister Pamela is sending home descriptive of her awful encounters with a male member of the Booby family. He writes to her, telling her how he is evading the traps set for him and confessing that there have been occasions when he could not have resisted the charms of Lady Booby had he not been inspired by Pamela's spotless example. Joseph's immediate reward for his virtue is not the hand of Lady Booby in marriage, but dismissal from her service.

Consoled by the thought that he has remained constant to Fanny, Joseph sets out by night, alone and on foot, to seek her in the parish far in the West. Despite the occasional aid of horse, stage, or coach, it took him eight days to make the journey, owing to a succession of adventures which began with his being robbed, stripped, and left for dead by the wayside. Thus Fielding enters upon his great epic of the road, as it has been called, swarming with men and women—highwaymen, innkeepers and their wives, chambermaids, country squires, parsons, doctors, lawyers, constables, prudes, and jesters. Along with Joseph all the Boobys and their retainers are turned into the highway. Parson Adams is far on the road to London to sell three manuscript volumes of sermons; but having forgotten to bring them along, he decides, on meeting Joseph, to go back with him. Fanny, desiring to get news of Joseph, has also taken the road to London, and likewise faces about as soon as she has found him. Lady Booby, after trying in vain to overcome her passion for Joseph, orders her coach and horses to be got ready for the journey homewards. Finally, her nephew Mr. Booby and "the illustrious Pamela," just married, leave town in a coach and six for a brief visit with Lady Booby before going on to their seat in the next parish. Through all the varied scenes of the road the narrative glides without friction, as if it were nature itself. If a long story is introduced, it is to fill up an uneventful hour in the stagecoach between adventures or to provide a means of keeping a group awake through a long night when there are no beds for them to sleep in. At times perhaps Fielding lets his narrative stand perfectly still as a burlesque of the suspense characteristic of Richardson.

His characters once assembled at Lady Booby's Hall for the concluding scenes, Fielding plays with the dénouement, in gay imitation of a common type of the drama known since Aristotle's time as that of "discovery and revolution." There has been a mistake in the parentage of Joseph and Fanny; and when the truth becomes known, they enter upon their happy future. Here Fielding assumes a mock gravity as if he were solving the riddle of Oedipus; and here, Pamela and her husband coming upon the stage for the first time, he gives them the finishing touches. Pamela is a snob disposed to look down upon her family connections since she has attained her exalted position; while her husband, Squire Booby, is so good-natured, shallow, and

harmless that one wonders how the deuce she ever had any
trouble with him. It is an amusing scene preliminary to the
dénouement, where Pamela tries to persuade Joseph to
give up Fanny because the marriage would throw down the
Andrews family again just after it had been raised by her
own marriage with a gentleman. She would have her
brother pray "for the assistance of grace" against his love
for Fanny. Following close upon this scene, it comes out
that Fanny is really Pamela's sister, and that Joseph is not
her brother at all, but the son of a Mr. Wilson, a retired
gentleman of good family. Joseph, when a child in the
cradle, had been stolen by a gypsy and afterwards ex-
changed in another cradle for Fanny, who was subsequently sold to Sir Thomas Booby for three guineas. The
identity of Joseph is proved by a birthmark. Standing in
Booby Hall, he unbuttons his coat and displays to the
company his left breast, whereon is seen "as fine a strawberry as ever grew in a garden." Pamela can interpose no
further objections to the match, for her sister as well as
herself will now have a gentleman for a husband. Nothing
more happens, except an incident at the marriage service,
which is performed by Parson Adams in the little church
of Squire Booby's parish. The good man, who would permit
no light conduct in his presence when he had his surplice on,
"publickly rebuked Mr. Booby and Pamela for laughing in
so sacred a place and on so solemn an occasion."

So much for "Joseph Andrews" as a burlesque of
"Pamela." It would be easy to go on and show just how
Fielding parodied certain high scenes in Richardson; but
that there are such parodies pervading the entire novel
may be taken for granted. No novel has ever survived
long in popular esteem because it parodied or burlesqued
another novel; something more is necessary to immortality. "Shamela" is a burlesque—a very fine one too, but
it is nothing more; and it has disappeared; only those who

read books that nobody else reads, have ever seen it. "Don Quixote" is a burlesque; it lives, however, not because it is a burlesque of the romances of chivalry, but because it possesses characters embedded in human nature and delineated with humour so genuine as to be ever fresh and modern. Cervantes built upon the picaresque novel, or the rogue story, the most realistic form of fiction then current in Spain. Fielding took Cervantes for his model; he built upon "Don Quixote" and the realistic fiction of France. Novels of this kind he mentioned by title in various places of "Joseph Andrews," and told the reader, in his honest way, what they had contributed to the novelist's art as he understood it. Novels outside of this class, that is, romances and impossible adventures, he either condemned or professed never to have read. To his favourite type of fiction he was indebted for his general plan and for an occasional scene. The epic of the road as a motif came from "Don Quixote," the "Roman Comique," or "Gil Blas," which you will, for in all of them a journey is the occasion of the humorous adventures.

A German scholar* once attempted to connect Fielding specifically with Marivaux's "Marianne." It is said that Fielding discovered his strawberry in this novel; for was not Marianne identified by a strawberry near her right eye? It happens, however, that the recognition scene in "Marianne" was not in the novel as Marivaux left it incomplete; it was added by another hand sometime after the publication of "Joseph Andrews." So the strawberry migrated, if it migrated at all, from Joseph's left breast to Marianne's right eye, and not the other way. The novel of Marivaux visible in "Joseph Andrews" is not "Marianne," but, as I have remarked, "Le Paysan Parvenu." In taking for his hero a young man from the country and placing him in the

* Erich Bosdorf, "Entstehungsgeschichte von Fieldings Joseph Andrews," Berlin, 1908, p. 40.

321

highly seasoned society of the town to see how he would behave, Fielding was certainly anticipated by his French predecessor. Fielding's Joseph so far derives from Marivaux's Jacob. Indeed, the crucial scene between Joseph and Lady Booby in her London boudoir bears a close analogy to one in "Le Paysan Parvenu" between Jacob and Madame de Fécourt. Perhaps a gaiety of tone in narrative and description also passed over from Marivaux to Fielding. Add this to the abandon of Scarron, and the result is something like Fielding. Half seriously, Fielding proclaimed himself the successor of Homer. The Greek bard, it used to be said, composed a comic epic which bore the same relation to comedy as the Iliad bore to tragedy. The spirit of this ancient comic epic, long since lost—it is a variant of the jest on the origin of "The Vernoniad"—Fielding would restore to modern literature in his "Joseph Andrews."

Most roads, however, lead to Cervantes as Fielding's master at this time, in so far as a genius may be said to have a master. This Fielding acknowledged in that phrase on the title-page of his novel which I have quoted: "Written in Imitation of The Manner of Cervantes, Author of Don Quixote." Certain correspondences are at once apparent: the grouping of the chapters into four books in the style of the epic; pleasant or facetious headings to the chapters, with similar sentences at the close to lure the reader onward; the introduction of episodes and stories—"The Curious Impertinent" and "The History of Leonora" being exact parallels—to relieve one's tension though at the expense of a halt in the main business; always a drollery of style, becoming mock heroic for a contest, and, with Fielding, for a sunrise or a sunset; always an eye for the absurd or ridiculous in incident, manners, and character, with no fear of frank grotesqueness in description and delineation. A reader will observe, too, that

JOSEPH ANDREWS

Fielding, as well as Cervantes, runs his narrative on two contrasted characters, and that he had authority for the introductory chapters on his art in the humorous prefaces to "Don Quixote." All these resemblances are as obvious as the fact that Fielding made the serious novel of Richardson his game much as Cervantes did the romances of chivalry. But they do not tell the whole story. Fielding was so saturated with Cervantes that analysis, beyond exteriors, is rendered almost helpless. Neither "Don Quixote" nor "Joseph Andrews" is, strictly speaking, a burlesque. Each begins in burlesque and on occasion returns to it, but each is in the main the comedy of real life. This may be truer of the English than of the Spanish novel. Fielding's tendency to exaggeration was checked by the example of his friend Hogarth, which showed him how in a sister art character and incident may be heightened for comic effect and yet escape caricature.

By a mysterious process of imagination, the character of Don Quixote, undergoing a sea-change, reappeared in Parson Adams. Don Quixote fabricated a world of men from the ideals of honour, courtesy, devotion, and loyalty to truth, such as he found exemplified in books of chivalry. Then his author sent him out into the real world of men where quite different ideals rule the majority, including the squire whom the knight took along with him. The humour and the satire arise from the clash of ideals. Now Fielding in his youth, as has been described, transferred Don Quixote and Sancho Panza to the English stage. It was a pleasant comedy wherein the knight and his squire remain essentially as they were in Cervantes, despite the fact that Sancho utters English instead of Spanish proverbs. This adaptation of "Don Quixote" never satisfied Fielding; he felt that he then lacked the experience and knowledge necessary for transmuting Spaniards into Englishmen. He did not give them English names even. With time came the experience and knowledge that he had lamented the lack of. He dropped the exotic knight and took up the country parson, whom he knew from intimate association. In fact, before the appearance of Parson Adams, he had made preliminary studies of the clerical character in "The Champion," drawing upon observation, sermons, books in divinity, and the laws of the realm. No essential aspect of the clergy there escaped him. It remained for him to give life and action to the essays and sketches that he had written for the readers of his periodical.

Mr. Abraham Adams was educated for the church at Cambridge, where he began to lay up a rare fund of learning. To a perfect mastery of Greek and Latin, he added, as the years went by, some knowledge of the Oriental tongues and an ability to translate French, Italian, and Spanish. He also studied the great moralists and divines in his own language, and pored over the Scriptures until he knew them almost by heart. By nature as well as by cultivation, he was honest, generous, and brave—never suspecting that the dark passions of malice and envy existed in the rest of mankind any more than in himself. These qualities and acquirements so endeared and recommended him to his bishop that he found himself, when well above fifty years of age, still the curate of Lady Booby's parish on an income of twenty-three pounds a year; "which," remarks Fielding, "he could not make any great figure with because he lived in a dear country, and was a little encumbered with a wife and six children." Something, however, may be said for the bishop and others in whose hands his preferment lay. The parson was a large man of powerful frame, with big fists and the muscles of a labourer; he was awkward in gait and figure, and very eccentric in his manners. He went about so shabbily dressed that Sir Thomas Booby could never receive him at his table, but in recompense gave him free access to his kitchen and cellar.

He was absent-minded, not ready with a reply when spoken
to, and had a way of giving natural vent to his honest
opinions and feelings, when the floodgates were once unloosed, irrespective of persons or circumstance. He had
no vices unless one wishes to regard some weaknesses as
such. He was a little vain of his learning; he gorged his
food and guzzled his ale like a giant; he would have died
but for the solace of his pipe and tobacco. In short, Parson
Adams was a humorist in the old sense of the word.

Thirty-five years in Lady Booby's parish confirmed and
increased both the parson's good qualities and his glaring
peculiarities. His character, as we say, was refined to pure
gold. The poor in his flock became as dear to him as if
they had been his own children. When a piece of good
fortune happened to any one of them or he saw a way out
of difficulty and danger, he had a habit, under the excitement, of snapping his fingers over his head and skipping
about like one possessed of a strange spirit. To the
brighter boys of his parish he gave instruction in the rudiments of Latin grammar, with or without pay, for money
counted but little with a man who "thought a schoolmaster
the greatest character in the world, and himself the greatest
of all schoolmasters" since the days when Chiron taught
the Greek heroes. All his leisure was devoted to the study
of ancient literature, especially Greek, at which he laboured
hard for many years. His favourite author was Aeschylus.
Too poor to purchase a fresh copy of the dramatist, he
transcribed from an old one the great tragedies, and always
carried the manuscript book in his pocket for perusal at
odd times as he sat by the fire or lay prostrate on the
grass. So it was that the present world in which he lived
and moved, gradually faded away and he substituted for it
the world of ancient books. So far as concerned him,
nothing had happened for a thousand years. As were the

Greeks idealized in heroic literature, so were the Englishmen of his own time.

Except for a few scattered authors, modern literature of the lighter kind was a sealed book to him. He once read Addison's "Cato" because it had an ancient hero, and Steele's "Conscious Lovers" because there were some things in it "almost solemn enough for a sermon." Of Pope he had heard great commendation, but he had never looked into that poet's works. On the other hand, he could discourse eloquently of Homer and the Greek tragedians, dwelling upon their great scenes and their nice discrimination in character—rapping out, as he did so, hundreds of Greek verses with "such a voice, emphasis, and action" that he frightened his hearers. There was not a character in human nature, he used to say, left untouched in the Iliad and the Odyssey. Though he had hardly wandered beyond his parish, he regarded lightly his lack of contact with various peoples, since he had travelled in his books much farther than any ships could take him. If he had never heard of the Levant (which he inferred from the etymology of the word must lie in the East rather than the West Indies), he knew where the unfortunate Helle fell into the sea and had sailed the Euxine with Jason in search of the Golden Fleece. He imagined that he was still living in the golden age as described by Virgil, when truth, justice, and all the primitive virtues were practised by mankind. One conviction that became fixed in him was to prove especially unfortunate. From a remark reported of Socrates, he concluded that the human face is an infallible index of character. Therefore, it was the parson's maxim that in all one's dealings full credit must be given to a man's countenance. Three years' attendance upon Lady Booby initiated Joseph Andrews into mysteries of conduct that Parson Adams never learned from his long perusal of old books. Of many things in the modern world the scholar was as ignorant as the infant just born into it, or as the cat that sits on the table.

This is the man whom Fielding sent out on the great highway to London in answer to an advertisement by a society of booksellers for manuscript sermons of the right sort. The parson borrowed a weak-kneed horse of his clerk and set forth, dressed in a short greatcoat from which emerged the patched skirts of an old cassock. His weapons of defence against anticipated attacks of highwaymen, with which the road was infested, were not a knight's lance and shield, but two fists, which rolled up like the knuckles of an ox, and a huge crab-tree stick with which he found it necessary to provide himself on the way. But for his very long legs the parson would have frequently received some mischief when his horse, without warning, fell to the ground; but as it was, the horse sometimes dropped on his knees while the rider remained standing, and at worst horse and rider always got up unharmed after rolling over one another in the mud or down a hill. For food and lodging on the way he took only a few shillings, for he expected to meet with the same hospitality that he was accustomed to extend to strangers who passed through his own parish. The parson's adventures at inns and alehouses, through woods and across the downs, with rogues of many sorts and occasional gentlemen, are conceived in that spirit of broad comedy which pervades "Don Quixote." It is these misadventures that give zest and life to the narrative.

But the character of Parson Adams and of all those whom he fell in with, is revealed not so much by misadventures as by conversations and disputes, which may or may not reach their climax in a humorous quarrel. The issue depends upon circumstance. The parson himself was always ready to fight, if necessary, for his opinions, but the courage of his adversaries might be in words only. He did not, of course, find a ready purchaser for his sermons. Though a clergyman named Barnabas introduced him to a book-seller at one of the inns, a bargain could not well be struck for sermons which had been left at home. Still, had the sermons been in his saddlebags, there would have been no sale, since the parson and the bookseller got into an alter-cation over doctrinal questions. The bookseller, if he could not obtain a sermon or two from a bishop, wanted some-thing in the line of Whitefield or Wesley, whose books sold as well as farces. On quizzing Adams, it was discovered that his sympathies were with the reformers in their efforts to restore to the church its ancient simplicity and piety, but he broke with them when they began to preach, as did Parson Williams in "Shamela," faith against works. That detestable doctrine, he said, was coined in hell. All his own sermons threw the emphasis, where it belonged, on good works. Did they not do this, he declared eloquently, "I should belye my own opinion, which hath always been, that a virtuous and good Turk, or heathen, are more accept-able in the sight of their Creator, than a vicious and wicked Christian, tho' his faith was as perfectly orthodox as St. Paul's himself." The bookseller hurried away in disgust, remarking that opinions like that would be cried down by both clergy and people. Nobody cared anything about the poverty and self-denial of the early church, he said, while everybody was interested in a doctrine that enabled one to substitute faith in place of good works. Barnabas, who took part in the discussion, agreed with the bookseller; on hearing Adams place some heathen above Christians, he hurried out of the inn lest he should be contaminated by association with a devil who had crawled into the cassock of a clergyman.

A little later Parson Adams had experiences with another brother of the cloth. As he was preparing to leave an ale-house one morning, he found that he had only a scant six-pence to pay the reckoning, which amounted to seven

shillings, for himself, Joseph, and Fanny. In his perplexity
he called on Parson Trulliber, who held the cure of the
parish, and who, he thought, would gladly help a poor
brother in so small a matter. This Mr. Trulliber, like many
another rural parson, had made himself snug by cultivating
his glebe, keeping a dairy, and fattening swine for the
market. As Adams's cassock was concealed beneath his
greatcoat, Trulliber took him at first for a man come to
purchase some of his swine, and insisted upon an immediate visit to the pens, where an unsavoury mishap occurred. The interview, however, progressed in good
humour until Adams announced the business of his "embassy," as he called it. He told Trulliber that he would
probably be able to repay the small loan; but if he failed
to do so, it would be laying up treasure in a place where
neither moth nor rust doth corrupt. Thereupon arose a
most stormy scene, and it seemed for the moment as if
Trulliber might die of apoplexy. He rolled his eyes from
earth to heaven and then back again to earth. With Adams,
the injunction to lay up one's treasure in heaven meant
charity; with Trulliber it meant merely to have one's heart
in the Scriptures, where his had always been. It was impertinent for one clergyman to instruct another in his duty.
Each denouncing the other as not a Christian, Adams was
driven from the house amid cries of robbery from Trulliber
and his wife. In the end Adams was relieved of his distress by a poor pedlar who gave him his last penny and
wished that it had been more.

These are but two of many episodes in which Parson
Adams learned the dark ways of the world. He was made
aware that there were within his own sacred order worse
knaves than any depicted in ancient literature. For his
further enlightenment, Fielding brought him into conflict
with the Tow-wouses, who kept the Dragon Inn, with a
squire and a company of jesters, who played tricks upon

him, and with a justice of the peace, who came near committing him to jail on the charge of ravishing the girl whom he had rescued from that fate. Fielding did not take Adams to London; but instead of that, had him sit up all night to listen to the story of Farmer Wilson, who in his younger days had lived through all the dissipations of the town. It was a wonderful night of story-telling as the two men and Joseph sat by the fireside of the comfortable farmhouse—Adams often replenishing his pipe and drinking all the beer that was set before him. In return for the parson's account of his parishioners and for a glorious discourse on Greek literature, Mr. Wilson related in detail what occurs in the life of a young gentleman who goes up to London, as Fielding had done, to make his fortune in the Covent Garden district. With wonder, groans, and exclamations—"Good Lord! What wicked times, these are?"—the parson listened till morning, when under the influence of the last bottle he fell into a reverie from which he awoke a wiser man.

Before the parson reached home, he was subjected to a good deal of horse-play; he was run down by hounds, tied to a bedpost, and dipped in a tub of water. For these undignified mischances, which carry one back to Scarron and the picaresque novel, Fielding felt it necessary to apologize in his preface, where he says relative to the character of Adams: "It is designed a character of perfect simplicity; and as the goodness of his heart will recommend him to the good-natur'd; so I hope it will excuse me to the gentlemen of his cloth; for whom, while they are worthy of their sacred order, no man can possibly have a greater respect. They will therefore excuse me, notwithstanding the low adventures in which he is engaged, that I have made him a clergyman; since no other office could have given him so many opportunities of displaying his worthy inclinations." This is a fair statement. Fielding endowed Parson Adams with the choicest qualities of head and heart, giving him at the same time a blind side to keep him human. From all encounters the parson comes off triumphant. There was nothing which Fielding really detested more than that diversion called "roasting," notwithstanding its vogue with country squires and the polite part of the world. Whenever he was in a company where jesters attempted to play off a good but eccentric character, it was his custom, as related in "The Champion" and elsewhere, to turn the current of laughter back upon the wits with redoubled force. So it was in "Joseph Andrews." The reader's sympathies are never drawn away from Parson Adams. He is always on the right side, always weighty in his opinions, always a gentleman. All attempts to make sport of him eventually fail. "I defy," said Fielding, speaking through Joseph Andrews, "the wisest man in the world to turn a true good action into ridicule." Some of the characters in the novel tried this and earned for themselves only ridicule or contempt; for Fielding always, either directly or through Parson Adams, exposed them ruthlessly. In "Joseph Andrews" more perhaps than in "Don Quixote," it is the man practised in the ways of the world, not the idealist, who is satirized. Adams remains to the end one of the glories of human nature. His experience on the road in no wise altered his views on what men should be; but it enlarged his knowledge on what they actually are. In one respect only did Fielding let him become contaminated by the world. Mr. Booby persuaded the good parson to accept, while retaining his old curacy, a living in a neighbouring parish worth £130 a year. With a laugh in his sleeve, Fielding thus left Parson Adams to enjoy the fruits of a small pluralist.

II

Lying behind Parson Adams and most characters in "Joseph Andrews" is a definite theory of humour, which

THE HISTORY OF HENRY FIELDING

Fielding, as may be seen from several of his articles in "The Champion," had been working out for himself from the examples of his great predecessors and from various disquisitions that had got into literature on the source and the nature of the ridiculous. Neither of his compeers— Lucian and Cervantes—had proclaimed a theory of humour, but both showed by incidental remarks that they proceeded on lines clearly defined for themselves if not for the public. At the outset of "A True Story"—a burlesque of the marvellous tales and adventures related by Homer and Herodotus—Lucian said in substance that he had a plan, but that he would leave it to be divined by his readers, except for the clue that they should look everywhere for parodies on the old poets, historians, and philosophers. That skill in parody, in union with an assumed gravity, which one sees in "Joseph Andrews," was an art or manner learned from Lucian. It is a kind of parody which, though often direct, is never crude; and at its best defies analysis, for it is inherent in the mood and attitude of the author. If Cervantes had laid down a theory of humour, just hinted at in his preface to the first part of "Don Quixote," it probably would have been in agreement with the observation of Schopenhauer that the conduct of Don Quixote becomes humorous because the knight "subsumes the realities he encounters under conceptions drawn from the romances of chivalry, from which they are very different."[*] That is, the humour of "Don Quixote" lies in the incongruity between things as they appear to the general run of men and as they appear to a man who derives his knowledge of the world mostly from books. This is in accord with Bergson also. The French philosopher, it is well known, finds the essence of humour in a certain rigidity of thought and action resulting from absent-mindedness.

[*] "The World as Will and Idea," as trans. by Haldane and Kemp, Boston, 1887, II, 278.

That, in his view, is the supreme source of the comic. Don Quixote is systematically absent-minded. Throughout his adventures, his mind is on the romances of chivalry with which the business in hand is always coloured. Fielding had divined the character of Don Quixote, when he created, as a rival to the Spanish knight, Parson Adams living among the ancients as if they were his contemporaries. He deepened and varied this absent-mindedness, and humanized it to the point of forgetfulness. Like Cervantes, he let two worlds collide for the amusement and instruction of mankind.

In the process, Fielding quite naturally considered what qualities, characteristics, and actions are legitimate objects of ridicule. On this question he read what had been written by critics and moralists—by Aristotle, Cicero, the Earl of Shaftesbury, and the Abbé Bellegarde, who had published a treatise entitled "Réflexions sur le Ridicule"; but he was surprised to discover that their definitions of what constitutes the ridiculous were mainly negative. Aristotle remarked that villainy is not a proper object of ridicule, but nowhere postively asserted what is the proper object. Later writers—Cicero, for instance—described many species of the ridiculous, but none traced it to its fountain. In agreement with Aristotle and Cicero, Fielding held that all attempts to ridicule villainy were bound to fail, since the natural emotion awakened by great vices is abhorrence. He likewise agreed with Shaftesbury that a writer who understands his business will never think of ridiculing great qualities of head and heart, for the natural emotions awakened by these qualities are admiration and love. Indeed, when Fielding declared that he defied "the wisest man in the world to turn a good action into ridicule," he was hardly more than repeating—I wonder whether he knew it—a sentence from Shaftesbury, who said "One may defy the

world to turn real bravery or generosity into ridicule."*
Moreover, Fielding would ordinarily, though not always,
exclude from ridicule misfortunes, poverty, ugliness, and
all physical deformities, inasmuch as they should call forth
our pity.

As soon as he thus clearly saw that the border line between the serious and the ridiculous is neither fixed nor
straight, he was face to face with an unsolved problem.
Thereupon his reflections turned to the practice, sometimes conscious, sometimes unconscious, of English comedy
since Ben Jonson; wherein the characters are strongly
marked by some "humour," as it was called—that is, by
some trait, notion, idiosyncrasy, or mere affectation which
by the consent of everybody exposes them to ridicule. By
Fielding's time, opinion had become settled that affectations were the source of ridicule, that humour consisted in
portraying them. So Steele said; so Lord Chesterfield said.
Fielding did not dispute the common view; in fact, he may
have written the anonymous essays on wit and humour in
"Common Sense" which have been attributed to Lord
Chesterfield.† But when he came to write "Joseph
Andrews" and its preface, he saw the need of tracing back
further the affectations. Humour, it is true, has its source
in affectation; but what is the source of affectation? The
novelist answered his question by saying:

"Affectation proceeds from one of these two Causes;
Vanity, or Hypocrisy: for as Vanity puts us on affecting
false Characters, in order to purchase Applause; so
Hypocrisy sets us on an Endeavour to avoid Censure by
concealing our Vices under an Appearance of their opposite
Virtues. And tho' these two Causes are often confounded,

---

* "Essay on Wit and Humour," in "Characteristicks," 1714, I, 129.

† The essentials of the theory of humour which Fielding held, are stated
and illustrated in the leading articles of "Common Sense" for Sept. 3 and
10, 1737. Fielding either wrote these articles or appropriated in the preface
to "Joseph Andrews" the ideas which they contain.

(for they require some Difficulty in distinguishing;) yet, as they proceed from very different Motives, so they are as clearly distinct in their Operations: for indeed, the Affectation which arises from Vanity is nearer to Truth than the other; as it hath not that violent Repugnancy of Nature to struggle with, which that of the Hypocrite hath. It may be likewise noted, that Affectation doth not imply an absolute Negation of those qualities which are affected: and therefore, tho', when it proceeds from Hypocrisy, it be nearly allied to Deceit; yet when it comes from Vanity only, it partakes of the Nature of Ostentation: for instance, the Affectation of Liberality in a vain Man, differs visibly from the same Affectation in the Avaricious; for tho' the vain Man is not what he would appear, or hath not the Virtue he affects, to the degree he would be thought to have it; yet it sits less awkwardly on him than on the avaricious Man, who is the very Reverse of what he would seem to be.''

"From the discovery of this affectation," Fielding held, "arises the ridiculous—which always strikes the reader with surprize and pleasure.'' It is accordingly the province of the humorist to show that the vain man is deficient in the quality he professes to have, and that the hypocrite is the exact opposite of what he sets himself up to be. This process of unmasking, Fielding would say, not only gives delight to the spectator, but may induce him to correct similar faults in his own character and so do him as much good as a bishop's sermon. Reflections like these led Fielding to return to the point whence he set out and to inquire a little further into the question whether misfortunes or the imperfections of nature have any legitimate part in ridicule. His conclusion was that they must be avoided by the humorist unless there be some affectation involved in them. For example, ugliness and lameness move the compassion of all good men; but nobody can withhold his mirth when he sees an ugly man aiming at the applause of beauty, or a lame one endeavouring to display agility. On the other hand, Fielding could never bring himself to deal lightly with the blacker vices though they were affected; and yet, he said, "it is very difficult to pursue a series of human actions and keep clear from them." His solution was to represent the vices that were necessarily introduced into his novel as "rather the accidental consequences of some human frailty, or foible, than causes habitually existing in the mind," and never to set them forth as the "objects of ridicule but detestation."

On this theory of humour, Fielding claimed, not with full seriousness perhaps, to have built his "Joseph Andrews." Though differently expressed, the theory is essentially in harmony with what Cervantes, as explained by Schopenhauer, had in mind when he wrote "Don Quixote." Both sought humour in the incongruities of speech and conduct. The characters in "Joseph Andrews" for the most part move in half lights, their vision blinded by some affectation. They are bent upon transforming themselves from what nature intended them into something else, as it were for a masquerade, wherein they go through the dances, each unknown to another; but in the end they all betray themselves through some incident or remark when they are taken off their guard. Parson Adams, who has all the time supposed the masques to be real faces, looks on in wonder at the unmasking, while everybody else, suspecting that something of the kind would occur, laughs or smiles.

In some cases there is little or no disguise. Joseph and Fanny become humorous only from the violent manifestations now and then of their excessive love, as in the scene where for the moment it seems as if they were brother and sister and so cannot marry. In like manner Parson Adams has no fault, in the moral meaning of this word, except the harmless vanity of a learned man inclined to quote his Greek authors or to preach a sermon at unseasonable times; but even then his fine qualities always come to the front; whenever his masque is removed, nothing is discovered but unalterable goodness. When, for example, Joseph fears that he may lose Fanny by an ill turn of fortune, Parson Adams admonishes the young man to submit himself in peace and contentment to the will of heaven. "You are too much inclined to passion, child," he tells him, "and have set your affections so absolutely on this young woman, that if G— required her at your hands, I fear you would reluctantly part with her." Hardly had he uttered his rebuke of Joseph's impatience, before it was reported to the parson (by mistake, of course) that his youngest son Dick had just fallen into the river and been drowned. At first struck dumb by the news, the parson soon burst out in loud lamentation over the supposed death of his dearest child —"my little prattler, the darling and comfort of my old age—the little wretch to be snatched out of life just at his entrance into it; the sweetest, best-temper'd boy, who never did a thing to offend me. It was but this morning I gave him his first lesson in *Quae Genus*"—a chapter in the Eton grammar. In this way Fielding often found it necessary to call Parson Adams back to the natural human affections which no speculations on life and death can ever suppress. The humour arising here from absent-mindedness, in the Bergsonian sense of the word, only makes Parson Adams more lovable than ever. All good qualities, Fielding admitted in practice if not in theory, are heightened by association with some weakness, provided it does not become a grave fault. The dash of vanity that he gave to Parson Adams, in addition to his absent-mindedness, was the supreme touch in that humorous creation.

Of the vices, Fielding felt most at home with avarice, which, notwithstanding the views he expressed on the ridiculous, he had contrived to treat very humorously in "The Miser"—a comedy then performed at the London theatres many times every year. This vice, originating in a laudable desire to make one's self comfortable in the latter days of life, has long been regarded as fair game for the comic writer. Besides many others, there were Plautus and Molière, on whose "Aulularia" and "L'Avare," Fielding, to say the truth, had drawn freely in composing his own comedy. Of the two misers in "Joseph Andrews"—Parson Trulliber and Peter Pounce—Fielding is rather more successful with the latter, in whom is united a lust for gold and an ineffectual lust for young women. Peter is Lady Booby's unjust steward who has amassed a large fortune in land through concealed dishonesty and extortionate usury. Out of this reprobate, Fielding gets much humour by contrasting his pretensions with the real man, and by displaying the curious ways in which his mind works. If anybody calls him rich, he denies the compliment, fearing that it may be but preliminary to a request that he unloose his purse-strings. If anybody questions his wealth, he becomes enraged and boasts of his great accumulations. A memorable conversation takes place between him and Parson Adams while the two are jogging along in the coach towards Lady Booby's parish. The subject turns to charity, a word which, as usually understood, Peter most disliked of all the words in the English language. In the hope of a new definition, Pounce asks Adams what his notions are of this so-called virtue which, parsons keep repeating, is enjoined by the Scriptures.

" 'Sir,' said Adams, 'my Definition of Charity is a generous Disposition to relieve the Distressed.' 'There is something in that Definition,' answered Peter, 'which I like well enough; it is, as you say, a Disposition—and does not so much consist in the Act as in the Disposition to do it; but alas, Mr. Adams, Who are meant by the Distressed? Believe me, the Distresses of Mankind are mostly imaginary, and it would be rather Folly than Goodness to relieve them.' 'Sure, Sir,' replied Adams, 'Hunger and Thirst, Cold and Nakedness, and other Distresses which attend the Poor, can never be said to be imaginary Evils.' 'How can any Man complain of Hunger,' said Peter, 'in a Country where such excellent Sallads are to be gathered in almost every Field? or of Thirst, where every River and Stream produces such delicious Potations? And as for Cold and Nakedness, they are Evils introduced by Luxury and Custom. A Man naturally wants Clothes no more than a Horse or any other Animal, and there are whole Nations who go without them.' ''

Unable to endure these sentiments which quickly ran into insults to the cloth, Parson Adams leaped from the coach and pursued the rest of the way on foot. So abrupt was his departure that he forgot to take his hat, which Peter threw after him with great violence. This surely is a comic presentation of avarice.

But Fielding always found rather difficult a positive vice which had become ingrained. He rather excelled in his portraits of people in whom the common virtues have suffered considerably from want of exercise—of people whom the world has rendered selfish instead of kind and generous. They are not outright bad, but any good qualities which they may have can hardly be awakened except by an appeal to selfish motives. Into their composition goes vanity but far more hypocrisy. Of this kind is Mrs. Slipslop, the daughter of a country curate, and now waiting-maid to Lady Booby. As ignorant as she is vulgar, the woman thinks that her birth entitles her to be consulted on all affairs of Lady Booby's household and parish. Her imagined importance leads her to affect the use of hard words which, deceived by sound, she invariably gets wrong. One of her favourite topics of discussion with Parson Adams is on the "insense," as she terms it, of matter. She is the character in which Fielding developed farthest the comic in words.

Sheridan turned her into Mrs. Malaprop, and perhaps she is more suited to the drama than to the novel. Owing to a small slip that she made in her youth, she remains chaste thereafter until she reaches middle life, when she decides that it will be safe to make amends for her long self-denial. But of her fruitless endeavours it is unnecessary to write here.

The class of not very harmful hypocrites to which Mrs. Slipslop belongs, is represented with very great humour by those passengers in the coach which is brought to a halt by the cries of Joseph as he lies robbed, naked, and bleeding in the ditch. Nobody wants to take him in, and the postillion is reprimanded by the coachman for stopping the horses "as we are confounded late." Joseph would have been left there to die, had it not been for a lawyer in the party who, though he wished as much as any that they had passed by without notice, feared that it would not now be safe to do so, for he knew cases in the books where innocent men last in the company of a murdered man were held responsible for the crime. "He therefore thought it advisable to save the poor creature's life, for their own sakes, if possible." A prude protests against Joseph's being lifted into the coach until he is properly dressed, though she is all the while looking at him through the sticks of her fan. Seeing the poor boy shivering with cold, a wit suggests that she accommodate him with a dram—a request that she resents, for she never tasted such a thing. A little later it turns out that she has about her a small silver bottle containing some excellent Nantes, which her maid had put up for her by mistake instead of Hungary water. Neither the coachman nor the passengers can spare a coat to cover Joseph, for they are themselves cold or else fear damage to their clothing from the blood of a wounded man. "It is more than probable," remarks Fielding, "poor Joseph . . . must have perished, unless the postillion, (a lad who hath

been since transported for robbing a hen-roost) had volun-
tarily stript off a great coat, his only garment, at the same
time swearing a great oath, (for which he was rebuked by
the passengers) 'that he would rather ride in his shirt all
his life, than suffer a fellow-creature to lie in so miserable a
condition.' ''

"A comic writer," Fielding concluded, "should of all
others be the least excused for deviating from nature, since
. . . life every where furnishes an accurate observer with
the ridiculous''; whereas "it may not be always so easy for
a serious poet to meet with the great and the admirable."
And of his "Joseph Andrews," he added that it contained
"scarce a character or action" which he had not taken
from his "own observations and experience." These statements are perfectly just. It might be expected that a
novelist having an elaborate theory of the ridiculous, more
or less true, would do little more than illustrate it in the
plot and characters of his book; that the outcome would
be at best only a distorted or one-sided view of men and
their conduct. But for Fielding a wide and intimate acquaintance with real life acted as a corrective. With him
the imaginative faculty worked in the main, not from theory
to observation, but from observation to theory. Certainly
whatever he took over into his art, he first tested by personal experience. He rejected as well as accepted. No one
would say that Fielding arrived at a full and complete
explanation of what humour is. There are elements in the
problem that have baffled philosophers all the way from
Aristotle to Bergson. But Fielding's notions were sound
enough so far as they went; and when they failed him, he
disregarded them, as a wise man should, and followed the
natural bent of his genius, which was certain to lead him
aright. A situation, character, act, or gesture that appeared comic to him, he might be sure would appear comic
to others also.

Furthermore, wherever there is involved in his novel some hint or suggestion for his scene derived from Marivaux or Cervantes, no foreign note is ever struck; there is no transference of French or Spanish manners to his pages. Perhaps one might say that Parson Adams on horseback is a very close parallel to Don Quixote on Rosinante; that both meet with comical adventures at inns, alehouses, and elsewhere on the road. This would all be true. Cervantes gave Fielding a plan for organizing his adventures. And yet there is nothing Spanish in "Joseph Andrews." The novel is thoroughly English in colour, motive, and character. In 1740, parsons and country squires often made the journey to London on horseback. If their families accompanied them, they travelled by coach—either in their own chariots, as they called them, or in the public conveyances. The poor, of course, went on foot. As in Chaucer's day, there were inns at the usual stopping-places for dinner and lodging, and alehouses were scattered all along the route. These alehouses, "The Gentleman's Magazine"* complained, were "the nurseries and sanctuaries of highwaymen, footpads, pickpockets, gypsies, and strolling beggars; and all sorts of rogues and villains, which like state vermin prey upon the public." That is exactly the background of "Joseph Andrews."

Of the road Fielding wrote as if merely in memory of what he had actually seen. If he recalled the sign of an inn—a lion or a dragon—he gave it; if the sign had slipped from memory, the inn remained forever nameless. Likewise only a few of the many characters are endowed with English surnames—none outside the Adams, Andrews, and Wilson families. For two of these names, as well as for several in "Tom Jones," it was once pointed out,† Fielding had recourse to the list of subscribers appended to Bishop

* September, 1736, VI, 537-538.

† "Notes and Queries," 9 S. II, 426 (Nov. 26, 1898).

JOSEPH ANDREWS

Burnet's "History of his Own Times," a copy of which, I may add, was in his library. There he found, it is said, "Joseph Andrews, Esq." There, too, was "Abraham Adams, Esq.," who became in 1731 a director of the East India Company.* These may be, however, only coincidences, for they are common names, and the former is the only apt name that could be given to a virtuous brother of Pamela Andrews. Still, one wonders how well-known gentlemen, if they were living in 1742, liked the sight of their names in a novel for a lady's footman and an absent-minded parson. But to drop a fruitless speculation, Fielding usually either invented facetious names for his characters or left them without any at all. Names like Tow-wouse and Slipslop were chosen primarily to indicate the characteristic of the wearer. This was a practice long sanctioned by English comedy. A sobriquet might serve also as a disguise for someone whom Fielding did not wish to call by his real name; or it might be employed because he did not remember the name of the person whom he was describing, if indeed he ever knew it. One justice of the peace is only "a justice," while another is "Justice Frolic"; a constable who lets a robber escape is "Tom Suckbribe"; one lawyer is merely "a lawyer," while another becomes "James Scout." In these and many similar cases Fielding was apparently giving so much as he knew of people whom he had come into contact with. If an appropriate name for the character occurred to him, he applied it; otherwise he let him play his part without one.

And what has been said of the characters in the novel might be said with equal truth of the incidents. They all have the appearance of coming from memory. The incident that seems now most improbable is the exchange of Joseph and Fanny in the cradle. But if one considers the state of society in 1740, there is nothing fantastic about

* "The Grub-street Journal," April 29, 1731.

343

that. According to the newspapers, it was a common crime for gypsies to steal children in order to recruit their bands or to dispose of them to the best advantage as servants to the gentry. Test "Joseph Andrews" wherever you will, and you come face to face with real life.

Of course, no comic writer ever reproduces exactly what has come within his experience. His art requires for its effect emphasis on traits of character and some embroidery of incident. No man was ever so absent-minded as Parson Adams; no man in the course of a fortnight ever went through so many misadventures in consequence of this weakness. No woman within the same period ever made so many blunders as Mrs. Slipslop in the use of high-sounding words. The point I wish to make is that in delineating Adams, Slipslop, and other characters in his novel, Fielding kept his mind upon men and women of his acquaintance who possessed in a marked degree the humorous qualities that he developed and elaborated. Aware of this characteristic of his art, he protested in his preface that he had "no intention to vilify or asperse any one." "I have used," he said there, "the utmost care to obscure the persons by such different circumstances, degrees, and colours, that it will be impossible to guess at them with any degree of certainty; and if it ever happens otherwise, it is only where the failure characterized is so minute, that it is a foible only which the party himself may laugh at as well as any other."

Notwithstanding the caveat, the curious at once began to uncover his characters. "Parson Young," wrote Richardson in 1752, "sat for Fielding's Parson Adams, a man he knew, and only made a little more absurd than he is known to be."[*] This had been the general opinion ever since the novel appeared. The man to whom Richardson referred was the Rev. William Young whom Fielding knew in the West. Born at Hannington, a parish and village of North

---

[*] A. L. Barbauld, "Correspondence of Richardson," IV, 60.

JOSEPH ANDREWS

Wiltshire, Young matriculated at St. John's College, Oxford, on July 15, 1727, when he was twenty-five years old. Before this time he had kept a school at Romsey, a market town on the way between Southampton and Salisbury; and after leaving Oxford he was appointed curate of Fielding's parish at East Stour, where he remained, though living at Gillingham, for nine years, from 1731 to 1740. It was, of course, at East Stour that the two men met, and became so fast friends that when Fielding left the parish for good, the parson followed him to London and joined with him in projects for translations of Aristophanes and Lucian. It is probable, too, that Young collaborated with Fielding in other miscellaneous work; but of this there is less direct evidence. As already noticed, he was with Fielding when the copyright in "Joseph Andrews" was assigned to Millar and he put his name to the agreement as one of the witnesses.

The tradition that Parson Young was the original of Parson Adams has doubtless been adorned with several tales in part apocryphal. As an example of Young's absent-mindedness, it has been related, for instance, that the parson, while serving as chaplain in one of Marlborough's regiments in Flanders, strayed away, during a fit of reverie, into the camp of the enemy. "The officer, who commanded," we are informed by Murphy, ". . . seeing an innate goodness in his prisoner . . . very politely gave him leave to pursue his contemplations home again." This story, which had the authority of "a gentleman" who was in the wars at the same time, cannot be true in all particulars; for when Marlborough was relieved of his command in the Netherlands, William Young was but a boy nine or ten years old. At a later time he was, however, chaplain to Major-General Lascelles's Regiment of Foot, and so may have been on the Continent just before his appointment to East Stour. It was then if ever that he went over to the enemy and was sent home again. More likely to be true is the anecdote that he once threatened to knock down a man who casually addressed him as Parson Adams.

Another story takes us back to the time when he was a schoolmaster at Romsey, under the patronage of Sir John St. Barbe of Broadlands in the neighbourhood. In those early days, he was "so careless a man," it is said, "as to run into every tradesman's debt," and would have been sent to jail had not Sir John St. Barbe and other friends come to his aid. "All he knew of the matter was, he wanted the goods and had 'em." His London career was very well summarized by Herbert Croft, who wrote of him in his "Life" of Edward Young, the poet, with whom the parson had become confounded: "He supported an uncomfortable existence by translating for the booksellers from the Greek; and if he did not seem to be his own friend, was at least no man's enemy." Among his learned works, he revised Ainsworth's "Latin Dictionary" and Hederich's "Greek Lexicon," books widely used in the schools. Subsequent to Fielding's death the poor scholar retired to Chelsea Hospital, where he died on August 30, 1757.

Parson Young was clearly a man of kindly nature, who could not adjust himself to the ways of the world. He was a Greek scholar, particularly fond, we see, of Aristophanes and Lucian, and perhaps of Aeschylus. His absorption in study may well have developed in him not only absence of mind but the eccentric gesture of snapping his fingers over his head, or the habit of shouting "Heureka," when an idea suddenly occurred to him. Withal, his country breeding doubtless made of him a strong and awkward man, expert, like other village boys of the period, in cudgel-playing. On this social misfit, Fielding let his mind play and produced Parson Adams. He took such details from the man's life as he wished and suppressed or altered others. Both Young and Adams were schoolmasters, as well as parsons;

both held small church livings, and had large families, the children of each numbering six; while as a variation, the one was educated at Oxford, the other at Cambridge; nor were the two men made to correspond exactly in age, for Adams was much the older. In a most important respect they differed widely. Young was naïvely dishonest. Rather than see his family starve, he ran into the books of grocers and let his friends raise the money to settle his bills. But this is not the most amusing incident. Some months after his portrait had appeared in "Joseph Andrews," he secured the post of tutor to a young gentleman at £70 a year. Before assuming his duties, he wished to take a brief rest, but instead of frankly saying so he resorted to a ruse which he was unable to carry through. In words written at the time, "he endeavoured by a feigned letter to himself to get leave of his patron to spend a fortnight in the country; but this letter, containing the pretended invitation, he put into his patron's hand sealed and unopened, which piece of absence discovered the scheme, so little was he able to act this little piece of disingenuity." This streak of guile in Parson Young, which must have been as plain as day to Fielding, was generously left out of the portrait of Parson Adams in accordance with his rule that he would asperse no good man's character. The trait was left out, too, in the interest of art; for it had been predetermined that Parson Adams should be thoroughly honest and honourable. He might borrow, if he could, of a more prosperous brother, or he might forget to pay for a night's lodging, but in either case the debt would be a treasure laid up in heaven.*

We may, I think, take another step, and say, if we do not press the resemblance too far, that the parish of Parson Adams containing Lady Booby's seat, corresponds with

* For fresh information about William Young, given here, see Mr. J. Paul de Castro in "Notes and Queries," 12 S. I, 224-225 (March 18, 1916).

Fielding's own East Stour. Fielding once speaks of the parish as being in Somersetshire, whereas East Stour is over the border in Dorsetshire; but besides the fact that the original of Parsons Adams was curate of East Stour, there are several indications that Fielding's eye was often on his own home. Dick fell into "the river," not a pond, perhaps because there are no ponds at East Stour, but the river flows through the meadows below. Again Lady Booby's parish, like East Stour, was not very far from Salisbury, where the robber who attacked Fanny was committed to jail. As related earlier, there is a tradition that Parson Trulliber was drawn from the Rev. Mr. Oliver, Fielding's tutor and the curate of the adjoining parish of Motcombe. Some mistake may be involved in this identification; but beyond reasonable doubt Peter Pounce derived his salient qualities from Peter Walter, the wealthy lawyer and usurer living a few miles away at Stalbridge Park. With this aged skinflint Fielding was to deal again under his Latinized name of "Petrus Gualterus." The sobriquet given to him here—"Peter Pounce"—was at once a play upon his real name and "Peter Pence," then applied by the Opposition to any unjust or unpopular tax of the Walpole Government. It is not improbable that there had occurred between Peter Walter and Parson Young conversations on charity and riches having some resemblance to those between Peter Pounce and Parson Adams in "Joseph Andrews." They must have occasionally met, and a clash could not have been avoided between men so unlike in temper. Parson Young and Fielding, we may assume also, made many journeys together up to London, meeting with adventures on which were based those of Parson Adams and Joseph. They would go on horseback to Salisbury—having but one horse if they followed the method of "ride and tie" described in the novel. At Salisbury they would strike the main road, and proceed thence, if not on horseback, by coach to London. A return journey over this road from London to Salisbury is the main scene of "Joseph Andrews." Perhaps Fielding also incorporated into his story incidents that had occurred on his journeys between Bath and London or on the western circuit which he was then riding. Some day we may discover from the notes of an eighteenth-century traveller just where were the inns named the Dragon, the George, and the Lion.

The novel contains no portrait of the author, but Fielding lends a part of himself to two characters. Joseph Andrews —I have said it elsewhere—has Fielding's splendid physique, strong and symmetrical in legs, thighs, and arms,— and withal his nose inclining to the Roman. Fielding's great frame, with its broad and brawny shoulders, had been developed by cudgel-playing, just like Joseph's. So said "The Gazetteer" in a satirical biography of him some time before the appearance of the novel. While it would be a mistake to regard, as many have done, the account that Farmer Wilson gives of himself as an autobiography of Fielding, the story follows Fielding's own career in outline. Both Fielding and Wilson had their experiences in the life of the town—with taverns, theatrical managers, book-sellers, and strange philosophies—and both married women having similar lovable traits of character, and retired to the country in search of the golden age; Wilson for the rest of his life, Fielding for a few months. The biography, however, is clearly intended to be typical, and not personal to Fielding. This does not mean that Fielding did not weave into Wilson's story incidents intimately personal; he probably did do this, but it would be dangerous and mis-leading to attempt to run up a parallel. Fielding rather uncovers himself in occasional comment and incident. Just how this was done may be safely illustrated by one example. Mr. Wilson, after his sad experiences with the women of the town, railed at them, he says, in the gross language of

Juvenal, calling them "painted palaces, inhabited by Disease and Death." So Fielding when a boy just out of Eton railed at women by modernizing the Sixth Satire of Juvenal, which he was revising at this time for publication. He railed at them, however, not because he had been associating with harlots, but because he had lost a beautiful heiress down in the West. It is certain to be much like this when one can discover precisely the personal element in Fielding's works; one never quite reaches autobiography; it is but some incident, anecdote, or detail drawn from experience or observation, and then reshaped by the hand of an artist.

Rather strangely, there are no traditions as to where Fielding composed "Joseph Andrews," though several places have contended for the honour of harbouring him while at work on "Tom Jones." It is probable that Fielding, after ceasing to contribute to "The Champion" in June, 1741, attended the Assizes in the West as he had done the previous year, and then rested at Bath or Salisbury. Apparently he had been going to Salisbury for his vacations ever since he sold his lands at East Stour. If this be so, "Joseph Andrews" was perhaps begun there—either within the Cathedral Close or in the manor house at the foot of Milford hill—near the very road travelled by his characters. However this may be, the novel was completed and published—and, I daresay, largely written—in most distressful circumstances after Fielding's return to London, while he was living in Spring Gardens, Charing Cross, within sight of St. James's Park. About his residence in Spring Gardens, nothing is directly known beyond the bare fact of it. His name appears nowhere in the rate-books of the parish. The necessary inference is that he did not take an entire house but merely lived in lodgings. It would be but conjecture to add that his lodgings were perhaps in one of two houses, against which taxes were levied during this period in the name of Richard Browning.*

The scene in those lodgings is described briefly—though "Joseph Andrews" is not mentioned—in the preface to his "Miscellanies" of the next year. Although Fielding was but in his thirty-sixth year, his magnificent constitution already showed signs of breaking. Gout, which was eventually to cripple him, laid him up for the winter. High living may have had something to do with this; but Fielding was rather paying the penalty for incessant labour since he gave up the theatre. As barrister and editor, he had been doing the work of two or three men. While he was tormented with the gout, "a favourite child," he says, was dying in one bed, and his wife lay desperately ill in another. Mrs. Fielding partially recovered; but the child—it was their first child Charlotte, then in her sixth year—was buried on the ninth of March (within three weeks after "Joseph Andrews" appeared) in the chancel vault of St. Martin's in the Fields, the church which the family attended when in London. The rough notes of the sexton give the information that four men bore the coffin, that large candles were provided for the altar, and prayers were read—probably by Thomas Newton, afterwards Bishop of Bristol, then the preacher at Spring Gardens Chapel within the parish of St. Martin's. The body, it is expressly stated, was brought from Spring Gardens, and the fees for burial were five pounds and eighteen shillings, a large sum for a poor man to pay. By the sexton's slip the child's age is recorded as seven instead of six years. Fielding tried to calm the transports of grief by reading the philosophers and divines on life and death; but found nothing there so just and true as the remark of his wife at the birth and death of Charlotte. "I remember," he said the next year in a passage of great pathos, "the most

* Rate Books in Westminster City Hall.

excellent of women, and tenderest of mothers, when, after a painful and dangerous delivery, she was told she had a daughter, answering: Good God! have I produced a creature who is to undergo what I have suffered! Some years afterwards, I heard the same woman, on the death of that very child, then one of the loveliest creatures ever seen, comforting herself with reflecting, that her child could never know what it was to feel such a loss as she then lamented."* From this afflicted household came one of the most humorous books in the English language.

Illness and grief explain the presence of some inconsistencies in the novel and of many minor errors, due partly to the author and partly to the compositor, which a man experienced with the press would have ordinarily corrected. Fielding did in fact make some alterations in the proofs, which the printer charged against the book, but they could not have been many. Not until "Joseph Andrews" was printed did he discover that he had made Parson Adams sit up two nights in succession, whereas there should have been an intervening night of sleep. For this mistake he apologized in a note facing the first chapter, and requested the reader to excuse all other mistakes. An opportunity, however, for thorough revision, was afforded by the call for a second edition of "Joseph Andrews," which made its appearance in midsummer,† "with Alterations and Additions by the Author." The number of copies printed, according to the entry in Henry Woodfall's ledger dated May 31, 1742, was two thousand.‡ A reader of the new edition would observe for the first time a table of contents and two additional footnotes, neither of which has lost its interest. One of them states that the very fond letter from Leonora to Horatio was contributed by "a young lady,"—that is,

* "Of the Remedy of Affliction for the Loss of our Friends."
† "The Gentleman's Magazine," Aug., 1742, p. 448.
‡ "Notes and Queries," 1 S. XI, 419 (June 2, 1855).

by his sister Sarah probably, who was soon to publish volumes of similar letters. The other footnote is Fielding's comment on a blunder which "a great orator" in one of the public coffee-houses thought he had unearthed in "Joseph Andrews." This obtuse gentleman (so it was reported to Fielding) took him to task for permitting Parson Adams to commend the learning of Farmer Wilson. Now Adams unquestionably possesses learning, declared the orator, perhaps all that the author had; but Wilson nowhere shows any. Fielding replied that the humour of the parson's remark lay just there; in that he commended in another his own qualities and acquirements. This so-called blunder Fielding decided to let stand, but he corrected nearly all the real ones down to mistakes in punctuation. "Justice Trolick" now became "Justice Frolick," and "Dr. Sanglado" became "Dr. Sangrado"; and small words that had dropped out, if they ever were in, were restored. To use the phrase then current, Fielding "cured" his text.

As Fielding went along, he made, too, a number of changes in phrasing, for clearness, ease, humour, and irony. Pamela, who in the first edition was only Mr. Booby's "wife," now called herself that gentleman's "lady." Occasionally brand-new phrases, sentences, and whole paragraphs were inserted. These additions might merely heighten the scene, but at times they altered it considerably. In the first edition, it is not clear, for instance, how Parson Adams, while staying at the Dragon Inn, learned that he had left his sermons at home, though it is implied that he looked into his saddle-bags for them and found only shirts and shoes. In the second edition, it is related in two inserted paragraphs that Joseph, on lifting the saddle-bags, knew at once by the weight that they held nothing so heavy as manuscript sermons. A passage like this was necessary to remove a possible inconsistency in the character of Parson Adams, and to make definite his motive for returning home. But for Joseph's discovery the parson should have gone on to London. Again, Fielding enlarged, for the pure comedy of it, the scene where Parson Adams is summoned before the justice on the charge of robbery, and comes near being committed, as the second edition only has it, on account of his manuscript copy of Aeschylus, which is produced as evidence against him. In the excited dispute over what the strange writing was—whether it was merely a book of ciphers or a manuscript of one of the Fathers—Parsons Adams appeared to call himself by the fictitious name of Aeschylus; whereupon the justice ordered his clerk to "make Mr. Aeschylus his mittimus" for giving a false name. Other alterations involved interesting but not very important changes in incident, such as the details of a fray in the kitchen of one of the inns, the occurrences when the characters set out on their last day's journey to Booby Hall, and numerous new turns in the dialogue. Fielding hardly reworked his novel, but he subjected it to close scrutiny. Only one detail that needed serious attention escaped him. In the first edition he confounded Sir Thomas Booby with Sir John Booby, the father of Pamela's husband.* In consequence of this slip of the pen, Fanny was made to live at one and the same time in two different families twenty miles apart; and so far as I know, she has continued to live in both places ever since—in all subsequent editions of "Joseph Andrews."

A second edition of "Joseph Andrews" within a few months of the first, means that the novel rapidly made its way to the public. Its sale almost if not quite equalled that of "Pamela" during a corresponding period. But thereafter "Joseph Andrews" could not keep up the pace set by "Pamela." A novel that deals seriously with a risky situation is sure to have many more readers than one that parodies that situation. For a sober narrative

* Compare Bk. I, Ch. XI, with Bk. IV, Ch. XII.

354

with a moral purpose, real or affected, is understood by everybody; whereas humour and irony perplex the average mind. Richardson's novel ran its course down through all classes to the servants' hall, while Fielding's novel ran upward through a less numerous class to the gentry and nobility. Still, Fielding had in the aggregate a large audience. Further evidence of the demand for "Joseph Andrews" is afforded by the attempts of a bookseller to steal it in the autumn of 1742. Fielding or Millar obtained a writ of injunction against him, and the case came up at Westminster Hall during the Michaelmas term. The story is briefly told by Sir Dudley Ryder, the attorney-general (afterwards chief-justice) in a letter, indorsed October 23, 1742, to his wife then at Bath. The letter begins—

"My dearest Girl.— I can't help thinking of you in the midst of the noise of Westminster Hall. I have this moment sat down after endeavouring to rescue Jos. Andrews and Parson Adams out of the hands of pirates, but in vain; for this time we are foiled by a mistake in the attack. However, another broadside next week will do the business."*

The mistake in the attack to which the attorney-general refers was "an error in the jurat of the affidavits." The injunction was evidently granted the next week, for no pirated edition of the novel made its appearance in London at that time.

A third edition of "Joseph Andrews," comprising, it has just been discovered, three thousand copies, was published by Millar on March 24, 1743.† This was essentially a reprint of the second edition. Here first certain mistakes in numbering the chapters, which had run through both the

---

* John Lord Campbell, "Lives of the Chief Justices," 1849, II, 260.

† "St. James's Evening Post," March 22-24, 1743. William Strahan, in place of Henry Woodfall, printed for Millar the third edition, and also the fourth edition (of which there were 2,000 copies). Excerpts from Strahan's ledger to this effect are given by Mr. J. Paul de Castro in "Notes and Queries," Nov., 1917, p. 465.

other editions, were corrected; and here first the author put his name on the title-page—"Henry Fielding, Esquire"—as a protection against infringement on the copyright. To compensate perhaps for smaller type and poorer format, the publisher added illustrations from plates made by James Hulett, an engraver chiefly employed by the book-sellers. These cuts, which have been many times reprinted, are good but not very remarkable. It was from this edition that Fielding's novel, preceded by notices in French period-icals, made its way into France. "Les Avantures de Joseph Andrews et du Ministre Abraham Adams," bear-ing Millar's imprint and the date 1743, purports to have been translated by "une Dame Angloise" living in London. The next year it was reprinted with altered title-page and some corrections, in Amsterdam by the society of French refugees engaged in making known English books to their countrymen. Only the Amsterdam edition took over Hu-lett's engravings. The real translator, disguised as "an English lady," was the Abbé Desfontaines, who had ren-dered into French "Gulliver's Travels." It is a crude piece of work with many suppressions and some additions, in no way doing justice to the original. Desfontaines had the presumption to make alterations in Fielding's preface on the novelist's art, and to quote himself against the English author. The Amsterdam translation, however, contains a most interesting letter from the "English lady" to her friend, the wife of the "maître des comptes" at Montpellier. In this letter, Desfontaines describes in con-siderable detail the manners and customs on which the novel is based. Though anticipated by others, he is an early authority for the tradition that Parson Adams had a prototype, and that Parson Trulliber was one of Fielding's tutors. Of Parson Adams, Desfontaines says: "C'est un caractère vrai, & peint d'après nature. Car nous avons dans une de nos Provinces un Vicaire qui lui ressemble parfaitement, & il n'y a personne en *Angleterre* qui ne l'ait reconnu.'' Of Parson Trulliber, the words are: ''On assure que celui qui est peint ici sous le nom de *Trulliber,* a autrefois enseigné le Latin à l'Auteur de ce Livre. Si cela est, il n'est guères reconnoissant, ou le Maître ne s'est pas fait estimer & aimer de son élève.'' Rarely can one thus trace a tradition back to contemporary gossip.

Three London editions of ''Joseph Andrews,'' six thousand and five hundred copies altogether, in the course of thirteen months, with a French translation, twice printed, soon following, would indicate a body of readers numbering about half that enjoyed by ''Pamela,'' of which there were six English editions the first year. Two more authorized editions of ''Joseph Andrews'' were yet to appear in English during Fielding's lifetime—one in November, 1748, though dated 1749,* and the other in 1751. There were also two Dublin editions, the first of which came out in 1742, and the second in 1747. Counting translations, the novel was printed at least fourteen times before the author's death.

This demand makes it necessary to modify the assertion, very often repeated, that the novel at first took slight hold on the public. It is true that one hears more of it after the publication of ''Tom Jones,'' when the two novels provided a theme for people who like to discuss comparative merits. But there is nothing unusual in this, for it takes time for a novel to get into letters and memoirs outside an author's circle of friends. From the beginning, Richardson kept the letters of his admirers, and they make an imposing array. Only one letter to Fielding has survived, and that was written before the appearance of his novel; but this does not mean that people never wrote to him; it means that the correspondence was destroyed or lost by some accident. It is for this reason that one knows

* ''The Jacobite's Journal,'' Nov. 5, 1748.

so little about the first impression made upon the public by "Joseph Andrews." One knows, however, that the novel was talked about and that readers were curious to discover the originals of the characters. Parson Adams became from the first a person to whom Fielding and others could refer as if he were a reality. "Honest Abram Adams," says Macklin in the prologue to "The Wedding Day," "makes readers laugh in spite of the critics"; and he became one of the sober correspondents to "The Jacobite's Journal." A writer in "The Craftsman" for January 1, 1743, quoted Fielding on the nature of humour; the French translation was reviewed in the "Bibliothèque Françoise" for 1744;* and "The Gentleman's Magazine" twice mentioned facetiously Fielding's novel, publishing on the second occasion a poem supposed to have been written by Parson Adams's son Dick.† And when "Joseph Andrews" three years later reached Lady Mary Wortley Montagu, who was then living in Italy, she wrote back to her daughter Lady Bute that she sat up all night reading in that and Fielding's other works, and liked it better than "Tom Jones," which had been out a few months. Amused everywhere, Lady Mary was especially struck by Fanny as an exact and charming portrait of the English country girl.‡

And there is the poet Gray, who, on the recommendation of his friend Richard West, read "Joseph Andrews" just after it appeared. Gray seems to have lost West's letter; but the poet's reply has been preserved. Writing to West in April, 1742, he had this to say of Fielding's novel: "The incidents are ill laid and without invention; but the characters have a great deal of nature, which always pleases even in her lowest shapes. Parson Adams is perfectly well;

* Tome XXXIX, 201-215.

† See "The Gentleman's Magazine," Oct., 1745, p. 550, and May, 1746, p. 268.

‡ "Letters and Works," 1861, I, 186.

so is Mrs. Slipslop, and the story of Wilson; and through-out he [Fielding] shews himself well read in stage-coaches, country squires, inns, and inns of court. His reflections upon high people and low people, and misses and masters, are very good. However the exaltedness of some minds (or rather as I shrewdly suspect their insipidity and want of feeling or observation) may make them insensible to these light things, (I mean such as characterize and paint nature), yet surely they are as weighty and much more useful than your grave discourses upon the mind, the passions, and what not. Now as the paradisiacal pleasures of the Mahometans consist in playing upon the flute and lying with Houris, be mine to read eternal new romances of Marivaux and Cré-billon.''* West, whose mind responded more easily to new impressions, rallied Gray on his preference for Marivaux and Crébillon. ''I rejoice,'' he replied, ''you found amuse-ment in 'Joseph Andrews.' But then I think your concep-tions of Paradise a little upon the Bergerac.''† Still, Gray's measured praise, I daresay, was echoed by many readers. Long fed on romances, they hardly knew just what their attitude should be towards a novel essentially true to Eng-lish life and manners. For them it lacked invention, and yet was admirable in its characters and observations cover-ing all classes. As might be expected, full approval came from Hogarth, whose art had much in common with Field-ing's. Beneath that group of heads which he drew in 1743 for a subscription ticket to Marriage-à-la-Mode, he referred the public to the preface to ''Joseph Andrews'' for the proper distinction between characters and caricatures, whether in painting or in literature.

* ''The Letters of Thomas Gray,'' edited by D. C. Tovey, Vol. I, 1900, p. 97.

† D. C. Tovey, ''Gray and His Friends,'' 1890, p. 162. West's happy allu-sion is to Cyrano de Bergerac's fantastic description of the inhabitants of the sun and the moon.

CHAPTER XIII

THE MISCELLANIES

After publishing his novel, Fielding again fell back upon miscellaneous writing. His first opportunity came in the war of pamphlets over the career of Sarah Jennings, the aged Duchess of Marlborough. Following her dismission from the Court of Queen Anne, the Duchess prepared a statement of her side of the quarrel, but withheld it from the world on the advice of Bishop Burnet. Now, at the age of eighty, she called in Nathaniel Hooke, an historian of some consequence in his day, who was induced by a purse of £5,000 to assist her in enlarging her original statement into a book really amounting to her political memoirs. It reached the public early in March, 1742, bearing the title "An Account of the Conduct of the Dowager Duchess of Marlborough, from her first coming to Court, to the Year 1710." With the aid of Hooke, the Duchess justified her conduct at all points in a style at once fluent and vigorous. For three months the book became, to use Dr. Johnson's phrase, "the most popular topic of conversation." Before May was over, it had provoked a dozen pamphlets at least, which "reviewed" the Duchess's story, or "remarked" upon it, or "explained" her "party gibberish." There were also several burlesques of it, such as a poem in Hudibrastic verse called "The Sarah-ad; or, A Flight for Fame." The most complete reply to the Duchess, however, was a book of nearly five hundred pages from Fielding's former associate, James Ralph, who, under the assumed

360

name of "a Lady of Quality," gave "The Other Side of the Question," taking as his text the words attributed to Solomon: "He that is first in his own cause seemeth just, but his neighbour cometh and searcheth him."

Few ventured into print in defence of the Duchess; for she had indeed proved too much. Of these few was Dr. Johnson, who reviewed her book on the whole favourably, in "The Gentleman's Magazine" for March. Another was Fielding. In the next month, he let fly a shilling pamphlet entitled "A Full Vindication of the Dutchess Dowager of Marlborough: Both with regard to the Account lately published by her Grace, and to her Character in general; against the base and malicious Invectives contained in a late scurrilous Pamphlet . . ."* Fielding's fire was here drawn against "Remarks upon the Account of the Conduct of a certain Duchess. In a Letter from a Member of the last Parliament in the Reign of Queen Anne to a young Nobleman," wherein the young lord addressed was warned not to accept the Duchess's narrative as a true account of her transactions. This pamphlet, signed "Britannicus," gave the lie direct to the Duchess. Fielding, scenting a lord under the fictitious name, gave him in turn the lie direct, answering each important charge and proving, he thought, its falsity. "Britannicus" had intimated that he would take up the subject again in another pamphlet. Fielding dared him to proceed. Thereupon "Britannicus" rested his case, and so Fielding never had occasion to write a second pamphlet for which he declared himself eager. The "Vindication," however, went into a so-called second edition, really a reissue of the first, with no change except in the title-page.

The sincerity of Fielding's admiration for the Duchess has been questioned. It has been surmised that he as well as Hooke (whom Fielding knew and praised) was paid

* "The Gentleman's Magazine," April, 1742, p. 224.

liberally for his defence of a quarrelsome old woman. The suspicion is most ungenerous, for there is no evidence that Fielding received more for his pamphlet than the five pounds and five shillings which his publisher gave him. The fact is, Fielding's heat over the attacks on the Duchess was most natural. The Duke of Marlborough he always classed with the greatest military heroes; but lamented that little remained to show for his glorious victories besides "the torn colours in Westminster Hall." Fielding's father had served under Marlborough; and the Duke's brother, General Charles Churchill, had married his mother's cousin, Mary Gould of Dorchester. After the Duke's death, the Duchess sided with the young Patriots, of whom Fielding was one, against the policies of Walpole, and in the last years of the struggle she unloosed her purse-strings—for which both Chesterfield and Lyttelton expressed profound obligations. Fielding, the friend of these political leaders, certainly knew whence came the sinews of war, and had as certainly profited indirectly by the Duchess's liberality during the time that he conducted "The Champion." It was thus the better side of the Duchess that he had seen. Her pride and haughtiness appeared to him but an elevation of mind that would not stoop to mean things. As if personally acquainted with her (as he doubtless was, for he had visited Blenheim*), Fielding declared that no one could equal her in "affability and condescension" to people beneath her in rank, provided they knew their place. To Fielding she was a "glorious woman," the widow of the great Duke, the benefactor of his party. Her political enemies treated her like an oyster-wench. Fielding's chivalry was aroused, and he came to the rescue.

At the same time, Fielding projected a translation of the eleven comedies of Aristophanes. William Young was to collaborate with him, and the publisher was to be T. Waller

---

* "A Journey from this World to the Next," Ch. IV.

362

in the Temple Cloisters. Fielding and his Parson Adams labouring together over a crabbed Greek text is a sight very pleasant to the imagination. But they never got beyond one play, which they announced in "The Champion" of May 4, 1742, for speedy publication. It would be followed, said the advertisement, by all the rest, "if the public show proper encouragement to the translators." The comedy they selected to test the town with was "Plutus, the God of Riches," which duly appeared, as a two-shilling pamphlet, on the last day of May, with the names of "Henry Fielding, Esq." and "the Revᵈ Mr. Young" on the title-page.* A dedication to Lord Talbot paid a high tribute to the heart and understanding of his father, the late Lord Chancellor, who had befriended the poet Thomson, and asked for his lordship's protection in the present "distressed and . . . declining state of learning." Like Fielding, Lord Talbot was an Eton boy and an ardent Patriot, inclining to the Duke of Bedford in factional disputes. The dedication clearly pleased him, for his name is among the subscribers to Fielding's "Miscellanies" of the next year for two sets printed on royal paper. A preface, containing sensible remarks on translating Aristophanes, set forth an intention of adding to the complete work "a very large dissertation on the nature and end of comedy, with an account of its original, rise, and progress to this day,"—from the wit of Aristophanes down to "that pretty, dapper, brisk, smart, pert dialogue, which hath lately flourished on our stage," degenerating at last into that inane stuff, called "genteel comedy," in which Colley Cibber "succeeded so excellently well both as author and actor." The comedy was rendered into idiomatic and vigorous prose, the knack for writing which the translators claimed to have learned from Pope's "Essay on Man." "Large Notes, Explanatory and Critical"—just the kind

* "The Daily Post," May 31, 1742.

Fielding had burlesqued in "The Vernoniad"—completed the apparatus.

How the translators divided their work cannot be exactly determined. Apparently, Young did the hardest part of it, and Fielding then went over it all carefully, for the humorist's hand is visible everywhere in light and facetious touches. The dedication, though signed by both, was written, as the style shows, by Fielding. This conclusion is confirmed by an amusing anecdote which dates back to the very year 1742. Lord Talbot, it was said, sent Young five guineas as a gratuity for the dedication, but the parson for a long time refused to touch it on the ground that he had had no hand in the dedication and so the money did not belong to him. "At last," so the story runs, "he took it, but not for himself, but Fielding, who writ the dedication. He saw him daily for five days, but still forgot the five guineas. At last, upon a dispute, he pulled out the money to lay a wager; being questioned about it, he said 'twas χρυσος Αριστοφανικος and belonged to Fielding; and so told the manner of his coming by it. 'Twas with great difficulty he could be persuaded to take any part of it, but at last, they, upon the judgment of the company, divided it; but he still insisted upon paying Fielding's reckoning out of his share."* The scene of the anecdote, it is implied, was at a London tavern or coffee-house. The parson who wanted to bet, was responsible for much of the preface following the dedication. Perhaps he wrote most of the paragraphs running on the pronoun "we," while the few running on the pronoun "I" came from Fielding. Apparently Fielding found the preface as prepared by Parson Adams a little dull, and so put in the passage on translation, the hit at Cibber, and the compliment to Pope, the sweetness of whose numbers was declared to be "scarce inferior to that of Theocritus himself." The translation

* Mr. J. Paul de Castro, "Notes and Queries," 12 S. I, 224 (March 18, 1916).

of the comedy itself may be safely assigned to Young except for some rephrasing here and there. Most of the notes, though Young may have brought together the material for them, have the wit, humour, and banter peculiar to Fielding.

The two men professed to have translated the comedy directly from the Greek. This they doubtless did, using for the purpose one of those current editions of Aristophanes with the Greek and Latin text on opposite pages, such as the Amsterdam folio of 1710, which Fielding had in his library. Nevertheless, for the interpretation of doubtful passages, they relied to a great extent upon the French translation of "Plutus" made a half-century before by Madame Dacier. They had at hand, too, a good English translation which Theobald had more recently published. Yet Theobald was their butt. They liked to rally him on mistranslations of occasional words and phrases, especially where he followed the errors that had been made by Madame Dacier; the inference, of course, being that Theobald hardly went back of the French for his original. Mr. Theobald, Fielding thought, should not be offended at the banter, inasmuch as he was "a critic of great nicety himself, and great diligence in correcting mistakes in others."

Quite unexpectedly, the preface and notes throw a ray of light upon the relations existing between Fielding and Pope. In his boyhood verses, Fielding had expressed admiration for Pope's genius, but was later irritated by the attacks of the poet's newspaper, "The Grub-street Journal," upon "The Modern Husband" and other plays. Then followed the unfortunate dispute between the friends of each over whether Pope attended a performance of "Pasquin" and so gave his approval to the piece. Since that time, the Tories and the Patriots had come together in a closer alliance for the final struggle against Walpole; and as a result of it, the two men now had more friends in common. In "The Champion," Fielding referred to Pope's support of the Opposition, besides going out of his way to praise him extravagantly. In return, Pope made a handsome allusion to Fielding's dramatic satires in "The New Dunciad," now known as the fourth book of the complete poem, which appeared by itself in March, 1742. Comedy, it is there said, was becoming dull and lifeless when satire came to her aid; and then satire in turn was forced from the stage by the Licensing Act, despite the eloquent protest of Lord Chesterfield. They are very fine lines:

> There sunk Thalia, nerveless, cold, and dead,
> Had not her Sister Satire held her head:
> Nor could'st thou, Chesterfield! a tear refuse,
> Thou wept'st, and with thee wept each gentle Muse.

Moreover, Fielding and Pope had the same antagonism towards Colley Cibber, though they showed it differently. Fielding pelted him with ridicule; Pope pelted him with satire and abuse. In the earlier books of "The Dunciad," Pope took Theobald for his hero; now he was preparing to substitute Cibber for him. It cannot be a mere coincidence that Fielding at this juncture again paid his tribute to Pope and riddled both Cibber and Theobald in the preface and annotations of "Plutus." Pope, as it will be related, was soon taking an active interest in Fielding. By this time or a little later, the poet and the novelist had met and conversed. The date cannot be fixed; but the fact is made certain by Fielding's own statement. When attacked long afterwards by a nest of serpents issuing from Grub Street, he recalled a sentiment, which, he says, "I heard drop from the late Mr. Pope," to the effect "that nature never produced a more venomous animal than a bad author."*

The good understanding between Pope and Fielding must have been threatened by the great literary scandal of 1742. Several contemptuous references in "The New Dunciad"

* "The Covent-Garden Journal," Jan. 18, 1752.

to Cibber aroused the laureate to a terrible revenge in "A Letter from Mr. Cibber to Mr. Pope"; wherein was related in detail a most shameful occurrence in the private life of Pope, which had enough truth in it to be unanswerable. Though Pope professed that Cibber's letter merely amused him, it really made him writhe with anguish. Thereupon, he rewrought the first books of "The Dunciad" in order to enthrone Cibber in place of Theobald. But it was too late for Pope to save himself. For once Pope had met his match in abuse and vituperation. Cibber's letter, out in July, was immediately followed by half a dozen squibs in verse and prose and by a print depicting the indecent incident that the laureate had described. Two of these scurrilous pamphlets against Pope had the appearance of coming from Fielding, for they both bore the pseudonym that he had employed in "The Champion." Both were published in August. "Blast upon Blast and Lick for Lick; or, a New Lesson for P–pe . . . By Capt. H——s Vinegar," was a short rehearsal of the quarrel between Pope and Cibber, running on the lines of the story of Cain and Abel. The parody so diverted Horace Walpole that he sent a transcription of it to Horace Mann in Italy, with the remark that it was "supposed to be Fielding's." This pamphlet, however, is not so good a performance as the other one— a long verse satire which turned Pope's own heroic couplets against him. It had as title-page: "The Cudgel, or, a Crab-tree Lecture. To the Author of the Dunciad. By Hercules Vinegar, Esq. . . . Printed for the Author, and sold at his House, the Crab-Tree, in Vinegar-yard, near Drury Lane."

Neither of these pieces has the earmarks of Fielding's style; both of them are in the interest of Cibber, his archenemy; and they appeared at a time when Fielding was probably out of London for the summer. The unknown authors may have been trading upon Fielding's name as an

aid to the sale of their wares; they may have been enemies
who wished to involve him in difficulties; or their use of his
pseudonym may have been a mere jest, for it was, indeed,
a comic situation to represent Fielding taking sides with
Cibber, the man whom he had many times belaboured with
the club of Captain Hercules Vinegar. These facetious
pamphlets which the town was disposed to lay at Fielding's door, so annoyed him that he took occasion, in the
publication of his "Miscellanies" the next spring, to give
a list of all his works, since June, 1741, not included in that
collection. He did this, he said, because he had been "very
unjustly censured" for what he had never written, as well
as for what he had written; and though he was quite willing
to assume the responsibility of his own works, he must
protest against having attributed to him "anonymous
scandal," such, of course, as the two scurrilous pamphlets
in question, which he did not deign to mention by name.

In the meantime, Fielding was trying the drama once
more, not by writing new plays but by reworking old ones.
Many of his comedies and farces still diverted the public
every season; and it was but natural that he should make
use of their run for bringing out similar pieces that he
had by him. One of them, dating back to the spring of
1735, was a ballad farce, called "Miss Lucy in Town,"
which he wrote in collaboration with some unknown playwright as a sequel to "An Old Man Taught Wisdom; or,
the Virgin Unmask'd." Lucy, it will be remembered,
married Thomas the footman, in preference to all the other
lovers her father provided for her. In the continuation,
she and her husband come up to London, six weeks after
marriage, to see the usual sights—the Tower, the lions,
Bedlam, Westminster Hall, and the great Abbey; but being
"fresh and raw out of the country," they take lodgings by
mistake in the notorious house of a Mrs. Haycock, which
becomes the scene of the action. The farce was first per-

formed at Drury Lane as an afterpiece to "Othello" on May 6, 1742,* and was published the same day by Millar, who gave the author ten pounds and ten shillings for the copyright. During the next few weeks, "Miss Lucy" was used variously with "The Old Bachelor," "The Beggar's Opera," "The Virgin Unmask'd," and "The Miser." Mrs. Clive, the original Lucy, took the part of the girl turned wife; Macklin, who had also been in the original cast of "The Virgin Unmask'd," became the Jew of the new farce; and Beard, the famous tenor, appeared in the rôle of Signor Cantileno. The great hits of the piece were the songs in burlesque imitation of the waning Italian opera. Horace Walpole, after attending a performance, wrote to Horace Mann, preliminary to sending him a copy of the play: "There is a little simple farce at Drury Lane, called 'Miss Lucy in Town,' in which Mrs. Clive mimics the Muscovita admirably, and Beard, Amorevoli intolerably."† For some reason, Walpole never liked Beard's voice, fine as it was. One of the songs that Beard sang, it may be remarked in passing, seems to have been written by Fielding in honor of Miss Cradock in the days of their courtship. It begins:

> To beauty compar'd, pale gold I despise,
> No jewels can sparkle like Caelia's bright eyes.

The little one-act farce, having a few songs, met with misfortune, because of its personalities. There could be no objection to mimicking Italian singers—that was relished by the audience. Of more questionable expediency was the character of Mrs. Haycock, whom the audience immediately recognized as a direct presentation of Mrs. Haywood, the Covent-Garden bawd. She and her house had perhaps been introduced into the earlier "Covent-Garden Tragedy," but not in so specific a manner. In this farce, Mrs. Macklin, who took the part, played her off to the life, even to her squeamish airs and affected modesty.

* "The Daily Post," May 6, 1742. † "Letters," edited by Toynbee, I, 228.

Mrs. Haycock, however, would have passed without much censure, had not Fielding brought into her company a Lord Bawble, who also touched closely upon the life and character of "a particular person of quality" about town. It is in the theatrical anecdotes that his lordship protested to the Lord Chamberlain against being thus exposed to public scandal, with the result that further performance of the farce was prohibited. Though the details of the story cannot be verified, the Lord Chamberlain or his licenser, Mr. Chetwynd, did intervene on or about the twenty-first of May, after the author had enjoyed two benefit nights. The next day the farce was withdrawn for the rest of the season. The prohibition, however, was removed by October, when "Miss Lucy" began a second run with Mrs. Haycock renamed Mrs. Midnight. This reversal of attitude on the part of the Lord Chamberlain was of course occasioned by the remonstrance of the manager of Drury Lane. After the episode was over, an anonymous spectator came out with a sixpenny pamphlet telling the story so far as he knew it, which was but vaguely. It was "A Letter to a Noble Lord, to whom alone it Belongs"; that is, to the Duke of Grafton, the Lord Chamberlain. The nameless author denounced the late Ministry for passing the Licensing Act because of Fielding's political satires, and then—strangely enough—rebuked the Lord Chamberlain for permitting plays like "Miss Lucy in Town." At the same time, he congratulated Mr. Fielding on "his happy genius." Because of this compliment, I suppose, the pamphlet has been attributed to Fielding himself; but he could not have written so incoherent a piece of irony had he tried.

Garrick was then coming into his first fame. Two or three years before this, he had shown his extraordinary talent in various amateur performances among friends gathered at the house of Edward Cave, the conductor of "The Gentleman's Magazine." Cave lived over St. John's

Gate, Clerkenwell, whence issued every month his periodical. One of the plays in which Garrick there appeared was Fielding's "Mock Doctor," for which he composed an epilogue. In the audience was probably young Samuel Johnson, who introduced Garrick to Cave; and the epilogue was duly printed in Cave's magazine for September, 1740, wherein may be seen also Johnson's skill in reporting parliamentary debates without ever having heard the speeches. Following other performances, some of which were professional, Garrick took London by storm on October 19, 1741, when he appeared as King Richard the Third at Giffard's theatre in Goodman's Fields. The second piece that night was Fielding's "Virgin Unmask'd." As Goodman's Fields was an irregular theatre, the Licensing Act of 1737 had to be dodged, as I have explained in a previous chapter, by performing the two pieces gratis between the parts of "a Concert of Vocal and Instrumental Music," for which tickets were sold at the usual prices. Concealing his real name in the playbills under that of "A Gentleman," Garrick rapidly increased the number of his rôles in both tragedy and comedy before the season ended. He played many times Jack Smatter in the dramatized "Pamela," writing, it is said, the part himself, and created a sensation with his Bayes of "The Rehearsal" by his burlesque mimicry of the voice, manner, and gesture of the leading actors at the other theatres. He thus displayed on the stage an art akin to that which Fielding had displayed in literature. The next season, Garrick was secured for Drury Lane, where his great career as actor and manager really began. Then or before, he fell in with Fielding.

It was a lifelong friendship in which each well understood the other. Fielding thought that the stage had never had Garrick's equal and never would have again. But if an anecdote in Macklin's "Memoirs" is to be believed, he was disposed to rally Garrick on a closeness amounting almost to avarice. On one occasion, near this time, it is related there, "Garrick gave a dinner at his lodgings to Harry Fielding, Macklin, Havard, Mrs. Cibber, &c, &c. and vails to servants being then much the fashion, Macklin, and most of the company, gave Garrick's man (David, a Welchman) something at parting—some a shilling, some half a crown, &c. whilst Fielding, very formally, slipt a piece of paper in his hand, with something folded in the inside. When the company were all gone, David seeming to be in high glee, Garrick asked him how much he got. 'I can't tell you yet, Sir,' said Davy: 'here is half a crown from Mrs. Cibber, Got pless hur—here is a shilling from Mr. Macklin—here is two from Mr. Havard, &c.—and here is something more from the Poet [that is, Fielding], Got pless his merry heart.' By this time David had unfolded the paper, when, to his astonishment, he saw it contain no more than one penny! Garrick felt nettled at this, and next day spoke to Fielding, about the impropriety of jesting with a servant. 'Jesting!' said Fielding, with a seeming surprise: 'so far from it, that I meant to do the fellow a real piece of service; for had I given him a shilling, or half a crown, I knew you would have taken it from him; but by giving him only a penny, he had a chance of calling it his own.' "* Garrick retaliated, so the story goes, by mimicking Fielding just as he had mimicked the actors.

One evening, early in 1743, Garrick remarked to Fielding that he was desirous of appearing in a new part, and asked him whether he had an unacted play by him. Fielding replied that he had one "almost finished," but that Fleetwood, the manager of Drury Lane, would hardly care to bring it out that season. Garrick, however, insisted; and Fleetwood was friendly to the proposal. So "The Good-Natur'd Man," really an old play revised, was ordered to be written into parts for the actors. But at the last mo-

* W. Cooke, "Memoirs of Charles Macklin," 1804, pp. 146-147.

ment, Fielding substituted for it another that had long lain by him. He saw, he said, on perusal, that "The Good-Natur'd Man" contained no considerable rôle for a favourite actor. The other piece, "The Wedding Day," was a comedy that Fielding began as far back as 1730—"the third dramatic performance,"* he said, perhaps not quite accurately, that he ever attempted—and would keep Garrick almost continuously on the stage. Its leading parts had been intended for Wilks and Mrs. Oldfield; but Mrs. Oldfield died before the play was finished and it was never shown to Wilks, between whom and Fielding arose a slight quarrel. Subsequently it was rejected by Rich. On examination, this juvenile production proved to be very crude in places, and Fielding set about to make it over by working night and day for a week. Hardly had he begun his alterations before his wife became so dangerously ill that he was rendered incapable of executing his task. He therefore let the comedy go to the players without thorough revision, in the expectation that Garrick's wonderful acting would blind the audience to the defects of the piece. Fielding was in distress at this time, he said frankly, and could not let slip an opportunity for relief. There was also some trouble with the licenser, who objected to certain passages, all of which Fielding struck out. It was nevertheless noised about that the play was indecent, and ladies were advised to stay away from the performance. In these unfortunate circumstances "The Wedding Day" reached the stage on February 17, 1743, and ran continuously for six nights.† It was then laid aside for good, though Fielding announced that he would rewrite it for the ensuing season. It completely failed. No more than five ladies were present on the last night, which was the author's benefit, so effective,

* See preface to "Miscellanies," 1743, for facts about "The Wedding Day."

† "The London Daily Post," Feb. 17, et seq., 1743.

said Fielding, had been the rumours against it. The manager of Drury Lane lost by it, and Fielding received only fifty pounds exclusive of what Millar, who immediately published it, may have paid for the copyright. The printed play evidently sold well, for there were two or more impressions of the first edition.

Though "The Wedding Day" is not a first-rate comedy, its fate was hardly deserved. Garrick, according to Fielding, made "a surprising figure" as Millamour. Macklin, who wrote and delivered a very humorous prologue, had a good part, and Mrs. Pritchard and Peg Woffington were the young ladies of the piece. As in "Miss Lucy," Mrs. Macklin played the bawd. It was a splendid company. One misses only Mrs. Clive, who had had the leading rôle in so many of the author's plays. A story got into print—it is in a poem that Hanbury Williams contributed to "The Foundling Hospital for Wit," which was published in March—that Fielding tried to persuade her to take the part of Mrs. Useful, and that she became in consequence furious. She wanted the rôle of Charlotte or Clarinda, and would have none other:

> A bawd! a bawd! where is that scoundrel poet?
> Fine work indeed! By G—d the town shall know it.
> F—ld—g who heard, and saw her passion rise,
> Thus answer'd calmly: Prithee C—ve be wise,
> This part will suit your humour, taste, and size.*

The play failed, according to Murphy, on account of one unfortunate scene; but for that Garrick would have won over the audience. It is not clear just what Murphy had in mind. It may be that the audience resented the scenes where Garrick assumed the rôle of a quack physician, though they are excellent comedy, or the one where Stedfast marries by mistake his own daughter. Probably, however,

* Reprinted in "Works of Sir Charles Hanbury Williams," 1822, II, 190.

THE MISCELLANIES

Garrick was interrupted more than once at some very cynical but very brilliant epigrams that Fielding put into the mouth of Millamour early in the play. I doubt whether Garrick got through the second scene—the one between Millamour and Mrs. Useful—without a hiss. Scenting failure, Macklin advised the author in his prologue to abandon the stage and to stick to "honest Abram Adams." It was on the whole good advice.

Everything known about Fielding at this time points to the conclusion that his affairs had been drifting into a desperate state since he left "The Champion." The law, upon the practice of which he entered late, had not been sufficient for the support of his family in the way he wished to live. Hence his numerous cheap pamphlets, his test of the market for a fresh translation of Aristophanes, and his readiness to bring upon the stage old plays which had been discarded as not up to the theatrical standard. His gout, for one winter at least, had interfered with the law; and the continued illness of his wife after the death of Charlotte was unnerving him. "When I look a year or two backwards," he wrote on publishing his "Miscellanies" in the spring of 1743, "and survey the accidents which have befallen me, and the distresses I have waded through whilst I have been engaged in these works, I could almost challenge some philosophy to myself, for having been able to finish them as I have; and however imperfectly that may be, I am convinced the reader, was he acquainted with the whole, would want very little good-nature to extinguish his disdain at any faults he meets with. . . . And now, my good-natured reader, recommending my works to your candour, I bid you heartily farewell; and take this with you, that you may never be interrupted in the reading these Miscellanies, with that degree of heart-ach which hath often discomposed me in the writing them."

Besides illness and death, Fielding hints here and else-

375

where at other troubles, which were, he says, "very proper decorations" to the scene of woe. What he meant by this remark may be partially uncovered in the records of the Court of Common Pleas. On March 27, 1741, he gave his note for £197, payable on demand, to one Joseph King. After repeated demands for payment, King brought suit to recover the debt during Trinity term of the next year. Fielding himself, who was in the West, did not appear in court; and his attorney, a certain Thomas Buckle, who appeared for him, presented no answer to the complaint, saying that his client had none. Judgment was accordingly rendered in favour of the plaintiff to the full amount of the debt and fifty shillings more as damages. The order of the court bears the date of July 7, 1742.* This incident, though it cannot be followed further, tells the story. Fielding was borrowing money and was unable to pay. His friends came to the rescue.

Among them was Ralph Allen, the postmaster at Bath. This generous man, whose virtues were praised by Pope, Pitt, and Warburton, acquired a large fortune—twelve thousand pounds or more a year—as farmer of the cross-posts over western England. He devised, it is said, these short routes for the delivery of mail, to the great convenience of the rural districts as well as to his own emolument. He also worked several quarries of white stone, out of which were built the new Bath and his own mansion at Prior Park, beyond Widcombe and two or three miles southeast of Bath. His gifts to charity were munificent, and he was always ready to relieve anyone in distress. He had a large number of friends, who, after the completion of

* Common Pleas, Trinity Term, 1742, 16 George II, Roll 522 (Record Office). There are also in the King's Bench docket entries in Trinity Term, 1742, showing that Henry Fielding was the *plaintiff*, and Randolph Seagrim the *defendant*, in a case where the "judgment for debt" was given against the latter; but the roll containing this case is apparently no longer in existence. Accordingly it cannot be determined whether there is any connection between the two cases.

his mansion, visited him for long periods. There, in the winter of 1741-1742, Pope and Warburton spent several weeks together; there, too, at near the same time had been "courteously entertained" Henry Fielding. Twice Fielding referred to Allen in "Joseph Andrews"—"a commoner, raised higher above the multitude by superior talents than is in the power of his prince to exalt him; whose behaviour to those he hath obliged is more amiable than the obligation itself." To his new friend Fielding attributed all the qualities that Pope had bestowed upon the Man of Ross in the book of verses. Fielding and Pope may never have met at Prior Park, but its owner must have contributed to an understanding between them. Thereafter Fielding began to praise the scholarship of Warburton also.

According to a rumour which spread from Bath, Allen read something of Fielding's that he liked and sent the author £200 for his encouragement. A positive statement to this effect was made in a letter dated May 10, 1763, from Samuel Derrick, the master of ceremonies at Bath.* Although it may not have been precisely this way, Fielding had certainly received unsolicited assistance from Allen just before the publication of "Joseph Andrews." Such is the inference from Fielding's language in that novel. The only doubtful points in the story are the amount of the gift and whether it was made before or after a personal acquaintance. Whatever the amount and circumstances of this first gift, perhaps £200 came from the postmaster at Bath to release Fielding from the clutches of Joseph King. Instead of going to Salisbury after the summer Assizes of 1742, Fielding, his wife probably with him, went to Bath to drink the waters. Allen had just been elected mayor. While in the Pump Room one day, Fielding wrote extempore some pretty verses to a Miss H—and, concluding with a tribute to the skill of Dr. Thomas Brewster, a phy-

* Samuel Derrick, "Letters," 1767, II, 58.

sician at Bath, who may have been prescribing for Mrs. Fielding as well as for Miss H—and. The lines run:

> Soon shall these bounteous springs thy wish bestow,
> Soon in each feature sprightly health shall glow;
> Thy eyes regain their fire, thy limbs their grace,
> And roses join the lillies in thy face.
> But say, sweet maid, what waters can remove
> The pangs of cold despair, of hopeless love?
> The deadly star which lights th' autumnal skies
> Shines not so bright, so fatal as those eyes.
> The pains which from their influence we endure,
> Not Brewster, glory of his art, can cure.*

The lady with those fatal eyes, it has been shrewdly conjectured, was Jane Husband, the daughter of a baronet, whose surname Fielding partially suppressed just as he was accustomed to do in publishing poems of his youth addressed to the belles of Salisbury. The story of Miss Husband is all in Lord Campbell's life of the man whom she afterwards married. She was, says the biographer, "a very young girl of exquisite beauty, who, from illness, had lost the use of her limbs so completely that she was only able to appear in public wheeled about in a chair. She was the daughter and co-heiress of Sir John Husband, of Ipsley, in Warwickshire." Just as Fielding predicted, the waters completely restored her, and the next year she became the wife of Fielding's friend Robert Henley, subsequently the Earl of Northington and a Lord Chancellor. The marriage ceremony was performed by Thomas Newton, afterwards Bishop of Bristol, but at that time a preacher at the Chapel in Spring Gardens. He was the divine who probably read the service for the dead over Fielding's daughter Charlotte. Henley, who travelled the Western Circuit, seems to have first met Miss Husband at the time Fielding paid his tribute to her beauty; and struck by her

* "Miscellanies," 1743, I, 114.

charms, he "contrived to be introduced to her, when he was still more fascinated by her conversation." Was it Fielding who introduced them? Not long afterwards Miss Husband hung up her crutches as a votive offering to the nymph of the spring and led in the dance with her handsome suitor. Was it love or the waters that wrought the miraculous cure?*

Fielding's visit to Bath in 1742 was, I take it, the beginning of a residence there; sometimes for several months of each year. The first house in the neighbourhood with which tradition has associated his name is at Twerton on the lower Bristol road, a mile and a half from Bath. It is a seventeenth-century house built all of stone—roof as well as walls—now known as "Fielding's Lodge," from the rear of which is a view down the River Avon. A brass tablet by the doorway informs the traveller that once lived there "The Father of the English Novel." At a later date, tradition has it, Fielding settled at Widcombe in the lodge belonging to Widcombe manor, an estate which Allen had recently purchased. It is a beautiful situation by an ancient church dedicated to Thomas à Becket, well up the hill, from which may be seen in full view the mansion of Prior Park rising still higher. Much of that scene was destined to be reproduced in "Tom Jones"; and all the qualities of Fielding's benefactor were there to be fused into a character of perfect goodness.

Other friends gave support to Fielding's literary activities in the way most common in the eighteenth century. For some time, even before the publication of "Joseph Andrews," Fielding had been preparing to bring out by subscription such of his miscellaneous writings in verse and prose as he wished to preserve, along with new essays

---

* On the identification, see Mr. J. Paul de Castro, "Notes and Queries," 12 S. I, 483-484 (June 17, 1916). See also John, Lord Campbell, "The Lives of the Lord Chancellors," 1846, V, 179-180.

and fictions—enough of them to give freshness to the collection. On June 3, 1742, Henry Woodfall printed for him seven hundred proposals to be sent out to possible subscribers;* and two days later appeared in "The Daily Post" the following advertisement—a reprint of the circular letter—clearly written by Fielding himself:

"*This Day are publish'd,*
Proposals *for* printing *by* Subscription,
MISCELLANIES in Three VOLUMES Octavo.
By HENRY FIELDING, *Esq*;

"The first Volume will contain all his Works in Verse, and some short Essays in Prose.

"The second Volume will contain, a Journey from this World to the next.

"The third Volume will contain, the History of that truly renowned Person Jonathan Wyld, Esq; in which not only his Character, but that of divers other great Personages of his Time, will be set in a just and true Light.

"The Price to Subscribers is One Guinea; and Two Guineas for the Royal Paper. One Half of which is to be paid at Subscribing, the other on the Delivery of the Book in Sheets. The Subscribers Names will be printed.

"Note, The Publication of these Volumes hath been hitherto retarded by the Author's indisposition last Winter, and a Train of melancholy Accidents scarce to be parallell'd; but he takes this Opportunity to assure his Subscribers, that he will most certainly deliver them within the Time mentioned in his last Receipts, viz. by the 25th of December next.

"Subscriptions are taken in by Mr A. Millar, Bookseller, opposite St. Clement's Church in the Strand.

"As the Books will very shortly go to the Press, Mr

* "Notes and Queries," 1 S. XI, 419 (June 2, 1855).

THE MISCELLANIES

Fielding begs the Favour of those who intend to subscribe to do it immediately."

But those books were not to be in the hands of subscribers at Christmas. For the greater part of the winter of 1742-1743, Mrs. Fielding was again extremely ill; and her husband's first thought—they are his own words—was for "one from whom I draw all the solid comfort of my life." Her condition, which, as we have seen, kept him from making over "The Wedding Day," also interfered with his completion of the new pieces that were to go into the "Miscellanies." Publication was accordingly delayed until April 12, 1743—the date given in "The London Daily Post." The subscription copies were "printed for the author" and "sold by A. Millar"; that is, the bookseller merely acted as the author's agent in the distribution, so that all profits might go to Fielding. After the subscribers had been supplied, the remaining copies were bound up, later in April, without the list of subscribers, and labelled "The Second Edition." On the new title-page, "printed for the author" was displaced by "printed for A. Millar." This so-called second edition, differing from the first only in its preliminary pages, went to the general public at fifteen shillings a set. The sale was slow, for we find Millar still advertising the second edition of the "Miscellanies" in "The True Patriot" for February 18, 1746. The publication, however, served its immediate purpose. There were, all told, 427 subscribers, who took 556 sets, of which 214 were on royal paper. This means that the total receipts from subscribers amounted to 770 guineas, a very handsome purse for an author in need of money.*

It was a notable list of subscribers, with the Prince of

* The printer's bill for the third edition of "Joseph Andrews," numbering 3,000 copies, was £45. (See "Notes and Queries," Nov., 1917, p. 465.) The bill for printing the "Miscellanies" must have been under £100. Hence Fielding's profit was nearly seven hundred guineas.

Wales at the head, who had use for fifteen sets on the best paper. Dukes and Earls were there—among the rest, Argyle, Bedford, Chesterfield, Devonshire, Denbigh, Marlborough, Newcastle, Richmond, and Westmoreland. Even Walpole, just elevated to the peerage, sent in his name for ten sets. Did he read the scathing allegory of his own career in the life of Jonathan Wild? Duchesses and Countesses, too, were there—to cite a few, Pembroke, Strafford, Richmond, and Shaftesbury; and to the beauty of the last two Fielding referred in his verses. Political leaders outside the nobility were there also—Pitt and Lyttelton, Dodington and Hanbury Williams of course. The Church was represented by Bishop Hoadly of Winchester, royal chaplains, and humbler members of the clergy. Medicine had its quota in Dr. Edward Wilmot, physician to his Majesty, and Dr. William Wasey, of St. George's Hospital, down to Dr. Thomas Brewster of Bath and Dr. John Barker of Salisbury, an authority on epidemic fevers. Admiral Vernon was a subscriber; and Charles Fleetwood, manager of Drury Lane Theatre, took twenty sets, perhaps to be distributed among the players; while Mrs. Clive and Mr. Garrick subscribed on their own account, the latter for the cheap paper. But what pleased Fielding most was the array of judges and lawyers, whose names comprised "more than half the list," he said in thanking them for their good feeling towards "a late and unworthy member" of the profession. Members of Gray's Inn, Lincoln's Inn, and the Inner Temple, as well as of his own Middle Temple, nearly all put down their names for the benefit of a brother whom they saw come and go every day—"a tall man with a grey coat and a long chin."

Certain names were conspicuous for their absence. One looks in vain for Pope and Ralph Allen. A list of subscribers, however, is never complete; some names fail to appear through delay, oversight, or the desire of the subscriber. It thus happened in Allen's case and probably in Pope's likewise. Pope, writing to Allen, on April 12, 1743, about Martha Blount and Warburton, remarked casually:

"Fielding has sent the Books you subscribed for by ye Hand I imployed in conveying ye 20^{ll} to him. In one Chapt^r of ye Second vol. he has payd you a pretty Complement upon your House."[*]

Who was that unknown "hand"? Some London or Bath friend who acted as intermediary in a three-cornered friendship. The "pretty complement" which Pope had observed in the second volume of the "Miscellanies" may be found in "A Journey from this World to the Next," where the travellers, coming in the allegory to the parting of the ways—the road to greatness and the road to goodness,—take the latter and so have in view during all the rest of the journey "a handsome building . . . greatly resembling a certain house by the Bath." What fine compliments to Pope, too, here and there in the volumes!

Fielding introduced his "Miscellanies" with a preface, from which I have quoted, invaluable for its autobiography. He there set forth his intent in the more important pieces and gave a partial account of their origin and history. Concerning the poems, which came first after the preface, he begged the reader to pass upon them lightly as "productions of the heart rather than of the head"; for though he had written verse since boyhood, it had never been his pursuit. It was his aim, he said, to include in the collection all his occasional poems, with one or two exceptions, that he could recall or procure copies of. He purposely excluded the songs and mock-heroic verses of his plays, as well as the long burlesque named "The Vernoniad." One of the poems which he omitted—if indeed it had then been written—has since been restored to his works; it is a rather pretty poem in Hudibrastic metre called "Plain

[*] Letters from Pope to Ralph Allen, British Museum, Egerton MSS., 1947.

Truth,''* on the reigning beauty at Bath. The "plain truth" was that Venus, when visiting the waters, always wore the face of Betty Dalston. Other verses not found in the "Miscellanies" might be doubtfully culled from the original files of "The Champion"; but they have no significance. Except the shorter lyrics such as those to Celia, most of the juvenile poems which Fielding brought together betray by their allusions extensive revision; and the best of the long poems were composed near the time of publication. As a sort of dedication to his friends or patrons, Fielding opened the first volume with "True Greatness, an Epistle to George Dodington, Esq," "Good-Nature, to his Grace the Duke of Richmond," and "Liberty, to George Lyttleton, Esq." In the same category belong "To a Friend on the Choice of a Wife," evidently complimenting Lyttelton on his marriage in the summer of 1742, and "To John Hayes, Esq.," one of Fielding's associates in the Middle Temple. "True Greatness," as we have seen earlier, had been published separately in 1741; and four lines of "Good-Nature," varying somewhat in phrase, had been worked into the sixth number of "The Champion." All these semi-dedicatory epistles are average Popean verses depicting the characters of real and imaginary men and women, with praise of the Patriots, of the poet Young —the Muse's darling—of Handel, Quin, and Garrick. Placed first, they struck the keynote of the "Miscellanies," that there is no necessary connection between goodness and greatness; that the good man is not sure to thrive in this world, that the great man is often a rogue.

Here Walpole saw, if never before, the two poems addressed to him by the poor bard who looked down from his garret upon the house of the Prime Minister in Arlington Street; and Mrs. Fielding consented to the inclusion of the

* Dodsley, "A Collection of Poems in Six Volumes by Several Hands," 1758, V, 302-305.

poems in which her lover had extolled her above all the nymphs of Salisbury, though he suppressed, perhaps by her persuasion, all lines that reflected on her rivals. The burlesque modernization of Juvenal's "Sixth Satire," which Fielding sketched out after being jilted by Sarah Andrew in his boyhood, was filled in with numerous allusions to contemporary incidents and persons, in the way of banter or satire. He referred, for example, to the "perfect Pamela"; mentioned Clive, Woffington, and Beard, all of whom had taken parts in his last plays; and drew the character of Mrs. Theophilus Cibber, who was living apart from her husband. In the manner of Pope, Juvenal's Latin ran along on opposite pages with the burlesque translation; and both texts were elaborately annotated as if it were a serious undertaking. To this kind of humour, the world has since grown callous. One rather turns to Fielding's shorter poems for his wit and cleverness, to poems like the lines "Written Extempore on a Half-penny," the first version of which had appeared in "The Champion." Better still are occasional epigrams, such as the one on John Watts, the former publisher of Fielding's dramatic pieces, who falls into a rage on seeing a play damned which he has agreed to take; or the epitaph for Butler's monument in Westminster Abbey with its sting in the last line:

> What tho' alive, neglected and undone,
> O let thy spirit triumph in this stone.
> No greater honour could men pay thy parts,
> For when they give a stone, they give their hearts.

In defiance of the critics, Fielding reprinted "The Wedding Day," in company with "Eurydice,"* that unpublished farce which had been hissed from the stage six years before. For the first time appeared here also "An Interlude between Jupiter, Juno, Apollo, and Mercury, which was orig-

* Fielding thus altered the spelling from "Euridice."

inally intended as an Introduction to a Comedy, called, Jupiter's Descent on Earth.'' Had Fielding finished his comedy, it would have been a light social satire like his "Eurydice"; they would have been companion pieces. Probably the failure of "Eurydice" had discouraged him from proceeding with "Jupiter's Descent on Earth.'' So he moulded the four scenes which he had by him into an interlude complete enough to be enjoyed by itself. This he did, as is clear from the fragment, while his translation of "Plutus" was fresh in memory. The interlude lays out a good situation for a farce. Jupiter has decided to visit the earth for two reasons. In the first place he wants a rest from the tongue of Juno, with whom he has just had a quarrel. In the second place he has been reading some of the recent dedications of authors to their patrons, who are described therein as greater than the gods; he would like, he says, "to take a trip to earth and spend some time in such God-like company.'' By the aid of Mercury, these gentlemen, "feeding on soft dedication,'' were to be stripped of their divine attributes. The interlude is, of course, but a trifle; and the same may be said of another strip of drama, not fashioned for the stage, which Fielding called "A Dialogue between Alexander the Great and Diogenes the Cynic,'' in which each character is cleverly made to show up the cruelty and meanness of the other. Fielding liked neither the military hero nor the cynic.

Some other little things also found their way into the "Miscellanies"—perhaps merely to fill out the number of pages. Such, for example, is a translation of "The First Olynthiac of Demosthenes.'' It is probable that Fielding made and published this translation somewhere in 1739 or 1740 as an address applicable to the political situation in those years. Both Athens and England had a Philip to contend with; with both the question was a supply of men and treasures for a war; and Demosthenes was the Patriot of the Athenians. Let Pitt stand for Demosthenes, and the analogy becomes complete. Lest this surmise seem fanciful, it may be added that, in the winter of 1737-1738, "Common Sense"* had as its leading articles three abridged translations of Demosthenes, "occasioned by Philip's insulting the Athenians." The parallel was obvious to readers of that day.

A grave seriousness was given to the volumes by three lengthy essays. As hinted at in the first of them, called "An Essay on Conversation," his dull friend James Harris of Salisbury, was then at work upon "An Enquiry into Happiness," which duly appeared the next year as "Concerning Happiness" in the philosopher's "Three Treatises." Harris lent Fielding his manuscript on happiness, from which were derived some reflections on man as "a social animal." From this beginning, Fielding developed in his "Essay on Conversation" a dissertation on good breeding, mingled with classical quotations, anecdotes, and allusions to his friends, and ending with very interesting remarks on wit, humour, and raillery in so far as they have a bearing on the conduct of the complete gentleman, of whom the Earl of Chesterfield was taken as the pattern. Here the country gentleman might learn how he should treat a visitor, the visitor might learn how he should conduct himself, and everyone received directions for his speech and behaviour when associating with persons of his own station or below or above him. Good breeding, Fielding held, is confined to no rank or fortune, but consists in an endeavour "to cultivate the good-humour and happiness of others." The only raillery that he would permit was "a gentle animadversion on some foible; which while it raises a laugh in the rest of the company, doth not put the person rallied out of countenance, or expose him to shame and contempt. On the contrary, the jest should be

* Nov. 26, Dec. 24, 1737; and Feb. 4, 1738.

so delicate, that the object of it should be capable of joining in the mirth it occasions.''

With this conclusion, Fielding moved forward into ''An Essay on the Knowledge of the Characters of Men,'' replete with practical observations on how to read men by their faces—on what one may expect of the austere countenance, the fierce aspect, the glavering smile, and the squire's chuckle. It was his favourite theme of hypocrisy carried out to a humorous unmasking of the formal saint. The physiognomist, it is admitted, may make mistakes, and he should, therefore, usually hold his judgment in suspense, until he can observe a man's behaviour when off his guard or when there is no motive for deceit. ''See whether he hath acted the part of a good son, brother, husband, father, friend, master, servant, etc.; if he hath discharged these duties well, your confidence will have a good foundation; but if he hath behaved himself in these offices with tyranny, with cruelty, with infidelity, with inconstancy, you may be assured he will take the first opportunity his interest points out to him, of exercising the same ill talents at your ex-pence.'' On the other hand there are faces which may be accepted at once; such as the ''sprightly and penetrating look,'' ''the cheerful composed serenity,'' and the ''fiery cast of the eyes,'' which are, taking them in order, almost certain tokens of understanding, good nature, and courage. The essay itself is more penetrating, more wise, more just, than can be inferred from any brief account of it. Throughout are displayed those unusual perceptive powers that made a novelist of the author.

More intimate was the third essay—''Of the Remedy of Affliction for the Loss of our Friends,'' coloured if not occasioned by the death of his daughter Charlotte. For so intense grief he could discover no complete remedy; he could not reach the heights of Cicero and Seneca—those ''glorious writers'' who prescribed a Stoical philosophy as

"a certain and infallible method" to calm all the per-
turbations of the mind. He himself belonged to a lower
order of mortals, to the great class of common men who
share in "the more amiable weaknesses of human nature,"
who cannot meet with indifference sudden and unexpected
bereavement, who in the first agonies of grief cannot re-
strain the tears and lamentation which philosophers look
down upon as "marks of effeminacy" or "a contemptible
imbecility of heart." All that he can prescribe is confined
to "some palliative remedies" such as he administered to
himself when suffering from an anguish of the mind which
exceeded a hundred-fold the torments of the gout. "And
if Montaigne," he added, "be right in his choice of a physician, who had himself had the disease which he undertook to cure, I shall at least have that pretension to some
confidence and regard." Fielding's meditations for the
comfort of the distressed took a wide range through philosophy and religion, in reflections on the shortness of life,
the certainty of death, and the accidents to which one is
exposed, on to the conclusion that we should be thankful for
the friends that fortune has given us rather than rail at
her for taking them away sooner than we expected. Speaking from his own experience, he gave as his opinion, that
though there is "more real happiness in life than the wisest
men have allowed," it is overbalanced by the evil. Wherefore "death is not that king of terrors as he is represented
to be"; to the good man it can be no misfortune, for it is
but the beginning of another existence where the virtues we
loved him for will become "the foundation of his happiness
and reward in a better world." And finally, religion—read
Sherlock in his "Discourse on Death"—further assures us
that our friendships will be renewed and cemented in a
union everlasting. "This is a hope," declared Fielding,
"which no reasoning shall ever argue me out of, nor millions of such worlds as this should purchase: nor can any

man shew me its absolute impossibility, 'till he can demonstrate that it is not in the power of the Almighty to bestow it on me.''

Meditations on life and death were, however, but streaks in volumes where humour, irony, and banter became more and more the prevailing colour as the author progressed. In ''An Essay on Nothing,'' which took its cue from Lord Rochester's facetious stanzas ''Upon Nothing,'' Fielding proved that ''nothing'' has all the attributes of matter so-called, that it is really the ''immaterial essence'' or ''immaterial substance'' which Hobbes and other philosophers have written and disputed about. ''Nothing,'' as common speech shows, can be seen, heard, smelled, tasted, touched—and thus completely known. To say nothing of the moderns, did not the wisest man of antiquity confess that he *knew* nothing? Contrary to the adage, *ex nihilo nihil fit,* everything proceeds from nothing, and in nothing all things of this world find their eventual rest. From nothing to nothing come and go the honours paid to courtiers, the ''bustle and hurry'' of misers, the godlike passions of ''Alexander, Caesar, and all the rest of that heroic band.'' And ''true virtue, wisdom, learning, wit, and integrity, will most certainly bring their possessors—nothing.'' So Fielding prattled on delightfully for pages over ''nothing,'' with nothing in his head, stopping once for a compliment to Lord Chesterfield and the young poet James Hammond, just dead.*

One of these playful satires got into print some weeks before it appeared in the ''Miscellanies.'' Roberts published it on February 16, 1743,† as a sixpenny pamphlet under the title: ''Some Papers Proper to be Read before the R——l Society, Concerning the Terrestrial Chrysipus, Golden-Foot or Guinea; An Insect, or Vegetable, resem-

* ''Notes and Queries,'' 12 S. II, 443 (Dec. 2, 1916).
† ''The Daily Post,'' Feb. 16, 1743.

bling the Polypus, which hath this surprising Property,
That being cut into several Pieces, each Piece becomes a
perfect Animal, or Vegetable, as complete as that of which it
was originally only a Part. Collected by Petrus Gualterus,
But not Published till after His Death.'' This skit had its
origin in a paper contributed in November, 1742, to the
"Philosophical Transactions of the Royal Society"* by
Abraham Trembley, a distinguished Swiss naturalist and
Fellow of the Royal Society. He was then living at Sorg-
vliet near The Hague, where he discovered several new
species of fresh water polypi or polyps and carried on
experiments in their regeneration as novel and startling to
biological science as they were ridiculous to men like Swift
and Fielding, who knew little of science and cared nothing
for it. To them all scientific pursuit was sheer waste of the
intellect upon trivial things. As if in response to Fielding's
waggish invitation, Trembley sent over in 1744 another
communication to the President of the Royal Society, and
published at Leyden a full account of his experiments and
discoveries in "Mémoires pour servir à l'histoire d'un
genre des polypes d'eau douce, à bras en forme de
cornes.'' Subsequently he became governor to the young
Duke of Richmond, the son of Fielding's friend, and travelled with him in Italy and Germany. Trembley's papers
and book brought him great and deserved fame. He was
indeed a century in advance of his age in methods and results; for at that time little or nothing was known concerning nature's reproduction of the lost parts or the destroyed
organs of animals. Trembley cut his polyps transversely,
split them lengthwise, and found that the several parts
quickly developed all that had been lost by the process, each
section becoming a perfectly formed polypus. When he
turned them inside out, they still lived, and the stomach

* "Philosophical Transactions, Abridged and Disposed under General
Heads,'' IX, 17, *et seq.*

lining changed to skin. They ate and thrived just as if
nothing had happened to them. Enlarging upon the characteristic behaviour of polyps, the scientist had much to
say of their adherescent quality; they would, for instance,
attach themselves so closely to the hand that it was difficult
to make them quit their hold. Here lay matter for a jest
were one so disposed.

What Fielding did in his "Chrysipus" was to run up
a burlesque parallel on the Dutch experiments. The polypus became the chrysipus, or the English guinea; and for
the learned Trembley was substituted the late "Mynheer
Petrus Gualterus"—that is, Peter Walter, the miser and
unjust steward whom Fielding had satirized in "Joseph
Andrews" as Peter Pounce. The terrestrial chrysipi, says
Fielding, should be looked for in "scrutores, and behind
wainscotes in old houses," except during the Parliamentary elections, when "these animals swarm in England all
over the country, like the locusts." Any one of them may
be divided, as easily as the polypus, into twenty-one parts,
each as large as the original; and if one goes on with the
subdivision, each part becomes rather heavier than the first
chrysipus, although the colour changes from golden yellow
to white or silver and finally to copper or the "complexion
and substance of many human faces." Under the prudent
management of a Peter Walter, each will creep, and eat, and
grow, whatever its colour; and the pouch may be turned inside out as readily as an old stocking. In their adhesiveness,
there is one marked difference between the polypus and
the chrysipus, for the former clings to the hand of its own
accord, whereas it is the hand that clings to the latter. "A
single chrysipus," says Fielding, "stuck on to the finger,
will make a man talk for a full hour, nay will make him say
whatever the person who sticks it on desires: And again,
if you desire silence, it will as effectually stop the most lo-
quacious tongue. Sometimes, indeed, one or two, or even

twenty, are not sufficient; but if you apply the proper number, they seldom or never fail of success." To illustrate how the chrysipus sticks to a finger, the pamphlet was adorned with the "figure" of a ruffled hand just touching the crown of a guinea with a forefinger, preliminary to a firm and lasting grasp.

CHAPTER XIV

THE GLORY OF THE MISCELLANIES

"Chrysipus" and "An Essay on Nothing" were experiments in those brief Menippean satires such as Lucian sometimes composed. Of the same class, too, was "A Dialogue between Alexander the Great and Diogenes the Cynic"; while "An Interlude between Jupiter, Juno, Apollo, and Mercury" was a variation on one of Lucian's "Dialogues of the Gods." Fielding was, however, more fond of the "Dialogues of the Dead," and that masterpiece of burlesque and irony called "A True Story," which parodies tales of adventure and takes the reader down into Hades for conversations with the Greek heroes quite different in tone from those given by Homer in the Odyssey. As already described, Fielding had long ago descended into the lower world for the scene of his "Pleasures of the Town" in "The Author's Farce"; and in "The Champion" of May 24, 1740, he had adapted one of the Charon dialogues—it is one that boys read at Eton—to the society of his own time, introducing among others himself and the laureate. In a similar vein but with more use of "A True Story," he now wrote "A Journey from this World to the Next," which surpasses in humour and irony all other attempts by himself or anyone else to modernize Lucian. Except for an incident here and there, it is not an imitation; it came from an imagination filled with the literature of Hades as one finds it not only in Lucian but almost equally in Homer and Virgil. Just as Cervantes, had he flourished in the England of George the Second, might have written

394

something like "Joseph Andrews"; so Lucian, had he been living then, would have more surely given the world a satire like Fielding's "Journey," dwelling in the same way upon death as the stern unmasker of all pretence and deceit.

When Fielding composed his "Journey," comprising more than half of the second volume of the "Miscellanies," is a question which has perplexed his biographers. Although no positive statement can be made, it is probable that he sat down to it near the first day of December, 1741, the date with which the narrative opens; but that he was compelled to suspend work owing to his other literary projects, especially the publication of "Joseph Andrews," and to the severe illness of his wife and daughter as well as of himself. The satire contains, says a footnote, passages that relate to events within "this year or two." There is, for example, a reference to "our last Lord Mayor," whose virtues carry him so easily into the Elysian Fields. Here, then, should be an index to the date of composition. It happens, however, that two Lord Mayors of London had recently died in office—Humphrey Parsons on March 21, 1741, and Sir Robert Godschall on June 26, 1742. Although Godschall appears to have been an estimable man, it was Parsons, president of Bridewell and Bethlehem hospitals, who was beloved by the people. He is "the good Lord Mayor," whose praises were sung by Dr. Atterbury and others. To him "the incorruptible" hero whose death was lamented by the citizens of London, Fielding would allude rather than to the colourless Godschall. The inference, then, is that Fielding had written the seventh chapter of "The Journey," where the late Lord Mayor is welcomed into Elysium, some time before the death of Godschall, and that he let the passage stand. It is also worth notice, in passing, that in the tenth chapter Fielding speaks of St. Chrysostom's fondness for the plays of Aristophanes, which a servant placed on his pillow every night, so that the volume might be ready for the pious bishop's eyes in the morning. The story is likewise told in the preface to the translation of "Plutus" which Fielding and Young put together in the spring of 1742. Again, Parson Adams is mentioned in the introduction; and in the eighth chapter, Fielding clearly has in mind the death of his daughter Charlotte when he writes of the child met in the Elysian Fields. These and some other considerations point clearly to the conclusion that the "Journey," though probably begun before "Joseph Andrews," was mainly written during the weeks immediately succeeding.

Among the ancients, the way to the entrance of Hades was usually by boat over distant seas; but as more in harmony with English custom, Fielding made the journey by land in a stagecoach that set out on a cold winter's night from Warwick Lane under the very shadow of Newgate, the prison-house where many ladies as well as gentlemen in the eighteenth century passed the remnant of their mortality. Though the seven passengers who squeezed into that immaterial coach were but shades, their conversation, reflecting mortal whims and passions, gave Fielding a chance for social banter and satire in the manner of the famous journey in "Joseph Andrews" down towards the West. Everywhere the scenes and characters are intensely real; for the author could not detach himself from the life about him, however much he might try. The protagonist, who died of a "fever on the spirits," was a vague likeness, though not a portrait, of Fielding himself; and several of the characters, it is definitely stated, resembled certain unnamed contemporaries. In its general effect, the "Journey" is an allegory of life, ending before the gate of Elysium, where everyone must cast aside his hypocrisies and be judged by the quality of his deeds. Few pass through the portal, and none who is without charity.

Twice the coach halted before reaching "the banks of

the great river Cocytus.'' Some hours were first passed
at the dreadful City of Diseases, for a description of which
Fielding drew upon the Covent Garden district, with its
taverns, brothels, and tawdry women, and upon The Hague
in summer, when the stench rising from the canals is unendurable to anyone but a Dutchman. In that city flourished
all the fashionable diseases that carry people off, and all
the physicians who spend their time in experiments ''to
purge away the immortality of the soul.'' A hoary miser
was undergoing there the torture of giving away a shilling
a day from his immense accumulations; after they should
be exhausted he was to return to the earth for another
seventy years to play again the part of a miser; and then,
his character ''being purified in the body of a hog,'' he was
destined to enter the human species for a last trial. Not
far distant was the Palace of Death, resembling in outward
splendour nothing on earth so much as the palace at Blenheim. None of the trophies of Marlborough, however, were
to be seen; for the great Duke never sent a soul to the Court
of Death if he could help it. The real heroes were Charles
the Twelfth of Sweden and Alexander of Macedon, between
whom stood Death the Emperor, extending a hand to be
kissed by all in attendance. A little more jolting brought
the company to Cocytus, where they left their coach, and
after crossing the river in a boat, performed the rest of
the journey on foot. Once they stopped to admire an
immense wheel of fortune presided over by an ugly woman,
who allotted to spirits about to enter the world their virtues, vices, passions, and occupations. Chance settled the
question whether a man should become a king, a philosopher, or ''a miserable damned poet,'' and so on through
the list of man's labours. Those who drew the highest
prizes were most discontented, and often exchanges were
made in consequence. Such had formerly been the case
with Alexander and Diogenes; but for an exchange of

tickets, he that was afterwards Diogenes would have been Alexander.

At length, purged of all earthly passions, the travellers reached the gate of Elysium, and stood by, in a prodigious crowd of spirits, to watch the procedure of Minos the judge as he let one through, or sent another back to the earth to purify himself in a second life, or thrust those guilty of heinous crimes through a little back gate into the bottomless pit. The beau, the coquette, the virtuoso or collector of butterflies, the patriot, the military commander with his army of invaders, and a parson who had let four of his parishioners die of starvation, were all told to return to the upper world. A poet who expected to be saved by the strict morality of his works—meaning thereby his "dramatic works"—narrowly escaped the same fate; but when it transpired that he had once lent the whole profits of a benefit night to a friend in distress, the gates flew open, and Minos requested him, in view of this act, to spare the further "remembrance of his plays." Another spirit, fearing that he might be kicked into Tartarus, approached the judge, and in trembling voice begged him for mercy, saying "he hoped Minos would consider, that tho' he had gone astray, he had suffered for it, that it was necessity which drove him to the robbery of eighteen pence, which he had committed, and for which he was hanged: that he had done some good actions in his life, that he had supported an aged parent with his labour, that he had been a very tender husband and a kind father, and that he had ruined himself by being bail for his friend. At which words the gate opened, and Minos bid him enter, giving him a slap on the back as he passed by him." Of the company that had come in the stagecoach from Warwick Lane, a fair spirit was admitted without hesitation, though she had died of a fever brought on by overdancing herself at a ball; while a grave lady of the coach "was rejected on her first appearance, Minos declaring, there was not a single prude in Elysium." "The judge then," says the leader of the company, "address'd himself to me, who little expected to pass this fiery trial. I confess'd I had indulged myself very freely with wine and woman in my youth, but had never done an injury to any man living, nor avoided an opportunity of doing good; that I pretended to very little virtue more than general philanthropy, and private friendship.—I was proceeding, when Minos bid me enter the gate, and not indulge myself with trumpeting forth my virtues."

It was in a delicious orange grove of the Elysian Fields that this fortunate gentleman, walking with his beautiful companion of the stagecoach, first saw his little daughter whom he had lost several years before. "Good Gods! what words can describe the raptures, the melting passionate tenderness, with which we kiss'd each other, continuing in our embrace, with the most extatic joy, a space, which if time had been measured here as on earth, could not be less than half a year." He soon fell in with Leonidas of Sparta, whom he told of the great honours that had been recently paid to him by Mr. Glover in a noble poem; and then attended a concert in which Sappho sang and Orpheus played the violin. Old Homer was present, and Madame Dacier, his critic and expounder, sat in his lap. The ancient bard inquired after Mr. Pope, whom he hoped to see some day, whose translations of the Iliad had given him as much pleasure as the original had given other people. Milton, Dryden, and Shakespeare were there. To Shakespeare, the actors Betterton and Booth were appealing for the proper accent of a line in "Othello," but the dramatist could not help them. "Faith, Gentlemen," he told them, "it is so long since I wrote the line, I have forgot my meaning." When other obscure passages were called to Shakespeare's attention, he was not inclined to talk much and

THE HISTORY OF HENRY FIELDING

referred all inquirers to the commentators, saying "if Mr. Theobald had not writ about it sufficiently, there were three or four more new editions of his plays coming out, which he hoped would satisfy everyone." Forming a little group apart, stood Virgil, Addison, and Steele, all of whom Fielding pleasantly characterized, exposing Addison's blind side and paying at the same time a fine compliment to Warburton, who, in "The Divine Legation of Moses," had recently given a symbolic interpretation to the descent of Aeneas into Hades. To quote the passage with its original capitals—

"Virgil then came up to me, with Mr. Addison under his Arm. Well, Sir, said he, how many Translations have these few last Years produced of my Æneid? I told him, I believed several, but I could not possibly remember; for that I had never read any but Dr. Trapp's.—Ay, said he, that is a curious Piece indeed! I then acquainted him with the Discovery made by Mr. Warburton of the Eleusinian Mysteries couched in his 6th Book. What Mysteries? said Mr. Addison. The Eleusinian, answered Virgil, which I have disclosed in my 6th Book. How! replied Addison. You never mentioned a word of any such Mysteries to me in all our Acquaintance. I thought it was unnecessary, cried the other, to a Man of your infinite Learning: besides, you always told me, you perfectly understood my meaning. Upon this I thought the Critic looked a little out of countenance, and turned aside to a very merry Spirit, one Dick Steele, who embraced him, and told him, He had been the greatest Man upon Earth; that he readily resigned up all the Merit of his own Works to him. Upon which, Addison gave him a gracious Smile, and clapping him on the Back with much Solemnity, cried out, Well said, Dick."

There were some surprises for the visitor. Thomas Thumb unexpectedly came up and took him cordially by the hand as one honoured, not disgraced, by that little

400

farce in which a cow swallowed him. Near them Adam was conversing with Milton, Aeneas and Julius Caesar with Virgil, Achilles and Ulysses with Homer. It was a glorious company of epic poets and heroes to which the friend of Tom Thumb was welcomed far beyond his merits. He could but stare when he saw Oliver Cromwell leaning on the shoulder of Charles Martel, for his grandmother had told him that Cromwell had been "carried away by the devil himself in a tempest." Cromwell denounced the report as a lie, but admitted that hell would have taken him, had not the former part of his career been "more to his honour than the latter." In consideration of this fact, Minos had ordered him, he said, back to the upper world to be born a poor cavalier, to suffer terrible wounds and untold miseries in the service of James the Second, and finally to die half-starved and broken-hearted, having been reduced to the occupation of "cleaning shoes, and snuffing candles at the opera" over in Paris, whither he had followed his unhappy master after the Battle of the Boyne. As soon as Cromwell had thus been made to feel acutely some of the misfortunes of that House which he had bitterly attacked in his first life, Minos decided to let him into Elysium. Anne Boleyn, whom some of the histories had painted "as black as hell," had also gained admittance. She gave a most charming and feminine account of her career, keeping back, however, none of her weaknesses. Minos had hesitated a little over her case, she said, but finally told her to enter, since anyone who "had suffered being a queen for four years, and been sensible during all that time of the real misery which attends that exalted station, ought to be forgiven whatever she had done to obtain it."

But the shade whose presence most startled the company was that of Julian the Apostate, whom, it was supposed, had long been undergoing torments in the bottomless pit.

This renouncer of Christianity explained that Minos had indeed rejected his first claims to Elysium, but instead of kicking him through the little gate to the realm below, decided to put him through a score or more of pilgrimages on earth as a punishment greater than any that hell offered for his despicable conduct. Thereupon Julian began the long story of the transmigration of his soul through the centuries, relating, for instance, his experiences as a slave, a Jew, a beau, a monk, a wise man, a king, a fool, a beggar, a poet, and a dancing-master. Had he gone on, he would have told how he was three times a bishop before he suffered martyrdom at the stake in the body of Hugh Latimer, thus atoning for his first wretched and shameful career.

This part of the "Journey" has become of less interest than the rest. Perhaps it has not been quite understood. Fielding, as his library shows, read widely in the history of Europe from the most ancient times. He possessed the Greek and Latin histories, and most of the histories of England, beginning with the mediaeval chronicles. He even owned and cited such out-of-the-way books as the translation of Mariana's "General History of Spain." His quarrel with history was that it may tell you when an event takes place but that it is helpless when it proceeds to the motives of the actors. Just as Lucian burlesqued tales of adventure in his "True Story," Fielding here gave his version of certain episodes in general history. Events as such he was careless of, and changed them at will; with him the characters were the main thing. The result is that his accounts of Cromwell, Anne Boleyn, and the Emperor Julian become, as they were intended, an ironic rendering of history. It is a jest well worth entering into. Furthermore, over the whole narrative is thrown a modern atmosphere. The sentiments, anecdotes, and allusions are of the eighteenth century. None of the characters through which Julian's soul passed were remote; they had actual

402

existences or analogues among the men whom anyone
might see in the London of George the Second.

After all is said, however, the story of Julian's many
pilgrimages did not work out very well. In length, the
narrative is out of all proportion to those brief and vivid
first chapters; the humour lags; the style labours; and
who cares what happened to the Emperor Julian? Fielding knew all this, and stopped, leaving the tale incomplete,
and by a device common in his time, he pretended for the
reader's benefit that the manuscript of the "Journey"
had been found in the garret of a stationer doing business
near the shop of Andrew Millar in the Strand. Its frag-
mentary character, he told the reader, should not be laid
to the editor but to the carelessness of the stationer who
used parts of it in wrapping up his wares. With the approval of Parson Adams, the editor now published so much
of the manuscript as he could make out and put together,
in the hope that it would not be held against him as an
atheistical book, for its intent was clearly to teach the
moral, "that the greatest and truest happiness which this
world affords, is to be found only in the possession of goodness and virtue." Notwithstanding this reasonable request, Fielding's enemies, according to Arthur Murphy,
charged him "with an intention to subvert the settled
notions of mankind in philosophy and religion." Doubtless, the scenes before and within the gate of Elysium gave
offence to many who could not appreciate Fielding's
humour, irony, and insight into character. Withal, the
frank avowal of the hero's weaknesses, written between jest
and earnest, could not have escaped the denunciation of
those who take in soberness all that they read in a humorist.

The glory of the "Miscellanies" is "The Life of Mr.
Jonathan Wild the Great," or to give the second title, "The
History of the Life of the late Mr. Jonathan Wild the
Great," comprising four books and filling the third and

last volume. This mock-heroic biography contains no scene quite equal in humour to the best in "A Journey from this World to the Next"; but as a sustained piece of irony, occasionally breaking into burlesque, there had been nothing in our literature comparable with it outside of Swift. The Lucianic dialogue adopted in the "Journey," always admirable if kept within bounds, failed at the point where Fielding began stretching it out, through the transmigration of souls, into obscure history with which few but himself were acquainted. On the other hand, everybody knew about the career of Jonathan Wild, the thief and thief-taker, who had been executed within the memory of all men in middle life. Moreover, the biography of this gentleman, as anyone might read it in numerous pamphlets, was a compact and well-ordered story quite different from the loose narrative inherent in the design of "A Journey from this World to the Next." Fielding could not have had a better subject for a piece of perfect irony.

The real Jonathan Wild was a scapegrace born of humble but industrious parents living at Wolverhampton in Staffordshire. Soon after reaching his majority, he deserted a wife and child, came up to London, and worked for some time at buckle-making; but being idle and extravagant, he did not thrive in this sober trade; and it was not long before a debt that he could not pay sent him to the prison in Wood Street, where he fell in with a loose woman who introduced him, when released, to several gangs of sharpers. Owing to an Act passed in the time of King William making it a felony to receive stolen goods, if they were known to be stolen, thieves and pickpockets found it difficult to dispose of their "purchases," as they called them; at best the risk of meddling with stolen goods was so great that dealers paid little for them, and the poor thief's occupation was accordingly losing its ancient lucre. The clear-headed Jonathan at once set his mind at work on a state of affairs that

JONATHAN WILD,
Thief Taker General.
of Great Britain
and Ireland 1725.

was bringing into distress a large part of the London underworld. The problem, as he rightly saw it, was to render theft and robbery, despite the law, reasonably safe for all engaged in the profession and to devise at the same time a sure means of obtaining the full value of all "purchases." Beginning in a small way, he eventually organized a large corporation of thieves, pickpockets, and highwaymen, who under his strict supervision plied their trade all over London. His men usually worked in gangs so that the actual thief or robber might be easily rescued by his fellows in case the exploit threatened to miscarry because of haste, commotion, or attempted arrest. If the thief were caught, as would sometimes happen, then it was necessary for his friends to perjure themselves in order to prove an alibi.

When the system was completed, the old receiver of stolen goods—always a danger point—disappeared from view; he still existed but lay concealed behind a sort of broker's office which Jonathan opened near the Old Bailey and managed himself with the aid of a corps of clerks. It quickly became known that the only certain way to recover valuables of which one had been robbed, was to enlist the aid of Mr. Jonathan Wild. This could be obtained by paying him a commission accompanied with a promise to give the porter who should deliver the goods a fixed sum without asking any impertinent questions. There was always some delay, for Jonathan professed to have difficulties in finding the thief or robber; but in the end the delivery was made, provided the man bereft of his goods was willing to pay for their return what they were really worth, or considerably more if they happened to be heirlooms or especially prized gifts from friends. As Jonathan himself never touched the goods or permitted them to be deposited in his office, he adroitly evaded the law. While thus restoring property, he was also sending out his gangs to commit more robberies.

It was for him an endless circle of crime and profit. Suspicion of Jonathan's real character—if there was any—was allayed by his frequent aid in the apprehension of criminals who could not otherwise be reached. He became known in consequence as a thief-catcher, an honest citizen who was employing his intimate knowledge of the underworld for the benefit of society. In keeping with his assumed character, he wore, when on the streets or elsewhere in public, a laced coat and carried a silver staff as a token of authority. To all appearance he was a complete gentleman.

Those behind the scenes could have told another story. Jonathan was so cruel that he seemed to his men to have no heart at all. Under threats of the gallows he extorted from them most of their winnings; the small share he allowed them to keep would make them, he well knew, more desperate and eager for new crimes. If he turned a man over to justice and hence to death, it was someone with whom he had quarrelled, someone whom he feared or could not control, or someone belonging to a gang outside his own corporation. As time went on Jonathan became bolder, and as a result of it his disguise wore thin. For example, one Joseph Blake, known as Blueskin, who was convicted of robbery on evidence supplied by the gang, attempted to cut our hero's throat in the bail-dock, shouting, as he inflicted an ugly wound, that Wild had first made a thief of him and then abandoned him. Though the gash did not prove mortal, it rendered mute Jonathan's voice for that trial. Soon after this, the great man himself was trapped by a law enacted some years before, which declared it a felony to take money or reward under pretence of helping any person or persons to stolen goods or chattels. On May 24, 1725, Mr. Jonathan Wild was hanged at Tyburn in the presence of an immense mob that had pelted him all the way from Newgate to the place of execution.

THE GLORY OF THE MISCELLANIES

It was an eminently successful career in that the hero accomplished what he set out to do. The closing scenes, it is true, were clouded with dishonour; but the struggle was then over. Public curiosity for details of Jonathan's life was fed by newspapers and pamphlets which claimed to have fresh and startling facts unknown to others. Just after his arrest, appeared, for instance, "An Authentick Narrative of the Life and Actions of Jonathan Wild (Citizen and Thief-Taker of London)," embellished with a portrait—"drawn from life"—of the man sitting in his cell, trying to lighten a careworn face with his pipe and a mug of ale. It was a moment of most serious reflection, and of anxiety also, for his fate still hung in the balance. Of similar biographical sketches issued as cheap pamphlets, two that were published after the execution were certainly from the pen of Defoe, though his name did not appear on the title-page. The first of them was called "The True and Genuine Account of the Life and Actions of the late Jonathan Wild; not made up of Fiction and Fable, but taken from his own Mouth, and collected from Papers of his own Writing." In a preface, Defoe denounced his brother scribblers for romancing the life of an "infamous creature," for making out of it a light jest or a tale for the chimney-corner, and then constructed a picturesque narrative of his own with pauses of abundant moralizing. Jonathan had, readers were told, six wives or concubines—not all at once of course, but Bluebeard style in rapid succession; and in order to maintain control of his gangs, he had sent to the gallows in the course of sixteen years more than a hundred confederates in crime. After whetting the appetites of purchasers with these tales, Defoe put out another and larger pamphlet costing twice as much. This was, to abbreviate the title, "The Life of Jonathan Wild," written not by an outsider but by "H. D., late clerk to Justice R," that is, to Chief Justice Raymond, before whom Jonathan had been tried and convicted.

Had the story of Jonathan Wild remained where Defoe left it, it would have been long forgotten. But it did not remain there; for it appealed to the imagination. As soon as Robert Walpole came to the front in English politics, people saw in his private life and public career certain correspondences with the rise and progress of Jonathan Wild. There were hints of this identification in "The Beggar's Opera" (1728). Peachum, the receiver of stolen goods, who was drawn from Wild, more than once compares his trade with that of the statesman, to his own advantage and honour. "In one respect, indeed," he remarks to Lockit, "our employment may be reckon'd dishonest, because like great statesmen, we encourage those who betray their friends." Other characteristics of Wild which were likewise applied to Walpole, appeared in Macheath, the highwayman who forcibly takes money and watches from reluctant travellers and puts them into his own pocket. It was a parallel between a statesman's taxes and a robber's booty. A few months later, the Government prohibited the performance of Gay's continuation of "The Beggar's Opera" called "Polly," because it reflected too closely, in the characters of Macheath, Lucy, and Polly, the relations existing between Walpole, his wife, and his mistress Miss Skerrett. Fielding, himself, as we have seen, played facetiously with the intrigues and intimacies of Walpole in his "Grub-Street Opera," though he did not then bring in a comparison with Wild; and when he later attacked the Prime Minister in "Pasquin" and "The Historical Register," it was mainly on the score of bribery. The sober parallel between the methods of Wild and Walpole was the work of the Opposition newspapers, beginning with "The Craftsman." The parallel was continually obtruding itself in the political articles of "The Champion" during the

years that Fielding conducted that newspaper. "Common
Sense" on one occasion gave a sketch of Wild with remarks
on his levée, crowded with "personages of the first rank,"
among whom Jonathan moved as one "rather born to a
ribband than to a rope"; and on another occasion, it declared that the House of Commons could be no worse were
it given over to a Jonathan Wild and his gang. When Walpole fell from power in 1742, the allegory became complete.
Of two great men, one had been hanged and the other had
met his fate at the hands of an indignant people. So said
"Common Sense"* in firing its last shots at the nation's
"robber and oppressor."

Beyond reasonable doubt, it was at this time that Fielding wrote his "Jonathan Wild," retaining the political
undercurrent of the story but giving it a wider sweep.
Most critics, I am aware, place the composition of the
piece, except for certain added passages, at a much earlier
date—in some cases as far back as 1737, and never later
than the period when Fielding was director of "The Champion." Recently it has been surmised that Fielding wrote
an ironical account of Jonathan which appeared in "Mist's
Weekly Journal" for June 12 and 19, 1725, and afterwards
expanded it into his novel. He may indeed have read that
account and derived hints from it, but he was altogether
too young in 1725 to have written that early psychological
study of the Newgate hero.† It seems impossible to the
critics that Fielding, after discovering himself in "Joseph
Andrews," should have at once experimented in another
type of fiction. Logically, they say, "Jonathan Wild" ante-
dates "Joseph Andrews." Logically, one might add,

---

* July 10, 17, and Oct., 16, 1742, as quoted in "The Gentleman's Magazine," July and Oct., 1742. See also "The London Magazine," Dec., 1738;
and "The Scots Magazine," Nov., 1739, for other abstracts of articles in
"Common Sense."

† "Notes and Queries," 11 S. II, 261-263 (Oct. 1, 1910); and 12 S. II,
442 (Dec. 2, 1916).

Fielding should never have wasted his time on another newspaper after leaving "The Champion." The fact is, however, that he was still to conduct three more similar periodicals within a decade. To this kind of logic the exigencies of life can never be safely adjusted. Again, as pointing to an early date for "Jonathan Wild," attention has been called to certain parallels between that work and several political papers in "The Champion." There are, indeed, these marked parallels in thought and expression. Scattered through "The Champion" and the poems that Fielding was then writing, one may find much that received more complete expression in "Jonathan Wild." One may also find much, if he looks for it with equal diligence, that eventually got into "Tom Jones" many years afterwards. The fact is, resemblances in thought and style, if unsupported by other considerations, cannot be relied upon for fixing the dates of Fielding's works, for it was his custom to revamp his old ideas, presenting them from fresh points of view in the light of a free play of the imagination. It is probable that Fielding, losing interest in his "Journey from this World to the Next," took up "Jonathan Wild" in the spring of 1742, soon after Walpole went down to defeat. This event is what gave force and piquancy to the analogy between the careers of Walpole and Wild; this is what gave point to the phrase in Fielding's second title-page—"The Life of the *late* Mr. Jonathan Wild the Great," for the real Jonathan had died seventeen years before. Everybody had the analogy in mind, the newspapers were dilating upon it, and it was the best and easiest subject for Fielding, who had before him the task of filling up three volumes of miscellanies for which subscribers were paying him in advance.

This conclusion receives support from various allusions in the book. A letter from Peter Pounce refusing aid to a poor bankrupt and a reference to fortune's allotting to

spirits not yet clothed in the flesh the stations they are to
occupy in the world, are details reminiscent respectively
of "Joseph Andrews" and "A Journey from this World
to the Next." Moreover, there is reproduced a scrap of
the conversation between Adams and Barnabas on the
possible salvation of a sincere Turk. One of his similes
Fielding says was made while he was travelling over "the
hills near Bath." Fielding had travelled over these hills
more than once; but we know that he was at Bath in 1742,
and the inference, taken with what follows, is that he
wrote parts of his "Jonathan" during the visit. Again,
in disclaiming all knowledge of supernatural causes of
events, he ironically refers to "many occurrences of the
phaenomenous kind which have lately appeared in this our
hemisphere." When Fielding revised his "Jonathan" just
before death, he altered "recently" to "formerly"* as
the more appropriate word, since the strange occurrences
were then no longer recent. This banter about the supernatural explanation of unusual phenomena was almost
certainly occasioned by the comet of 1742, which made its
appearance on February 20, and remained visible through
March. From the north and the south letters from Whis-
ton and others came in to London periodicals describing
its course from day to day; "wond'ring mortals" sat up
nights to gaze at it; and many superstitious people feared
that it threatened some national disaster, perhaps indeed
the Last Conflagration, while the political wits told them
it meant nothing more than the overthrow of the Ministry,
and so should be hailed as a blessed portent.

Of several political allusions, one belongs definitely to
the summer or autumn of 1742. After the fall of Walpole,
Pulteney, who had led the Opposition in the House of
Commons, turned courtier and accepted a peerage, being
created Earl of Bath on July 13, 1742. Immediately his

* Edition of 1743, Bk. II, Ch. XIII; edition of 1754, Bk. II, Ch. XII.

THE HISTORY OF HENRY FIELDING

former associates fell upon him with a torrent of vituperation that crushed him forever. No word in the English language was vile enough to describe the character of this renegade, who, said Hanbury Williams in "An Epitaph on the Political Memory of the Earl of Bath," was

Curs'd, scorn'd, and hated, e'en by those he lov'd.

Fielding, still having some sympathy with Pulteney, appears to have put him into a proverb with a hard hit at Walpole and his mistress. The proverb, afterwards suppressed, read "Debauching a Member of the House of Commons from his principles, and creating him a peer, is not much better than making a woman a whore, and afterwards marrying her."*

With these passages in view, woven into the text here and there, no one should greatly doubt when Fielding wrote "Jonathan Wild." It is the last production worthy of his genius before the advent of "Tom Jones."

His design Fielding explained in the preface to the "Miscellanies" and repeatedly enlarged upon it during the progress of the story. The subject of "Jonathan Wild" was to be greatness, concerning which he had written piecemeal in "The Champion" and several poems. He held that people are continually confounding the ideas of greatness and goodness as if the former quality must include the latter. If a man is great they think that he must be good also. No inference could be more false. The elements of goodness belong to the heart; they are "benevolence, honour, honesty, and charity." It is these that make the good man. The elements of greatness belong to the will and the understanding; they are called "parts," or ability, and courage. These qualities alone are sufficient to render a man great. True, the elements of greatness and goodness sometimes appear in the same person—in a Lyttelton, for example—and then we have a great and good character

* Edition of 1743, Bk. II, Ch. XII.

412

who "at once fills us with love, wonder, and delight"; but this perfect equipoise is rare in human nature. On the contrary, most of the good men that we love are lacking in the efficient virtues, they are often called fools or cowards; while many of the great men that we admire have but assumed the virtues of the heart in the service of their ambitions. Into the composition of great men frequently go the worst vices—"pride, ostentation, insolence, cruelty, and every kind of villany."

This species of bombast greatness one sees—to paraphrase Fielding—in the world's conquerors and tyrants, in statesmen and prime ministers, who have attained to power, riches, and honour through deceit and humbuggery. "In the histories of Alexander and Caesar," said Fielding, "we are frequently reminded of their benevolence and generosity. When the former had with fire and sword overrun a whole empire, and destroyed the lives of millions of innocent people, we are told as an example of his benevolence, that he did not cut the throat of an old woman, and ravish her daughters whom he had before undone: And when the mighty Caesar had with wonderful greatness of mind destroyed the liberties of his country, and gotten all the power into his own hands, we receive, as an evidence of his generosity, his largesses to his followers and tools, by whose means he had accomplished his purpose, and by whose assistance he was to establish it." This is the highest order of greatness. Somewhere below it lies an inferior greatness represented by Jonathan Wild; who, in justifying his crimes against a poor family—robbery, perjury, and attempted seduction,—appealed to the heroes of antiquity. "What is the life of a single man?" Jonathan asked himself. "Have not whole armies and nations been sacrificed to the humour of ONE GREAT MAN? Nay, to omit that first class of greatness, the conquerors of mankind, how often have numbers fallen, by a fictitious plot, only to satisfy the spleen, or perhaps exercise the ingenuity of a member of that second order of greatness the Ministerial! What have I done then? Why, I have ruined a family, and brought an innocent man to the gallows. I ought rather to weep, with Alexander, that I have ruined no more, than to regret the little I have done.'' The implication everywhere is that the qualities which made Jonathan Wild great have also made great in the world's eye Alexander, Caesar, and a contemporary statesman known pre-eminently as the Great Man.

The reader is, however, warned against a sweeping generalization. There are statesmen of unquestioned patriotism, and there are military commanders who, disregarding foreign conquest, have fought nobly in defence of their religion and their country. Rome had her Brutus, and England her Marlborough. ''I do by no means intend in the character of my hero,'' Fielding declared, ''to represent human nature in general. . . . But without considering Newgate as no other than human nature with its mask off, which some very shameless writers have done, a thought which no price should purchase me to entertain, I think we may be excused for suspecting, that the splendid palaces of the great are often no other than Newgate with the mask on. Nor do I know any thing which can raise an honest man's indignation higher than that the same morals should be in one place attended with all imaginable misery and infamy, and in the other, with the highest luxury and honour. Let any impartial man in his senses be asked, for which of these two places a composition of cruelty, lust, avarice, rapine, insolence, hypocrisy, fraud and treachery, was best fitted, surely his answer must be certain and immediate; and yet I am afraid all these ingredients glossed over with wealth and a title, have been treated with the highest respect and veneration in the one, while one or two of them have been condemned to the gallows in the other.''

414

THE GLORY OF THE MISCELLANIES

This is the thesis lying behind "Jonathan Wild." As a further preliminary, the public was cautioned not to expect a faithful portrait of the Newgate hero such as was drawn by "that excellent historian"—Daniel Defoe—who had access to "authentic papers and records." "To confess the truth," remarked Fielding, "my narrative is rather of such actions which he might have performed, or would, or should have performed, than what he really did; and may, in reality, as well suit any other such great man, as the person himself whose name it bears." That is, the aim was not a real so much as an imaginary biography with an undercurrent of social and political satire very like that in "Pasquin" and "The Historical Register." Accordingly, Fielding retained of the old biography of Wild only the merest outline—the beginning and end of his career, a few incidents, and two or three characters, most notably Blueskin.

Having once attained the Newgate point of view, he let his imagination play at will in fashioning new scenes and characters from slight hints or from none at all. It had not been recorded by the pamphleteers, for example, that the sound *th,* most difficult for children to utter, was "the first that came with any readiness from young Master Wild"; nor that, when in the prime of life he met his fate on the scaffold, his last act was to pick the pocket of the parson who attended him, of a corkscrew, "which he carried out of the world in his hand." A sufficient number of Wild's confederates are made to live and act their parts handsomely. Besides Blueskin, there are Fielding's own Count La Ruse, from whom Wild learns his trade, and Bagshot and Fierce and Fireblood, to mention the chief of them. The roundhouse where Wild was confined for a brief time in his youth is described as if at first hand. Mr. Snap the bailiff has two charming but disreputable daughters, one of whom—the wanton, sordid, and shrill-tongued Laetitia—makes the great man's life miserable, and deserts him in his misfortunes, thus compelling her chaste lover to seek the favours of Miss Molly Straddle. An Ordinary of Newgate had been but a colourless clergyman. Fielding individualizes him; lets us see him giving spiritual consolation to Jonathan until the superior intellect of the thief overpowers the feeble conscience of the parson. Jonathan, becoming drowsy over the Ordinary's exhortations, proposes a bottle of wine as a surer antidote than religious conversation against the low spirits into which both seem to be sinking. The Ordinary has scruples against wine-bibbing, and suggests punch in its stead, if they must drink, for two reasons; first, because punch is nowhere spoken against in Scripture, and second, because of all liquors it agrees best with his constitution. A bowl of punch is straightway ordered, and thereafter punch takes the place of religious instruction as a preparation for the gallows.

But most conspicuous of all the new characters are the Heartfrees—a London jeweller and his wife—whom Fielding created as a foil to his hero. They are representative of the perfectly good and honest tradespeople that Wild looked upon as his spoil. The husband, though the friend of his boyhood, he drove into bankruptcy and almost to the gallows on a trumped-up felony; the wife he lured away by the blackest arts that he might ravish her. In the end Fielding metes out the strict poetic justice of a Samuel Richardson. Virtue is rewarded, and vice receives the severest punishment known to the law. For those who want a moral neatly expressed, Fielding adds: "Whoever considers the common fate of great men must allow, they well deserve, and hardly earn that applause which is given them by the world; for, when we reflect on the labours and pains, the cares, disquietudes, and dangers which attend their road to greatness, we may say with the divine, that a man may go to heaven with half the pains which it costs him to purchase hell."

In rather vague phrases, Fielding advised his reader not to identify too closely the portrait of Jonathan Wild with that of any great man then living, for there were many rogues in the kingdom—certainly more than one—on whom the resemblance might be fixed. "I have been so far from endeavouring to particularize any individual," said Fielding, "that I have with my utmost art avoided it." This apparent disclaimer of having in mind a particular rogue while describing the species could have been but a jest at a time when the newspapers were holding up Walpole as no better than a Jonathan Wild, when they were calling him in irony the Great Man, the very phrase that Fielding had used in "Tom Thumb" and now applied to the hero of Newgate. In Wild's organization of his gang, and his perfect mastery of it from behind the scenes, in his clever schemes for pocketing most of the booty, his quarrels with a Fierce or a Blueskin, his betrayal of friends, his impudence, and utter heartlessness, a reader would see depicted by way of allegory the political career of the Prime Minister. Had not Walpole built up his power at the head of a horde of placemen that preyed upon the nation? Had he not been relentless in punishing subordinates who questioned his supremacy? Had he not acquired vast wealth for himself and a few favourites to the great distress of the people, whose estates were dwindling under heavy taxation? But a reader would be quite aware that Fielding was not running up a plain and consistent allegory on the Prime Minister, that in the current fashion he sometimes avoided or, more exactly, disguised the personal application, letting the satire overflow into other characters for perplexity or amusement. On closing the book, he would say that Walpole's career was a general shadow of Wild's, at times clearly outlined, and then indistinct and purposely confused.

A reader, nevertheless, could not help observing that when the narrative began to drift into unrelated incident, it had a way of suddenly coming back to its political significance. Then a character would bring in a comparison between a Prime Minister and a common thief, or the author *in propria persona* would comment upon a disgraceful transaction. Thus, after Wild had made adroit use of an accomplice to turn Fierce over to the hangman, Fielding remarked: "With such infinite address, did this truly great man know to play with the passions of men, and to set them at variance with each other, and to work his own purposes out of those jealousies and apprehensions, which he was wonderfully ready at creating, by means of those great arts, which the vulgar call treachery, dissembling, promising, lying, falshood, &c. but which are by great men summed up in the collective name of policy, or politicks, or rather *Pollitricks;* an art of which, as it is the highest excellence of human nature, so perhaps, was our Great Man the most eminent master."

As in this passage, the quarrels between Wild and his men almost always assumed a political colour; and there were times when Fielding quite forgot that he was writing of a gang of thieves, so intent was his mind upon a gang of politicians. It would be understood by everybody that when he described the exploits of Prigs (the cant word for thieves), he meant the exploits of the Whigs. Of course he did not intend to bring under the opprobrious name the entire body of the party—for Fielding himself was a Whig—but rather those hungry politicians who were always scrambling for office in order to satisfy their greed. They were ready to follow Walpole or anybody else who could assure them of luxury without labour. Of these Prigs or Whigs, there were at one time, says Fielding, two

418

bitter factions ever at war over what they called their principles, which were none other than the shape and style of their hats. One faction wore "hats fiercely cocked," while the other preferred "the nab or trencher hat, with the brim flapping over their eyes." At intervals it was necessary for the great man to appear and warn the factions against letting their foolish differences go too far. So long as their quarrels were counterfeited as a cover to picking the pockets of the crowd, he did not object to them; but there was always danger, he said, of their coming to a close fight in earnest. They must know, as well as he, that a Prig is no less a Prig in one hat than in another; that they were all engaged in the great and glorious enterprise of robbing the public; that the only value of a hat lies in the amount of booty that it will hold. Moved to shame by this exhortation, the Prigs all tossed up their hats together. A scene like this could be regarded only as a burlesque of the very able speeches whereby Walpole often kept in line those members of his party who showed signs of disaffection. Many a time when the Government's measures were threatened, the Prime Minister's eloquence and promises saved the day.

Of more specific reference is a scene in Newgate. On his entrance to this castle, Wild found that the Prigs there were already organized by "one Roger Johnson, a very great man," for the plunder of the debtors who swarmed through the place. By playing upon the grievances of these Prigs against their leader, Jonathan broke them up into two parties, with whom the crowd of debtors took sides, so that the walls of the old prison, hitherto quiet, now resounded, day and night, with "Wild for ever" and "Johnson for ever." Jonathan, being cleverer at promises than Roger, quickly succeeded to the place and power of his rival. Whereupon he stripped Johnson of his finery—a silk nightgown, embroidered waistcoat, and velvet hat—

and arrayed himself in these insignia of office, defending his conduct, whenever any surprise was expressed, with the claim that the clothes "fitted him much better than they did Johnson, and that they became him in a much more elegant manner." The debtors first grumbling and afterwards becoming indignant at Wild for his appropriation of spoils which they thought should be sold "for the good of whole," as they called it, "a very grave man" in the company severely rebuked them for their stupidity in supposing that they could improve their condition by overthrowing one rogue in favour of another. Their only hope of preserving "the liberty of Newgate," he told them, was by reforming "the manners of Newgate." Not only must they keep apart from the Prigs, neither eating nor drinking with them, but they must also eradicate from themselves all Priggish instincts and desires shown in their own disposition to pillage one another. This was Fielding's way of burlesquing a change in the Ministry.

And no one needed to be informed that the Prigs were place-hunters or placemen, and that the unfortunate debtors were the people who paid the heavy taxes, whichever faction might be in power. But precisely what change in Ministry the author had in mind, was left—purposely, I think—to conjecture. A reader who wished to keep the allegory whole and consistent, would see in the rivalry between Wild and Johnson a reflection of the old contest between Walpole and Townshend in which the former emerged triumphant as Prime Minister after there had been a scuffle with drawn swords. The "very grave man" who gave the poor debtors such excellent advice, expressed of course the views of the Opposition formed against Walpole back in 1730, immediately after he became supreme. The remembrance of this old quarrel between Walpole and Townshend had not yet grown stale; it was commonly read into "The Beggar's Opera," and Fielding alluded to it elsewhere in

THE GLORY OF THE MISCELLANIES

"Jonathan Wild." "The Great Man . . . ," he said, "ought to keep himself as much behind the curtain as possible," though "two very great men, whose names will be both recorded in history, did, in former times, come forth themselves on the stage; and did hack and hew, and lay each other most cruelly open to the diversion of the spectators."

Political allegories, however, have the oblique glance; that is their charm. Humorists have ever had the habit of breaking the continuity of an allegory, so that the reader himself may become responsible for any direct application. This had been the method of Swift, Gay, and political writers in the newspapers. Fielding likewise drew his portrait of Wild in such a way that it might not always point to Walpole; in such a way that there should be differences as well as resemblances. Though no one could really doubt that the author wrote in the main with his mind on "a certain great man," a reader would meet everywhere with incidents and sometimes with qualities that could not be made to tally with the assumed original. These inconsistencies appeared especially in the quarrel just described between Wild and Johnson. Walpole's enemies charged him with vice and crime, but they all acknowledged his uncommon endowments of intellect and will. How, then, could Fielding say, as he did in the prison scene, that Johnson's cast-off garments fitted Wild, despite that gentleman's assertion to the contrary, "very ill, being infinitely too big for him"? By general consent of all parties, Walpole was a much abler leader than Townshend. The remark may have been an inadvertence, but it is safer to assume that it was made deliberately; that the allegory at this point was intentionally given a squint towards the last dissensions in the Walpole Cabinet preceding its downfall.

Walpole as Prime Minister was succeeded by the Earl of Wilmington, who, though he had held office under the late Government, was cool towards his chief, sometimes intrigued against him, offered him no assistance when the crisis came, and stood by to take the cast-off clothes of office which he believed Walpole had stolen from his own shoulders many years before. The clothes proved a ludicrous misfit; Walpole's hat must have made the new Minister's head ache; for Wilmington was only a dignified nonentity, lacking in the intelligence and decision necessary to leadership. By reversing the allegory in the Newgate quarrel, making Johnson stand for Walpole, and Wild for Wilmington, the scene may be made to fit the change in Ministry that occupied men's minds when Fielding was writing his novel. That Fielding quite intended this complete reversal is not probable; he rather suggested it, I think, in a mischievous spirit; and thereby furnished a subject for hot discussion among coffee-house politicians over who was meant by Roger and who was meant by Jonathan, in the strife for the dirty symbols of office. These wiseacres might debate also the identity of the "very grave man," for his political philosophy was as sound in 1743 as in 1730. Indeed, it reads much like Fielding's own as one sees it in "The Champion" and "The Opposition."

Minor hits at Walpole's private as well as political life, once clear enough, appear in many places. Professor John Edwin Wells,* the only writer who has adequately considered this aspect of the novel, was the first to observe that Fielding, in fabricating a genealogy for Wild, was perhaps burlesquing that one of Walpole which had appeared a few years before in William Musgrave's "Brief and True History of Robert Walpole and his Family." This pamphlet, having altogether but seventy-eight printed pages, devotes thirty-eight of them to the great man's ancestors. Robert Walpole's father was named Robert, and his grandfather, Edward. Similarly Wild's father was put down, without

* "Publications of the Modern Language Association of America," Vol. XXVIII, No. I, March, 1913, pp. 1-55.

any authority from the pamphlets, as Jonathan, and his grandfather as Edward. The coincidence seems to have been intentional, for Fielding, as may be seen by examining the genealogy of his hero, first called Jonathan's grandfather James, and immediately began writing of him under the name of Edward as if his mind were on Walpole's ancestry. One of the most humorous passages in the book is a conversation between Jonathan and his wife Laetitia one morning a fortnight after marriage. They accused each other of infidelity, but after emitting a torrent of abuse, they patched up the quarrel with the agreement that thereafter neither should interfere with the liberty of the other. This scene was in accordance with current gossip concerning Walpole and his wife. Just like this, Walpole was to have Miss Skerrett, and his wife was to have Lord Hervey; there was to be no more talk about it on either side. Much else, too, was mixed with the scene. Finally, for we must stop somewhere, Walpole's feeble religious nature was touched upon with excellent ridicule in those conversations between Wild and the Ordinary of Newgate. The great man was uncertain whether he was an atheist or a Christian. As the day of "death and damnation" approached nearer, he took more and more to punch and then to laudanum, in order to make the transition as easy as possible.

The personal satire of "Jonathan Wild" has long since spent its force. This is due partly to the obscuration that comes with time and partly to the fact that the novel in the form in which Fielding first published it has been superseded by a later version. Near the end of life, when his old political animosities were but a memory, Fielding thoroughly revised his fiction. Two entire chapters, one of which is largely political, were eliminated, and the word "Prime Minister" gave way in most cases to "Statesman." The new edition was accompanied with an advertisement written by Fielding, in which the author deprecated the allegorical interpretations which had been given to his book, and yet really acknowledged that an allegory was there. The general effect of the alterations and the advertisement has been to blur and darken the political undercurrent. It is this second "Jonathan Wild," carefully made over from the first one, that has come down to us in popular editions. This is perhaps as it should be. To the modern reader, "Jonathan Wild" is hardly a political pamphlet. Time and Fielding's hand have subordinated its political purpose to a parody on the lives of so-called great men, among whom one thinks of Caesar and Alexander, but not at all of Walpole, unless one's attention is called to the fact that he lies concealed under the title of Statesman or Prime Minister.

Fielding's method was irony as he had learned it from Lucian and Swift, but it was less bitter than Swift's and it was sometimes coloured by banter and burlesque. A capital burlesque of extravagant tales told by shipwrecked sailors, such as one finds in Defoe's books of adventure, he cut from the first edition because it was irrelevant and hindered too much the main narrative. He nevertheless let stand a parody of the grand tour in connection with an accident that befell Jonathan in his youth, compelling that gentleman to pass seven years in his Majesty's American colonies. The composition of that chapter, though the shortest in the book, was most difficult, said Fielding, because nothing occurred worth recording. We tried, he added, to fill out the narrative from the adventures of other young gentlemen abroad; "but to our great sorrow could not extract a single incident strong enough to justify the theft to our consciences." Occasionally, too, Fielding was betrayed into direct statement under the sway of deep emotion at Wild's cruel treatment of the Heartfrees; and then he could not refrain from denunciation of his hero's treachery. But except for these very human lapses, Fielding kept the cool masque of irony tight over his face; he described the adventures of Jonathan Wild as if the thief were really a great man, and the distressful experiences of the Heartfrees as if the honest jeweller and his wife were silly and contemptible creatures. Barring a few misadventures and an unhappy marriage, Jonathan Wild's career was one long triumph from the first pocket that he picked down to the last when he relieved the Ordinary of a concealed corkscrew. There was no flinching; he met his fate with the careless fortitude of the martyrs, certain that he would soon be among the ancient heroes, with Caesar and Alexander of Macedon. After closing the book, Coleridge declared that its irony exceeded anything in "Lilliput" or "A Tale of a Tub." And the critic was probably right.